Protestant women's narratives
of the Irish rebellion of 1798

Protestant women's narratives of the Irish rebellion of 1798

John D. Beatty

EDITOR

FOUR COURTS PRESS

Typeset in 10.5 pt on 12.5 pt Ehrhardt by
Carrigboy Typesetting Services, County Cork for
FOUR COURTS PRESS LTD
Fumbally Court, Fumbally Lane, Dublin 8, Ireland
e-mail: info@four-courts-press.ie
and in North America for
FOUR COURTS PRESS
c/o ISBS, 5824 N.E. Hassalo Street, Portland, OR 97213.

A catalogue record for this title is available
from the British Library.

ISBN 1–85182–625–4

Printed in Great Britain
by MPG Books, Bodmin, Cornwall

CONTENTS

5

ACKNOWLEDGMENTS

There are many people who should be thanked for their assistance in compiling this book. Kevin Whelan of University College Dublin offered much assistance with notes, giving this editor the benefit of his encyclopedic knowledge of Wexford families and helping to place them into the political spectrum of the time. Brian Cleary was instrumental in helping me obtain a photocopy of the original version of the Elizabeth Richards diary. My colleague, Steven W. Myers of Fort Wayne, offered advice throughout the compilation of this work.

I am also indebted to the following institutions for giving permission to publish some of the items in this work: the Manuscript Department of Trinity College Dublin for allowing the publication of the original manuscript version of Dinah Goff's diary; the Deputy Keeper of the Records, Public Record Office of Northern Ireland in Belfast for granting permission to quote from the Goff Papers and for allowing the publication of a manuscript version of Alicia Pounden's account; the Council of Trustees of the National Library of Ireland for granting permission to reprint its version of Barbara Lett's narrative; and the British Library for permission to publish the original, unaltered account of Jane Adams, which was subsequently bowdlerised by Crofton Croker.

This work is by no means an attempt to publish all known women's accounts of the Irish Rebellion of 1798; rather, its focus is predominantly on Protestant women with either loyal or neutral sympathies. Left out are the letters of Margaret Dobbin née Cochrane, daughter of a rebel sympathizer, whose unpublished papers are housed at Trinity College Dublin. These letters, though worthy of publication and scholarly editing, are better fitted for another work with a broader focus. Similarly, the letters of Lady Louisa Conolly, aunt of the United Irish leader Lord Edward Fitzgerald, contain much about the rebellion through her contacts with her nephew and other family members. Her letters do not lend themselves to a narrative format, however, and extensive abstracts have previously appeared in print in such works as Brian Fitzgerald's *Lady Louisa Conolly, 1743–1821: An Anglo-Irish Biography* (London, Staples Press, n.d.).

I hope that this edition will encourage further study of the involvement of women in 1798. Though their voices were stifled by the patriarchal

7

culture of the time, they remain sensitive, perceptive witnesses, both to the warfare which surrounded and often enveloped them, and to the brutality and martial law which followed in the rebellion's wake. They have much to teach revisionists in search of a more complete picture of that time.

JOHN D. BEATTY
Fort Wayne, Indiana
March 2001

INTRODUCTION

Until recently, the role of Protestant women with loyal or neutral sympathies in 1798 has received only scant attention from historians of the Irish Rebellion.[1] In the immediate aftermath of '98, loyalist historians made peripheral use of women's depositions in their accounts of the rebellion, seeing little need to make them central characters in a drama that was primarily played out in the meeting-hall and on the battlefield and gallows, where women typically had little direct influence. Because loyal women were widely considered to be both non-political and non-combatants, the male-dominated, politically-charged historiography that followed 1798 deemed their involvement in the rebellion to be, at best, only minimal and not worthy of close study. Sir Richard Musgrave used the observations of several women to illustrate his thesis that the rebellion was a Papist plot to exterminate Protestants. Yet even he was hard-pressed for evidence that loyal women had been murdered or raped in large numbers at the hands of the rebels or had played anything but the most passive of roles in the conflict. To be sure, he would have played the propaganda card if they had suffered.[2]

Of course, there were exceptions, and some Protestant women did lose their lives, and loyalists made note of their martyrdom. Many women and children, both Catholic and Protestant, died in the terrible fire at Scullabogue which followed the battle of Ross in County Wexford, while in neighbouring County Kildare, several high-profile murders of women took place. Hannah Manders of Glassealy and two of her sisters died in a house fire set by rebels, who may have sought vengeance against Manders's nephew.[3] Near Athy, a group of rebel youths apparently stoned to death Catherine Dale, wife of Joseph Dale, a Protestant who forced to join the rebel army or face death. In spite of his action, the youths had stormed Dale's house and murdered his wife, apparently after calling her an 'orange

---

1 See my previous essay on this subject, John D. Beatty, 'Protestant Women of County Wexford and Their Narratives of the Rebellion of 1798', in Dáire Keogh and Nicholas Furlong (eds), *The Women of 1798* (Dublin: Four Courts Press, 1998), 113–136. Other essays in this work, cited elsewhere in this book, represent the first effort to address this neglect in more than one hundred years.   2 Sir Richard Musgrave, *Memoirs of the Different Rebellions in Ireland* (4th ed., Fort Wayne: Round Tower Books, 1995).   3 Ibid., 260–1.

9

whore'.[4] Outside of Kildare, a party of rebels piked to death George Crawford, a sergeant in Captain Taylor's Yeoman Cavalry, together with his fourteen-year-old granddaughter who had attempted to shield him, while Crawford's wife hid herself in a hedge. In telling this story, Musgrave cites a deposition given in Dublin by Crawford's widow in August of 1798, but the story itself remains unverified.[5] These stories, perhaps sensationalised, stand virtually alone in loyalist propaganda as examples of rebel murders of loyalist women.

On the opposite side, Catholic historians, whose revisionist history was equally martyr-based, ignored loyalist women altogether. They remain invisible in the memoirs of Miles Byrne and Thomas Cloney, who perceived women as playing no role of importance in 1798. Indeed, the enormity of the widespread suffering of Catholic women, raped and brutalised by invading English and Hessian armies, may have eclipsed any interest in the role of loyal women, who suffered only minimally by comparison.

Almost from the beginning of the rebellion, Protestant women, particularly from middle and upper social ranks, received official protection. The United Irish leadership regarded loyal women as non-combatants, along with the Quakers, and specifically ordered their soldiers not to violate them. Except in only a few instances, this order was respected.[6] Even the Protestant historian James Gordon conceded in 1801: 'In one point, I think we must allow some praise to the rebels. Amid all their atrocities, the chastity of the fair sex was respected. I have not been able to ascertain one instance to the contrary in the county of Wexford, though many beautiful young women were absolutely in their power.'[7] This protected status marginalized women in the eyes of subsequent writers who refused to view them as having any role.

Part of this lack of interest also stemmed from the social attitudes of the eighteenth century. In a society where male and female roles were sharply defined and rigidly enforced, Protestant women were relegated to the sidelines of the political and military arenas. They suffered, mourned, and bore witness; they gave alms, baked bread, and dressed the wounded; they negotiated for fair treatment, and they supported their families – but they assumed no public role, and with a few exceptions on the rebel side, they remained non-combatants. Protestant women, more than their Catholic counterparts, were viewed by men as ornaments of domesticity. Nature had rendered them incapable of political thought or military skill.

4 Ibid., 690–1.   5 Ibid., 226–7.   6 See Kevin Whelan, 'Reinterpreting the 1798 Rebellion in County Wexford', in Dáire Keogh and Nicholas Furlong (eds), *The Mighty Wave: The 1798 Rebellion in Wexford* (Dublin: Four Courts Press, 1996), 28.   7 Revd James Gordon. *History of the Rebellion in Ireland in the Year 1798* (2nd ed., Dublin: J.D. Dewick, 1803), 213.

Yet women remained close to the events of 1798. The official British policy of free quarters forced households to board soldiers. In this context, women heard first-hand accounts of the fighting and the suppression of the uprising. From their windows and doorways, they witnessed unspeakable acts of violence and brutality committed by both Catholics and Protestants against one another. Many had family members in yeomanry regiments who were killed in the fighting. Many more watched the burnings of rebel houses, the floggings on the triangle, and the executions of rebel leaders, whose severed heads impaled on spikes served as grim reminders of the conflict months after the imposition of martial law and the restoration of order.

As witnesses, then, women played an important role in 1798, despite being relegated to the periphery by the male leadership of the time. A small number left behind narrative accounts, offering their perceptions of the rebellion in a style not mirrored in the writings of their male counterparts. They provide a view of 1798 that is less polemical, less injected with partisan hyperbole, yet revealing much about their times, their fears, and their beliefs. Rather than attempting to explain the root causes of the fighting, they offer instead their perceptions of personal relationships strengthened and strained by the conflict, of the numbing and inexplicable acts of violence committed by both sides, of favors granted and slights inflicted. They listened intently to reports of the rebellion from their Catholic neighbours and servants, and they made careful notes of their own treatment by them. In short, they reveal in their writing a glimpse of a personal side of the rebellion in all its subtlety that their male counterparts either ignored, did not experience, or deemed unimportant.

These female narrators were by no means of a single voice or common mind. Living in several counties across Ireland in 1798, they witnessed different theatres of the rebellion and endured different hardships. Some held sharply contrasting world views that were shaped by a variety of factors, including their age and social station, the political affiliations of their families, and their religious upbringing. Most were Anglicans and part of the eighteenth-century ruling Ascendancy, though the level of their personal sense of piety and the degree to which they drew upon their faith in times of crisis appear to have differed. Their faith offered stability, and through its liturgy a structured understanding of God, to whom they turned when afraid. Elizabeth Richards of Rathaspick and Jane Adams of Summerseat, both in County Wexford, relied heavily on their faith, with Richards refusing repeatedly all attempts to convert her. Isabella Brownrigg of Kilpipe, also in County Wexford, related some of her own and her daughter's observations to her faith, while Lady Roden of Dundalk, County Louth, frequently appealed to God's mercy when fleeing her estate. By contrast, Jane Barber of Clovass and Barbara Lett of Killaligan, both of County Wexford, made few religious allusions, and Maria Edgeworth of County Longford and Alicia Pounden of Daphne, County Wexford, offered none at all.

The reasons for this apparent disparity of piety are not altogether clear. Some may have simply been less religious. Lett and Barber both came from lower social stations than Richards, Brownrigg, Adams, and Lady Roden, and hence may not have received as thorough a religious instruction in their youths. Adams, the sister of an Anglican clergyman, attended church regularly before the rebellion and resumed her attendance as soon as she was able at the end of the rebellion. Richards professed a devout attachment to her faith, had clearly received a well-grounded religious education, and when challenged, remained confident that her faith was the true one. For both women, together with Brownrigg and Roden, the Church of Ireland upheld the social order – the very fabric of Protestant society – and was integral to the maintenance of that system. Pounden and Edgeworth, both members of the landed gentry, had undoubtedly received a similar Anglican upbringing, but their faiths may not have seemed important later in writing their accounts. Edgeworth, moreover, was clearly influenced by the Enlightenment views of her father, which had led her to a more rational, less religous, approach to life. She polished her subsequent writings for publication, which none of the other narrators did.

Two other writers, Mary Leadbeater of Ballitore, County Kildare, and Jane Goff of Horetown House, County Wexford, belonged to the Society of Friends. For them, God was more experiential than rationalistic and logical. Their faith had instilled in them radically different notions of peace, egalitarianism and social justice, which had profound implications on how they viewed Irish society. Since few Quakers were landlords, they did not fit into the usual social hierarchy that had stratified Ireland at that time.[8] Nor did they observe the niceties of class and distinction in their treatment of others. Their belief in the universality of an inner light had led them to accept their Catholic neighbours as equals and fellow Christian travelers, rather than as idolatrous Papists. The families of both women opened their homes to the suffering, both Protestant and Catholic, in the wake of the rebellion.

Quaker beliefs clashed with those of the establishment Ascendancy in other ways. Quakers refused to pay tithes, did not recognize marriages performed before a priest, and their devotion to the principles of non-violence was so great that they abjured any involvement in or support for the local yeoman militia. Leadbeater's social idealism allowed her to offer

8 See Kevin O'Neill, 'Mary Shackleton Leadbeater: Peaceful Rebel', in Keogh and Furlong (eds), *The Women of 1798*, 141. See also Maurice J. Wigham, *The Irish Quakers: A Short History of the Religious Society of Friends in Ireland* (Dublin: Religious Society of Friends in Ireland, 1992), 58–60.

limited, non-military support to United Irish organizers in County Kildare, but she resolutely abjured the violence that soon seemed to pervade her village. Although her house was robbed, her non-combatant status generally shielded her family from the reprisals of both the rebels and the English. By contrast, in the more volatile climate of County Wexford, the Goff family's well-known pacifism made them the easy targets of renegade rebels, who often threatened Dinah Goff's father with death, knowing he would not fight back. The religous beliefs of these women led to different aspirations as the rebellion progressed. While some of the Anglican women hoped for a decisive English victory to quell all aspirations of Catholic nationalism, Leadbeater and Goff longed simply for an end to the violence without regard to politics or religion.

Despite the lack of interest most Protestant women had for the political arena, the views of their families had undoubtedly some influence on their own perceptions of Catholics and the social order. Yet the nature and degree of that influence remains unclear. The nuances of the liberal-conservative spectrum that preoccupied so many men of the period may have influenced some of their female relatives more than others, and the process may have varied greatly from family to family. Indeed, other factors such as social status may have played an equally important role in shaping this outlook. Elizabeth Richards came from a liberal gentry family, whose reputation was well known to the rebels. Three of her cousins were United Irishmen, and the family often socialized with Catholics, especially the Tooles of Monaseed. Mary Leadbeater's social altruism, stemming from her faith, led her and her family to accept radical notions of equality and improving the living conditions of the poor. Her brother Richard Shackleton opened his home to refugees during the rebellion. Maria Edgeworth's father, Richard Lovell Edgeworth, a member of the landed gentry, voted with the liberals in Parliament, treated Catholics even-handedly, and allowed them to serve in his yeomanry unit. Suspected of being a rebel sympathizer, he was nearly killed by an angry mob of Orange loyalists. Alicia Pounden's husband, also a member of the gentry, had a reputation for moderation, and after his death, Alicia received protection from her Catholic tenants. Dinah Goff's family sheltered a Catholic family during the rebellion and fed hundreds of others who had camped on their lawn. None of these women seem to have held bigoted views of their Catholic neighbours.

Those women from more conservative families include Isabella Brownrigg, Barbara Lett, and Jane Adams. Brownrigg came from the professional middleman rank, a position just below that of gentry; her husband John had been a commissioner. Lett's father, William Daniel, had been a Surveyor of Excise in Enniscorthy, a social rank slightly below that of the Brownriggs. Both were governmental positions, which suggested that the two men had owed their posts to the patronage of the conservative Lord Ely, thus making it highly likely they held similar conservative views. Neither family was isolated in an Orange cocoon, however. Like many Anglican families, Brownrigg and Lett maintained a wide circle of acquaintances that included many liberals. Brownrigg enjoyed the hospitality of Ebenezer Jacob, the liberal mayor of Wexford, in whose family's home she stayed during the rebellion. Lett's husband Newton's family was exceedingly well-connected to the United Irish: his brother Stephen had actively supported liberal causes and Stephen's widow was a niece of Bagenal Harvey. These liberal influences appear to have had only a marginal impact on the outlooks of the two women. By the end of the fighting, they had hardened toward the rebels, and neither showed any sympathy for Catholics. Although both had endured considerable suffering, the conservative views of their families had probably affected their attitudes.

Jane Adams remains a more complex case study. A Dublin native, she and her family were outsiders in Wexford, but they had achieved enough status to rank with the professional middlemen on a par with the Brownriggs. Adams's brother, the Reverend Roger Owen, was a clerical magistrate who held conservative views and treated Catholics under his control in harsh terms. He was so despised by the Irish at Camolin and Gorey that during the rebellion he was imprisoned, pitchcapped, and marched under guard to prison in Wexford. Only through his sister's intervention was he spared an almost certain death.

In sharp contrast to her brother, however, Jane behaved with humanity toward local Catholics. She entertained the local parish priest at dinner and wrote a letter in praise of his humane conduct out of gratitude for his help in obtaining her father's release from prison. She opened her house to a wounded rebel soldier and wrote cards of protection to her Catholic neighbours, urging them to nail the cards to their cabin doors. Many rebels found refuge in her outbuildings. Far from harbouring a cry for vengeance, she reacted to the rebellion with a sense of pragmatism, and her actions illustrate the danger in labeling a family 'orange' on the basis of the views of only one of its members.

Conceding that these women narrators came from different classes and traditions, some common themes emerge nevertheless in nearly all of their writings, and they suggest issues that were common to many Protestant women in 1798. Each of the women perceived the rebellion as a period of confusion and terror. They all report witnessing wanton acts of violence, either against their own family or others in their neighbourhood, and they express fear of their own personal safety. To a few, the rebels alone seemed demonic and villainous, while others even-handedly observed acts of cruelty committed on both sides. Lett reported the cruelty of the English soldiers, who mistook her husband for a 'croppy villain'. Leadbeater described the unjust executions of several of her neighbours by the English, while Edgeworth focused a fair portion of her narrative on the vigilante mob mentality of the loyalists in Longford. Most of the women, Richards, Brownrigg, and Adams in particular, believed their own deaths to be imminent.

Most of the writers from County Wexford reported attempts of religious conversion, and the stories offer evidence of a widespread rumour that all Protestants would suffer death if they did not convert to Roman Catholicism. Elizabeth Richards wrote of her family's Catholic friend, Mary Byrne, who convinced Richards's mother and sister to convert and save themselves. Dinah Goff reported the efforts of Fr John Byrne, a Carmelite of Goff's Bridge, who met with the family in order to convince Dinah's mother to allow him to put the sign of the cross on her children. Jane Barber's young siblings were handed a Catholic prayerbook by an Enniscorthy baker as a means of protection. Isabella Brownrigg heard reports that a number of prominent local Protestants had gone to chapel in order to be rebaptized. After leaving the prison-ship, she was entreated by a boatman to find a priest in order to save her soul, a request she resolutely refused. Barbara Lett wrote that Mrs Williams, in whose house she stayed after the fall of Enniscorthy to the rebels, attempted to convince her to see a priest so that she would no longer be regarded as a heretic. A servant of Jane Adams begged her and her daughters to be rebaptized as a means of protection. Later, when her father was arrested and taken to jail, the rebel guard said that the family should have sent for a priest long ago.

The similarity of these conversion stories lends powerful support to the view that the masses of participants in County Wexford believed the rebellion to be a religious war. Although United Irish leaders and local parish priests did not promote the canard, they did not actively discourage it. Richards, Goff, Lett, and Adams each reported meeting with different parish priests, all whom were reassuring and did not pressure them to convert. None of the women reported abjuring their faith and becoming Catholic; the wall surrounding their faith was, for them, insurmountable. In every instance they politely rejected the conversion attempt. Indeed, when Adams did so, she seemed to gain the esteem of Fr Roderick O'Connor of Rathmacnee, who told her that a conversion under duress was hardly valid or respectable.

Many of the women reported acts of politeness, even gallantry, on the part of some of the rebel men, especially those in the United Irish leadership. The age of the women, their social station, and their reputations for kindness seem to have influenced the behavior of some of these United men. Elizabeth Richards and Alicia Pounden, both members of the gentry with solidly liberal reputations, fared reasonably well. Richards's family received reports about the rebellion from friendly rebels throughout

May and June of 1798, when the fighting reached its height in Wexford. Pounden suffered greatly when she learned that her husband had been killed in the fall of Enniscorthy, but she and her family were otherwise reasonably well treated, especially by her tenants who knew of her family's moderate reputation. One tenant retrieved her husband's corpse and had it properly buried; other tenants welcomed her back into her home and reassured her that her husband would not have been harmed had he not died in battle. Her house at Daphne had received a specific note of protection signed by United army leaders.

For Jane Barber, Isabella Brownrigg, Barbara Lett, and Jane Adams, prior acquaintances with rebel neighbours sometimes helped them through difficult situations. When Barber found her father's corpse lying on an Enniscorthy street, she burst into tears and sobbed uncontrollably. An angry rebel struck her with the handle of his pike, but another, a business acquaintance of her father, came to her rescue and protected her from another blow. He and a family servant helped Barber to a place of safety on the estate of William Barker, a rebel general who had opened his estate to refugees. Lett obtained a letter of protection from Martin Fenlon, a rebel leader and childhood friend, who urged her to get a pass from Barker. Barker granted it courteously. Brownrigg received a similar letter from Bagenal Harvey, who had been an acquaintance of her husband and who seemed greatly affected by the degree of her suffering. Adams received the protection a squad of rebels led by one Captain Butler, who told her that she had once offered him hospitality while working as a coachman. Old kindnesses were repaid with new ones, perhaps as often as old wrongs were avenged.

More striking, however, is the help that came from total strangers. After the battle of Enniscorthy, Pounden and Lett both received shelter and protection from local Catholic families whom they did not know. The liberal connections of both women in that town may have played a role in winning that protection, though there is no indication of it in their accounts. Adams begged for bread and cheese from a woman distributing it to United army soldiers, but was rebuffed. A passing soldier tossed her his own ration and refused payment for it. Another group of rebel soldiers consoled her when they found her crying at the side of the road and offered to guard her safely back to Summerseat. In attempting to win her controversial brother's release from the Wexford jail, Adams negotiated at length with William Kearney and eventually won custody at considerable risk to Kearney's own reputation.

While the narratives also contain numerous examples of rudeness and incivility committed by rebels against women, this thread of politeness and deference, particularly among the United leaders and the better-educated, runs through many of the accounts. It affirms the view that a number of the insurgents, from the military leadership to some foot soldiers, not only heeded the warnings of the United Irish political leadership and treated women as non-combatants, but went a step further by affording them formal courtesy. An eighteenth-century gentlemen's code of behaviour regarding the deferential treatment of women and, perhaps the personal religious convictions of some of the rebels may have played a part as well in shaping this response. Many appear to have accepted the view that a lady of a certain wealth, age, and station deserved respect, regardless of her loyalties or faith. For this group, whatever social changes they perceived the rebellion bringing, the behaviour code would not change.

By contrast, rebel women did not often govern themselves by the same code of conduct. Appearing frequently in the narratives of loyalist women (more often, in fact, than in the writings of male historians), they often assume different guises. In the case of Adams's servant Alley, loyalty to her mistress prevailed above everything, including the pull of her own family. She stayed at Adams's side throughout the rebellion, even after her own mother urged her to flee when it appeared Summerseat would be burned. When one rebel suggested to Alley that the rebellion now allowed her to change roles and be the master of Adams, she burst into tears and refused. Similarly, Molly Martin, the mother of one of Jane Barber's servants, continued to offer help to the family, even though she was sometimes saucy in her responses to Barber's questions. When Barber asked her where she got a new beaver hat, Molly retorted, 'Hush! tis not for one the like of you to ask me where I got it'. Nevertheless, her past loyalty to the family led Molly to help Jane find the corpse of her father, and she offered consolation when Jane became deeply emotional.

For some rebel women, the rebellion offered a chance to evangelize for Roman Catholicism. It emboldened them in their dealings with the Protestant women, who had never before perceived them as their social equals. When Mary Byrne prevailed on Elizabeth Richards and her mother and sister to meet with Fr John Corrin, the parish priest of Wexford, in order to be rebaptized, she exuded a sense of delight which Richards found irritating. Richards also noted Mary's apparent hypocrisy, concealing her glee when news reached them of a rebel victory and feigning sympathy for the Richards' predicament. The wife of George Williams, who sheltered Barbara Lett after the battle of Enniscorthy, boldly urged her to seek a priest. Even Alley stepped outside the boundaries of her usual servitude and urged Jane Adams to seek rebaptism, though she did so out of concern for the family's welfare.

Other rebel women evinced outward hostility toward their loyal counterparts, without any hint of the deferential decorum shown by men. Adams provided two dramatic illustrations. Once after meeting her brother in prison she was so overcome with emotion that she entered a Wexford ale-house and fainted. Her daughter repeatedly begged a group of women inside for a glass of water but was ignored. Only after the women were scolded by a male rebel was any assistance rendered. Later, when Adams took in a wounded young rebel soldier as a humanitarian gesture, she reported meeting with the boy's mother, who angrily rejected Adams's offer of medical treatment and ordered him removed from Summerseat. The mother had added, 'All was not over with them yet'.

Brownrigg and Pounden both encountered the incivility of Margery 'Madge' Dixon when they were briefly held prisoner on a ship in Wexford Harbour. Madge Dixon, who had been violated by a soldier some time previously, was bent on revenge and filled with hatred for Protestants. With her husband, Captain Thomas Dixon, she was among the principal instigators of the massacre on Wexford Bridge and whipped up local hysteria against Protestants, at least several of whom were moderates. Brownrigg and her daughter managed to gain her confidence through a slight acquaintance, and in spite of their fears managed to escape the ship unharmed, though they lossed all of their possessions to her.

Pounden faced the additional indignity of returning to her home at Daphne and finding it occupied by strangers. Though she was welcomed and protected by her tenants, other women were less accomodating. In the evening after her return a group of these strangers sat up late at night dancing to a fiddle. Her loyal servants protested that it was cruel to do so just after the mistress had returned home, but the female strangers replied, 'If she does not like it, we will turn her out'.

For Barbara Lett, rejection came from members of her own family. Her husband's deceased brother, Stephen Lett of Newcastle, had been a liberal with rebel sympathies; Stephen's widow Mary (Moore) was a cousin of Bagenal Harvey, the Wexford United Irish leader. Barbara met with Mary and her daughters at the height of the rebellion after she had been driven from her home. She found her in-laws dressed in green and openly embracing the rebel cause. After relating the story of her distress, Barbara begged accomodations for the night, but Mary scornfully rejected her request by saying that since her principles were so well known, she was surprised that Barbara could make the request. In this instance, pressure from Mary's rebel friends may have affected her response.

Rebel women sometimes appeared both negatively and positively in the same narrative. Dinah Goff offered two jarring glimpses of rebel women. When a mob of rebels threatened to plunder Horetown House, it was thwarted by a rebel leader who seemed sensitive to the fact that the Goff family was non-partisan and Quaker. A group of crones was turned away at the same time. They had stared into the windows in the hope of pillage, but when the soldiers retreated, they shouted, 'You are a set of chicken-hearted fellows'. Yet in another incident, her father was led out into a field surrounded by a group of pikemen, who threatened him with death. They hesitated beginning to stab him, and as Dinah writes, 'at this critical moment some women came in great agitation through the crowd, clinging to their husbands and dragging them away'.[9] Thus, in at least some situations, contrary to the image of Madge Dixon, some rebel women appear to have acted in ways to blunt the violent actions of their rebel husbands.

The narratives that follow in this work offer a view of 1798 as a small group of literate, Protestant women perceived it. Some of the words were written during the rebellion; others were penned years after the event, when memories had perhaps dimmed and the memory of their own actions may have seemed more dramatic. Nevertheless, the accounts have the ring of forthrightness and truth, rather than exaggeration and sensationalism. They reveal the complexity of the social conditions of the time. The rebellion was neither a peasant rebellion nor religious war waged by villainous Papists. Rather, in their eyes, it was a chaotic, fearful time of great social instabilty, where neighbours helped one another nearly as often as they harmed. They challenge all scholars of the rebellion to continue taking a broader view of the conflict.

9 Dinah Wilson Goff, *Divine Protection through Extraordinary Dangers during the Irish Rebellion of 1798* (Philadelphia, 1856), 21–2.

CHRONOLOGY OF EVENTS

This chronology of events associated with the rebellion of 1798 is designed to help the reader place the women's narratives into a larger historical context. An especially useful source for more detail on these events is Daniel Gahan's *The People's Rising: Wexford, 1798* (Dublin: Gill & Macmillan, 1995).

1795	Orange Order is organized in southern Ulster as an Anglican secret society sworn to oppose the political aspirations of Roman Catholics; Catholics form an opposing society called Defenders.
1796 December	French army of 12,000 almost lands at Bantry Bay but is thwarted by bad weather.
1797–1798 Winter	Rebellion planned by United Irish leaders. Orange lodges spread, including three formed in County Wexford.
1798 12 March	Arrest of United Irish Directory. Manufacture of pikes is widespread and noticed by some loyalists.
30 March	Martial law in Ireland is proclaimed, and the Privy Council declares Ireland to be in a state of rebellion.
18 April	Declarations of loyalty from several Catholic parishes in Co. Wexford are presented to the Lord Lieutenant.
25 April	Twenty-seven magistrates meet at Gorey to proclaim County Wexford for the United cause.
27 April	North Cork Militia arrives in Wexford and imposes draconian policies upon the Catholic population. United Irish leaders meet in Wexford.
17–18 May	National Directory of United Irishmen meets.
23 May	All Catholics possessing arms are ordered to surrender them within fourteen days. Anthony Perry is arrested by the North Cork Militia and tortured, leading to the arrest of many United Irish leaders in Wexford.
24 May	Thirty-five suspected United Irish prisoners are shot at Dunlavin Green. Archibald Hamilton Jacob and his yeoman cavalry from Enniscorthy march to Ballaghkeen, where they flog a man to death.
25 May	Twenty-four United prisoners shot at Carnew; a United Irish attack on Carlow ends with 460 rebels killed.

26 May	Formal outbreak of the rebellion in County Wexford at The Harrow. Battle of Kilthomas fought near Ferns, Co. Wexford. Signal fires are lit on surrounding hills. Rebels mobilize under the leadership of Fr John Murphy of Boolavogue.
27 May	Battle of Oulart Hill is fought; rebels rout the North Cork Militia under the command of Col. Foote. Rebels under Fr Murphy overrun the house of the Revd Robert Burrows at Kyle, killing Burrows and several others.
28 May	Battle of Enniscorthy fought and captured by rebels after fierce fighting.
29 May	Arrest of United leaders Harvey, Fitzgerald and Colclough in Wexford; garrison in Wexford reinforced by troops from Duncannon under Col. Maxwell. United Irish camp formed at Three Rocks.
30 May	Rebels ambush English troops under Maxwell's command at Three Rocks, paving the way for rebel control of Wexford. Many Protestants are taken prisoner by a gang led by Captain Thomas Dixon.
31 May	Bagenal Harvey made commander-in-chief of United army; Matthew Keogh is governor of Wexford town. United Irish conference at Windmill Hill camp. Civilian government is established in Wexford consisting of four Catholics and four Protestants.
1 June	Rebel attack on Newtownbarry (Bunclody) repulsed; fighting also on Ballyminaun Hill. Rebels execute suspected Orangemen at the Vinegar Hill camp.
2 June	North Cork Militia leader Lord Kingsborough arrested and held in Wexford. Government troops under General Loftus reach Arklow.
3 June	Government troops continue to march toward rebel positions. Dixon's gang shoots Francis Murphy, an alleged informant, in the Bullring in Wexford.
4 June	Battle of Tubberneering won by rebels; Gorey falls to the rebels.
5 June	Battle of New Ross fought; the town is successfully defended by government forces commanded by Gen. Johnson. Over a hundred prisoners held in a barn are burned to death by rebels at Scullabogue.
6 June	Rebellion begins in Ulster led by Henry Joy McCracken, who issues a proclamation calling all United Irishmen to arms. Dismayed by the fall of northern County Wexford, Gen. Lake orders 1,000 government soldiers under Lt-Gen. Needham to march from Dublin to Arklow.
7 June	Rebel Gen. Edward Roche assumes command of the United Irish forces in County Wexford from Harvey. Carnew, County Wicklow, is burned by rebels.
9 June	Battle of Arklow fought; rebels are defeated and retreat to Gorey. Roche issues a rebel proclamation declaring four Orange leaders, Hunter Gowan, Archibald Jacob, James Boyd and Hawtrey White, as outlaws.
12 June	Failed rebel attack on Borris, County Wexford.

13 June   United Irish in the north are defeated at the battle of Ballinahinch, County Antrim.

14 June   Dixon whips up hysteria in Wexford town against Col. Le Hunte, who is nearly killed.

15 June   Dixon's radicals temporarily oust Keugh and take control of Wexford.

16 June   Wexford and South Wicklow United Irish overrun a small garrison at Mountpleasant, near Tinahely, County Wexford. Dublin is reinforced by 1,000 British troops.

18 June   Keugh regains control of Wexford. Rebels fight a stalemate at the battle of Kilcavan Hill near Carnew.

19 June   Gorey retaken by government forces under Gen. Needham; British forces advance into County Wexford under Generals Lake and Moore.

20 June   Battle of Foulkesmills or Goff's Bridge; in a decisive engagement, the day is won by government forces under Gen. Moore. The rebels retreat to Three Rocks. Dixon's gang orders the massacre of prisoners on Wexford Bridge; ninety are killed.

21 June   Battle of Vinegar Hill fought; rebel troops defeated by Gen. Lake's forces in the most decisive battle of the rebellion. Many civilians are massacred. Wexford's United Irish leaders meet and send Kingsborough to Lake with terms of surrender. Loyalist prisoners are freed. Enniscorthy is retaken.

22 June   Rebels scatter. Harvey and John Henry Colclough flee to the Saltee Islands; another group under Fr John Murphy march to the Sculloge Gap. A small battle is fought at Killedmund, County Carlow.

23 June   Many rebels are arrested, including Harvey and Colclough. Rebel columns move into Carlow, Wicklow and Kilkenny. Battle at Goresbridge, County Kilkenny.

24 June   Pursued by government troops under Gen. Asgill, some rebels reach Castlecomer in County Kilkenny and capture it.

25 June   Another rebel column reaches Hacketstown, Queen's County, and is defeated in a skirmish. Executions continue in Wexford, including Keugh and Fr Roche.

26 June   Battle at Kilcumney Hill, near Goresbridge. Asgill's soldiers kill any men they find on the suspicion that they are rebels. Cornelius Grogan and Edward Frayne are tried in Wexford. Yeomanry units seek revenge against Catholics, especially Hunter Gowan's Black Mob. Many innocent people are terrorized and killed.

27 June   Grogan convicted.

28 June   Harvey, Grogan, and Colclough are executed in Wexford.

29 June   Battle of Ballyellis near Monaseed; Ancient Britons are ambushed by rebels. Rebels encamp on Kilcavan Hill.

2 July	Fr John Murphy executed at Tullow, County Carlow.
10 July	Rebels attack Clonard but are repulsed.
12 July	Generals Lake and Moore march north to crush the rebellion in Kildare and Meath.
End of July	Rebellion in Wexford effectively crushed. Some rebels flee to the Wicklow Mountains.
22 August	French army of 1,000 under the command of Gen. Jean Humbert lands near Killala, County Mayo.
8 September	Humbert surrenders to Gen. Cornwallis at Ballinamuck, County Longford.

ELIZABETH RICHARDS

Elizabeth Richards was born in 1778 at Rathaspick, Co. Wexford, the youngest of two daughters born to Thomas Richards and his wife Martha Redmond. She was part of one of Co. Wexford's most liberal Anglican gentry families, and though her family remained loyal in 1798, it maintained close ties to both the local Catholic gentry and the United Irish.

The Richards family had settled in Co. Wexford prior to Cromwell's invasion. Thomas Richards of Park was the father of Thomas Richards, who became the first of the family to settle at Rathaspick. He married Jane, daughter and co-heir of Col. Loftus Codd of Castletown and Rathaspick, from whom also descended the Hores of Harperstown, Co. Wexford. His son, Thomas Richards III (1688–1768), grandfather of Elizabeth, married Elizabeth, daughter of Joseph Orne of Wexford. Their son, Thomas Richards IV, the father of Elizabeth, was born in 1722; in 1776, at the late age of 56, he married Martha, daughter of Matthew Redmond of Kilgowan.[1]

Thomas Richards allied himself closely with Co. Wexford's liberals during the 1780s and early 1790s, voting for the constitution, supporting Catholic emancipation, and allying himself with the Grogan-Colclough wing in local politics.[2] Unlike many of his more conservative contemporaries who viewed Catholics with suspicion, Richards felt no antipathy for his Catholic neighbours and often entertained several Catholic gentry families in his home. In her diary, Elizabeth recorded her frequent visits with the Tooles of Fairfield, one of the wealthiest Catholic families at that time in the county. Although Thomas Richards was dead by 1798, his liberal sympathies would not have made him or his family isolated from the growing radicalism of the early 1790s. Indeed, three of Elizabeth's first cousins, William Hatton, Michael Redmond, and John Cook Redmond, were early members of the Society of United Irishmen.

For all of these reasons, Elizabeth's diary offers an unusual glimpse of how a loyal, liberal gentry family viewed the events of 1798. Like many other Protestants, she joined in the prevailing hysteria by accepting the

---

1 'Richards of Macmine Castle', in *Burke's Landed Gentry of Ireland* (London: Harrison & Sons, 1912), 591. 2 For material on Thomas Richards' voting pattern, see Kevin Whelan, 'Reinterpreting the 1798 Rebellion in Co. Wexford', in Keogh and Furlong (eds), *The Mighty Wave*, 14.

rumour that all Protestants were targeted for death by the rebel army. Her diary, written contemporarily with the events she describes, is filled with lamentations of dread as she hears news of the rebel victory at Enniscorthy, the taking of Wexford, and the assembling of a massive force at Three Rocks. Nevetheless, she summoned her courage, renewed her Anglican religious convictions, and resisted attempts by several family friends to convince her to renounce her faith and be baptized a Roman Catholic. The Richards' political stance and their relationship to William Hatton apparently spared their home from being targeted for rebel reprisal. The family remained safe at Rathaspick throughout the rebellion, and the following year, her mother petitioned the crown for modest losses of cattle and a horse, with a bridle and saddle, totalling £50 (a modest sum compared to the losses of other Protestants).[3]

On 15 April 1802, ignoring her mother's reservations, Elizabeth married Frederik Willem van Limberg Stirum, a Bavarian nobleman, who was born on 7 December 1774 at Deventer, and died on 6 April 1858 at The Hague, Netherlands. Martha Richards had questioned Stirum's sincerity because of the swiftness of the courtship, but the marriage proved happy, and the couple reared ten children born between 1803 and 1820: Eliza Martha in 1803, Frederik Adriaan and Thomas Henry in 1804; Theodora Louisa in 1806; Menno David in 1807; Anna Frederica in 1809; Aurelia Elizabeth born in 1812; Julius Bernard in 1815; Frederica Johanna in 1817; and Albertina Catherina in 1820. Elizabeth's sister, Martha, had also married a nobleman, John Louis Gidson Ernest von Preberton Willmsdorff of Hanover.[4]

Elizabeth and her husband lived briefly in Pembroke before returning to Wexford to a house called Rockfield on the banks of the Slaney. The Willmsdorffs lived at the Richards's home at Rathaspick, until mounting debts and mismanagement forced them to sell the home and all of its contents in 1807. They were forced to flee to the Isle of Man. In 1810, after the Stirums had themselves lived several years in difficult circumstances, they sold the house at Rockfield and returned to the house at Rathaspick, although Elizabeth remained unhappy about the move. After living many years at Rathaspick, the family moved to the Netherlands, where Elizabeth's children gained prominence. Son Menno David served

---

3 'List of Claimants for Relief as Suffering Loyalists ... ', *Journal of the Irish House of Commons*, Appendix [1800], cccxi. Hereafter cited as 'Claimants'. 4 Martha Richards von Preberton died in 1855. She had four children: Thomas William Frederick of Rathaspick, who died unmarried; Henrietta, who married Capt. Frederick Dayrolles; Anne, who married John Craven Mansergh and died in 1844; and Elizabeth, who died unmarried in 1898 (*Burke's Landed Gentry of Ireland* [1912], 519). For material on Rathaspick Manor, the Richards' house, see Dan Walsh, *100 Wexford Co. Houses: An Illustrated History* (Enniscorthy: Mill Park Productions, 1996), 82.

as minister of War for Holland, while daughter Aurelia Elizabeth was dame du Palace to the Queen of the Netherlands. Elizabeth died in 1863 at The Hague, where the original manuscript of her diary is preserved.[5]

THE ACCOUNT

Rathaspeck [sic], *May 27* [recte 26th] *1798, Saturday*
We this day quitted Clonard after spending a happy week there; we came through Wexford where we learned there had been a general rising in the Co. of Kildare, but that the insurgents had been defeated. It was also reported that the neighbourhood of Gorey and of Oulard has much disturbed. Our trunks of clothes that went off this morning for Dublin are, I think, in some danger. I much fear that the people of this country are more inclined to insurrection than is apprehended. Sullen melancholy was expressed this day on the countenances of every individual of the lower classes. It can have no cause but the banishment of their priest Dixon[6] and of 10 men found guilty by the magistrates of the county assembled at Wexford of disloyalty. These rebels were sent off this day to Duncannon Fort escorted by a troop of yeomanry.

5 The manuscript diary of Elizabeth Richards is housed at The Hague, Netherlands; in 1919 it was owned by her grandson, Jonk Groenix van Zoelen of The Hague. The manuscript was transcribed during the Great War by Major W.E. Gatacre of the King's Own Yorkshire Light Infantry, who in turn permitted Goddard H. Orpen, the well-known and respected historian of Norman Ireland, to copy it shortly afterward. This version was lost, but a transcript made by Orpen's brother, the Revd Thomas H. Orpen, was preserved. This version is available at the National Library of Ireland, Microfilm 36486. It contains several slight errors from the original, such as Keugh written erroneously as Keagh, but for the most part is a faithful transcription. A photocopy of the original diary was graciously supplied to the editor by Brian Cleary of Wexford. The reader should be aware that the diary does have a problem with dates. She began her '98 account on Saturday, 26 May 1798, giving an erroneous date of 27 May. The dating remained erroneous through Thursday, 31 May, when the problem was remedied.   6 Fr Thomas Dixon of Castlebridge was a cousin to another priest Dixon, Fr James Dixon of Crossabeg, as well as cousin to Nicholas and Thomas Dixon, who were active United Irishmen in Wexford (see David Goodall, 'Dixon of Castlebridge', in *Irish Genealogist* 6 [Nov. 1984]:633). Little is known of Dixon's early life. Whelan has noted that the Dixons were active as shopkeepers, cornfactors, maltsters, brewers, and innkeepers (Kevin Whelan, 'The Catholic Priest in the 1798 Rebellion', in Kevin Whelan and William Nolan (eds), *Wexford History and Society* [Dublin: Geography Publications, 1987], 302–3). Bishop Caulfield removed Dixon as curate of Our Lady's Island in 1794 because of his 'drinking, dancing, and disorderly conduct' (see Caulfield-Troy Correspondence, Troy Papers, Dublin Diocesan Archives). Later, Caulfield sent him to Blackwater as curate under Fr David Cullen, where he became actively involved with the United Irish. He was again removed by the bishop on the testimony of his cousin, Fr James Dixon. Arrested in the spring of 1798, he was sentenced to transportation at the May assizes, but he died of a fever soon after while confined at Duncannon.

Whitsunday May 28 [recte 27th] *Clonard.*

At church to my unspeakable astonishment I heard that Bagnal Harvey, Edward Fitzgerald and John Colclough[7] of Ballyteague had been taken up on suspicion of disaffection to government and lodged in jail, that the rebels in great force had attacked Carlow, nearly destroyed Tullagh Street, but at length had been repulsed. After divine service we walked to Fairfield. The news we had heard was the subject of conversation. It was treated lightly until a servant of Mr Sutton's[8] rode up in haste to the hall door, and told us that his master and mistress had sent him out to let my mother know that the people at the other side of the water were up, that they judged the county to be very unsafe, and begged we would go to town immediately. Horror-struck, we ran home. My mother had the lower windows barred, and in breathless anxiety, we awaited the return of our servants, whom she had sent to town to take the oaths of allegiance.

An hour had lapsed when I saw my nurse running down the avenue. I asked her what was the news. She said 'good news'. The people had dispersed and the danger was over. My mother had the hall door opened and we ventured to come out. At that moment a strange man came from the shrubbery and we were running back to our fortress. My nurse knew him to be one of Mrs Hatton's[9] workmen. I ran to ask him for his mistress. She was at Clonard, he said, and begged we would go to her immediately.

7 Beauchamp Bagenal Harvey, Edward Fitzgerald, and John Henry Colclough were leaders in the political wing of the United Irish in Co. Wexford. Harvey, an Anglican, was born in 1762, entered Trinity College Dublin and was called to the Irish Bar. He was named President of the rebel Committee, but he professed to have little influence over the masses of rebels and openly deplored the massacre of Protestants, of which he was one. He was captured at the Saltee Islands and executed on 27 June 1798. For a sketch of his life, see Helen Skrine, 'A Glimpse of Bagenal Harvey', *J. of the Wexford Historical Society* 14 (1992–3): 92–100; see also Richard R. Madden, *The United Irishmen: Their Lives and Times* (London: Catholic Publishing, 1860), 4: 462–94 (cited herafter as Madden). Fitzgerald, a Catholic and maltster, was born about 1770 at Newpark, Killisk, Co. Wexford, the son of a wealthy Catholic middleman. He was also called to the Bar and later joined the Committee, becoming a prominent United Irish organizer in Wexford town. Following the Rebellion, he fled to Hamburg and died there in 1807 (see Madden, 4: 550–63). Colclough, also Roman Catholic, was a native of Ballyteigue and an active United organizer. He was captured with Harvey at the Saltee Islands and executed on 28 June 1798 (Ibid, 4: 476–83).   8 Sutton's identity is uncertain, but he was probably a son of Caesar Sutton of Longraigue. Caesar Sutton married Elizabeth, daughter of Jacob Goff of Dublin and had several sons, including Jacob, Joshua, John, and Charles (see David Goodall, 'Freemen of Wexford', *Irish Genealogist* 5 [Nov. 1977]: 457; cited hereafter as Freemen). Goff was admitted Freeman of Wexford, 2 July 1782.   9 Elizabeth, daughter of John Wray of Castle Wray, Co. Wexford, married John Hatton of Clonard on 29 Oct. 1757 (see 'Hatton of Clonard' in *Burke's Landed Gentry of Ireland* [1912], 303). Her husband John was the son of Henry Hatton, attorney, by his wife Edith, daughter of Thomas Richards of Rathaspick. Thus, the Hattons were cousins of the Richards (see Freemen, 322). They had four sons: Henry of Clonard; William, a member of the Dublin Society of United Irishmen; George, M.P. for Lisburn; and John, a Major-General in the Army.

She sent to my mother a note she had received from a lady in Wexford, by that we learned that the insurgents were in force and had put to death some men who would not join them. The danger seemed evident to my mother, and she determined to wait no longer for the carriage, but to walk across the fields to Clonard with the man who had brought the note. I often turned round to look at Rathaspeck. I fear that the sadness with which I gazed at it is prophetic.

In the evening, flying reports reached us that a detachment of North Cork Militia, consisting of 200 men, had been sent against the rebels, and was cut to pieces with the exception of Col. Foote,[10] who commanded it, and five privates. This was thought to be impossible – too soon we found it to be a dreadful certainty. From the back windows we saw several houses in flames – Good God! What a scene!

Monday, May 29th [recte 28th]
The morning passed in listening to reports and looking through a spy glass. At about 3 oc. George Read rode out to demand Mrs Hatton's fire-arms. He confirmed the dreadful intelligence of a second defeat of the King's troops at Enniscorthy, of the burning of part of that town, of the murder of Mr Burroughs,[11] of D'Arcy Howlin,[12] &c. He represented in

---

10 On 26 May 1798, Colonel Foote was commander of all government forces at Oulart Hill, including North Cork Militia, which had a notorious reputation for lack of discipline. Foote was overrun by the United Irish army; he survived the battle but lost 105 of his complement of 110 men: see Brian Cleary, 'The Battle of Oulart Hill: Context and Strategy', in Keogh and Furlong (eds), *The Mighty Wave: The 1798 Rebellion in Wexford*, 79, 96. Little else is known of his career. Pakenham states that he had served in America before being sent to Ireland (Thomas Pakenham, *The Year of Liberty* [Englewood Cliffs, NJ: Prentice-Hall, 1969], 151). Musgrave includes Foote's account of the battle in his work (see Sir Richard Musgrave, *Memoirs of the Different Rebellions in Ireland*, 4th ed. [Fort Wayne, IN: Round Tower Books, 1995], 319–20).   11 Revd Robert Burrowes was vicar of Ballyvaldon and curate of Millenagh, a post to which he was nominated by Henry Hatton (see James B. Leslie, *Ferns Clergy and Parishes* [Dublin: Church of Ireland Printing, 1936], 120). His alliance with the Hattons reflects his liberal political views. His brother Peter Burrowes was a United Irishman, and their mother was Roman Catholic. Burrowes entered Trinity College Dublin in 1767, received his B.A. in 1772 and M.A. in 1775. He married Mary, daughter of William Clifford of Castle Annesley (*Ferns M.L.*, 1782). On 28 May 1798, his house at Kyle was occupied by a party of local parishioners seeking sanctuary, knowing his liberal views would likely protect them. Shortly afterwards, the house was approached by a party of United Irish led by Fr John Murphy. When someone in the house fired a shot at the party, they stormed it and killed all of its occupants, including Burrowes. See Patrick Comerford, 'Euseby Cleaver, Bishop of Ferns, and the Clergy of the Church of Ireland in the 1798 Rising in Co. Wexford', *J. of the Wexford Historical Society* 16 (1996–7):79. For a biased account, see Musgrave, 310, 315–16; see also H.F.B. Wheeler and A.M. Broadley, *War in Wexford* [London: John Lane, The Bodley Head, 1920], 87–8.   12 Edward Howlin D'Arcy of Ballynahown, son of Maurice Howlin D'Arcy of Coolcul by his wife Eleanor, sister of Sir John Tottenham, was a local magistrate and member of Hawtrey White's Ballaghkeene Cavalry, which held Orange views and was widely disliked. He was shot dead 'near the gates

the strongest colours the dangers which we should be exposed by remaining in the country, assured us we should be perfectly safe in town, it would be fortified, he said, in such a manner that the rebels, if they did attack it, would not be able to make the least impression.

My mother and Mrs Hatton seemed fearless of danger, yet the latter was not totally disinclined to go to Wexford. I wept and supplicated my mother to make an effort to save our lives and properties. I represented to her that there would be time enough that evening to go to Rathaspeck, take our papers from thence and proceed to Wexford. She scolded me for my tears and forced me to silence. What will be our fate? I will not go to bed. The rest of the family can sleep as usual. The smoking ruins of Enniscorthy are in sight. How can they rest?

Tuesday, 30th [recte 29th] *May*
The Donegal Militia commanded by Col. Maxwell[13] is arrived at Wexford, also Col. Colville, Capts. Young and Soden[14] of the 13th, who have volunteered their service for our defence. My mother and sister are gone to Rathaspeck to secure our papers and anything of value that is portable. Mrs Hatton and Miss Tench[15] to town. I wished to go with them but there was not room for me in the car. Their absence was spent in questioning every passenger and looking towards Rathaspick through the spy-glass. I was uneasy for my mother and sister. At length we all again were

---

of the then fine avenue at Ballynahown' on 27 May 1798, allegedly as he was endeavouring to rescue his mother (see P.H. Hore, *History of the Town and Co. of Wexford* [London: Elliot Stock, 1911], 6:566–7; see also Freemen, 118; Musgrave, 315). His asssassin was allegedly Timothy Whelan. D'Arcy's mother, Elinor Howlin D'Arcy, claimed losses in 1799, including 'House burned, Cattle, Furniture, Wine, Cloaths, [and] Corn' (Claimants, App. cccxlv).   **13** Col. Richard Maxwell, commander of the 200-man Donegal Militia, played a major role at the battle of Three Rocks, leading a retreat of British forces to Duncannon in response to the defeat of two companies of the Meath Regiment (Wheeler, 97–8). Taylor distinguishes him from Barry Maxwell, later Lord Farnham, who commanded a different militia (George Taylor, *A History of the Rise, Progress, Cruelties, and Suppression of the Rebellion in the Co. of Wexford in the Year 1798* [Belleville, Ireland: M. Bowell, 1864], 111; see also Musgrave, 357, 360, 364–66). Maxwell's report to Col. Eustace on the evacuation of Wexford is published in Charles Dickson, *The Wexford Rising in 1798: Its Causes and Its Course* (Tralee, Ireland: The Kerryman, n.d.), 234–6.   **14** Colonel Colville, with Captain Young and Lieutenant Soden of the 13th Regiment, left Duncannon Fort on the orders of Gen. William Fawcett to join the forces of Maxwell's Donegal Militia at Wexford (see Daniel Gahan, *The People's Rising: Wexford, 1798* [Dublin: Gill & Macmillan, 1995], 62; see also Revd James Gordon, *History of the Rebellion in Ireland in the Year 1798* [London: T. Hurst, 1803], 119). Nothing further is known of their careers.   **15** Mary Tench, called 'Molly' later in the narrative, was undoubtedly related to Samuel Tench of Spa Well, Co. Wexford, who left a will dated 1774 (see Freemen, 458–9). Samuel had married Margaret, daughter of Highgate Boyd of Rosslare and had a daughter Margaret, who married Henry Hatton of Clonard. In spite of his alliance with the conservative Boyds, the Tenches, like the Hattons and Richards, were a liberal Protestant family in Wexford.

assembled. Toward evening we heard that the rebels were collecting on the mountain of Forth.

Wednesday, May 31st [recte 30th]

At four o'clock my mother called us during the night; the rebels had collected in great force at the Three Rocks. Through the telescope we plainly saw them in large bodies marching and counter-marching and tossing their pikes as if in jig. Numbers on horseback were also performing a sort of exercise. About 6 o'clock we saw part of the garrison march towards the rebels. They were met by them on the high road that leads from Wexford by the Mountain of Forth to Taghmon. A volley of musketry was fired. We saw one officer fall from his horse. We afterward learned it was Col. Watson[16] and in the course of a few minutes the King's troops began a precipitate retreat. Our distress, aggrevated by uncertainty of the fate of the army and what our own might be so near to a conquering mob, at first approached despair. At length a stupid horror pervaded my senses. I feared without being able to grieve at the extent of our misery – that was most dreadful.

In the course of the morning a man rode into the courtyard with a white handkerchief tied round his hat, a green bough in front of it, and a drawn sword in his hand. Everyone crowded round him; the servants seemed joyful. He demanded or rather commanded that provisions should be sent to the camp. 'We are starving, Ma'am', said he to Mrs Hatton, 'Send us provisions or – ' he struck his sword with violence on the head of a pump rear which he had stopped his horse, and without remonstrance from Mrs Hatton.

'Government may confiscate my property for assisting rebels'. 'If you do not comply we shall be murdered' was the reply by all. An old man was dispatched to the Three Rocks with a car loaded with bacon, potatoes, &c &c, for which Mrs Hatton received thanks from the rebel chiefs.

16 Lt-Col. Jonas Watson, a retired officer with the rank of Sergeant in the Shelmalier Cavalry, was a moderate whose wife Harriet was the daughter of Revd Thomas Colclough and his wife Florence (Molesworth). She was thus a cousin of John Henry Colclough, the United Irish leader (see *Burke's Landed Gentry of Ireland* [1912], 120). Watson, whose military career included service in America, took charge of the Wexford Yeoman Cavalry after the fall of Enniscorthy. He set up barricades in town, and then led his men in a retreat to Three Rocks, where he was killed on 30 May 1798. (See Pakenham, 176–7; Dickson, 82, 85; Musgrave, 360; see also the memoir of his son Edward Watson, 'Memories of Col. Jonas Watson', ed. by Hilary Murphy, *J. of the Wexford Historical Society* 15 [1994–5]: 115–18.) He was buried in Carrick churchyard, where his inscription states, 'he had been actively employed for thirty years in the service of his country, during which period his life had often been preserved against the shock of Battle, but pleased the Almighty that he alone should fall whilst gallantly leading on the Yeomanry of this county to attack the Rebel Force which was posted on the Three Rocks ...' (see Brian Cantwell, *Memorials of the Dead*, vol. 6 [East Wexford], 233; cited hereafter as Cantwell).

Reports had reached us that the yeomanry had abandoned their posts, got on board vessels with their families, and that the town was nearly deserted. About 10 o'clock Mrs Clifford[17] came to Clonard from Wexford. She looked distracted. 'Ladies', she said, 'I am sorry to be the messenger of bad news: the army has left Wexford. It is in the possession of the rebels. Every Protestant is to be murdered tonight. You cannot escape; all we have to do is prepare for death'.

I looked around me with horror. I felt there was no possibility of concealment or flight. The infernal pikes seemed already to glitter at our breasts. I shrieked and for a moment was all but mad. Crowds of Enniscorthy victors now began to fill the house, some of them wearing the uniforms of the murdered yeomen, flushed with victory and glorying in the blood that they had shed. They told us that they or some of their friends had met the 13th regiment on its way to Wexford and that not a man but the commander had escaped. (It was one or two companies of the Meath Militia that had been defeated by the rebels. They had two field pieces which were taken by the latter and contributed to the defeat of the Donegal Militia at the Three Rocks). Some of Mrs Hatton's servants repaired to their victorious confederates as soon as they knew to a certainty that the army had retreated. The mask was cast aside. Those men who the Sunday before had solemnly taken the oaths of allegiance did not scruple to join the rebels.

About 6 o'clock a vast number of the insurgents on horseback and on foot marched in a tumultuous manner from the Three Rocks to take possession of the town. They passed by the gate of Clonard and to our inexpressible satisfaction promised protection to Mrs Hatton.

An evening of listless anxiety was followed by a night of apprehension. We could hear shouts or rather yells of joy from the town that struck terror into our hearts. I sat up late; death, I imagined, would have additional horrors if unthought of, and notwithstanding the assurances of safety that had been given to me, to that only did I look forward.

Thursday, May 31 [dates now correct]
Mrs Hatton received a threatening letter from a man with whom she had had some money dealings. He required that she should give him up some lands or £700. A rebel guard which had been sent to protect her by

17 Jane Staunton, daughter of Richard Ousley Cormick of Mullockmore, Co. Galway, married William Clifford of Wexford, son of William Clifford of Castle Annesley by his wife Alicia, daughter of William Moore of Tinraheen (see *Genealogical and Heraldic Dictionary of the Landed Gentry of Great Britain and Ireland for 1850* [London: Henry Colburn, 1850], 231). Jane died on 28 Nov. 1867, aged 91; her husband died on 2 Apr. 1835, aged 61. They are buried in St Patrick's Churchyard, Wexford (see Cantwell, vol. 6 [East Wexford], 274). Mary Clifford, their daughter, married Revd Robert Burrowes (see Freemen, 115; Leslie, 120).

General Roach[18] (a tenant of Mrs Hatton's) confined the bearer of the letter in the guard house, and sent information of the threats contained in it to the rebel camp at the Wind-mill Hills. The guard was reinforced.

Our servants and an old cotter came from Rathaspeck to see us. They wept for us; the marks of attachment they showed for us made me cry too.

Some people who had flown from Wexford to Clonard told us that a massacre of the Protestants was intended and would undoubtedly take place. A servant of Mrs Hatton's of the Protestant religion once heard some Papists say that they would first murder the Orangemen and the Protestants too, although it should be five years afterwards. William Hatton,[19] who is an original United Irishman, assured us there would not be a 'massacre', but that if we were 'uneasy', he would endeavour to procure us a boat to take us to Wales.

It is said that Captain Boyd[20] has been taken and put to death at the Three Rocks. We spent a melancholy evening; although we know him but little, some of us, some of our tears were for his sufferings.

Friday, June 1st
On foot, unattended, and bearing in our hands green boughs, the emblem of unity, Mrs Hatton, my mother, my sister and I set out from Clonard. We met several parties of armed men on the road. They suffered us to pass unmolested. The great body of insurgents had been drawn off towards Ross. One or two corps were exercising on the Windmill fields. The town presented a melancholy spectacle: houses gutted, the streets strewn with broken glass, pieces of furniture, and articles of ladies' dress. Confusion, astonishment, ferocity were alternately expressed in the faces of those we met, and some viewed us with exultation, while others invoked the saints and angels to guard and bless us. William Hatton met us and accompanied us into town. He desired us to hide our sorrows. Everyone succeeded but me. In hopes of seeing Genl. Roach and by his means, forwarding our scheme of departure, we walked long on the Quay. He had set off for Gorey or Vinegar Hill an hour before we arrived there.

---

18 Edward Roche of Garrylough was born about 1758; he was a Sergeant in the Shelmalier Yeoman Cavalry, which was typical of the liberal corps infiltrated by United Irish in order to get recruits. During the Rebellion, he became a General in the United army, surrendering in August, 1798. Subsequently he was tried and sentenced to transportation, but died at Newgate about 1799. See L.M. Cullen, 'The 1798 Rebellion in Wexford: United Irishman Organisation, Membership, Leadership', in Whelan and Nolan (eds), *Wexford History and Society*, 250, 257–8; see also Goodall, 'Dixon of Castlebridge', 633.   19 William Hatton, son of John and Elizabeth (Wray) Hatton, was a member of the Dublin Society of United Irishmen (see R.B. McDowell, 'Personnel of the Dublin Society of United Irishmen', *Irish Historical Studies* 2 [1941]: 12–53). He married Elizabeth Ross and had several children (see *Burke's Landed Gentry of Ireland* [1912], 303).   20 Captain John Boyd was the son of Highgate Boyd by his wife Amy Phillips, and a brother of Captain James Boyd, notorious

Disappointed and fatigued, we reached Mrs Hatton's house in George's Street. There a more distressing scene than any we had passed through awaited us. Several Protestants, terrified at the report that a massacre of all those who professed their religion was intended, had abjured their faith and suffered themselves to be christened by Romish priests, from whom they had obtained written *Protection*, which ran nearly as follows: 'I beseach you for Christ's sake, protect A.B., his (or her) children and property, whom I certify to be a true friend to the Roman Catholic cause, signed Corrin,[21] Parish Priest of Wexford'.

A lady who had conformed through fear was very urgent with us to follow her example. My mother consented, my sister did not object, my heart reviled at such hypocrisy. Mrs Hatton condemned it, fortified with her approbation. I became resolved to avoid even the appearance of a change of religion. Mrs Roche[22] in the strongest terms represented the danger to which we would expose ourselves by refusing to submit to the ceremony of being christened by a Priest. She knelt to Mrs Hatton, she shed tears, she caressed, she coaxed me. My determination she could not shake, although she heightened the struggle between the love of my religion, the dread of committing sin should I seem to renounce it, and the fear of a violent death. I wished for madness to end the conflict – madness that had hitherto seemed to me of all evils the most dreadful!

Mrs Hatton, ever thoughtful, had sent for Mr Corrin. She would enquire from him if there was any foundation for Mrs Roche's fear. He answered her that there was not and gave us protection, omitting the words

---

commander of the Wexford Yeoman Cavalry, and together with Hawtrey White, Hunter Gowan, and Archibald Hamilton Jacob, one of the most despised magistrates in the county. John, whose political beliefs are unknown, had married Jane Danby in 1789 (Ferns M.L.). On 30 May 1798, on disembarking a ship, he was recognized by his enemies, chased, piked, and left for dead, bleeding to death for many hours on Wexford Quay. His death should be seen as a public execution, ordered out of hatred for his brother (see Edward Hay, *History of the Irish Insurrection of 1798* [Boston: Patrick Donahoe, n.d.], 162; see also Freemen, 112; Musgrave, 421). **21** Fr John Corrin was born in Wexford in 1750. He was educated in Europe and ordained in 1779 in France. Appointed parish priest of Wexford in 1780, he lived on Bank Street and formed friendships with many local Protestants. During the Rebellion, he offered protection for many refugees and is credited by Taylor for stopping the massacre of prisoners on Wexford Bridge with his passionate plea for mercy (Taylor, 152–3). As with most parish priests, he was a pacifist and upheld the status quo. After 1798, Corrin was harrassed, and the windows of his house were broken, but he was never accused of complicity in the Rebellion. His effigy, housed in a glass case in the Church of St Francis, Wexford, notes that he remained parish priest for 54 years. He died in Wexford in 1834. (See Cantwell, vol. 6 [East Wexford], 268; see also Whelan, 'The Catholic Priest in the 1798 Rebellion', 312). **22** Probably Margaret, daughter of John Dixon of Castlebridge and a sister of Thomas Dixon, rebel leader in Wexford. She married Edward Roche of Garrylough, rebel general, who died in prison in 1799 awaiting transportation. She was listed as a widow in Garrylough on 14 Nov. 1806, when she was party of a lease to Edward Dixon of Poulreagan. See Goodall, 'Dixon of Castlebridge', 633.

'friends to the Roman Catholic cause'. A little tranquilized, though disappointed in our hopes of getting to Wales, we then returned to Clonard. Exhausted by the emotion, and fatigues of the day, I lay down on the bed as soon as I came in. After an hour of refreshing sleep I went to the dining room; dinner was nearly over. I had not sat five minutes when Miss Mary Byrne[23] crossed the court yard, accompanied by a servant of Mrs Sutton's, bearing an enormous pike. She entered our parlour with an air of exultation. Her coutenance was glowing and had much of the expression a painter would give to a Bacchante. She begged to speak to my mother in private. They left the room together. Her escort had followed her in. He was asked by William Hatton to sit down. He drew a chair to the table where my sister and I sat, we whom he had so often waited on. We rose at that moment we were sent for by my mother. Miss Byrne had informed her that the massacre of the Protestants would take place that night. Unless we consented to be christened by a Priest, we must die.

The conflict of the morning was now renewed. Miss Byrne threw her arms around me, kissed off my tears, professed her utmost sincerity, the tenderest regard for me, and entreated that I would only consent to become a Christian.

'Oh', she exclaimed, 'this is a glorious day for our religion, not a creature put to the sword. You knew what was to have happened, we were all to have been *murdered*.'

I was too much exhausted to attempt arguing with her. I told her no force could induce me to change my religion, that it was not from the prejudice of education, but from conviction that I was a Protestant, that I could die, but not become a Roman Catholic.

'Well then, my dear Eliza, I will die with you. I will stay here with you tonight. We shall be murdered, but I too can die!'

She then urged the insignificance of the ceremony that would save our lives: 'merely to suffer the priest to make a cross on our foreheads'. Mrs Hatton was as unwilling as I was to submit even to that, but at length overcome by entreaty, and seeing Miss Tench inclined to go to town, she ordered the mule and car to be got ready for her and for me, who were unable to walk. Miss Byrne was in rapture, I in despair.

'Never,' said I, 'will I abjure my religion.'

'Nor I, my dear girl, we will speak to Mr Corrin in private, we will explain our sentiments, we will stand together. Let others do as they please.'

We soon reached the gate of the Chapel yard. We alight. Several pikemen were in the yard and some unfortunate Protestants, returning as I supposed from abjuring their faith for sorrows were painted on every

23 Mary Byrne is unidentified, but she may have been related to Luke Byrne of Oulartard, one of the largest Catholic farmers in Co. Wexford.

countenance. Mrs Sutton[24] was among them. I went to her and entreated she would let me know what ceremonies she had been obliged to go through. Miss Byrne endeavoured to prevent her answering me. I perceived she wanted to hide the truth from me. I turned to her with a haughtiness I wonder I dared to show and desired she would leave us as I wished to speak to Mrs Sutton alone. She seemed confused and left us. Mrs Sutton told me she had been obliged to say she believed in Transubstantiation, Saints, in short the whole creed of the Papists. Miss Byrne had deceived me. I was in the snare. How alas, should I escape?

I was called to go into the convent. We went up a narrow, dirty staircase, at the head of it a door jay open. I looked in and saw a low room filled with wretched converts to fear. The sight of those unhappy beings, together with the heat and close small, overcame me. I felt sick and scarcely knew how I got down stairs. We were taken into a room on the ground floor to wait for the priest, who was, it was said, engaged 'preparing souls for heaven'.

Mrs Hatton said she would not see any priest but Mr Corrin, and she insisted on his being sent for. Whilst we were waiting it occurred to me that I should be christened by force. I determined if I could not escape from the convent to feign madness. I thought that by doing so I should escape what I dreaded infinitely more than either death or madness. It began to grow dark, my agitation increased. I pretended to be near fainting and have an excuse for leaving the room. Mrs Hatton came with me.

I said to her, 'Oh, Mrs Hatton, we may now get away and the guards will not mind us; we may escape.'

She agreed that we would return together to Clonard. We had walked on for some time when she recollected that she had left her little granddaughter in the convent. She said that she must go back there for her. This was a dagger in my heart, but I made no opposition to her wishes, and we returned to the Convent. Mr Corrin had come there during our absence. He assured us that no massacre was intended, reproached Miss Byrne for having unconsciously alarmed us, offered us protection, his house, and behaved with that benevolence one expects should characterize ministers of the Gospel. He accompanied us to Mrs Hatton's house in George's Street. On the way he harrangued several groups of men on the wickedness of giving out such a report. 'If', said he, 'any of you have such intention and execute it, you will draw down on you the vengeance of God and Man.' They unanimously protested that they had not, yet there was something in their countenances I did not like. They seemed astonished but not convinced by his words.

24 Perhaps Sarah (Reade), wife of Jacob Sutton (*Ferns M.L.*, 1793). She may also have been the wife of Joseph Sutton, a member of the Wexford Yeoman Infantry,

We slept or rather lay in town this night. I scarcely closed my eyes. When I did, I was touched by terrific dreams.

Saturday, June 2nd

This morning brought us some consolation. Lord Kingsborough[25] (Colonel of the N. Cork Militia) and two of his officers have been taken prisoners by the crew of an armed boat that has been fitted for the sea by order of Mr Keugh, the rebel commander of the town. Letters were found with them which say that 10,000 men had marched from Dublin against the Wexford rebels. Oh! What joy for us!

Mr Keugh[26] came into a Lady's [house] where we had gone to see some friends. He had Lord Kingsborough's sword. My mother addressed him as 'Capt. Keugh'. He scarcely noticed what she said. He laid his hand on the hilt of his sword, exclaiming, 'I am now Colonel. This is Lord Kingsborough's sword.' In a pompous, conceited manner, he then mentioned his intention of sending an express to Govt. offering to spare the

---

25 George King, Viscount Kingsborough and later 3rd Earl Kingston, was born in 1771. He was a leading national figure in the Orange Order and commanded the North Cork Militia, a much-despised unit stationed in Wexford in April, 1798, ostensibly to keep order by spreading terror in the Catholic community (see Whelan, 'Reinterpreting the 1798 Rebellion in Co. Wexford', 20). After the outbreak of the rebellion, he was arrested on the water in Wexford while attempting to join his regiment. He was not harmed while in captivity, because 'such a man was a useful hostage, and the insurgents apparently thought that he could make terms with the Government, or at least with any of the loyalist generals, on their behalf should it be necessary' (Wheeler, 154–5; see also Musgrave, 431–3). On 21 June, Kingsborough was told to inform the King's troops of the surrender of Wexford and that all, except murderers, should be protected in person and property. Kingsborough ascended to the earldom in April, 1799 and died in 1839 (see G.E. Cokayne, *The Complete Peerage* [London: St Catherine Press, 1929], 7:300).   26 Capt. Matthew Keugh of Wexford was born of a Protestant family about 1744. He married Grace (Thornton), the wealthy widow of Lawrence Grogan, a half-brother of Cornelius Grogan (Freemen, 320). He had enjoyed a lengthy military career, rising from Private to Ensign during the French and Indian War, then being gazetted to the 60th Foot in 1763. Mrs Brownrigg states derisively that he had once been a fifer, though Madden claims he was a drummer in the 33rd Regiment (see Richard R. Madden, *The United Irishman: Their Lives and Times* (London: Catholic Publishing, 1860), 4:513; hereafter cited as Madden). Returning to Ireland, he became a Lieutenant in the 45th Foot and later transferred to the 27th or Inniskilling Regiment of Foot in 1772. He retired to his estate in Wexford in 1774, became a J.P., but was removed from the bench in 1796 for radicalism. Whelan states that he serves as an example of the apprenticeship of many involved in the Rebellion, 'intially in liberal, then in independent and finally in radical circles in the 1790s' (Kevin Whelan, 'Politicization in Co. Wexford and the Origins of the 1798 Rebellion', in Hugh Gough and David Dickson (eds), *Ireland and the French Revolution* [Dublin: Irish Academic Press, 1990], 170). An early member of the Wexford Society of United Irishmen, he became a colonel in the United army in Forth and Bargy baronies (Gahan, xi), and later rebel governor of Wexford. He was subsequently arrested at the fall of Wexford in June, and executed there on 25 June 1798, despite the testimonies of George Le Hunte and Lord Kingsborough as to his humanity (see Goodall's account in Freemen, 329).

lives of the prisoners the people had taken, if those of their party which were in the hands of the Govt. were protected. Miss Lahunte[27] begged he would enclose a few lines from her to her brother. He said he would, adding, 'Make haste, and do not write fiddle-faddle. I shall be obliged to read what you write.'

Lord Kingsborough had been conducted to Mr Keugh's house. The mob wanted to see him and to have him taken. Mr Keugh's authority availed to keep the people quiet, but he could not induce them to disperse. A boy of about 14 of the name of Lett,[28] a relation of Beauchamp Bagnal Harvey, rode up asking if they should not get a pitch-cap for Lord Kingsborough. 'No, no,' he [Keugh] replied, 'we will have none of these doings,' and such was his influence that it was pressed no further.

We returned to Clonard more tranquil than we had left it, although fully convinced that we were prisoners. No application for our removal from Wexford would be listened to by the committee. 'For some time', said William Hatton, 'you must content yourselves here.'

Sunday, June 3rd
My mother and Miss Tench went to the Catholic Chapel. After dinner Miss Byrne paid us a visit. She seemed elated we were dejected, our conversation certainly far from lively, yet once or twice she put her hand to her face. I believe to have the appearance of attempting to conceal her exultation. I happened to say something of our servants. She repeated after me with a sneer 'your servants that were your servants – I did not mean that,' she said with some confusion.

[Monday, June 4th, no entry]

Tuesday, June 5th
All [of] Mrs Hatton's servants had been summoned the day before to the neighbourhood of Ross to be ready for an attack on the town. Judging from what I had already seen, I expected it would fall into the hands of the rebels. About 4 o'clock a servant of Mrs Hatton's returned. He was immediately asked (not desired) to come into the parlour to tell the news.

---

27 Possibly Anne Le Hunte, who married Simon Purdon, or Editha Le Hunte, who married Sir Henry Meredyth. They were daughters of George Le Hunte of Artramont, and sisters of Col. William A. Le Hunte of Artramont, commander of the Shelmalier Yeomanry. See 'LeHunte of Artramont' in *Burke's Landed Gentry of Ireland* (1912), 394–5.   28 James Lett was the son of Stephen Lett of Newcastle and his wife Mary (Moore), a cousin of Bagenal Harvey. He was thirteen in 1798 and of small stature. He played a prominent role at the battle of Ross, waving a bannerette and urging the pikemen to attack the forces of Gen. Johnson. He was later tried for his involvement at the battle but according to one source, 'he was so small that the warder had to hold him up in the dock to enable the Chief Justice,

'Is Ross taken?'

'Faith they have it now now, if they'll take it.'

'Were you in the town?'

'Oh, yes. I rode over the bridge two or three times.'

'What troops were in the town?'

'2,000, besides Orangemen.'

'But pray', said Mrs Chambers,[29] who had dined with us and was no friend to rebellion, 'How many men do you think you lost? 400 think ye?'

'Indeed I don't doubt but these might have been that killed.'

In the evening some more hords returned. They affirmed only 12 men had been killed, and to our astonishment, he who only a few hours before had owned a loss of 400, now agreed to their account.

Wednesday, June 6th

Some women who came to Clonard today said that the Barracks and Market House of Ross were still in possession of the King's troops. I was [now] in ecstacy of joy. I exulted over William Hatton. I reasoned with him. He listened to my loyal arguments with good humour, but without conviction, he provoked me. I left the room, and for revenge pulled the odious Green Cockade out of my had and trampled on it. It was a satisfaction to me to insult the rebel colours.

[Thursday, June 7th, no entry]

Friday, June 8th

At breakfast Miss Tench said with a tone of great kindness that she wished it was possible we could remain always together, but it could not be.

'And why not, Molly dear?', said Mrs Hatton.

'Oh! because Mrs Richards must go home and see about her own affairs.'

This was an unexpected speech. It was followed by a dead silence. Miss Tench interrupted it and manifested unusual vivacity.

Lord Kilwarden, to see him. When Kilwarden saw the little fellow who was being charged, he lost his temper and shouted to warder, "Send that child home to his mother"' (Joseph Ranson, 'A 1798 Diary', *The Past* 5 [1949]:148, note 5).   **29** Maryann Alcock of Wilton Castle, Co. Wexford was the daughter of Henry Alcock by his second wife Philippa Melosina, daughter of the Rt. Revd Richard Chenevix, Bishop of Waterford and Lismore (*Burke's Landed Gentry of Ireland* [1912], 3–4). She was the sister of William Congreve Alcock, who shot John Colclough of Tintern Abbey in a famous duel in 1807. She married, in 1786 (*Ferns M.L.*), Robert Chambers, a surgeon in Wexford, who claimed losses in 1799, including 'Cattle, Furniture, [and] Books' (Claimants, cccxxxvii). They are buried at Donoughmore, where their marker states Robert's death on 1 May 1804; aged 50, his wife, unnamed, on 11 May 1830, aged 75; and three sons (see Cantwell, vol. 5 [North Wexford], 183).

My mother had ordered a car to come for her from Rathaspeck this day, intending merely to visit it. Miss Tench's conduct determined my sister and me to accompany her and to remain at home. With a breaking heart I bade Mrs Hatton farewell. She was more affected at parting with us than I ever remember to have seen her.

This day was enchantingly fine – yet how melancholy did Rathaspeck seem! The hall still retained the marks of the crowds of rebels who had drank tea there. The furniture of the rooms was displaced. All seemed neglected, forlorn. I reflected on what we had been – what our future prospects were. I threw myself on the first chair. I listened to nothing that passed. I felt as if that moment I could have died of grief.

I sat up late reading proofs of that religion I glory to profess. Every word strengthened my resolution to suffer death rather than renounce it.

Saturday, June 9th

Early in the morning we were disturbed. William Hatton wanted to see my mother; he was in the court-yard. She spoke to him from her bedroom window. An idea of the most consoling presented itself to my mind. The English vessels, I thought, that had been for some days hovering on our coast might have landed troops. He came to inform us of it. My hopes were in vain. He said Mr Grogan's[30] servants had called him up twice saying that my mother had sent for him. She answered him she had not. This is extraordinary!

The messenger my mother had sent to town returned after dinner and brought what she called 'good news'. Arklow had surrendered to the rebels. 3,000 men coming to our relief had been cut to pieces. 150 soldiers of the garrison of Ross had deserted to the rebels (for now they acknowledged that part of the town held out against them) – and a cutter conveying 15 guns had been taken 'by Admiral Scillram's[31] gun-boats'. I listened with horror. The blood rushed to my head. I felt as if a cord was bound round my temples and a sensation resembling suffocation.

30 Cornelius Grogan of Johnstown Castle was born about 1738, the son of Cornelius Grogan by his wife Catherine, daughter of Andrew Knox (see Freemen, 320). He remained unmarried, though his sister Catharine married Sir Vesey Colclough, thus allying him as an in-law to the United Irish leader, John Henry Colclough (see Madden, 4:503). A wealthy landowner, he had been M.P. for Enniscorthy from 1783 to 1790, and had also served as High Sheriff. A political liberal, he was known for his humanity as a landlord (Gordon, 181; see also Whelan, 'Reinterpreting the 1798 Rebellion in Co. Wexford', 14). He was too old to fight in 1798, but accepted instead the post of Commissary-General to the rebel army. He was subsequently executed on Wexford Bridge, 28 June 1798, perhaps as a scapegoat for those prominent in liberal politics (see Kevin Whelan, 'The Religious Factor in the 1798 Rebellion', in Patrick O'Flanagan, Paul Ferguson, and Kevin Whelan (eds), *Rural Ireland 1600–1900: Modernisation and Change* [Cork: Cork Univ. Press, 1987], 81). Madden's account remains the most lengthy treatment of his life (Madden, 4:502–13).　31 John Scallan was a Catholic and owner of a sloop in Wexford. Whelan includes him on a list of

The Miss[es] Tooles[32] came to see us this evening. They are freer from bigoted zeal than I could have supposed Catholics to be. They did not speak of religion and seemed truly loyal. From the time they left us until we retired to our bedrooms we were gloomily silent. Alas! we could not speak comfort to each other.

Saturday, June 10th

My sister feigned illness and did not rise until it was too late for any of us to go to chapel as the servants seemed to suppose we should.

About 1 o'clock a heavy cannonading was heard towards Duncannon Fort. I do not well know why, but this gives me hope. Our guards do not seem to like it.

Betsey, having heard my sister was not well, came to see her. She says the people are determined no Protestant shall enjoy a fortune such as ours. They exult in our fall, no matter our being heiresses gives us no pride. The loss of fortune cannot humble us. But to think that a mean wretch says he will marry me 'tis too much'. Betsey says that a low shop keeper says he shall marry me as soon as affairs are a little settled. I will never consent to it. I am indignant.

The King's troops, the Misses Toole tells us, have retaken Arklow. A Mr Codd,[33] who was intended for the priesthood but now commands the Rathaspeck corps, sat two hours with us this evening. He says he thinks the lives of Mr Kellett[34] and Mr Edwards[35] 'are safe because their wives are Romans'.

those Wexford merchants radicalized in the 1790s 'schooled in the *Rights of Man* and conscious of their exclusion from the monolithically Protestant corporation ...' (Whelan, 'Reinterpreting the 1798 Rebellion in Co. Wexford', 25). 32 Probably daughters of William or Lawrence Toole, a Catholic gentry family formerly of Buckstown (Monaseed) and in 1798 of Fairfield, Co. Wexford (see Art Kavanagh and Rory Murphy, *The Wexford Gentry* [Bunclody: Irish Family Names, 1994], 168–9). The close relationship of the Tooles to the Richards reflects their liberality in politics. For further discussion of the Tooles and their place in Wexford politics in the eighteenth century, see Whelan, 'The Catholic Community in Eighteenth-Century Co. Wexford', 132–5. 33 Probably William Codd, a captain in the United army at Rathaspick and Wexford. Mr Codd, shopkeeper of Enniscorthy, was a rebel, but 'Francis Codd, another person of the same name, was very loyal' (Musgrave, 346). 34 William Kellett of Wexford was married to a Catholic. In 1798, he was arrested, together with Captain Bland and Nathaniel Crump, and placed on the prison ship in Wexford Harbour. His wife appealed to Fr Corrin to intercede on his behalf after Corrin had visited Clonard to baptize Kellett's child (Musgrave, 456–61). Later, when Kellett was taken to Wexford Bridge to be piked, he passed a note to a former servant with instructions to take it to Corrin, who later made an impassioned appeal for mercy for all of the prisoners. In 1799, after moving to Dublin, Kellett claimed losses of 'Furniture, Cloaths, Cattle, Rent, [and] Duty on Coach' sustained at Clonard during the Rebellion totalling over £753, for which he received £670 (Claimants, App. ccclxxxi).

Monday, June 11th

At 7 o'clock this morning, Mr Hay[36] (a rebel chief) sent a messenger to Rathaspeck with a letter for Mrs Hatton and another for me. In a note which accompanied this he said he had found them in the mail, which had been intercepted by the United Army. The rebels, an united army!

Today we drove to Clonard on a common car attended by two of our servants, armed with swords. Coming out of the avenue gate, we met three women who sneered at us and looked exultingly at our shabby equipage. I was vexed, but charming in the sight of a friend. Mrs Hatton's warm embraces banished every uneasy feeling. Miss Tench was all kindness. She seemed to wish we should forget her late behaviour to us.

Mrs and Miss Clifford were at Clonard, the latter related some of her adventures since the fatal battle of Oulart. To this battle she was an eye witness. The North Cork Militia, she says, fought with astonishing bravery. Cut off to two these gallant men disdained to submit. They were overpowered by numbers and died honourably. She had seen her uncle, Mr Burroughs (a clergyman), and 12 Protestants put to death by the rebels on Whitsunday morning.

Some of the insurgents were so unused to fire arms that they did not know how to fire off a double-barreled gun. They applied to Miss Clifford to teach them. 'How should I know how to fire it off,' said she.

'Oh, but we know you do,' one of them answered. 'We saw you firing last week at a mark.'

On her way to Wexford she met one of the murderers of her uncle. He pointed a musket at her breast. She perceived it had no lock, told him so, and that he could not shoot her. Whether it was that circumstance that preserved her life or the interference of the rebel guard that accompanied her, I do not recollect.

From Clonard we proceeded to Wexford. Oh! what a dismal scene! The shops all shut, pikemen guarding every avenue to the town, distrust, fear, anxiety painted in the countenances of everyone we met.

We called on Mrs Sutton. Mr Hay had given her a newspaper. Its contents inspired us with hopes, which we did not dare manifest in her presence. It mentioned the defeat of the Rebels at Ross, the numbers slain, the marching of a strong force to our relief, the success of the English at Ostend.

35 Thomas Edwards of Wexford is mentioned in Musgrave as being a prisoner on the prison-ship in Wexford Harbour and like Kellett was saved for having a Catholic wife. 'It was asked by one rebel, whether he had ever prevented his wife from going to mass? Another, who was friendly to him, answered in the negative, and said, he had often attended his wife to chapel, and had gone for her when mass was over; on which he was discharged' (Musgrave, 457, App., 804).   36 John Hay of Newcastle was a brother of Edward Hay, the rebel historian, and of Philip Hay, a Colonel of the 10th Lancers (see Wheeler, 121, 173; Dickson, 210–11). He was hanged by a party of yeomen near his house, 21 June 1798.

Mrs Sutton told me she had heard that the burning of a barn at Scullabogue had been ordered by one of the rebel chiefs. That such an action was permitted will be shame, eternal shame, to the Irish name.

Tuesday, June 12th

Mr and Mrs Sutton, William Hatton, and Count Rerstrat dined with us. Whilst we were at tea, a party came to search the house for Mr Ogle.[37] They had got information from the camp at Vinegar Hill that he was concealed here or at one of the Clonards. They were civil to us, but talked of the punishment they would inflict on those who concealed Mr Ogle in a manner that made us shudder. Some one assuring the Rebels that Mr Ogle was not in our house, he took up the French Count's stick, saying 'there is an old rascal here at any rate'.

It was said that sailors were committing great excesses in town. My mother requested William Hatton to stay this night at Rathaspeck. He consented, but got so drunk after supper that had the house been attacked by them, he could not have afforded the slightest protection.

Wednesday, June 13th

I drew the whole morning. The weather is too warm to take exercise. It is the finest I have seen in Ireland. How little are our feelings in unison with the bright sunshine.

A woman whom my mother sent to town today brings word that Lord Kingsborough and his officers have been taken out of jail (Mr Keugh's influence could not prevent their being confined there) and put on board a ship, where they are in danger of being devoured by rats. 25 prisoners, she says, have been brought in from the neighbourhood of Gorey. They are to be confined in the Assembly room.

Some of our work people and servants took leave of us. They are going to the rebel camp at Lasken. Some of them go reluctantly. Ross is soon again to be attacked. Bagnal Harvey has resigned the chief command to a Priest of the name of Roach.[38] This is an age of wonders. The rosary is exchanged for the sword, and the ministers of the Prince of Peace, for the flames of civil discord.

37 George Ogle of Bellevue was born 14 Oct. 1742, the son of George Ogle, translator, of Dublin. Serving as M.P. for Co. Wexford, 1768–96, and for Dublin, 1798–1804, he was the leading conservative at that time in the Irish Parliament and a hated figure to both Catholics and Protestant liberals. During the Rebellion he commanded a much-despised corps of Yeoman cavalry nicknamed 'Ogle's Loyal Blues'. He married Elizabeth, daughter of William Moore on Tinraheen, and died without issue, 10 May 1810 (see Freemen, 450–1; see also Brian Cleary, 'Sowing the Whirlwind', *J. of the Wexford Historical Society* 14 [1992–3]: 9–71.
38 Fr Philip Roche was born about 1760 at Monasootagh, Co. Wexford (see Whelan, 'The Catholic Priest in the 1798 Rebellion', 306). He was curate to the Revd John Synnott at Gorey, and while there became involved with the United Irish in the early 1790s.

Thursday, June 14th

The insurgents have failed in their attack on Borris. They cannot conceal their disappointment. They thought there to have taken ammunition that would have enabled them to get possession of Ross. They speak of attacking it next Tuesday. Edward Roche, they say, will march through the counties of Carlow and Kilkenny and raise their inhabitants to assist at the siege of Ross.

After tea I walked with my mother. The evening was delicious. Sealed in the Elm-bower, breathing air perfumed with woodbine and syringa, my heart was heavy, all my thoughts gloomy. Forgive, O Merciful Father of the Universe, forgive my resigning at thy will. Since my birth thou hast showered down blessings on me. I acknowledge my unworthiness and that my chastisement is not equal to my offences.

Friday, June 15th

I had been drawing with some tranquility when Betsey came to tell me that Col. Lehunte[39] had been taken to prison. An orange-coloured screen found at Artramont by Mrs Dixon was the pretext for arresting him. She says the engravings on it are the symbols of the deaths the Orange faction had intended to have inflicted on the Roman Catholics. The people say that Col. Lehunte was the chief of that society, and that their meetings were held in a room in his house. On his way to jail some of the mob cut at him; others threw him down. He has not been materially hurt. He is to be tried and if found guilty, to be shot.

I am persuaded that this Orange business is only a pretext for murdering Protestants. The Papists know that our religion never ordered massacres, and though they now say that one was intended, they do not in their hearts believe it.

It is not, I think, possible that the rebels, although they may for a time be victorious, should ultimately obtain possession of Ireland, but I scarcely dare hope that we shall see the day of its deliverance from the savage

According to Bishop Caulfield, he was 'a proper man and would be useful' but that he 'indulged in excess of drinking and began to agitate', forcing Caulfield to remove him from his post (Bishop Calufield quoted in Caulfield-Troy Correspondence, Dublin Diocesan Archives). He was later made curate to the Rev. Thomas Rogers in Killgrey. During the Rebellion he assumed a prominent military role, eventually replacing Harvey as commander-in-chief. Gordon recorded several instances of his humanity to Protestants, noting that he was 'in appearance fierce and sanguinary, yet several persons ... owe their lives to his boisterous interference' (Gordon, 167–8). He surrendered after the battle of Vinegar Hill and was executed in Wexford, 25 June 1798.   39 Col. George Le Hunte of Artramont, Captain of the Shelmalier Cavalry, the son of George Le Hunte of Ballymartin and his wife Martha, daughter of Col. Oliver Jones (see Goodall, 330; *Burke's Landed Gentry of Ireland* [1912], 394–5). He married Alicia Mary Corry and had issue several children, including William Augustus Le Hunte, who succeeded him as captain of his yeomanry corps. A liberal in politics, his men were allowed to escape during the battle of Oulart Hill. He later lived natives! 'They will not long suffer hereticks to infect the air.' (This expression was used by the wife of one of Mrs Hatton's cotters, a woman to whom she had been very kind.) We shall be murdered; I am convinced we shall, if we cannot effect an escape – and of that there is no possibility.

Saturday, June 16th

A party of ruffians came to search the house for arms. An English 74 gun ship, they assert, is stranded in the Barony of Forth. 'We want a few muskets', they say, 'to enable us to get possession of her'.

My mother answered them she had not any, but they were welcome to search the house. Some would have taken her at her word, as William Hatton assured them also that she had not. Others were not so believing and went over every part of it. On a loft they found a blunderbus covered with dust and without a lock. It served, however, as a pretext for reproaching my mother with a breach of faith. One Cornick, who had found the blunderbus, insisted on my sister's opening her writing-desk. He thought, he said, it might contain pocket pistols. The impertenance of the man and the tone of authority assumed by the whole party overcame my mother's spirits, and she wept bitterly. I felt indignation and a will to be avenged.

Sunday, June 17th

We did not go to Chapel. I dare say, the people wonder. No one, however, has asked us to go there since Miss Byrne's ineffectual attempts to make us Catholics.

I am very sad today. William Hatton tells us the North is in open and successful rebellion, that Dublin is up. I know him and the principles of his party, so I cannot have implicit faith in what he says – yet it does make some impression on my mind. A spirit of disaffection has long been prevalent in the North. This is the time for it to blaze out in the fury of rebellion. William Hatton's intelligence is, I fear, too true.

After dinner, my sister and I walked to Fairfield. The Misses Toole returned with us. There was a strange-looking old man at the Lodge. I entered into conversation with him. He spoke of the rising in the North. The present disturbance had been foretold, he said, 25 years ago by a stranger, who came to his father's house. He told me, 'he said it would be better for me to put the value of a cow into the land in '97 than that of a hen in '98 and that we should not have peace till '99'.

---

some days undisturbed in Wexford until being falsely accused by Thomas Dixon as an Orangeman. An angry mob of sailors, aroused by Dixon's allegations, nearly succeeded in taking his life, but several rebels intervened and saved him (see the account of Mrs Brownrigg, Chapter 4; Musgrave, 438–9). Musgrave includes him on the list of prisoners in the Wexford gaol (Musgrave, 806).

He seemed to speak with restraint to me. I understood from the hints he gave Miss J. Toole that part of the prophesy was that the Roman Catholic cause would be victorious. The reason he assigned to the failure of the rebels before Ross was their being commanded by B.B. Harvey. 'But now,' he said, 'they have got one of the right sort at their head. They'll take it with all pleasure.'

Father Murphy,[40] he said, had been cruelly treated by the army at Arklow. 'They wanted to burn his chapel and he in it, Miss, but his head would not burn; no, not all the faggots in the county would have burned it. So at last they sent in a soldier for him and cut it off'. Had I not been afraid I would have said to him that the head of the soldier, who entered the flaming chapel, must have been made of the same material as the Priest.

Monday, June 18th

This day has been gloomy – so have my thoughts. Futurity seems a frightful wilderness, the past a lovely garden, whose gates have closed on me forever. How black seems the first cloud of adversity! But I will raise my eyes to Heaven. I will look forward to another world, where I'll not be a prey to the pangs of fearful suspence. The darkest visions of this world fade away. All here is uncertainty and cannot enter lasting happiness.

Tuesday, June 19th

We are told that Ross is to be attacked. Then our fate will be decided.

My heart beats so violently when I see a stranger coming down the avenue that I am obliged to lay down my pencil. I have not courage to ask if there is any news. In uncertainty there is a mixture of hope that enables us to bear its pain, but the knowledge of inevitable pain, I feel as if I could not survive the fall of Ross.

Wednesday, June 20th

The Rebels have been driven from the camp at Lackon! McDonald, with a faltering voice, told us so. Such a good omen, so unexpected, so unhoped for! It has been confirmed by a number of flying, trembling wretches, who faintly endeavoured to conceal their terrors.

With exhilerated spirits we walked to Fairfield, from thence through a telescope we plainly distinguished 11 English ships of war. We con-

---

40 Fr Michael Murphy, curate of Ballycanew, was born about 1760 at Ballinoulart. He was educated at Bordeaux and ordained in 1785 (see Whelan, 'The Catholic Priest in the 1798 Rebellion', 308). He was probably a captain in the United Irish army as early as 1797 and is often mentioned in connection to loyalty oath made to Lord Mountnorris in the spring of 1798 (see Wheeler, 57–9). He was tortured and beheaded by a group of yeomanry at Arklow on 10 June 1798, after leading his men in battle.

gratulated each other on a speedy deliverance. We were cheerful. The entrance of Mr Heyter of Gortinnanogue, with a sad countenance, increased my satisfaction. I guessed he had heard what was good for us – bad news for him. Mr Toole asked him, 'What was the matter?'

With a broken voice and tears in his eyes he exclaimed, 'The prisoners! Those devils from Enniscorthy are murdering them!'

1,500 men were marched from Enniscorthy this day to murder the prisoners. Not one Protestant would have escaped their furious zeal had not Edward Roach told them the King's troops had attacked Vinegar Hill and if their aid did not go to succour their friends, they would all be lost. Expresses, he said, had been sent for them, and three times the drum beat to arms before they obeyed. A pause of horror and silence followed this speech. Never before had I felt a combination of all sensations that constitute misery.

It was late when we left Fairfield. The evening was cold and blustery. At intervals we heard the roar of the cannons. Some men we met told us there was an engagement at Foulkes Mill. My mother and I resolved not to go to bed until we knew the event. She would not have the candles lighted for fear we might direct to the house some of the Enniscorthy wretches who had remained in the neighbourhood after the comrades had marched to Vinegar Hill. My sister and I sat in the back parlour. The wind whistled through broken panes of glass. Dark clouds flew across the sky. We were silent; our thoughts were on our murdered countrymen. The wind suddenly rose to a pitch of violence that made the house shake. The dismal howling of the storm, the darkness, we could not take alone. We rushed out of the room to seek for my mother. She was at a front window, listening to the sound of musketry, which was heard now and then in the intervals of the storm. We stayed there until the firing was no more to be heard. We returned together to the parlour. The window shutters were closed and lights were ordered.

About 11 o'clock we were so anxious to know what the result of the engagement had been that my mother begged of the housemaid to go and enquire of the guard that was kept at the cross-roads, if they had received any intelligence from Foulkes Mill. She soon returned and brought word that some men she had spoken to said that when they left Foulkes Mill, the King's troops were giving way, and by this time they supposed they were beat. It seemed so odd that any part of a conquering army should quit the scene of action that we gave but little credit to this account.

Thursday, June 21st
At 2 o'clock in the morning one of our servants and one of our guards returned from Foulkes Mill. (Mr Grogan of Johnstown, who was tried by Court Martial and sentenced to be hanged for the share he had in the

rebellion, had given us a guard composed chiefly of our servants and cotters.) The girl who opened the door for them brought us word that the King's troops had been defeated. Edward the guard had himself killed two soldiers. One of their firelocks he brought away. The remains of the army had retreated towards Ross. My mother left the room to enquire further particulars of the action. Despairing and almost broken-hearted, I threw myself on a chair in my bedroom. I knew not how long I remained there. I was stupified with grief. At length I lay down. I fell asleep, and for several hours was insensible of our wretchedness.

After breakfast we walked to Mr Toole's.[41] There we heard that the rebels had been defeated at Foulkes Mill, this morning at Vinegar Hill, and that they were flying in all directions. How happy we were now! I was as gay as I had been sad the night before.

On our return home we saw from the garret windows houses in flames. I ought to be ashamed perhaps to own it, but it gave me pleasure. I considered this as a sign of the approach of the army.

About 5 o'clock we walked to the avenue-gate. The green boughs and pikes had nearly disappeared. Crowds of women and children and a few men were flying from Wexford. Many sought refuge at our house. They said the King's troops were encamped at the Wind Mill Hills, that they plundered every house and shot every man they saw.

We again went to Fairfield. Mr Codd, who had commanded the Rathaspick corps, and a Mr O'Brien,[42] nephew of Mr Corrin, the Priest, were there. They wore their swords, cross belts, and green collars. The deep, the manly regret that Mr O'Brien seemed to feel for the overthrow of his party interested me for him. His countenance expressed despair. His arms were folded, his mind seemed abstracted from the surrounding objects. Some one observed, 'We shall now have the blessings of peace restored.'

'Yes,' he replied with a smile of agony and indignation. 'There will be peace, but we shall all be slaves.'

Friday, June 22nd
More troops have marched into Wexford. A body of rebels that had encamped at Killinick, and afterwards at Bensville, have retreated. They

---

41 Probably Lawrence Toole, son of William Toole, formerly of Buckstown and at the time of Fairfield (see note 32). He belonged to one of the few Catholic gentry families in Co. Wexford (see Kavanagh and Murphy, *The Wexford Gentry*, 168–9). Lawrence married Mary, daughter of Revd John Jacob, from a liberal Anglican family in Wexford. Also related to this family was William Tool of Edermine, who claimed losses of cattle and a gold watch (Claimants, App., ccccxxxi).   42 Patrick O'Brien, a schoolteacher near Johnstown Castle, was a captain in the United Irish and was sentenced to transportation for nine years. (see Whelan, 'The Catholic Priest in the 1798 Rebellion', 304).

have not been pursued. Two of Lord Mount-norris' cavalry[43] shot at a man within a short distance of Rathaspick, an unfortunate rebel who had sought protection here. I thought he would have lost his senses when he heard the report of the gun. He cried, he tore his hair. His pusilanimity made me feel more contempt than pity for him.

All the morning we listened to the shrieks, the complainings of female rebels. They almost turned my joy into sorrow.[44]

As we were going to dinner the father and brother of the rebel I before mentioned rode to the door. They were let in and endeavoured to vindicate their conduct to my mother. The father showed a protection given by Lord Kingsborough 'to the county of Wexford at large'. He cannot have a right to give one. I think it will not even protect Mr _____ when he goes into town.

Dinner was scarcely over when Capt. Toole sent us word he was arrived at Fairfield. My sister and I ran there without event.

[The next entry is dated 22 January 1801.]

---

43 Arthur Annesley, Viscount Valentia and first earl of Mountnorris (1746–1816) was a substantial property owner in Co. Wexford and a moderate. He attempted to pursue a conciliatory policy toward the Catholics before the Rebellion in the belief that he could 'deliver' their loyalty to Dublin Castle. Though several congregations professed allegiance, the ensuing insurrection invalidated his policy and all but destroyed him in the eyes of hardliners such as Ogle. Mountnorris was captain of the Camolin Legion, which incorporated both the Camolin Cavalry and the Loyal Mountnorris Rangers (Padraig O Snodaigh, 'Notes on the Volunteers, Militia, Yeomanry, and Orangemen of Co. Wexford', *The Past* 14 [1983]: 31; see also Cullen, 'The 1798 Rebellion in Wexford', 249–50, 265–6). Some of his correspondence was published in Wheeler and Broadley. 44 Here the writer offers important evidence of the rape and mistreatment of Irish women, probably at the hands of Gen. Lake's army. Gahan notes that as a loyalist, Elizabeth was 'relieved that the rebellion was over, but from her entry in her diary that night it is clear that she regarded what was now being done to the local people ... with deep horror' (Gahan, 224).

2

DINAH GOFF

Dinah Wilson Goff was born in 1784 at Horetown, Co. Wexford, to Jacob and Elizabeth (Wilson) Goff, a family of gentry Quakers. Her father was descended from the Reverend Stephen Goffe, rector of Bramber and St Botolph's, Sussex, whose son, Richard Goffe, was a regicide and an M.P. under the Cromwells. Richard's son, Richard Jr, settled in Co. Waterford and joined the Society of Friends. His son, Jacob Goff of Dublin, married Mary, daughter of John Fade, an officer in Captain Dubourguy's Regiment, and was the father of Jacob Goff of Horetown. This younger Jacob, Dinah's father, was born in 1736 and left a will dated 9 Dec. 1798 and proved 4 July 1799.[1] Her mother, Elizabeth, was the daughter of Benjamin Wilson of Mount Wilson, King's Co., and the granddaughter of Thomas Wilson, an early leader of the Society of Friends in Leinster.

The Quakers remained neutral pacifists during the rebellion and hence were regarded as non-combatants by the United Irish leadership. This fact placed the Goffs in a slightly different position than the Richards, who were liberal but still loyal. The Goffs felt no particular loyalty to the crown and, moreover, were forbidden by their faith from swearing oaths of allegiance to either side.

Dinah, the youngest of Jacob Goff's daughters,[2] was only fourteen when she witnessed the incidents described in her narrative. Her subsequent writing shows no trace of political bias, except to see the restoration of order that the conclusion of the rebellion would bring. Because her family home, Horetown House, was located near the rebel

---

1 See *Burke's Landed Gentry* (1969), 250–1; *Burke's Landed Gentry of Ireland* (London: Harrison and Son, 1904), 224. For a sketch of Jacob Goff, see also Richard S. Harrison, A *Biographical Dictionary of Irish Quakers* (Dublin: Four Courts Press, 1997), 48–9. See also 'Goff of Horetown' in Art Kavanagh and Rory Murphy, *The Wexford Gentry* (Bunclody, Ireland: Irish Family Names, 1996), 2: 88–100. Jacob Goff married Elizabeth Wilson at the Edenderry Meeting House on the 8th of 4th month 1759. Some of the Goff family papers are preserved in the Public Record Office of Northern Ireland, Ms T1621.   2 The six sons and twelve daughters of Jacob and Elizabeth (Wilson) Goff included: William (who m. Rebecca Deaves); Joseph Fade (who m. Eliza Penrose); Elizabeth (who m. John Lecky of Ballykealy, Co. Carlow); Sarah (who m. Richard Sparrow); Anne (who m. William Penrose); Jane (who m. Thomas Christy Wakefield of Moyallon, Co. Down); Lucy (who m. J. Pike); Mary (who m. [ ] Watson); Lydia; Hannah; Arabella (m. [ ] Fennell); and Dinah, the youngest. Two daughters died in childhood; the rest are not known (see Kavanagh, *The Wexford Gentry*, 2: 96; less reliable is *Burke's Landed Gentry of Ireland* [1904], 224).

camps of Carrigbyrne and Corbett Hill, her family had an unsual window for many events of 1798, including the battle of Goff's Bridge, which occurred on their property. The location of their home acted as a magnet for rebel activity, with hundreds of rebels encamping daily on their grounds. In spite of their neutrality, the family suffered a number of trials, and Jacob Goff nearly lost his life on several occasions. His family would attribute his death from natural causes later that year to the anxiety he suffered during the rebellion.

Little is known of Dinah's life after 1798. At her father's death her eldest brother William inherited Horetown House, and her mother moved to Dublin. Dinah remained unmarried, despite one source that confuses her with her sister Sarah and claims she married Richard Sparrow.[3] Dinah moved eventually to England, but the date of her removal is not known. She resided at Falmouth during Third Month 1850, when she first dictated her account, apparently to her friend Mary Forster of Tottenham. This version was written in a small notebook and preserved for many years among descendants of the Forster family until it was acquired by Trinity College, Dublin, where it remains today.[4] Six years after this initial dictation, she had apparently moved to Penzance in Cornwall, where with the help of an editor she prepared a revised version for publication. This second document was dated 23rd, Twelfth Month, 1856.

The two accounts are nearly identical. The order of narrative was changed slightly in the second version, several persons received more identification, certain religious passages were expanded, and several references to wine were removed, probably at the urging of an unknown editor. Several more paragraphs were inserted at the end, giving more details of her mother's life after the Rebellion and summarizing her religious philosophy, making the account more useful as a religious tract. She dated the second account 23, 12th month, 1856 and gave it the title, 'Divine Protection through Extraordinary Dangers during the Irish Rebellion of 1798'. It was printed subsequently both in Philadelphia and London by the Tract Association of Friends and distributed as a Quaker pamphlet.[5]

Printed here for the first time is the original version from 1850. The editor has included in brackets and in footnotes numerous material from

---

3 *Burke's Landed Gentry of Ireland*, 224. 4 Ms No. 5116, Trinity College Dublin, used by permission of the Trustees of Trinity College Dublin. The manuscript contains a note written by Frances Arnold Forster dated 15 Mar. 1911: 'Dictated by D. W. Goff in 1850 to a friend at Falmouth (query Mary Forster of Tottenham?), as she lived a good deal at Falmouth, and the book was found among Forster documents'. 5 Dinah W. Goff, *Divine Protection through Extraordinary Dangers during the Irish Rebellion of 1798* (Philadelphia: Tract Association of Friends, 1856). It was subsequently reprinted in John Grubb Richardson, *Six Generations of Friends in Ireland, 1655 to 1890* (London: Headley Brothers, 1895), 135–84.

the 1856 version, especially when it appeared that Dinah herself intended to expand a particular passage. In a number of other instances, however, the original version offers greater clarity of events than the edited second version and occasionally includes traces of Dinah's original speech pattern (for example the use of 'Ma'am' for 'Madam'). The original also uses quotation marks erroneously, denoting approximate quoted statements rather than exact quotes.

THE ACCOUNT

It has often occurred to me that I ought to leave some little memorial of the preservations extended to us in seasons of deep trial by our heavenly Father to my beloved parents & of the remarkable faith and patience with which my dear parents were favoured under circumstances of a very peculiar character.

It was about the middle of the 5th month, 1798 that the county of Wexford became a scene of open rebellion, headed by Bagnall Harvey, and two Roman Catholic Priests, Murphy[6] and Roach,[7] their aim being to extirpate the Protestants & bring Ireland again into subjection to the Pope.[8]

[About ten days before the rebellion broke out, a Roman Catholic, who resided near, called on my father, and desired to speak to him in private. He then informed him that the county would, in the course of a few days, be in a state of general insurrection. My father replied that he could not credit it, for that he had frequently heard such rumors. The person assured him that he knew certainly it was so, and that he had procured a vessel, now lying at Duncannon, to convey himself and family to Wales; and that, as a friend, he gladly offered accomodation to our household. My father thanked him for this act of friendship, but said that it felt to him a matter of great importance to remove from the position allotted him by Providence, yet that he would consider it, and consult his wife. After having endeavored to seek best wisdom, my dear parents concluded that it

---

6 Fr John Murphy was born at Tincurry in 1753, educated at Seville, and ordained in 1779. He was appointed curate of Boolevogue in 1785, and he held that post to the end of his life. Initially hesitant about the aims of the United Irish (he had once refused the sacrament to United Irish who had not abjured their oath), he eventually joined them in response to the excesses of the local yeomanry. When the rebellion broke forth, he assumed an active leadership role at the battles of Enniscorthy and Oulart Hill. He was captured near Tullow in July 1798, and executed. For a thorough biography, see Nicholas Furlong, *Fr John Murphy of Boolavogue, 1753–1798* (Dublin: Geography Publications, 1991).   7 Fr Philip Roche. See Chapter One, note 38.   8 In the 1856 version, this passage was removed in favour of: 'The aims of the insurgents were various; some were more cruelly disposed than others; all determined to liberate themselves by force from the unequal yoke, as they believed it, of the British government, and to become a free people; some to bring all Ireland to

was right for them to remain at home, placing their dependence and confidence in Him who alone can protect, and who has promised to preserve those that put their trust in him.]

The house of Jacob and Elizabeth Goff, Horetown, in that county, was situated between two camps,[9] which caused a constant demand for provisions, with which they were daily supplied, the insurgents often saying that the lives of the family were spared for that purpose.[10]

Early in the morning of [ ] we were roused by the sound of cannon at a distance & soon heard that an engagement had taken place between the Wexford Yeomanry & the rebels at the mountain of Forth, in which the former were put to flight with a considerable loss of life.[11] 60 or 70 men were buried in the same grave. Two of my cousins[12] were officers in that corps & made their escape to our house under the cover of the darkness of night. On their arrival they found that ther Father, Mother, & 9 children

Catholicism, etc'. **9** These camps are identified as 'Carrickburn' [Carrigbyrne] and 'Corbett Hill' [Corbitt Hill] in the 1856 version, 'one on each side of the house, at distances of two and five miles from it'. **10** Several letters exist in the Goff papers which attest to the loss of provisions. On 22nd 6th Month 1798, Dinah's sister, Elizabeth Lecky, wrote to her parents: 'Tho numerous the terrors by which we have been surrounded, yet I can truly say an apprehension of what yours may have been hath more than doubled our sufferings ... I know not how I can most serve you, but I only say make every use of me & mine where by you can be served or by which your wants may be relieved, if you are easy to come to me commanding my conveyances, if you are deprived of such conveyances which it probable is the case. I have often felt consolation in remembering that even in the midst of the fiery furnace there was preservation & the same Almighty hand is able to save in this day and for ever ... I would now send a car with provisions of which I fear you are in need, but fearing it would not be permitted to go forward ... Our apprehensions of your being in want of provisions has been truly distressing'. (Goff Papers, T1621/1, PRONI). Another sister, Jane Wakefield, wrote on the 24th of 6th Month: '... Surely my dear Mother if you have all escaped without any personal injury it will be a cause of thankfullness which I trust I with you shall never forget from accounts my beloved Father has suffered exceeding in his property...' (ibid., T1621/2). Son-in-law Richard Sparrow, who had married Dinah's sister Sarah, wrote an undated letter, probably about the same time, to offer provisions: 'Having learned this this Day that the Kings Troop had got as far as Wexford, I presumed the Road was clear to Horetown & we all being anxious to learn your Situation, that under divine protection, Joseph might be permitted to go forth as the Dove from the Ark to bring us glad tidings respecting you, I to know whether any thing we possess would in any Degree be acceptable to you. I have a milch cow, a fat cow, some sheep & other necessaries ready to go at a [ ] warning, having heard thou was deprived of nearly all thy cattle, do let me hear particularly how you have fared & be assured t'will give more real pleasure than I can well express to thee to render thee & thine a service of any kind ...' (Ibid., T1621/2). **11** Dinah refers here to the battle of Three Rocks, 30 May 1798. **12** In the 1856 version they are identified by the surname Heatley, whose mother had married out of the Society of Friends. John Heatley, Esq., of Rockview, Co. Wexford, had married a sister of Elizabeth (Wilson) Goff, and was a local magistrate. In 1799, he claimed losses in cattle, corn, a gun, and clothes (Claimants, App. ccclxxi). He was the father of the sons mentioned in the narrative, one of whom was William Heatley, Captain in the 63rd Regiment, who claimed losses at Wexford, including clothes, arms, horses, saddles and bridles (ibid.).

had been turned out of their comfortable home & had fled for refuge to my Father's, where they were affectionately received. We had all retired to rest when these young officers arrived; the thankfulness of their parents, who had never expected to see their sons again, passes all description. They were much affected, & immediately returned thanks on the bended knee for the preservation of their children.

These two young men remained for some days in the house, [hiding from room to room, sometimes under the beds, as there was a frequent search for arms and Orangemen by the rebels.] Some of the heads of the rebel army, [having information of their being with us], called on them to tender the United Irishman's oath, which they resolutely refused, saying they had taken an oath of allegiance to their sovereign a few days before & would never perjure themselves. On this, one of the rebels said in great irritation 'that were it not for the respect they had for Mr Goff, blood should be spilt & their lives be the forfeit of their loyalty'. After a short time they were taken prisoners to the Camp, where their lives were remarkably preserved.[13]

Two [Roman Catholic] men servants in our family and lodging in the house were compelled to join the rebels in their own defence – they were armed with pikes – the first we had ever seen. On my dear mother hearing that they had brought these weapons, she said that she could not allow any thing of the sort to be brought into her house; so each night they left them outside the door. [They behaved quietly and respectfully throughout, generally returning home at the close of the day.] A Roman Catholic family from Enniscorthy, 7 in number, also came apparently in great distress & received a hospitable welcome from my dear Father & remained with us the whole time, my mother often remarking with reference to her large family that like the cruise of oil and the barrel of meal, the necessary provisions never seemed to fail.

Twenty surrounded our dinner table each day, besides the number in the kitchen, [four of whom were members of our Society; which my mother considered a great advantage at that awful period.] She would also say that it seemed as if hind's feet were granted her in getting through the very much that now devolved on her in the way of household arrangements – strength was indeed remarkably granted and the precious promise again verified – 'As thy day so thy strength shall be'.

A rebel once inquired of her whether she thought they would gain the day, & feeling it to be rather a serious question, after a pause she replied, 'The Almighty only knows'.

13 In the 1856 version, this passage is expanded: 'At length, my cousins left our house at night, intending to make their way to Ross, and took shelter in the cottage of an old Roman Catholic nurse employed by the family; but they were betrayed, and handed over to the rebels, who took them prisoners to the camp. The lives of these interesting young men were, however, remarkably preserved, after they had endured much hardship in prison'.

He answered, 'You are right, ma'am – have a good heart, not a hair of your head shall be hurt, but when this is over, the Quakers are all to be driven down into Connaught, where the land is worth about two-pence an acre, & you live on that as you can'.

My dear mother smiled & said, 'I hope you will give us a good portion as we have a large family'.

My Father had a fowling piece which he broke to peices [*sic*] on hearing of the approach of the rebels, thus evidencing fidelity to his principles. It proved a source of satisfaction when afterwards the magistrates called for the fire arms of the inhabitants according to the orders of Government.

A day or 2 after the commencement of the rebellion two carts were brought to the door, the cellars emptied & all the salt provisions with a supply of cider, beer, &c. taken off to the camp. Fourteen beautiful horses were also carried away as well as other cattle. Orders were sent each week from the camp to have a cow & some sheep killed as supplies for the united army and these were sent for at stated times.

Hannah and Arabella [afterwards Fennell], with Dinah W. Goff, [aged about thirty, nineteen, and fourteen], were the only daughters at home at this time. The two former walked 3 miles & a half on First Days to their meeting-house at Forest, accompanied by 2 of the women servants who were Friends, though they met with a great deal of interruption from the rebels, who wanted them to go to their Chapel as they were passing it. They were enabled to pursue their way & sit quietly with the few Friends who were able to meet there, & these they remarked as peculiarly solemn opportunities.

Some of the rebels were heard to say, 'They even dare us by going through the streets, but they shall not go long'. On one of these occasions, having been more than usually threatened, they remarked that a strange dog, which they could not recollect to have ever seen before, followed or rather accompanied them home as an escort. On seeing them safe to the house he could not be prevailed on to enter & so left them.

[This circumstance, though simple, seemed remarkable at the time. I fully believe that their minds were not resting on outward help, but on that Omnipotent arm which was mercifully underneath to sustain. They were enabled regularly to pursue their way, and to unite with the few Friends that were permitted to meet, remarking those opportunities as being peculiarly solemn. Our dear parents would gladly have joined them, but were unable, from the infirmities of age, to walk so far, and had no horses left to draw a carriage.]

The following 1st day after a decisive battle near Vinegar Hill, when Friends met together as usual, numbers of these misguided people actually assembled about the doors and windows of the meeting house as a place of safety & refuge for themselves & remained there till the meeting had concluded & Friends had withdrawn – before which time they had asserted that if the Quakers ever attempted to meet in that meeting house, it should be burned.

My cousins Richard and Ann Goff[14] had been observed by the united men to persevere in attending their meeting & were apprised that if they continued this practice & refused to unite in the Roman Catholic forms of worship, they should be put to death & their house burned, which brought them under deep mental exercise accompanied with fervent prayers that they might be enabled to come to a right decision. They collected the family together in a degree of humble confidence that best direction might be afforded; after little solemn retirement they laid the matter before their children – the noble and intrepid language of [Fade] Goff, their eldest son (then about 17 years of age) as this memorable is worthy of being recorded, 'Father, rejoice that we are found worthy to suffer'. His parents were much affected & their minds so much strengthened that they proceeded next morning to their place of worship & expressed satisfaction in being enabled to accomplish what they considered to be their duty.

One evening, whilst we were assembled & had been listening to my dear father's reading, which was our constant practice after the hurry of the day, a priest came in & remarked on the question which prevailed. My Mother told him that this was our usual practice after the business of the day was over – he said he came with good news for we were all of one religion now the world over. My mother queried 'What religion he meant?' He said 'The Roman Catholic, for an edict from the Pope had arrived & he has seen the express passing over the bridge, therefore it was high time for her to put the cross on herself & children. She asked what he meant by the cross. He said, 'The outward sign'.

She answered, '*that* they should never do; but she believed that her Heavenly Father was enabling her to bear the cross, & she hoped He might enable her to do it to the end'. I was standing near, when he drew me towards him, saying, 'My dear child, we shall have you all to ourselves', & turning to my Father & laying his hand on his shoulder, said, 'And Mr Goff, you shall be one of our head senators'. He then withdrew. This unhappy man afterwards lost his life whilst attacking a Protestant gentleman on whose kindness and hospitality he had thrown himself when his own house was burnt down by the English troops, but to us he was

14 Richard Goff of Hopefield, Co. Wexford, was the son of Fade Goff and wife Anne Neville (see *Burke's Landed Gentry of Ireland* [1904], 224).   15 This is perhaps a reference to Fr John Byrne, a Carmelite of Goff's Bridge, whose convent was in a state of decline. He took an active role in the rebellion, attending the rebel camps in the south of the county. He was described by Bishop Caulfield as 'a drinking, giddy man' and by Veritas as 'a very zealous, active rebel' (see Whelan, 'The Catholic Priest in the 1798 Rebellion', 309, 538). Though the bishop admonished him to leave the diocese, he continued to seek alms with effrontery. His death occurred in a bizaar manner at Clougheast Castle when visiting

uniformly kind, [and we thought his attention might, under providence, have had some influence on the minds of the rebels.][15]

Many hundreds of the rebels were daily on our lawn, & our constant business was to hand them great tubs of milk & water at the different doors & in the hall & also prodigious quantitites of bread and cheese. The women servants were obliged to sit up almost every night, baking bread for them. My mother and sister cut the bread and cheese as they would otherwise take off the whole loaf and cheese at the end of their pikes.[16] They took the large knives from the pantry to stick on the ends of poles & thus convert them into instruments of cruelty. My mother, on seeing this, had the remainder locked carefully up. They often used these times to go into hideous details of their own cruelties to the great distress of my sisters, saying for instance one day 'They had had fine fun the day before to see the fine young officers when they sickled them under the short ribs with their pikes. They curled up like wood lice and screamed like asses'.[17] [One day after a battle, they related many such acts. I was handing them food at the time, and could not refrain from bursting into tears, throwing down what I had in my hand, and running away into the house.]

We were greatly struck by observing that, however outrageous a party of visitors might come, there were generally some among them who were disposed to promote peace & would say, 'You ought not to treat them so – the poor ladies who have been up all night making bread for you with their own hands'.

A barn belonging to a gentleman living at Scullabogue, about 2 and a half miles from us, was converted into a prison, where 180 were confined, men, women & children. From Sixth until Third-day, they were kept without receiving any provisions except some sheaves of wheat which were occasionally thrown in, that the rebels might have the amusement of seeing them scramble for the grains. One day [on the day of the battle of New Ross], 60 of them were brought out and one by one were offered liberty if they would change their religion & they all refused, some of these after being half tortured to death firmly replied, 'Give us more powder and ball first'.[18]

Richard Waddy. Waddy, who had captured Harvey and Colclough on the Saltee Islands, had become deranged and after inviting Bryne to dinner, suspected the priest of trying to attack him. As Byrne fled the castle, Waddy dropped the portcullis on top of him, pinning him under it and killing him.   16 The 1856 version contains this variant: ' ... my mother and sisters often made their hands bleed in cutting the bread and cheese ...'   17 This statement was excised from the 1856 version.   18 Much has been written about the atrocity of Scullabogue on 5 June 1798, which claimed about 200 victims, both Catholic and Protestant. It followed the battle of Ross earlier that day, when a number of innocent Catholics died at the hands of British troops. Although the massacre was used by loyalists to justify subsequent hardline measures against Catholics, it was clearly not sanctioned by the United Irish leadership. Dáire Keogh is correct in asserting that the incident 'occurred when the United Irish discipline broke down, not when it was in place' (Dáire Keogh, 'Sectarianism

One woman of the name of Jones,[19] whose husband & brother attended our meeting, held her husband's hand whilst he was being murdered by inches, one limb after another being broken, & each time that the question was asked him, 'Will you have the priest?' he stood firm in his refusal & looking quietly in his wife's face said repeatedly, 'My dear, I am not hurt'. She then opened her handkerchief & implored them to take her life also, which they refused, saying they would not dishonour the Virgin by taking the life of a woman. His brother was killed at the same time in the same horrible way. I saw this woman afterwards sitting in a cart with the remains of her husband & brother. They set fire to the barn soon after, when all other unfortunate prisoners were destroyed. Whilst the barn was on fire, some of the poor imprisoned women threw their children out of the windows in order to preserve their lives, when the merciless creatures took them up on their pikes and tossed them back into the flames. Scullabogue barn belonged to Francis King.[20] I saw & smelled the smoke of its burning [and cannot now forget the strong and dreadful effluvium which was wafted from it to our lawn.]

in the Rebellion of 1798: The Eighteenth-Century Context', in Keogh and Furlong (eds), *The Mighty Wave*, 45. Possibly the most authoritative study of Scullabogue is Sean Cloney, 'South-West Wexford in 1798', *J. of the Wexford Historical Society* 15 (1994–5):85–97. **19** John and Samuel Jones of Abbey Brainey or Kilbrainey, near Ross, were the sons of a Quaker who had married out of unity. They attended the meeting at Forrest, though they were not members. From Hancock's account, there is some evidence that the two men had been in conflict with the Catholic community. Samuel, the younger of the two, was 'of meek and tender spirit ... As preparations for the impending conflict were going forward, he became very thoughtful, apprehending that some serious calamity would befall him from the Insurgents. About a month before the lamentable event took place, he told his wife that he did not expect to die upon his bed ... The last time he attended the meeting at Forrest, it appeared as if he considered it to be a final parting with his friends ... He was taken prisoner soon after, with his elder brother John, and conveyed to the mansion of F. King at Scullabogue, his wife accompanying them. John lamented his situation and former manner of life, signifying that he was ill prepared to die; but Samuel encouraged him ... When the two brothers, with Samuel's wife, were brought out on the lawn ... to be put to death, some person said, 'They were Quakers'. It was replied that 'if they could make it appear they were Quakers, they should not be killed'. As they were not in reality members of the Society, this was not done. Those who had taken them into custody took Samuel aside, and on certain conditions offered him his life; but, whatever was the nature of these conditions, he firmly rejected them; and when the *holy water*, as they termed it, was brought to them, he turned his back upon it' (Thomas Hancock, *The Principles of Peace, exemplified by the Conduct of the Society of Friends in Ireland during the Rebellion of the Year 1798*, 3rd ed. [New York: Garland Publishing, 1974], 153). Musgrave's account of the brothers' deaths is similar to that of Goff's (Musgrave, 401). The brothers were allegedly buried in the Friends Burying Ground at Forrest with their father.   **20** Capt. Francis King of Scullabogue was the son of Richard King. In 1778, he had married Anne Browne of Tullibards and had 22 children (see Cloney, 'South-west Wexford in 1798', 86–7. He fled his home in 1798 along with other Protestants in Ross, and later claimed losses in 1799, including 'Cattle, Meadow, Furniture, Plate, Liquors, [and] Provisions' totalling some £554. His claim, however, was disallowed (Claimants, ccclxxxiii).

Previous to this circumstance a party came leading two horses to say that they had orders to take my dear Father and J. Heatley, my cousin, to the camp. It was between 10 & 11 a.m. My mother had gone to give some orders in the kitchen. I ran to her on seeing them seize their prisoners & told her that they were forcing my dear Father on a horse, on which she pressed through a dense crowd on the lawn & preemptorily demanded, 'What are you doing with my husband?' & on their replying that they were going to take him to the Camp, she said in the same tone as before, 'You shan't take my Husband. He is in poor health, and if you put him in a prison, I think he could not live many weeks'. They were then quite silent & my Mother said, 'We have got what you call protections from the generals'. These were sent for and read: 'Let no one molest Mr Goff or his family, they being hostages to the United Army'. Signed in the camp by the Generals, Harvey and Roach.[21] At which they seemed perfectly satisfied & desisted on my Mother's saying that my Father would be there at any time they wished as he could not leave his house.

But all our entreaties were in vain with respect to my cousin Heatley, who was taken away. He had been for many years a Captain in the navy. They then put him on board a prison ship at Wexford, where he remained until the enemy was totally defeated. He saw many of his fellow sufferers & acquaintances taken out of the same ship & put to death, with many cruel circumstances, on Wexford Bridge. They were called out two & two; when it came to his & his friend's turn, he said to his companion, 'We have taken many good bottles of wine together & there is one left; let us take it & die like men'. The rebels were now calling them to come up from the hold of the vessel, but they remained to finish their bottle. Before they had quite done, a rumour reached their guard that the English were marching to the town, on which they all took flight in all directions & Wexford was left in possession of the English, to the great joy of my cousin, J.H., who often related the circumstance, saying that the bottle of wine under Providence was the means of saving his life. His nice mansion had been inhabited by the rebels, who left it a complete wreck. Those in the neighbourhood said it was most laughable to see the country people parading about in the silk and satin trains, which they found amongst my cousin's property.

A party, who had assumed the rank of officers in the rebel army, came to our house one day, desiring to have dinner, & on my mother's requesting the servants to lay to lay the table in the hall, they asked in indignation, 'And is it there you are going to give us our dinner? Show us into the best parlour in the house'. & on my Mother assuring them that she had seen noblemen sitting in that hall, they were perfectly satisfied. They then asked for spirits & wine, & on my Mother telling them that there were none in

21 Bagenal Harvey and Edward Roche. See Chapter One, notes 7 and 18.

the house, they were greatly irritated & said they would have it, & on being spoken to by my Mother in the plain language, they desired her not to say thee & thou, as if she were speaking to a dog; & on her saying 'thou' to one of them, he flourished his sword over her head, saying 'No more of your theeing and thouing for me'. They ate their dinner, however, and went off peaceably.

We were now informed that orders had been given to take my dear Father's life, & my mother was most particular in keeping us all close together around him, saying that if he were taken, we might all support one another or else go together. About 12 o'clock one day a large party appeared on the lawn, carrying a black flag, which we knew to be the signal for death. My dear Father advanced to meet them as usual with his open, benevolent countenance, & my mother, turning to me, said, with her sweet, placid smile, 'Perhaps my stiff stays may prevent my dying easily'. On which the Roman Catholic who had taken refuge with us, said, 'Have faith in God, ma'am; I hope they will not hurt you', on which she went forward & joined her husband, who was surrounded by a large party on the lawn. My Father observed to them that he feared they would injure each other as their muskets were prepared for firing; when one of them replied, 'Let they who are afraid keep out of the way'. My Mother distinctly heard them say, 'Why don't you begin?' and each seemed looking to the other to commence the work of death. Some of them presently muttered, 'We cannot'.

At this moment some women came in great agitation through the crowd, clinging to their husbands & dragging them away. A Higher Power appeared evidently to frustrate the intentions of the murderers, and he was again graciously delivered from their hands. [One man said there was 'no use taking Mr Goff's life', but his two sons, if there, should be killed and then the estate would be theirs.]

One morning a most outrageous party advanced toward the house, yelling & roaring like savages, evidently for some wicked design; but two young men who looked serious & sorrowful called out to my Father to shut the hall door as the consequences would be dreadful if the mob were allowed to come in. They then stationed themselves on the steps of the Hall door, flourishing their swords, declaring that not one of them should pass, pleading at the same time for us in the kindest manner, saying, 'Why would you injure Mr Goff or his family who are constantly feeding and providing for you?'[22]

22 Musgrave relates an apocryphal story that Fr John Keane, the suspended parish priest of Ballymader (Bannow), had 'refused his blessing to some rebels, unless they brought him the head of Mr Goff, of Horetown, a quaker, who was universally and justly esteemed; and it is said, that he would most certainly have been assassinated, but for the victory of Gen. Moore …' He adds: 'A party took possession of Mr Goff's house, under the command of [Dick] Monk, and they were attended by father [John] Byrne, a priest, who was purveyor to the

After a long struggle, they relinquished their design. [The young men were quite overcome with the exertion and heat: my father warmly thanked them and gave them silk handkerchiefs to wipe their faces, inquiring their names – one of them called Dennis ___ of Gorey.] A party of [wicked-looking] women outside, evidently waiting for plunder, seemed much disappointed & told the men they were 'chicken-hearted fellows' for not doing as they intended. They had surrounded the house, making hideous faces & shaking their clenched hands at us [as we stood at the windows.]

A young man, who, with his mother, kept a public house, used to walk into our drawing-room at all hours, lay his sword on the table, & amuse me and my cousin by giving us his beautifully decorated hat to admire. [One afternoon] he tried to prevail on my cousin & me (we were 16 & 14 years of age) to go one evening with him to the Camp, saying it was such a beautiful sight, such as we might never have the opportunity seeing again. On my saying that I did not think my Mother would permit us to go, he desired us not to tell her, for he would soon bring us safely back. At this moment, my Mother was crossing the Hall, & seeing us together, came over to inquire what he was saying. On our telling her, she asked him how he dared to request the children to go to such a place? She then reasoned with us on the impropriety of listening to such invitations, saying she should never have expected to see us again if we had once gone.

An English army of 300, [accompanied by] Hompesch's German hussars[23] had landed in the middle of the Sixth month at Duncannon Fort about 6 miles from us & found an encampment on my uncle [Caesar]

party; and he compelled the miss Goffs, young and amiable women, to bake bread, and do every other menial office to supply the rebels' (Musgrave, 452). According to Whelan, Keane was mentally unbalanced, and together with the fact that he was suspended from his post gave him special potency in Irish folk tradition, especially as a thaumaturgist. His insanity saved him from retribution after the Rebellion (see Whelan, 'The Catholic Priest in the 1798 Rebellion', 296, 305, 308–9). **23** According to one source, the leader of these Hessians, a Catholic, was the brother of Ferdinand Joseph, baron von Hompesch (1744–1805), Grand Master of the Knights of Malta: 'He had commanded in Ireland in 1798, a corps of banditti, recruited in all the military prisons of Europe, and which were officially called 'Hompesch's Mounted Riflemen', or more generally 'Hessians', and by the lower orders of the people 'Hussuans'. They were more dishonest, and to the full as cruel, as their co-operating cavaliers, the Ancient Britons' (see Andrew O'Reilly, *Reminiscences of an Emigrant Milesian*, 3 vols [London: Richard Bentley, 1853], 265). The *Neues Allegemeines Deutsches Adels-Lexicon* identifies this brother as Carl Franz von Hompesch, chancellor of Pfalz-Bayern and Bayern, who married (1) Antonette von Hacke, and (2) Theresia, Marquise von Hoenbroech (see Ernst Heinrich Kneschke, *Neues Allgemeines Deutsches Adels-Lexicon* [Leipzig: Verlag von Friedrich Voigt, 1863], 4:471). Taylor writes that the Mounted Hussars, a regiment of trained mercenaries, were attached to the brigade of General Moore, together with two rifle companies of the 60th regiment, and were encamped at Foulke's Mill (Taylor, 139). They were later dispatched to Co. Mayo, where they joined forces with Lord Roden's Foxhunters, attacking a group of Irish attached to the French army (see Sean Cloney, 'The Hessians', *J. of the Wexford Historical Society* 14 [1992–3]: 113–28.)

Sutton's[24] lawn at Longgrague [about two miles from us]. This was announced by the firing of cannon early in the morning. [On my mother's entering my room, I expressed much pleasure at the intelligence, when she replied: 'My dear, we must rejoice with trembling; having much to dread from being strangers, and we know not what may be permitted; we have only to place our trust in Him who hath hitherto preserved us!']

One day whilst we were sitting at dinner, it was rumoured that the rebel forces were coming from Wexford in thousands. They intended surrounding the English encampment, but the royal troops, [commanded by General Moore],[25] having had previous information, were on the alert and met them on the road near our lawn. We counted 24 pieces of cannon belonging to the rebels, [which passed our entrance.] A dreadful scene was now enacted partly in our view and lasted for 3 hours. The firing was awful! Having closed the doors & windows [in the lower part of the house] as much as we could, we all retired to an upper room, and there we remained in a state of awful suspense, the cannon balls flying around the house. [On one of my sisters raising the window to look out, a ball whizzed by her head, and this, with many others, we afterwards found.] Seeing the rebels fly in all directions, we learned that they were routed.

Two of them came to the house to have their wounds dressed, [which my sister Arabella did as well as she could; one had a ball in the cap of his knee, and both bled profusely. They expressed much thankfulness and hoped they might soon be able again to fight for their freedom. A fine young man coming, who had received a severe wound in his side and shoulder, my dear mother used means to relieve him and dressed him comfortably in clean linen, while he frequently exclaimed, 'Do, ma'am, try to stop the blood. I don't mind the pain, so that I may but fight for my liberty'. Observing him in danger from the great injury, she spoke to him in a very serious strain and also recommended his going to the Wexford Infirmary. We heard afterwards that he died on the way a few hours after he left us.] This battle was at Goff's Bridge on the 20th of Sixth month. Several hundreds [of the insurgents] were killed, but not many among the military.

Soon after the firing had ceased, we observed two of the cavalry moving slowly & suspiciously up our avenue; on which my father went down to the hall door to meet them and advanced towards them with open arms, at which one, who was a German, embraced him, saying in his broken

24 Caesar Sutton of Longraigue, presumably the eldest son of William Sutton and wife Eleanor Maria (Colclough), married Elizabeth, fourth daughter of Jacob Goff of Dublin and sister of Jacob Goff of Horetown. He served as Burgess of Enniscorthy, 1767–93. (See Chapter One, note 8; see also Freemen, 457).   25 Major-Gen. Sir John Moore (1761–1809) was a native of Glasgow and had an extensive military career as the Hero of Corunna. See *Dictionary of National Biography*, 13: 813–819.

English, 'You be Friend – no enemy', and gave him a kiss of peace. And although we were much affected by the scene which had just taken place, we could not but rejoice to see them & got them eggs & milk & refreshed them after their excessive fatigue.[26]

[The evening before this engagement, one of my sisters, passing through the servants' hall, observed the coachman leaning on his arm, apparently much distressed. When she requested to know the cause, he hesitated and said he could not tell her; but on her entreating him and adding that she should like to know the worst, he said that he had heard it planned at the camp, that, if they conquered the royalists, we were all to be murdered, and the generals were to take possession of our house. He then added, weeping, 'Oh, our plans are too wicked for the Lord to prosper them!' My sister remarked that we trusted in a Power stronger than man and able to protect us in the midst of danger, or to that effect.]

After the battle of Goff's Bridge, our house was surrounded in the night by the military who slept on the lawn.[27] The next morning 20 or 30 of the officers breakfasted with us & told us of the marvellous escape we had on the previous evening. The cannon had been placed on the bridge & pointed at our house in order to batter it down. Even the match was lighted, when an officer came forward and told them the house was occupied by loyal Protestants. They had fancied it a nest of rebels. Some of them almost shed tears when they reflected on the danger we had been in, & became so ultimate with the family that when drinking our health in milk, as all the wine was gone, they would say 'If this be war, may we never have peace!'.

A battle was afterwards fought at Ross, in which the insurgents were again defeated. [This was an awful scene of conflict and bloodshed, continuing with but little cessation for nearly twelve hours. It is stated that two thousand persons were killed. The king's troops retreated twice, and the town was in the hands of the rebels, when a reinforcement was understood to have come up and put them to flight. Some asserted that no reinforcement arrived, and that the assailing multitude fled when there was none to pursue them. General Johnson,[28] who commanded the royalists, said that the success of that day was to be attributed to Providence and was not the work of men.] Several Friends of that place had fled to Waterford; [others who remained were remarkably preserved, though the town was set on fire in different quarters.].

---

26 Goff's view of these German mercenaries differs from Gordon's, who noted that they had 'a grim reputation for cruelty' (Gordon quoted in Cloney, 122). They were greatly despised by the Irish for being mercenaries and for their lack of discipline. Pakenham notes they had 'an orgy of looting and rape' near Wexford (Pakenham, 266). 27 In the 1856 version, the soldiers are specified as Hompesch's cavalry 'who slept on the lawn wrapped up in their grey coats'. 28 Major-General Sir Henry Johnson (1748–1835) was one of the British commangers who suppressed the rebellion. A native of Kilternan, Co. Dublin, he

The decisive battle was at Enniscorthy, after which some degree of order was restored to our afflicted country. It occurred 2 days before our quarterly meeting for Leinster. David Sands[29] was then in Ireland & his companions[30] as they passed through the town had to alight to remove the dead bodies from before the wheels of the carriage. The meeting was remarkably solemn & favoured, though small, so many, ourselves amongst the rest, being deprived of their usual means of locomotion as the rebels had taken away all the horses they could find.

David Sands and his companions proceeded after the 2 M to our house & were joyfully received by us. My dear Mother said D.S'.s visit was like that of the good Samaritan pouring oil into our wounds. The three families who now occupied our house all assembled with him in a solemn sitting, when his communication was affectingly impressive, inducing tenderness of heart in all. He addressed us first in allusion to the trials we had been brought through, and afterwards offered an acceptable sacrifice of thanksgiving & praise to the great Preserver of our lives. The Roman Catholics had never before witnessed such an opportunity, but they all united in prayer on their knees, & the mother said, 'I never heard anything like that gentleman; he must be an angel from Heaven sent to you!' He then proceeded on his way.

The rebellion was now at an end, but some consequences remained; not only houses in ruins, burnt and torn in pieces by both armies, were to be seen everywhere, but many of the rebels who were outlaws took up their abode in caverns in the Wood of Killoughran & sallied forth by night to

served under Sir William Howe during the American War of Independence, and later commanded the 17th Foot in Nova Scotia. In 1798, he led a contingent of 3,000 men, which occupied New Ross. On 5 June, his forces succeeded in repulsing and defeating the rebel army, which proved a turning point in the suppression of the Rebellion in Co. Wexford. **29** Revd David Sands (1745–1818) was a native of Cow Neck, Long Island, New York. A leading Quaker preacher and abolitionist, he assisted in organizing Quaker meetings in New England. His visit to Ireland in 1798 brought him by chance into contact with the rebellion. In his journal he made no specific mention of the Goffs. but he described his visit to Enniscorthy, where 'we were presented with a view of all the horrors of war: the houses had been set on fire the day before, the inhabitants mostly having fled ...' After visiting several Friends in town, he journeyed two miles into the country. 'In our way we saw great numbers of dead bodies, that were slain the day before, some of which we had to remove, to make way for our carriage to pass'. At the quarterly meeting, he observed that 'though we came through many discouragements, yet we rejoiced, not only in seeing our friends, but under a sense of the Lord's goodness, who had made way for us through many troubles ... I proceeded towards Waterford, taking meetings in my way that lay in the county of Wexford; and had many opportunities with Friends in their families, who had been greatly distressed by the insurgents. And I had also many public meetings, wherein I was often favoured to hold forth truth in a good degree of clearness, and some convincement appeared to take place' (David Sands, *Journal of the Life and Gospel Labours of David Sands* [London: Charles Gilpin, 1848], 178–9). **30** One of these companions is identifed in the 1856 version as Abraham Jackson.

commit depredations on the inhabitants, some of whom had again returned to their dilapidated dwellings. They visited us two nights, when our sufferings were greater than any during the whole rebellion. [My father had been urged to accept the nightly services of a guard of yeomanry, but always positively refused.]

On the first occasion we had all retired to rest. We were aroused by a frightful knocking at the hall door with their muskets. My dear Father raised the window & requested them to wait a few moments & he would open the door, but they continued knocking till he went down, calling outloudly for admission. He opened the door as soon as possible when they seized him & rushed up stairs instant by breaking his secretary to pieces with their muskets & demanding money. My Father handed them twenty guineas, which was all he had in the house; but they still persisted in asking for more & declared they would take his life if he did not give them more. I slept with a little niece in a room inside his, and we were desired by my sister not to rise, as we should be of no use. I endeavoured to keep still till I heard a dreadful scuffle & my father's voice saying, 'Do not murder me!'

I opened the door & saw one of the men, dressed in regimentals[31] with a drawn sword, rushing towards my dear Father, when my sister Arabella intercepted the stroke by throwing her arms round my Father's neck. I saw the point of the sword touch her side, but not so as to injure her. [In the struggle the candle went out, and they called most violently for light. The horror which I felt at this awful moment can scarcely be expressed. My sister went down towards the kitchen and found a man standing at the foot of the first flight of stairs; she asked him to light the candle; when he said she might go down, and he would stand guard and not allow any one to pass. This he performed faithfully, and she returned in safety.] I could not, after this, leave the party, but followed them about the house. The dreadful language they used [some of which was addressed to my sisters] shrilled through me still when I think of it. Money was their sole object that night. They were constantly asking for it. They forced my Father to kneel down & held a pistol to his forehead, asking for money & assuring him that if he did not give them more, they would take his life, saying from minute to minute, 'Now you are just gone'. Seeing myself the situation of my dear Father, I threw myself on the floor and clung to his knees, when the ruffians pushed me away saying, 'Go away. You'll be hurt if you stay there'. But my father put his arms round me & said, 'She had rather be hurt if I am'.

[They snapped the pistol several times, which perhaps was not charged, as it did not go off. When they found there was no more money], they got

---

31 In the 1856 version, he is described as 'dressed in scarlet regimentals with full uniform epaulettes, &c.'

several watches & then went away after eating & drinking all they could obtain, charging my Father to have more money the next time, or they would have his life. [So saying, one of them, who appeared in a great rage and had a cavalry sword in his hand, cut at the handrail of the hall stairs, the mark of which still remains.]

About a fortnight afterwards before the family retired, my Father had a presentiment that they might come that night & sat up later than usual. About 12 o'clock they arrived, knocking furiously as before, when they came fully prepared to plunder the house & accordingly emptied all the drawers & took all the wearing apparel they could get that did not betray the costume of Friends; [so that we were deprived of nearly all our clothes. On perceiving they were taking all, my mother begged one shirt and one pair of stockings for my father, which they threw at her face in the rudest manner, using dreadful language.]

They then behaved in a most outrageous manner, asking for money & watches [and spreading quilts and sheets on the floor, filled them with all sorts of clothing they could get] & then called for eating & drinking, desiring my sister to drink their health, 'Long life and success to the Babes of the Wood' [as they called themselves.].³² She refused, on which they put the cup to her lips & said that they intended coming again in two weeks & would take us all to cut bread & butter in the Wood for the Babes & there we should live with them. Their behaviour was so insulting, and my Father & Mother [were so fearful of those threats being realized, that they] determined to send us to Ross with our cousins Goff and Neville, [who were then merchants in Ross], until tranquility was perfectly restored to the country.

After they had finished their repast, they threatened to take my dear Father's life, appearing very outrageous & said they must take him to their main guard at a little distance and murder him there, as they did not like to do it in his own house. They then took him out. We all attempted to follow, when they pushed my dear Mother back, saying that she should not come – it would be too painful a sight for her to see her husband murdered. It was dark, but my sister Arabella positively refused to leave my Father & managed to accompany him.

Whilst walking across the lawn, the root of a beech tree caused my dear Father him to stumble, when he then sat down and said, 'if they determined to take his life, they might as well do it there'. My dear Sister stood by in a state of awful suspense. They then asked my Father if he had any

---

32 The Babes in the Woods were an unorganized band of rebel guerillas, possibly 300 in number, centered in Killoughram Forest, west of Enniscorthy. From here they launched raids against loyalists and yeomanry during the autumn of 1798 (see Daniel J. Gahan, 'The "Black Mob" and "The Babes in the Wood": Wexford in the Wake of Rebellion, 1798–1806', *J. of the Wexford Historical Society* 13 [1990–1]: 92–110).

thing to say, for his time was come. On hearing this, he was quite silent, &
they, not understanding it, hurried him to speak; when he said the prayer
that the Almighty might be merciful to him & be pleased to forgive him his
trespasses & sins, & also to forgive them, which he did sincerely. They said
that was a good wish & asked if he had any thing more to say. He then
desired that they would be tender towards his wife & family. On which
they said, 'Good night, Mr Goff; we only wanted to rattle the mocuses[33]
out of you'.

On their taking my dear Father out, my Mother, though much distressed, was favoured with extraordinary quietude and calmness. So strong
was her confidence that she even called to the servant, desiring to have
some warm water ready to make a little negus for my dear Father on his
return; when I said, 'My dear Mother, I suppose we shall never see my
Father living; they are going to murder him'. On which she replied: 'I have
faith to believe they will never be permitted thus to take his life'. In about
a quarter of an hour, my dear Father returned, pale & exhausted; and
throwing himself on the sofa, said: 'This work will soon finish me; I cannot
hold out much longer'.

This was literally the case, for his health sank under the repeated shocks
& trials he had endured during the whole of the fearful period: & on the
23rd of the 12 Month of the same year, surrounded by many of his family,
he quietly breathed his last, sustained by his dear Saviour in faith &
confidence whilst passing through the dark valley of the shadow of death
& comforted in having his family around him.[34] He expressed to one
whom he saw weeping on the night of his decease, 'Do not shed a tear for
me, my dear; but rejoice & be thankful that the Almighty has permitted me
to die in peace with my dear family around me, and not by the hands of
wicked and unreasonable men'. He took my hand & said, 'My dear child, I
must leave you all, but keep near to the Lord, and he will be a Father and a
Friend to thee when I am no more'. Jacob Goff had only attained his 62nd
year. His life was evidently shortened by the many shocks & trials he was
subjected to.

[Remarkable also was the protecting care vouchsafed to my uncle Joshua
Wilson[35] (my mother's brother), whose residence at Mount Prospect, near
Rathangan, was forcibly entered by a party of rebels. One night, after the
family had retired to rest, they were aroused by a tremendous volley of
musketry, which at once shattered the hall door; and a loud cry was raised

---

33 Mocuses was a colloquial term for guineas.   34 In the 1856 version, Dinah states that her
father was in his 63rd year of age: 'Our merciful Saviour sweetly sustained him in faith and
confidence … He never expressed a murmur, but in humble Christian patience and
acquiescence withthe divine will, often evinced his thankfulness for the mercies received'.
35 Joshua Wilson of Mount Prospect, Co. Wexford, was the son of Benjamin Wilson of
Mount Wilson, King's Co.

of 'Arms, money, or life!' with most awful swearing. My uncle went hastily down in his dressing-gown, followed by his wife, who heard them exclaim: 'You are a dead man!' and seeing one of the men present a pistol at my uncle's head, she rushed between him and the ruffian, exclaiming: 'Thou shalt not, and darest not, take my husband's life or touch him, for the arm of the Almighty is stronger than thou art!' The man appeared confounded and let the pistol drop from his powerless hand; it was very remarkable that the whole party left the house soon after without doing any further injury.]

[Many were the heart-rending sufferings that some families endured, being turned out of their peaceful homes and spending many nights in the fields and ditches. Others, who still remained in their houses, were wonderfully favored with faith and patience under great privations, conscientiously adhering to the revealed law of their God, and thus experiencing, to their humbling admiration, the name of the Lord to be 'a strong tower' in which the righteous find safety. On taking a retrospect of this awful period and of the strength of mind evinced by my beloved parents, sisters, and others, my heart overflows with living praise and thanksgiving to the Father of mercies and God of all consolation, who was, indeed, 'strength in weakness, riches in poverty, and a very present helper in the time of need'.]

[Horetown now passed to my eldest brother, William Goff,[36] and my beloved mother removed to Dublin. She survived her affectionate husband nineteen years and died in that city in the seventy-eighth year of her age in perfect peace. For several years she was in the station of an elder. She always endeavored to rule her own house well and was accounted worthy of double honor and much beloved by her many descendants. Sixty children, grandchildren, and great-grandchildren were living at the period of her decease in the year 1817.]

[She was granddaughter of Thomas Wilson, an account of whose religious labours is published with James Dickinson's.[37] Her last illness was short, being caused by a paralytic seizure of which she had previously had several. On the morning before the seizure, she entered the drawing-room with an expression of countenance remarkably solemn, and, kneeling down

36 William Goff of Horetown was born in 1762, and served as High Sheriff of Co. Wexford in 1807 and 1811. In 1784, he married Rebecca, daughter of Edward Deaves of North Abbey, Co. Cork, and had issue a son, Jacob William, and six daughters: Rebecca (m. Francis Davis of Waterford); Eliza (m. Jonathan Pim of Dublin); Mary (m. Thomas Harvey of Youghal); Sally; Lucy Anne; and Arabella (m. Jonathan Pim of Mountmelick). See *Burke's Landed Gentry of Ireland*, 224; see also Kavanagh, *The Wexford Gentry*, 2: 96–7. 37 James Dickinson (1659–1741), a native of Cumberland, was a Quaker missionary in England, Ireland, and Barbadoes. His journal was published in 1745 (James Dickinson, *A Journal of the Life, Travels, and Labour of Love in the Work of the Ministry, of that Worthy Elder, and Faithful Servant of Jesus Christ, James Dickinson* [London: Raylton and Hinde, 1745]; see also *Dictionary of National Biography*, 5: 940–1.

at my side, engaged in fervent vocal supplication for her numerous family that the blessing of the Most High might rest on them, and that He might be pleased to continue with her to the end. Many consoling expressions she uttered, and when near the close, she said to me: 'May the blessing of the everlasting hills surround thee, my dear child, when I am gone'. She was perfectly conscious to the last and sweetly resigned to her divine Master's will.]

[It is comforting to have a well-grounded hope that through the mediation and redeeming love of our blessed Saviour, the spirits of both my beloved parents have entered into mansions prepared for the faithful; and that they are, through unmerited mercy, united to the just of all generations, 'who have washed their robes and made them white in the blood of the Lamb', to whom be honor and glory, for ever and ever!]

[Thus have I cause to commemorate the great goodness and mercy extended by our heavenly Father to his unworthy creatures throughout a season of inexpressible trial and distress. May his gracious dealings never be forgotten by one who feels undeserving of the least of all his mercies, and who, in taking a retrospective view, can gratefully adopt the language, 'Bless the Lord, O my soul, and forget not all his benefits!']

[I am the only one now remaining of twenty-two children, and ever felt much attainment to my parents, whose pious and watchful care over their large family in our early years lives in my heart as a sweet memorial, calling for gratitude to Him who gives us pious friends. This feeling, I believe, was cherished by all the rest of their children, now, I humbly trust, through unmerited mercy and redeeming love, united them in that happy state, where all trials and sorrows are at an end, and where all is joy unspeakable and full of glory.]

[The forgoing has been written from memory after a lapse of nearly fifty-nine years, the affecting events being still vivid in my recollection.]

3

JANE BARBER

Jane Barber was born about 1783 at Clovass, near Enniscorthy, Co. Wexford, the daughter of Samuel and Elinor Barber. Descended from a Williamite family, her father was a tenant farmer, draper, and the owner of a small textile factory. In the hierarchy of Protestant society in the eighteenth century, the Barbers occupied a much lower rank than the gentry Goff and Richards families, and for this reason, Jane's account is most unusual and of considerable historical value.

Samuel Barber served, at least for a time, as a Private in the Enniscorthy Yeomen Cavalry under the command of Captains Solomon Richards and Joshua Pounden, two political liberals whose corps was more moderate than that of Archibald Hamilton Jacob, which was also based in Enniscorthy. William Barber, Jane's brother, also served in this corps. This fact suggests that the Barbers were themselves moderate in their outlook, and though they remained loyal, they were not Orangemen. Little is known of Jane's mother Elinor. In 1799, she petitioned Parliament for losses sustained in the Rebellion, including a 'House, Car, Beds and Bedding, Cloaths and Barley;' she recovered only a small portion of her original petition.[1] The following year she placed a second claim as a widow of a fallen soldier.[2]

Jane's life subsequent to the Rebellion remains obscure. It would appear from the last paragraph of her account that she continued to reside with her mother and brother at Clovass and died there unmarried.[3]

THE ACCOUNT

My father's name was Samuel Barber. He held a small farm within two miles of Enniscorthy, called Clovass; it contained but twenty-one acres, but it was rich ground and the rent was low. It had been in our family since the

---

1 See Claimants, App., cccxxi.   2 *A List of the Subscribers to the Fund for the Relief of Widows and Orphans of Yeomen, Soldiers, &c., Who Fell in Suppressing the Late Rebellion* (Dublin: William Watson & Son, 1800), n.p. Cited hereafter as 'Widows and Orphans'.   3 The whereabouts of the original manuscript of Jane Barber's narrative is not known. A typescript is housed in the Wexford Library, Wexford, Ireland, and in the National Library of Ireland (ir 920041).

battle of the Boyne, for I am descended from a Williamite. It lay in a pleasant valley between two hills, named Moyne or Mine, and the other Coolnahorna. On this last, a tradition said that King James, when fleeing, stopped to take a breath; and an old prophecy said that, before another hundred years should have elapsed from that flight, the Irish should again muster on that hill, strong and victorious. The truth of this prophecy I myself saw but too clearly confirmed.

We had four milch cows and sent milk and butter to Enniscorthy; several dry cattle and plenty of pigs and poultry; in particular we had a great number of geese, for a beautiful trout stream ran through our ground. Besides working horses, we had two very excellent ones, one of which we thought good enough afterwards to mount a rebel General. We kept but one servant girl, for both my mother and myself were active and handy, and we kept one labourer in constant employment – poor faithful Martin. Our kitchen was always open to the poor travellers, and many a handful of meal and boiling potatoes as my dear father encouraged us to bestow on those that wanted. It was not in this World he met a return for it.

Our farm, though productive, would hardly have supported us in the comfort and respectability we enjoyed, but that my father was also a clothier. He bought the fleece from the sheep's back and manufactured it into middling fine cloths and frieses, which he disposed of at the neighbouring fairs. He thus gave bread to six men and four women, besides those he employed in harvest-time, and no one, gentle or simple, had ever reason to complain of Sam Barber. Although all our neighbours of the better class were Protestants, for we lived in the midst of twenty-two families of our own persuasion, yet all those we employed were Roman Catholics, and we met with as much honesty and gratitude from them as we could possibly have desired.

My father was advanced in life when he married, indeed upwards of forty, but my mother was much younger and I was their second child. He had five more at the time I speak of; the eldest, William,[4] was a fine, well-grown boy of sixteen or upwards; I was eleven months younger, not much above fifteen, but I was considered a cute and sensible girl for my years. I had two sisters, one eleven, the other six, a brother of four, and my mother had lain-in another little boy only six weeks before the fearful times which I am now endeavouring to describe.

4 William Barber Sr and Jr, and George Barber, all of Clovass, were shown as tenants on the Portsmouth estate in 1829 (Cantwell, 10: 431). William Barber, Jane's brother, was buried at Ferns (Old) cemetery: William Barber, 'who died December 6th 18 [ ], aged 77 years/also his wife/Elizabeth Barber, who died 15th/March 1875, aged 92'. Also buried there is George Barber, apparently another brother: 'George Barber, in memory of his grandfather George Barber, who died June 24th 1866 aged [ ], [ ] died March 15th 1887, also the above George Barber/ who died the 28th of June 1916, aged 88 years' (ibid., 186).

During the entire winter of 1798, when my father would return from Enniscorthy, he would mention the rumours he had heard of the discontent of the Roman Catholics, and the hopes they cherished that the French would assist them, but we never had time to think on such things, much less to grieve about them. We never imagined that anyone on earth would injure us, for we had never injured anyone, and we relied on the strength of the Government, and in particular, on the bravery of the Enniscorthy Yeomanry, for putting down any disturbances or even for repelling the French, let them come in what force they might.

My brother, William, though so young, was one of the Yeomen. In the preceding February, Colonel Pounden[5] of that Corps came to ask my father to join his men, but in his advanced age and constant occupations, obliged him to decline doing so. Colonel Pounden then cast his eyes on my brother who, with his shirt-collar open and his fair hair curling down his forehead and cheeks, looked more like a fine shame-faced girl than a boy. This handsome lad, said he, is the very stuff for a soldier, but my mother wept and said she could not part from her son, 'till my father said he thought no danger could possibly come near him, and I hung about her neck persuading her to let him go, for I longed to see how handsome he would look in his uniform. In less than a month he was put on his first active service – to escort a party of prisoners (taken on suspicion of being rebels) to Duncannon Fort. He returned to us in a couple of days, and this short absence was followed by several others, but still, though the rumours brought home by him were far more alarming than any ever told us by my father, we never thought danger would reach our neighbourhood, so little did we suspect the storm that was soon to burst over us.

On Saturday, being Whitsun Eve, Martin, our labourer, was shovelling oats, and my father went out to look at him. When he saw his master drawing near he laid down is shovel and, looking earnestly at him, said, 'O master, if you would not betray or injure me, I would tell you something which would serve you and yours'.

My father answered, 'You ought to know me well enough by this time Martin to be certain that I would not injure anyone, much less you'.

'But master', continued he, 'I'm sworn never to tell anyone that won't take the same oath which I did, to be true to the cause'.

'No, you unfortunate man', exclaimed my father, 'I had rather see all belonging to me dead at my feet and die with them myself than be false to the Government that has sheltered me'.

---

5 Probably Joshua Pounden of Enniscorthy, who commanded the moderate Enniscorthy Yeoman Cavalry with Solomon Richards. Pounden was a liberal and initially was sympathetic to the United Irish; he later suffered Orange reprisals for his politics (see Whelan, 'Politicization in Co. Wexford and the Origins of the 1798 Rebellion', 162–3).

On this, Martin, with a heavy sigh, took up his shovel and went on with his work. My father had but little time to think on this, for he was obliged to leave two carloads of oats at the mill of Monart to be ground for the use of the family. Monart is rather more than two miles from Clovass, and Grimes the miller[6] was a Protestant and much-respected in the country. As soon as my father cast his eye on him, he saw that he also knew of something going on, for the utmost consternation was visible in his countenance, yet he hardly exchanged a word with him, for his heart, as he told us, was too full, and leaving the oats he turned back with the empty cars, anxious to rejoin us as soon as possible. When he had gone over about half the road, he saw imperfectly (for it was now dusk) a great dust a little before him and heard a confused murmur of voices; a moment after he fancied it might be a body of soldiers advancing for he imagined he saw their bayonets. The next instant he was surrounded by a party of two hundred rebels, who stopped and dragged him off the car on which he was sitting. My father was no coward, as he proved well in two days more, but he told us that at that moment the thoughts of all he had left at home came over him, his knees failed him, and if he had not clung to the head of the horse, he would have fallen to the ground. They asked him, all together, who he was and where he was going to, and he was utterly unable to answer, but one of them chancing to know him exclaimed, 'Oh, let him go, that is Sam Barber of Clovass; he is an honest man', and they set him free.

He came slowly home and, turning the horses over to the care of Martin, he walked in amongst us and his face told us the ruin that was coming upon us even before his words did. We thought little of eating the supper we had prepared for him and ourselves, and after hearing his story, we stepped out to listen if the armed ruffians were coming back. We heard nothing indeed, but we saw eleven distinct blazes in the distance, every one from its situation marking out to us where the house and property of some neighbour, friend, or relation was consuming. In immediate expectation of a similar fate, we instantly began to load our cars with whatever furniture and provisions were most portable, that at daybreak we might flee with them into Enniscorthy. Whatever we saw was impossible to carry, and particularly all the wool and cloths in the factory, we dragged out to the fields and concealed in the ridges of the standing corn, and it was but little of what we thus left we ever saw again.

We passed the entire night doing this, the poor children, hungry and sleepy, ate and lay down in the nearest corner, for we had already packed the beds on the cars. At the break of day, we milked the cows about the

---

6 Grimes the miller remains unidentified. He does not appear on the claimants list or on the list of millers who sent flour to Dublin in the 1780s and 1790s. He may have worked for the owner a mill near Enniscorthy.

field, for we could not make use of the milk, and if we had left them unmilked, their udders would have become sore. After several unforeseen yet necessary delays, we set off for Enniscorthy about ten o'clock on Whit Sunday morning, just about the same hour we expected to have gone to its church. I carried the infant and my mother, yet weak from a bad confinement, leaned on my father's arm. The other children followed us and led on of the horses, but Martin remained behind with his mother in the little cottage my father had built for them, and when we next saw him he was an armed rebel, for he joined them on the ensuing day. Yet, from his subsequent conduct to us, I cannot think that he ever was guilty of the same cruelties committed by many of his comrades. When we entered Enniscorthy, we went to the house of a relation named Willis,[7] who willingly received us, but when we entered, there was hardly room for us to sit down, it was so full of the Protestant inhabitants of the neighbourhood, who had fled into the town for protection. Few of these had had time to bring away anything, and those who, like us, had brought food, immediately gave it to be shared in common.

My father, on seeing us safe in the house, immediately went and enrolled himself amongst the supplementary Yeomanry and was provided with a musket and crossbelts to wear over his coloured clothes. There were more than two hundred of the gentry and farmers in the vicinity armed hastily in like manner; our regular Yeomen, who were clothed and disciplined, amounted to about as many more, and we had one company of the North Cork Militia, not ninety-one in number. Excepting these last, all our little garrison were neighbours or friends or near relations to each other, who, knowing the immense force of the rebels, which certainly amounted to more than fifteen thousand men and their cruelty, for they gave no quarter, knew they had no choice between dying like men with their arms in their hands or standing tamely like sheep to be butchered. And it was this handful of men, not amounting to five hundred, that we, in our simplicity, had thought could conquer all the rebels in the country.

When my father had left us and we had unloaded our furniture, my sisters and I were at first so unconscious of our danger that we were rather gratified by the novelty of the situation and passed some time looking out of the windows, watching the yeomen (some of whom were cavalry) passing hurriedly to and fro and disputing between ourselves which of our acquaintances looked best in his uniform or sat best on his horse. A very short time, however, changed our feelings, when seven or eight men

---

7 William Willis, private in the Enniscorthy Yeomanry and corn-merchant, was killed on Vinegar Hill, 20 June 1798 (Musgrave, 741). He m. Jane Burt in 1790 (*Ferns M.L.*). In 1799, as a widow, she claimed losses including 'Whiskey, Shop Goods and Furniture' (Claimants, App., cccxli). She also appears as a claimant on the list of soldiers' widows ('Widows and Orphans', n.p.).

covered with blood were borne into the house, and we were called upon to give up our beds for them to lie on. These were yeomen who had been skirmishing in the immediate neighbourhood and who, full as the house was, were brought into it for immediate relief. I now began for the first time to see some of the miseries that threatened us, and thus passed a few uneasy hours over us, when it suddenly occurred to me that the cows would be injured if they were not milked again, and the servant-girl and I set out about six in the evening, and without meeting anything to injure us, reached Clovass in safety. We found all as we had left it, with the poor cows standing lowing to be milked. We each brought away a large pitcher and on the road home met several Roman Catholic neighbours with whom we had been on the most friendly terms; we spoke to them as usual, but they looked in our faces as though they had never seen us before and passed on. I have since thought that they either looked on us with abhorrence, as those devoted to destruction in this world and in the next, or knowing our doom and pitying us, were afraid to trust themselves to speak to us.

It was late when we returned to the town, and even in the midst of sorrow, I could still see joy lighten the faces of my father and mother at our safety; the reports of the advance of the rebels had been so frequent, even during our short absence, that they feared we might have been intercepted on our return. The milk was most gratefully received as well by our own children and by the other poor little creatures sheltered in that crowded house. We prayed and endeavoured to rest on the bare boards (for our beds were filled with the wounded Yeomen), but, though worn out in mind and body, it was little rest I took that Sunday night with the moans of a wounded man in the very room with us and the heat and the closeness of the air, so different from our own pleasant, airy, little bed-chamber.

At the dawn I arose, and after inquiring in vain through the house for the maid-servant (who I afterwards heard had stolen off in the night to join her relations in the rebel camp), my father, seeing me anxious again about our cows, said he would go with me, for he hoped there would be no immediate want of him in the town. We went accordingly to the little farm and found that, as yet, all was safe, the cows waiting for us and the poor poultry and pigs looking to us for the food we had not to give them.

My father went to look at his deserted factory, and I attended to the cows. I then thought of some griddle-cakes of coarse meal, which we had forgotten on a shelf and went to break some to the fowls; my father followed me into our desolate kitchen, and taking a piece of bread, asked me for a mug of the warm milk, which I gave him. When turning to the door and casting my eyes to the top of Coolnahorna Hill, which was not a quarter of a mile away, I saw the ridge of it filled with men armed with pikes, the heads of them glistening in the morning sun. I called in much trouble to my father, and scarcely knowing what I was doing, took up a large vessel of milk I intended to have carried into town for the children, but my father looked at me as if for the last time and said, 'Lay that down, Jane, it is most likely we shall none of us ever want it'. I obeyed him and we hastened back to Enniscorthy, where we arrived about nine in the forenoon. As we advanced towards it, we heard the drums beating to arms, and on entering, we heard that the enemy were closing in on all sides of it in a vast force. We saw our friends and neighbours hurrying through the streets to the different posts assigned to them; the North Cork Militia were placed on the bridge of the Slaney, which ran on the east side of the town; our infantry, amongst whom were the supplementary yeomen, were placed at the Duffry Gate at the opposite extremity of town toward the west. A guard of yeomen was placed over the Market House, where there was a great store of arms and ammunition, and where a few prisoners were confined; some more mounted guard over the castle, where some dangerous rebels were lodged, and in the midst of this confusion, my father, after leaving me with my mother, put on his belts, took up his musket, and joined my brother (whom we had never seen all this time) at the Duffry Gate, the post assigned to them.

In the course of this morning, Willis, in whose house we were sheltered, put his wife and two infants on a horse, and mounting another, fled with them to Wexford. He never mentioned to us his intentions, nor could we blame him, for a calamity such as that in which we were all involved would have made the most generous man selfish. He was a friendly man, but he could not save us all so, as was most natural, he took with him that were dear to him.

At eleven in the forenoon, the videttes brought word from the Duffry Gate that the rebels were advancing to the town from the northwest in a column that filled the road and was a mile in length; they were calculated by some of our garrison, who had served abroad to exceed six thousand in number. They soon closed with our Enniscorthy yeomen, and the shots and shouting fell sharply on our ears. I was at first greatly terrified, and the children hid their faces in my lap, but in a short time I became accustomed to the noise and could speak to my mother, endeavouring to give her some comfort, but she seemed stupified and could say nothing in answer, except to lament feebly that her son, William, was in the midst of such danger. She seemed not to comprehend that my father was equally exposed, more especially as he, seeing that the disaffected inhabitants of the town had now begun to set it on fire in several places, twice or thrice, on the enemy being partially repulsed, had quitted his post to run down and see were we yet safe and to tell us that his William was behaving like a brave man and a soldier. He then, on hearing the advancing shouts of the rebels, would rush back to the fight, and this imprudence in which he did, but initially too many of his comrades gave fearful advantage to the enemy. Yet they did not act thus from want of courage – for they all showed proofs of even desperate bravery – but from their anxiety for all that was dearest on earth to them and from their being totally unacquainted with the duties of a soldier, for the greater part of the supplementaries till the day preceding.

The fearful firing had now continued three hours, when the King's men fell back into the town, for our little garrison was now reduced to less than two hundred; and though they did not fall unrevenged – for more than five hundred of the rebels were slain – yet so numerous were these last that they never felt the loss. The North Corks were now forced to provide for their own safety, and I have heard it said that they neglected to sound a retreat, which, if done, would have enabled many more of the Enniscorthy men to have escaped in time. As it was, some few dispersed over the field and gained Duncannon Fort in safety, amongst whom was my brother, and the rest, with whom was my father, slowly retreated through the town, now blazing in many places. They fought in the burning streets, and though so few in number, more than once repulsed the enemy, who, crowded into a narrow space, impeded each other by their own numbers; then this handful of brave men would retreat again from the hundreds that still pressed on them, till at last they gained the Market-house, disputing every inch of ground.

The house which sheltered us stood exactly opposite to this building, and though none within it dared venture to the windows, yet we knew from the increased uproar that destruction had now come near us. At last the house caught fire over us, and we all rushed out from the flames into the midst of the fight. I don't know what became of the wounded men within it, but if they were consumed, it was a more merciful death than they would have met from the rebels. We fled across the square to the Market-house, leaving all that we had so anxiously saved the day before to be burned, without bestowing one thought upon it, and I, who had never seen a dead body, had now to step over many corpses of the rebels, who had fallen by the fire of our men in the Market-house, whilst whichever way I cast my eyes, dozens more lay strewed around. The doors were hastily unbarred and we were admitted, and once more I clung round my father, and then, stupified with fear, we sunk down amongst barrels of gunpowder, arms, provisons and furniture piled up in heaps together.

Amongst those who defended the Market-house was Grimes, the miller, who was one of the most eager to admit us into the already overcrowded place, and who, through the loopholes in the doors and walls, was one of the most active in defending it. But, in less than an hour, it, too, took to fire, and all within it, armed men, helpless women and infant children, were forced to leave it and throw themselves into the midst of the rebels who now surrounded it in hundreds, or they would have been destroyed by the explosion of the gunpowder, which took place shortly after. As we were on the point of rushing out of the building, Grimes, determined on a desperate attempt for our safety, stretched his hand out of the half-open door and seized the pikes of two of the enemy who had falled close to it, then turning to my father, he said, 'Act as I do, Sam; lay down that musket and take this pike; tear one of those little green frocks of your children to put on the pike for a banner and perhaps you and they may be spared'.

But my father replied, 'Never! I will never quit the King's cause nor my musket while I have life!'

Grimes then stuck his pike into a large flitch of bacon, and bidding us to follow, he marched out of the burning Market-house, as though he were joining the rebels and triumphantly carrying provisions to them. My father, shouldering his musket, followed him. I came closely after him, carrying my little brother of four years old; the two little girls clung to my skirts, and my mother with the infant came after me. As we stepped from the door, my father turned round to me and said, 'Jane, my dear child, take care of your mother and the children!' They were the last words I ever heard him speak.

As we left the Market-house, a fine infant of four years old, the son of Joseph Fitzgerald,[8] a near neighbour of ours, a child whom I had a hundred times nursed on my knees, came out beside me. Unfortunately, one of the rebels, who had some particular hatred to its father, knew the child and explaining, 'That's an orange brat', pushed him down, as I thought, on his back. The child gave a faint cry, and I was stooping down to raise him when I saw the pike drawn back, covered with its blood. A shiver for an instant shook its limbs – it was dead! I had strength given me to suppress a shriek, and I hid my face in my little brother's bosom, whilst the two other little creatures, without uttering a single cry, only pressed closer to me; my mother, whose eyes were never removed from my father, fortunately never saw it.

We were allowed to pass over the square without being injured, and we still were following Grimes towards the river when I noticed one pikeman following us closely and at last pushing between my father and me. In my fear and confusion I did not recollect the man, but I was told afterwards that he was one Malone, whom I had many times seen, and who, of all men on earth, we had least reason to fear. His mother had been of a decent Protestant family, but had married a profligate of the opposite persuasion; he had deserted her and one infant when she was near being confined of this man, and my father's mother took her home, and on her dying in childbirth, my kind grandmother put the deserted child to her own breast and thus preserved its life for some days till she hired a nurse for him. Our family reared him till he was able to provide for himself, and he was now a

8 Joseph Fitzgerald of Enniscorthy, a nailor, claimed losses of 'Furniture, Cloathing, Nails, Iron and Provision' (Claimants, App., cccxli). The claim was disallowed.

leather-cutter. I did not know him, however, for his face was covered with dust and blood; his appearance consequently was horrid, and his action was suspicious; so as though I could save my father, I determined not to lose sight of him and with his three young children kept close to both.

Concealed in a chimney at the corner of a lane we were now about entering, there was a yeoman, who, it was said, fired more than a hundred shots that day and made everyone tell. He, at this moment, took aim at a pikeman within a few paces of us, who staggered a few steps and fell dead behind me, exactly across my mother's feet. She dropped in a dead faint beside the corpse; I turned to raise her and to take the young infant from the ground on which it had slid out of her arms. I thus lost sight of my father and of the fearful pikeman that was following him and never saw him alive again. But Providence thus spared me the sight of his murder by the very man that had drawn his first nourishment from the same breast with him. He followed him into Barrack Lane and piked him at the door of Mr Sparrow's brewery;[9] a man named Byrne,[10] in charge of the place, saw him commit the act and saw him, too, with his leather-cutter's knife, disfigure his face, after emptying his pockets and stripping him of the new coat and hat he had on.

In a few minutes after I had lost sight of my father, my mother came to herself. She arose and we both, unconscious of our loss, went with the children towards the river, thinking we might perhaps rejoin him. My mother was quite bewildered and unable even to speak to me, much less advise me, and I, although born so near the town, had seldom been in it, but to church or to market, and was quite ignorant where to seek for shelter. We asked at many doors would they admit us, but we were constantly driven away and sometimes even with threats and curses. At last we came by chance to the house of one Walsh,[11] a baker, who knew my mother and spoke kindly to us; he opened his door, but we hardly had time to enter, when five or six pikemen followed and ordered him to turn us out or they would burn the house over our heads. He dismissed us unwillingly and put

9 William and Joseph Sparrow, of Back Street, Enniscorthy, were listed as victuallers in Richard Lucas's *General Directory of the Kingdom of Ireland, 1788* (see *Irish Genealogist*, 3:10). According to Goodall, William also registered as a banker in Aug. 1804 (Freemen, 456). In 1799, Samuel Sparrow, victualler, of Enniscorthy, claimed losses in 'Cash and Bank Notes, Flour, Corn, Whiskey, Shop Goods, Groceries, Wine, Furniture, and Plate' totalling over £5,000, of which he recovered £4,669. Joseph Sparrow gave testimony at Thomas Cloney's trial (see Thomas Cloney, *Personal Narrative of 1798* [Dublin: James McMullen, 1832], 272). Atkinson observed in 1814 that Thomas Sparrow of Enniscorthy was 'the principal merchant of the place' (Atkinson, 504; Freemen, 456).   10 Probably Luke Byrne of Oulartard, a captain of the United army in the barony of Scarawalsh. Musgrave maligns him as an 'opulent farmer and brewer' who, 'though advanced in years, was remarkably cruel and sanguinary; and his two sons, Morgan and Mogue, were little less so' (Musgrave, 346).   11 Walsh, baker of Enniscorthy and a Catholic, differs from Nicholas Walsh, whom Musgrave calls a 'shopkeeper' at Enniscorthy, and 'reputed rich' (Musgrave, 346; Thomas Handcock, 'Reminiscences of a Fugitive Loyalist in 1798', *English Historical Review*, 1 [1886]: 538).

a little open book into the hands of one of the children. When we had gone a few steps I saw it was a Romish prayerbook, which he seemed to have purposely opened at a picture of the Crucifixion; but whether he meant that this was to be a token to insure our lives or that it was to prepare us for the fate that seemed to await us, I cannot tell; I only recollect that I desired the child to lay it down, that we might not deny our religion in our last moments.

We now followed some other desolate beings, like ourselves, who led us into the garden of one Barker,[12] who had borne a high command that day amongst the rebels. His family did not seem as though they noticed us, and we sat down with many more on the earth under the bushes. All were women and children, and I have since heard that thirty-two new-made widows passed the night in that garden. Many of these new their loss, yet fear had so completely conquered grief that not one dared to weep aloud; the children were as silent as their mothers, and whenever a footstep was heard to pass along, we all hid our faces against the earth. The moon shone brightly that night, and at one time I saw a man led into the garden pinioned, but Barker, who was then in the house, was so humane as not to put him to death amongst us, but ordered him off to Vinegar Hill.

As the night advanced, a rebel named Lacy,[13] who knew us, perceiving my mother to shiver violently with fear and cold, went out and soon

12 William Barker, 'a brewer and a merchant of Enniscorthy, was a general in the camp' at Vinegar Hill and a leading United Irish figure in Co. Wexford (Musgrave, 346). Miles Byrne relates that Barker had served 'with distinction' in France in Walsh's regiment (Miles Byrne, *Memoirs of Miles Byrne* [Paris: Gustave Bossange, 1863], 1:66). He became actively involved in the rebellion following the fall of Enniscorthy, although he later protested his loyalty, claiming that until that time, he gave large quantities of flour and wine to the wives of soldiers, and that he gave shelter to loyalists, until 'compelled by menaces of death and destruction of his property' to turn them out and join the rebels (see Charles Dickson, *The Wexford Rising in 1798: Its Causes and Its Course* [Tralee, Ireland: The Kerryman, n.d.], 206–7). He later testified that he 'ever avoided having any concern whatever … in the cruelties, murders and atrocities committed by them, but did, to the utmost of his power and at the imminent hazard of his life, interfere when present to save and did save the lives of many persons …' (Barker in ibid.). He claimed further that he was forced to defend Vinegar Hill, but, in retreating to an adjoining wood, was wounded in his lower right arm by four soldiers; the arm was later amputated. Byrne depicts him as having a more active role, claiming that he advocated an immediate advance of rebel forces on New Ross instead of Wexford, but was outvoted (Byrne, 66). He also asserts that Barker's conduct at Vinegar Hill was 'brilliant' and that he actively 'commanded the important post at the Duffrey gate' (ibid.). Barker, said Byrne, lost his arm on the bridge of Enniscorthy, not at Vinegar Hill. Dickson states that Barker was acquitted on all charges at his courtmartial in 1799, and was set at liberty (Dickson, 207). Byrne contradicts this statement by relating that Barker's brother Arthur obtained his release from the Wexford jail on grounds of health prior to the courtmartial (Byrne, 1: 175–7). He and his family fled to Hamburg; he later joined the Irish Legion at Marlaix, where Byrne met him in 1803. His son Arthur served in the French army.
13 William Lacy, a rebel, was a 'shopkeeper at Enniscorthy and a brother to Father Michael Lacy' (Musgrave, 347). He was an early United Irishman in Enniscorthy, and during the Rebellion served as commissary-general to the camp on Vinegar Hill.

returning, threw around her about four or five yards of coarse cloth and spoke some words of pity to us. She, in her terror, endeavoured to cast it away from her, for she said she could be killed for having on her what was not her own, but I, with some difficulty, made her keep it; still, as she would throw it off her, drawing it around her again and placing the shivering children beneath it, till at last she seemed to forget how it was given to her. Except the clothes we wore, that was the only covering we had for ten weeks to sleep under.

In the dead of night I began to take somewhat more courage, and hearing a strange noise in a lane which was divided from the garden only by a low wall, I crept my hands and knees into it and saw a sight that soon drove me back to my mother's side. Some wounded men had been dragged to die in that lane, and some young boys of the rebel side had mounted on horses and were galloping up and down many times across their bodies, they only showing signs of life by their groans; but Barker, when he heard of this, put a stop to it and let them die in peace.

In the house, a Protestant lady of great respectability was sheltered with her children. As a mark of goodwill towards her, a thin stirabout was made early the next morning for them. She saw our desolation from the house, and beckoning me to her, gave me a plateful of it for our children, but though they tasted it, none could eat but the little boy; fear had deprived the others of the least appetite.

About nine, I felt such a desire to rejoin my father that I might bring him back to me, that I left my mother and went ot the garden gate. The first person I saw was Martin's mother, dressed completely in new and excellent clothes, and in particular, a remarkably handsome beaver-hat. I was so astonished at this, for she was very poor, that forgetting for the moment all my anxiety and fear, I asked her who had given her the hat. She answered me sternly, 'Hush! tis not for one like you to ask me where I got it'.

'But Molly', said I, 'have you seen my father?'

'I have', said she, 'and he is dead'.

I forgot what I said or did for some minutes after hearing this, but I then found that Molly Martin had drawn me away from the garden-gate, lest, as she told me, my grief should tell my mother what had happened. I clung to her and entreated her to take me to him that I might see him once more; at first she refused, but at last, to pacify my violence, she consented.

We went about a quarter of a mile to Barrack Lane, where, lying in the midst of five or six other bodies, with two pikemen looking on, I saw and knew my father. He lay on his back, with his hand across his back and one knee raised; his shirt was steeped in blood; the lower part of his face disfigured with the gashes of the ruffians knife, and his mouth filled purposely with the dirt of the street. Beside him lay our large mastiff, which followed us from Clovass, which had licked all the blood off his face.

This creature, though he was heard the ensuing night howling pitwously round the ruins of our cottage, was never seen afterwards by anyone.

I can now describe what then nearly killed me to look upon. I felt a suffocation come over me; I thought, as I looked on him, I could have given my mother, my brother, and all, even my own life, to have him brought back. I fell on my knees and, whilst kissing his forehead, broke out into loud cries, when one of the rebels gave me such a blow with the handle of his pike in my side as laid me breathless for a moment beside my father and must have broken my ribs, but for a very strong bodice I wore. He was going to repeat the blow, but then his comrade levelled his pike at him, crying with an oath, 'If you strike her again, I will thrust this through your body! Because the child is frightened, are you to beat her?' I now knew him to be one Jack O'Brien, who but the preceding week had purchased some cloth from my father at a fair to which I had gone with him. He spoke with kindness to me, and he and Molly Martin brought me back to the garden where I had left my mother, advising me not to tell her what I had seen lest she should perish with terror and sorrow.

We remained without food all that day, but we wanted none, and towards evening, Barker's family turned us all out of the garden, telling us it was not safe for us to remain there any longer. I now thought of taking my mother home, for as she was quite stupified and had never spoken all day, she was quite incapable of advising with me, so I was left entirely to myself and had to lead her after me like one of our children, but just as we reached the outskirts of the town and were slowly walking along the river, a party of rebels on the opposite bank ordered us back into the town again, threatening at the same time to fire on us. We then tried to quit it by another outlet, when we were surrounded by a large party of pikemen and marched off with many more prisoners, whom they had previously taken, to Vinegar Hill.

This hill lies close to the town of Enniscorthy. It is not high, but rather stout, and the rebels were assembled on it in thousands. They seemed to have a few tents made of blankets, but the greater number were in the open air. I could see that some were cooking at large fires, whilst others lay scattered about, sleeping on the ground. It was about sunset when we were taken to the hill, where the men who were our fellow-prisoners were separated from us and driven like sheep higher up the hill; whilst we and many more women and children were ordered to sit down in a kind of dry ditch or trench about half-way up it. We had not been long here when we were accosted by a female neighbour named Mary Donnelly; she was a Roman Catholic and had come that day to join her husband on the hill. She wept over us and sat down close to my mother, who, feeling that her presence was a protection, would cower down beside her when she heard the slightest noise.

And the entire of that night we heard fearful sounds above us, as the men who were brought with us to the hill were massacred one by one. We could hear plainly the cries of the murdered and the shouts of the executioners. Towards dawn, I saw in the bright moonlight what terrified me more than any sight I had yet beheld; I saw a tall white figure rushing down the hill directly towards us; as it came nearer I saw it was a naked man, and I felt my heart die within me, for I thought it was no living being. He passed so close to me that I could see the dark streams of blood running down his sides. In a few seconds, the uproar above showed that he was missed, and his pursuers also passed close to us. One saw me looking up and asked had I seen any one run past, but I was given courage to deny it. This – as I afterwards heard – was a singularly fine young man, not quite twenty, named Horneck,[14] the son of an estated gentleman in the neighbourhood. He had been piked and stripped, but recovering, had fled thus from the hill. He waded in the Slaney and ran six miles to the ruins of his father's house, where his pursuers reached him and completed their work of destruction.

On Wednesday, about eleven in the forenoon, owing to the intercession of Mary Donnelly, we were allowed to leave the hill. When we had gone about a furlong, I cast my eyes on my mother and was shocked at missing the infant from her arms. I cried, 'O Mother, where is the child?'

'What child?' she said, 'Oh, I believe I left it in the trench in which we sat'. I went back and found the poor little creature asleep on the ground, my mother being so crazed with grief and fear that she had forgotten it.

---

14 Jane refers here to Robert Hornick, who was shot near Enniscorthy, 30 May 1798. The Hornicks of Garraun (Killan) were of Palatine descent and were politically conservative. George Hornick Sr had two sons: George, who served with Ogle's yeomanry corps, and Robert, an apothecary's apprentice in Enniscorthy. The elder Hornick had angered local Catholics, when, in July, 1775, he successfully defended his home against a Whiteboy attack and later formed the Whiteboy Defence League, which paraded under arms to Killan Church in a show of force. During the battle of Enniscorthy, the younger George was killed while his corps was retreating to Wexford. As he was being piked to death, Fr Roche is said to have asked him sarcastically, 'Do you remember 9 July 1775 now?' (see Whelan, 'Religious Factor in the 1798 Rebellion', 75). Robert was captured by Robert Carthy and taken to Vinegar Hill, where, according to Musgrave, Carthy sent a dispatch to the elder Hornick, who was keeping a garrison house at Grange (Musgrave, 350). The rebels demanded the surrender of his arms in exchange for the life of his son, who would be inducted into the United army. George Sr refused, stating he had already given his oath of allegiance. The boy was stripped, shot, knocked on the head, and left for dead. He revived about midnight and fled Vinegar Hill for his father's house. On finding it abandoned, he was intercepted by another band of rebels, executed, and his body thrown into a gravel pit (Ibid., 350, 742; see also Taylor, 130–1). In 1799, George Hornick claimed losses of 'Furniture, Corn, Provision, Crop, House, [and] Horses' (Claimants, App. ccclxxv). Other Hornick sufferers included Thomas of Garrane, Elizabeth of Mount Nebo, and John and Peter of Old Ross, all of whom were probably related.

In our progress towards home, we met a poor silly fellow, a wood-ranger, who called himself a pikeman, but was armed only with the handle of a shovel with no pike head on it; he took my little sister on his back and my brother in his arms and offered to leave us at our home. When within half a mile of it, we met a Roman Catholic lad, a school-fellow of my own, whose name was Murphy; he wept bitterly on seeing us and perceiving us sinking with weakness, he led us to the next house and insisted on our being admitted. He then flew off to his mother's house for bread and milk, but we could only drink. We were allowed to rest here till evening, but were then obliged to leave it, for the woman of the house said that its safety was endangered by our stay. Murphy again gave my mother his arm and towards dusk we, at last, reached the house we had so long wished for and found but a heap of ashes. The house and haggard had been burned to the ground; the side walls had fallen in, and nothing was left standing but one chimney and a small outhouse, from which the door had been torn. Our factory, with all our wheels, looms, presses and machines, was burned; all our wool and cloth which we had concealed in the corners carried off; our young cattle, pigs and horses (all but one) were driven to Vinegar Hill; all our hay and corn burned down, and yet we stood looking on all this destruction in utter silence as if we could not comprehend that it was ourselves on whom it had fallen.

My father's brother[15] lived within two fields of us; his wife, whose maiden name was Reinhart, was the daughter of one of those German colonists, or Palatines as they were called, who were settled in our county, as well as in several others, many years before. She was uncommonly charitable to beggars, or poor travellers as the called themselves, and had even made my uncle build an outhouse purposely for a lodging house, which she had constantly filled with clean straw for them to sleep on. One of these, a woman, when she saw them on the preceding Sunday pre-paring, like us, to shelter in Enniscorthy, clung round their feet, and between entreaties and threats, prevailed on them to remain in their house. She stayed to protect them, and by her courage and presence of mind, she

15 A reference to either John or Thomas Barber, both of whom resided at Clovass and claimed losses in 1799. Neither are listed in the Ferns Marriage Licenses. Miss Reinhart, who married one of the Barber brothers, was undoubtedly a descendant of Henrich Rhinehart, a Palatine originally of Holland, who was first documented in Co. Wexford in 1715. Five years later he resided with Abel Ram of Gorey. In 1750, a Henry Rinhart, probably a son of the earlier Henry, was listed as a freeholder (see Henry Z Jones, *Palatine Families of Ireland*, 2nd ed. [Camden, ME: Picton Press, 1990], 96–7). A number of Rineharts were claimants in 1799, including Henry and Thomas of Miltown, James of Cavenagh's land, John of Ballymore, John of Clonhastin, Robert of Garrimtrowlin, Humphrey Rynhart of Ballygullin, and of Tubberincering, Henry Rynhart Sr and Jr, Mary Rynhart, widow, and Peter, a linen weaver (Claimants, App., cccxi, cccxv). Henry Rhynhart appears as a loyalist prisoner (Musgrave, 807).

saved the entire of their property from destruction. She turned back more than one party of rebels who came to plunder or burn, always running out to meet them with songs and cries of joy and constantly giving them whatever food could be procured for them, and which in the intervals my aunt and herself were busily employed in cooking for them. My uncle, hearing that we were standing at the ruins of our own house, came to us and brought us to his, and there we found nearly fifty women and children of the better class, who had no other place in which to lay their heads, nor a morsel to satisfy their hunger, which (now that they were no longer in immediate fear for their lives) they began to feel.

All the provisions in the house had been given to the different parties of rebels, but we milked all the cows, both my uncle's and our own (for the milch cows had been left) and made curds, which, for two days, was our only nourishment. On the third day poor Martin came to see us and gave us two sacks of barley-meal, which he and his comrades had, of course, plundered from some other distressed creatures, but which want forced us gratefully to accept. In a day or two after he came a second time with some tea and sugar, and I almost wept with joy at receiving it, for my mother was unable to take any nourishment, and the infant was perishing for want at her breast. I have often thought their lives were prolonged by this supply, but my aunt and myself scrupulously refrained from touching it, not that we thought it sinful, but to make it last longer. In a day or two more, my uncle found that two of our pigs, which had been driven off, had returned home, and he killed them, which gave us a great supply of food. In about a fortnight the greater number of those creatures he had sheltered departed to what homes and friends were left to them, but still, for many weeks, we and several as desolate were almost totally dependent on him.

On Friday, my aunt said to me, 'I shall tell your mother of your father's death, for it is better she should be in the most violent grief than in her present state'. She did so, and I cannot now bear to think of the manner my mother heard it; yet, in the midst of her anguish for his loss, the thoughts of his lying unburied seemed to give her most pain. My aunt, who was a woman of great strength, both of person and mind, and who loved my father as though he had been her own brother, now proposed that I should accompany her the next day (Saturday) to the town, with a little car, to seek for the body, and we agreed to lay it in one of those pits in which we were accustomed to burying our potatoes, but which were now empty and open. We went accordingly and met no molestation, but on reaching the place, the body was nowhere to be seen. No other corpse was in sight, yet the smell of putridity was so strong that my aunt fainted. I got her home again, and there we saw Martin, who had just brought the meal, and who told my mother that he had himself laid his master's body in a gravel-pit and covered it over; that I know was but a pretense to pacify my mother.

For some weeks afterwards we searched that gravel pit in vain, and I was afterwards told that the body of my father and all the others had been thrown into the Slaney, which ran close beside, but a few hours we had gone to seek for it. Martin called upon us several times afterwards, still anxious for our safety, but at Borris, on the 12th June, he was mortally wounded, and even then, when dying, made his comrades promise to bring his body and lay it in our ground. They accordingly brought it twenty miles on a car to his mother, waked it in our outhouse that was yet standing, and buried it next day in one of our fields near his mother's house. We attended his funeral, partly to conciliate the fearful men who accompanied it and partly from regard for his fidelity, and I shed some tears of sincere sorrow over his grave.

When I had been about ten days at my uncle's house, a young man named Morgan Byrne,[16] who was to have been married to one of my school-fellows, came on horseback with three more rebels of the better class, to demand from us the fine young horse which they had been unable to carry off before on account of his legs being fettered, lest he should have strayed away. They said they wanted him to mount their general and ordered me to unlock the fetters. In all our troubles, I had happened to preserve my mother's keys, though now totally useless, so I went with them to the field where the horses grazed, and when I had taken off the fetters, in a fit of careless anger at seeing this last act of plunder, I shook them at him, and the fine young beast fled at full speed. The rebels cursed me heartily, but galloped off to catch him, in which they did not succeed till he had run more than three miles, when they caught him as he attempted to swim the Slaney. Many weeks afterwards, when the rebellion had been completely quelled, my brother heard he was in the possession of a Protestant gentleman in Wexford. He instantly armed himself, rode thither, walked into the stable where the horse stood, and without exchanging a word with the man in whose possession he was and who was present, unloosed him from the stall and brought him off without the slightest opposition having been made.

The rebel power now began to decline, and we lived some weeks in dread, both of them and of the struggling parties of military sent in pursuit of them. From the first class we were protected by the female

16 Morgan Byrne of Kilnamanagh (Oulart), alias 'Santerre', was the nephew of Luke Byrne, maltster, of Enniscorthy and brother of Peter Byrne, a United Irishman (see Cullen, 292). Musgrave calls him the son of Luke Byrne and describes him as 'cruel and sanguinary' (Musgrave, 346). Mrs M (*q.v.*) states that he offered to save the life of her husband, provided that he join the rebel cause. Byrne played a prominent role at the battle of Oulart Hill, rallying the Unitedmen against the North Cork Militia at a key moment in the fighting (Cleary, 'Battle of Oulart Hill', 90–1).

beggar and by Martin's mother, who still lived with us, and neither of whom were ever afterwards deserted by our two families; but the last either not knowing that we were suffering loyalists, or not caring, often behaved with great insolence. The smaller the party was, the more we were in dread of them; and more than once, myself and a few more young girls, fearing to pass the night in the house, slept in the centre of a large holly bush at some distance from it. But after the rebels were repulsed from Newtownbarry and after the battle of Vinegar Hill, where they were totally routed, a regular camp was formed within a field's length of my uncle's house. We were then protected, for the soldiers were under better discipline, and we found an excellent market for our milk and butter, which enabled us to purchase a few indispensable articles of furniture and clothing, and to fit up the outhouse for a dwellinghouse. Lord Tyrone, too, who commanded these men, sent every day a baker's cart to distribute bread to the families of the suffering loyalists, and we frequently got two loaves each day from it.

On Vinegar Hill, being carried by assault, he sent to my mother desiring her to look if there was any of her furniture amongst the immense quantity of plunder that was on it; she went to thank him, but said she need not look, for all her's was burned in Enniscorthy. He smiled and called her a simple woman, and then asked her what she wanted most, for he would give it to her. She said if he could spare a feather-bed, she would be forever grateful, and he immediately ordered two of the best to be given to her. I shall not forget the joy we felt at being once more enabled to sleep in comfort for, till then, we had only loose straw thrown on the ground to sleep on. The latter end of July, a field of our barley, which had escaped the trampling, ripened; Mr Grimes, the miller, who had saved both his life and property, gave us back all our oats ready ground; our new potatoes were fit for use, and we never afterwards knew what want was. We did not, however, build a house till the next summer, and the blackened ruins of our little factory which (as he that managed it was gone) we never rebuilt, are yet to be seen.

A few nights after Vinegar Hill was taken by the King's forces, I went with a lantern to an unfrequented outhouse to bring in some straw. Martin's mother, when she perceived where I was going, followed me much agitated, but I had already reached the little building, and as I removed the sheaves, I was dreadfully shocked to see that they concealed three or four ghastly looking creatures who, on seeing me, entreated in the most piteous manner that I would not betray them. They were rebels, who had been badly wounded in the Battle, and the women who had sheltered them there and had supplied them with food from my uncle's house, now joined her entreaties to theirs, and I promised faithfully I would be silent. In four days more one died and was buried privately by the two poor women, and the rest were able to remove. I have since been blamed for not giving them up, but I have never repented for it.

It was just six weeks after the beginning of our troubles that, as I was passing near the ruins of our house, I was startled at hearing within it the deep sobs and suppressed cries of some person in sorrow. I ventured to look in and found they proceeded from a man who was sitting on a low part of the fallen wall with his head resting on his knees. When he heard my steps he arose, and I saw my brother, but if it had not been for the strong likeness he yet bore to my father, I should never have known him. From a fair, ruddy, robust boy, he had become a tall, haggard, sunburned man, so thin that his waist might have been spanned; and yet he was not seventeen, and this change had been wrought in him by the hardship and want in the space of little more than two months, for it was just so long since we had last met. He immediately turned when he saw me and fled from me at his utmost speed. In three days, however, he returned to us again, more composed and able to meet my poor mother with at least the appearance of calmness. He afterwards got occasional leave of absence to assist in our farming business, but he never was able to settle entirely with us till the winter was past.

In one of his short visits, sitting alone with him one night after all were gone to bed, I ventured to ask him how soon he knew of my father's death. He looked at me with a sterness and solemnity that awed me and said, 'I knew of it long before I was told of it; I knew of it when I was on guard at Duncannon Fort on the third night after the battle of Enniscorthy, for I saw him as plainly as I now see you. Overpowered with hunger and fatigue, I slept on my post, when he stood beside me and awakened me, and as I opened my eyes, I saw him clearly in the bright moonlight, and he passed away from before me and I knew by what I felt that he was no living man'. This might have been but a dream, yet who can say that he was not permitted to save his son from the death that inevitably awaited him if caught sleeping on his post.

I have now related the principal circumstances that fell under my own eye in the fearful summer of 1798 during which, besides my father, I lost fourteen uncles, cousins, and other near relations, but were I to tell all I saw and all I heard, I could fill volumes. Yet, before I conclude I must mention one evil not generally known that arose from the rebellion, but the ill effects of which may be said still to continue. The yeomanry was composed mostly of fine boys, the sons of farmers, some of whom had scarcely attained the age of sixteen. These, removed from the eyes of their parents with weapons placed in their hands, raised to the rank of men before they had discretion to behave as such and exposed to all temptations of idleness, intoxication, and bad companions, when peaceful times returned were totally unable to settle to their farms – too often, by their fathers' death, left to them alone, but continued the same careless, disorderly life, till they became quite unable to pay their rents. They then were ejected and emigrated to America, and on the very ground which thirty years ago were in the possession of old Protestant families, there now live the descendants of those very rebels, who may be said to have been the origin of all this evil. This, thank God, has not been the case with our family.

Clovass is still in my brother William's hands. My mother, now an aged woman, tries with him, and all the rest of the family have been married and settled in their own houses. But fears and suspicions still remain in the hearts of both parents in the Co. Wexford, and until the present generation and their children after them shall have passed away, it will never be otherwise, for those who, like me, have seen their houses in ashes, their property destroyed, and their nearest and dearest dead at their feet, though they may and must forgive, they can never forget.

4

ISABELLA BROWNRIGG

Isabella Brownrigg née Stanford, of Greenmound, Kilpipe, Co. Wexford, was born about 1768, the daughter of Daniel Stanford, an attorney of Dublin and Wexford, and his wife Mary Richardson. The Stanfords had come originally from Belturbet, Co. Cavan, her father being the son of John Stanford and grandson of Luke and Anne Stanford née Hecklefield of Belturbet.[1] Daniel Stanford was among the Freemen of Wexford voting in 1776, and the following year served as executor of the will of his kinsman Richard LeHunte of Artramont. Daniel's own prerogative will, dated 25 Apr. 1787 and proved 21 Feb. 1788, mentions his late wife Mary, who was buried at Finglas, his son John, daughters Elinor and Isabella, and brother-in-law Ralph Harman of Ballyhaise, Co. Cavan.[2] Young Isabella's roots were thus in the professional-middleman class in Cavan, Dublin and Wexford society, a position just below that of gentry but above the small farmer status of the Barbers.

In 1789, Isabella married John Brownrigg, a barrister, of York Street, Dublin and Kilpipe, Co. Wexford.[3] The Brownriggs of Co. Wexford were descended from two brothers, Henry and Giles of Yerton, Cumberland, who settled at Wingfield in Co. Wexford in 1685. Although several genealogies of the descendants of the brothers have been proposed, John's precise lineage remains unknown. His father Henry Brownrigg lived evidently at Kilpipe, near Wingfield Manor, which had been the family seat. Henry had several sons, including Thomas, Henry, and John, the

---

1 The prerogative will of Anne (Hecklefield) Stanford is recorded in the H. B. Swanzy manuscripts and abstracted in Andrew J. Clifford, 'Swanzy Will Abstracts', *Irish Genealogist* 9 (1997):471. She was the daughter of John Hecklefield, who left a will dated 18 Jan. 1677. 2 The will of Daniel Stanford of Dublin is recorded in ibid. For additional material on Daniel, see Freemen, 456. Bedell Stanford's will of Belturbet, dated 15 Mar. 1744, names brother Daniel Stanford of Dublin. That of William Stanford of Bilberry Hill, Co. Cavan, dated 13 May 1774 includes a bequest for a Bedel, son of Daniel Stanford of Dublin. Isabella's only surviving brother John was admitted to Trinity College in 1776. Some Stanfords of unknown relation include several 1799 claimants in Co. Wexford: John Stanford, farmer, of Tubberneering, and William, James, and Margaret Stanford, all of Clough (Claimants, App., cccxxiii). The latter was perhaps identical to Margaret of Tubberneering, whose husband was killed in 1798 (see Musgrave, 742). 3 *Ferns M.L.*

latter the husband of Isabella Stanford.[4] John Brownrigg's politics are not known with certainty, but he may have been a conservative. As a barrister, he appears to have divided his time between Dublin and Greenmound, Co. Wexford. That he is called 'commissioner' on a document presented in his wife's narrative suggests that he held a government post for which he owed patronage to Lord Ely. He was also an acquaintance of Harvey and like many Protestants had contacts in different political circles. His will is dated 21 Aug. 1792 and contains a codicil of 8 Apr. 1795; it was proved 31 May 1797. In it, he devised £6,000 to his widow Isabella, of which £2,000 was charged on the real estate of brother-in-law John Stanford; £2,000 on the property of father-in-law Daniel Stanford; and £2,000 from a covenant from his father Henry. Daughter Isabella Winifrid and son Henry John each received bequests of £3,000, and Henry received additionally an estate at Magheraberg, Co. Wicklow.[5] Widow Isabella moved to Bath, England, following the rebellion and died there in 1804.

Isabella's account of the rebellion is famous and often-quoted. She is perhaps best-known for her eye-witness account of the massacre of Protestant prisoners on Wexford Bridge on 21 June 1798 and her description of Wexford during the Republic. She appears to have written her account contemporaneously as a diary, for she had her writing box with her throughout her ordeal on board a ship in Wexford Harbour and later during her stay with Dr Ebenezer Jacob of Wexford. She may have embellished it at a later date for the benefit of Sir Richard Musgrave, who introduced it in his *Memoirs of the Different Rebellions in Ireland* as an account from 'a very amiable and respectable lady' whose 'name is concealed at her own desire'.[6] Musgrave bowdlerized much of the original text, adding and omitting sentences, changing portions of it from the first to third person while retaining the quotation marks, and often altering the wording of certain passages where it suited the flow of his narrative or served his thematic needs. He was particularly interested in her description of Wexford and treatment by rebel leaders, especially Harvey.

The disposition of the original manuscript after 1801 remains unclear. In the late nineteenth century, it was rediscovered by Francis Joseph Bigger, who transcribed it with some errors and reprinted it in two parts in

---

4 Freemen, 113. See also *Burke's Peerage* (1975), 385; an alternate pedigree of the Brownriggs of Wingfield is presented in John Carlisle Spedding, *The Spedding Family* (Dublin: Alex Thom, 1909), 83. 5 John Brownrigg's will in the Swanzy Manuscripts, *Irish Genealogist* 9 (1997): 447. Isabella Winifrid and Henry John, their children, survived their parents and were living in Bath in 1804. Henry John's prerogative will of Southampton and Chateau Duplessis L'Orient, France is dated 13 Apr. 1841 and proved 13 Feb. 1847. He mentions his uncle Henry Brownrigg of Wingfield, Co. Wexford; the property of his wife née Addington; four daughters, including Isabella, Henrietta, Mary, and Catherine Sarah; and a son Henry John (Ibid.). 6 Ibid., 422, 455–6, 463.

1895 and 1896.[7] This version with the same errors appeared again in 1910 in Wheeler and Broadley's *War in Wexford*.[8] Following this publication, it disappeared and has not resurfaced.

Isabella Brownrigg remained a staunch and uncompromising critic of the rebels, and her narrative reflects this tone. Her friendship with the Orange magistrate John Henry Lyster and her late husband's government commission are both suggestive of a conservative social circle, which may, in turn, have influenced her own beliefs. Yet her acquaintance with such liberals as Harvey and Jacob reflects the wide radius of contacts most Protestants had with others of similar status, regardless of politics. Her hardened attitudes toward Catholics in the wake of 1798 reflect the attitudes held by many loyalists, moderate and conservative alike, who were greatly disillusioned by the rebellion and eager to support the Act of Union.

THE ACCOUNT

Saturday, May the 26th. I was extremely busy at Greenmound making new cloaths for Henry and superintending a Walk by the River Side as we were to have a good many friends to dine on Whitsun Monday. About four o'clock Mr Lyster[9] returned from a ride to Wexford and brought an account of the alarm that reigned in Dublin, was in great spirits at what he thought the favourable prospect of affairs from Government's having full intelligence of all Plans against them, &c., &c. A Terror such as I never before experienced seized me, and I was obliged to sit down on the bank where I had been standing. Mr L said everything to dispel my fears, made me go to the house and take some wine – all was in vain, and the instant dinner was over I walked out to try and compose my mind. In about two hours I returned to the house and just at the door met a country girl almost

---

7 Francis Joseph Bigger, ed., 'Wexford in 1798: An Account of Events by an Eye-witness', *Waterford and South East of Ireland Archaeological Society Journal*, 1 (1895): 268–78; 2 (1896): 16–22. 8 Wheeler and Broadley, *The War in Wexford*, 162–199. 9 John Henry Lyster of Greenmound, Co. Wexford and Summerhill, Co. Dublin, was born on 8 Jan. 1759 and died on 11 Dec. 1808. He was the son of John Lyster of Rocksavage and Wexford and his wife Jane (Ducasse). He served as Barrister-at-Law from 1783 and married Catherine Dorothea, daughter of Benjamin Neal Bayly of Silverspring by his wife Lettice, daughter of Henry Archer of Ballyeskin (see 'Lyster of Rocksavage', *Burke's Landed Gentry of Ireland* [1912], 427). A conservative with probable Orange connections, he was closely allied with Ogle, serving in 1798 as lieutenant in Ogle's Loyal Blues (see Whelan, 'Politicization in Co. Wexford and the Origins of the 1798 Rebellion', 160–2). He was also a magistrate, who presided at the trial of Thomas Cloney (see Cloney, *Personal Narrative of 1798*, 139–140). He claimed losses in 1799, including 'Wine, Cattle, Furniture [and] Plate' (Claimants, App., ccclxxxix).

speechless with terror. With great difficulty she articulated that a gentleman had just rode by her cabin with a drawn Sword and desired that Mr
Lyster sh'd immediately join his corps at Bellevue. Mrs Lyster's situation
then engrossed me entirely. Mr L had gone out to walk and we cou'd not
find him for above two hours. He was as ignorant of the cause of the
Message we received as we were ourselves, and only stayed to put on his
Uniform and give his Keys to me, recommending Kate and her five
children to my care.

Such as night as we passed, surrounded I strongly suspected, and the
event has proved I was right, by Rebels who came to *protect* us and who
wou'd certainly have murdered us if they had been sure of the success of
their party. We walked the Court the entire night. One time we heard a
boat on the river, and were certain a party were coming over to attack us.
However, they went up the river. At daylight *our Guards* departed, and we
remained in anxiety till late in the day, when Mr Bayley[10] rode from
Wexford to intreat we would go there, and at the same moment a letter
came from Mr Lyster to beg we would come to Bellevue, where he had just
returned after marching with his corps 20 miles without seeing a rebel; but
alas he saw but too many proofs of their Execrable Barbarity. I was all
anxiety to go directly to Waterford and sail for England, but Mrs in treated
so earnestly that I would not run what she thought the only hazard, that I
suffered myself to be persuaded and consented to stay one day 'till I left
her with Mr L or in Wexford. We then all went by water to Bellevue,
where Mr Ogle's Corps were assembled, and spent a pleasing and almost
chearful evening. Mr Ogle knew the Rebels were approaching towards
Enniscorthy, but thought the Force there fully equal to its defence.

I must now tell you what I have always heard was the progress of the
business on Saturday. The rising began near Oulart, and let those
gentlemen who even now expatiate on the excesses of the Soldiery and the
oppressed state of the People remember that there was not a single soldier
from Gorey to Wexford, a distance of 21 miles, that there never had been
any there, nor could any possible excuse of that kind be assigned for what
ensued. One of their first steps was to attack Mr Burrows'[11] house and to
murder him in the presence of his wife, children, and a niece, whom I
[have] since conversed with in Wexford. They also broke into Mr D'Arcy's
house at Ballynation,[12] [and] offered to make him a Commander *provided*

10 Archer Bayly was the son of Benjamin Neale Bayly of Silverspring by his wife Lettice,
and was thus a brother to Catherine, wife of John Henry Lyster (see Freemen, 110).
Musgrave includes him on a list of privates who served in the Wexford Yeoman Cavalry
under Captain James Boyd (see Chapter One, note 20), indicating that he was probably allied
with the conservatives (Musgrave, 469). The name is transcribed erroneously as 'Bagly' in
Wheeler.   11 Revd Robert Burrowes. See Chapter One, note 11.   12 Edward Howlin
D'Arcy of Ballynahown, See Chapter One, note 12.

he wou'd turn Catholic. He said, 'No, he had lived a Protestant and wou'd die one'. He was immediately butchered.

On Sunday the 27th of May, when this account reached Wexford, 106 of the North Cork Militia, all picked men, and five officers of Col. Lehunte's[13] Yeomen Cavalry, all the rest were *not to be found*. This force marched on a hot day 12 miles, and, on ascending a Hill saw a Valley below them, and on the opposite Hill the entire Rebel Force. Two old officers who were in Lehunte's Cavalry spoke to Major Lombard,[14] who had the command given him by Col. Foote,[15] to hope they should all remain where they were and wait the approach of the Rebels, as their position from many circumstances was highly advantageous; but Major Lombard, a brave, spirited young Man, fearless of danger, resisted their remonstrances and intreaties and boldly rushed with his party down the Hill and half the opposite Hill, when he halted and made every one of his soldiers fire. At once the rebels, who were running back, saw the advantage he had given them, and whilst the soldiers were reloading, completely surrounded them. Col. Foote and 4 others only escaped to Lehunte's Cavalry, who got off without the least difficulty as the Rebels seemed not at all desirous of attacking them. They retreated to Wexford, from whence expresses were sent off to Waterford, Ross, &c., &c., requesting military assistance.

The Rebel Force, increasing every hour, and plundering and butchering every Protestant that they thought not absolutely favourable to their cause, proceeded towards Enniscorthy and attacked it on Monday morning the 28th. That day at the first dawn I was alarmed at Bellevue by loud talking under my window. I got up, and on listening heard a poor old Man give an account of the dreadful murders that had taken place round him. Shortly after an order came from Wexford that Mr Ogle and corps should march there. All was then confusion except the Master and Mistress of the house. She made breakfast for us all with her usual sweetness and composure. Our boat was got ready, and just before I went to it I saw from an upper window Enniscorthy in flames. Mrs L and I stopt at Greenmound, took in my trunks which I had packed on the first alarm and a few bundles of her own, and proceeded to Wexford. [During] our entire passage we never saw a living being. When we landed we found every man under arms. My entire object was to get any method of leaving it, and I walked about

13 Col. George Le Hunt, see Chapter One, note 39. Wheeler misread this name in the original manuscript and transcribed it as 'Lehante'. 14 Major Thomas Lombard of Lombardstown, Co. Cork, served in the North Cork Militia and was Col. Foote's second in command at the battle of Oulart Hill (see Cleary, 'Battle of Oulart Hill,' 87, 89–90). He led the charge against the United army, resulting in an ambush and the deaths of most members of the unit. Johanna Lombard, widow of Thomas Lombard, Serjeant in the North Cork Militia, later claimed compensation for his death (see 'Widows and Orphans', n.p.). 15 See Chapter One, note 10.

incessantly from one captain of a Ship to another to induce any one to sail with me to Milford and could not succeed. Spent a miserable night on a straw Matress on the floor by Mrs Lyster or wandering about the house.

Next morning, the 29th, at daylight Mr J. Grogan[16] and 12 of his cavalry marched in at the head of 200 of the Donegal Militia from Duncannon. This seemed to raise the spirits of many. It had not that effect on mine, so I set out again, and at last Capt. Dixon[17] agreed to take me to Milford and to sail that day. About 2 o'clock I went on board his Ship immediately, for the fate of Enniscorthy the day before, and the lamentable state in which some of the fugitives from it entered Wexford, gave me a terror of fire not to be expressed. I remained on board all night. Mrs L sent me a Matress and blankets which I spread on Deck and put the children on it with the blanket over them. There would have been room for me, but a lady I never saw till then laid herself down by them, so I sat all night on the handle of the Rudder with my head leaning on a bundle of ropes. Great God! What a night that was. The Horns of the Rebels I heard very plainly, for the ship just lay about half way from Ferry Bank and Wexford. I saw very clearly that the Captain of the vessel was not loyal. Of course, I had no chance of escaping to England, so sat in fearful expectation of my fate.

At the first dawn of day, May the 30th, the bridge was set on fire from the Ferry Bank side, all our crew were, or pretended to be, asleep. I awoke them, and if I had doubted their principles before could no longer doubt them. A wonderful scene of confusion now ensued. Boats of every description put off from [the] Shore, and our Ship and every other in the harbour was filled with women and children, some naked, several had been in Enniscorthy the day before entirely frantic. When day was quite clear I got a Spy Glass and saw a party of Rebels about half a mile from Ferry Bank. They were stationary, and seemed as if placed to watch the effect of the fire on the Bridge, that was soon extinguished. Several Gentlemen

---

16 John Knox Grogan of Johnstown, Co. Wexford was the son of John Grogan, Esq. and M.P. by his wife Catherine, daughter of Andrew Knox. He was also the brother of Cornelius Grogan, who served as commissary to the United army (see Chapter 1, note 30). The Grogans were split politically in 1798. Although John Knox Grogan was was a liberal and had been admitted to the United Irish in 1793, he remained loyal and headed the Johnstown Rangers in 1796 and Healthfield Cavalry in 1798. Another brother, Thomas Grogan Knox, was captain of the Castletown Cavalry and was killed at the battle of Arklow (see Freemen, 320). John was wounded in the retreat from Wexford (Gordon, App., 59). He visited his brother Cornelius before the latter's execution, and later succeeded in having Cornelius's forfeited estates regranted to him. He died in 1814 (see Madden, 503, 512). 17 Capt. Thomas Dixon, sea captain and innkeeper, was a native of Castlebridge, Co. Wexford. He became a Captain of the United Irish army in Wexford and is believed to have incited the massacre of prisoners on Wexford Bridge. His whereabouts after the Rebellion are not known. See Goodall, 'Dixon of Castlebridge, Co. Wexford,' 632–3.

rowed to our Ship to give us accounts of what was going on, and most curious as well as melancholy accounts they brought. The North Cork Militia was at various posts guarding the entrance of the town when every one of their officers but a young lad of 14 (of the name of Little) left them there and went on board the Ships. The Donegals and some Yeomen Cavalry marched with a field piece to the 3 Rocks, about three miles from Wexford, and a strong pass, to meet the Rebels. They did meet them, fired one volley, and seeing, I suppose, the immense disparity of numbers and that the rebels had got two field pieces, retreated to Wexford, marched through it to the barracks to refresh, and, of course, left all clear for the rebels, as the North Corks deserted by their officers and seeing the retreat of the Donegals quitted their posts immediately.

All this time, of course, the Rebels were advancing and increasing in numbers. I sat watching the Cavalry on the Quay. They began to disperse shortly after Mr Lyster come on the Shore, kissed his hands earnestly to me, lifted them to heaven, and went off. Several of the North Cork officers went back to Wexford from the Ships, and as I afterwards found, joined their Men who, with the Donegals, Mr Ogle and Corps, and some few Loyalists who knew of the retreat, fought their way and after incredible hardships arrived safe at Duncannon Fort. It appears very extraordinary that Col. Maxwell,[18] who commanded, neither sounded a retreat nor sent to acquaint the Yeoman Corps that he intended it. By this means those at distant posts never heard of it, and were standing perfectly ignorant of their situation when the Rebels poured into the town in numbers past all belief or description. As soon as the army had gone off, Capt. Dixon got into his boat avowedly to join them, and saying he wou'd *try* what he could do to save our lives in a manner that showed we had little hope. We were then, I suppose, about 40 women and children put into the hold of the Ship on Coals with which it was loaded, and sat expecting immediate death for above an hour.

Never can I forget the Scene; few have beheld such a one. Not a shriek or loud word was spoken, except by Henry, who was singing as if he was in perfect safety. My poor Isabella cried *quietly* by my side, *and* a Mrs Bland[19] sat patting *three lap Dogs*. At length Capt. Dixon returned, and said no woman or child shou'd be killed, but that no man should escape but 3 that he named. Numbers of Men had come on board in his absence, hoping to escape to England. One particular friend of mine, Mr T, asked me to shelter him behind me in the hold. I did so, and covered him with great

18 Col. Richard Maxwell, see Chapter One, note 13.   19 Captain Bland was held on the prison ship by the rebels. Musgrave writes that Mrs Bland, with Mrs Crump, entreated Fr Corrin to save the lives of their husbands, after which their release was obtained (see Musgrave, 456, 459, 803). George Bland of Drinah claimed losses of 'Furniture, Plate, [and] Cloathes' totalling over £933, which was disallowed (Claimants, cccxxv).

coats, &c. The Rebels now sent boats to bring the People into town from the Ships. What ferocious savages then appeared, intoxicated with Whiskey and victory, one *woman* brandishing the Sheath of a Sword and boasting of her exploits! She was sister to Mrs Dixon,[20] and an old acquaintance of mine, as her husband had been killed at Artramont. The first demand was for Arms which the Gentlemen [had] brought with them. Some Rebels jumped into the hold to search, one of them fixed his eyes on me and said, if *I* looked he wou'd be satisfied. This was a great relief, for I was certain before of seeing my poor friend killed by me, and perhaps sharing his fate for hiding him. I then crept on hands and feet under the deck, &c., and found several Guns, Pistols and Swords, which I handed to my Rebel *admirer*. He thanked me very graciously, told the rest not to molest me, and they all went off carrying with them a number of unfortunate men to Prison and to Death.

Observe that from the time Capt. Dixon returned, Pistols and Guns were incessantly firing around us, and he assured us there wou'd not be a life spared on board any Ship but his, and that his ship was excepted because he was brother-in-law to Roche,[21] the Commander of the Rebel Army. When the boat went off with arms, and my poor friend Mr T told me he wou'd go on Deck and meet his fate for he wou'd not involve me in it, I bid him stay and went to Mrs Dixon [and] told her who he was. She declared he was as safe as herself, so he went, most fortunately, on deck, for in half an hour another boat full came in very bad temper and said if they found one Gun or man below they wou'd burn the vessel and all in it. I thought it most probable they would find Guns, for I had not looked very carefully. However, they did not, but sent every one from on board the Ship but me and my family. I had no place to go. Mrs Lyster I knew had gone in a boat down the harbour, all my friends in town were loyal and I supposed were murdered. So I begged of Mrs Dixon to let me stay, and I must do her justice to say she consented with seeming good nature. The day passed in receiving boats full of Ruffians coming to search for men; to boast of their murders and to increase their Intoxication. One would not drink except *I* did first least he should be poisoned. I did drink; sincerely wishing (if it was God Almighty's will) that it might be poison. At night I lay down in the hold *on the Coals* with the Children, who slept quite sound. They had never eat nor asked for food that entire day, nor from 3 o'clock the day before, except one bit of bread. When the Crew thought us asleep their conversation exceeds description. What saved our lives or saved us from worse than Death was our all gracious God who still preserves us.

---

20 Mrs Dixon is known only as 'Madge' (see Revd Patrick F. Kavanagh, *A Popular History of the Insurrection of '98*, [Dublin: M.H. Gill, 1920], 181). Goodall cites a letter in the Rebellion Papers giving her name as Margery (Letter in the Rebellion Papers, 620/3a/175 in Goodall, 'Dixon of Castlebridge, Co. Wexford,' 633). **21** Gen. Edward Roche; see Chapter One, note 22.

At day light, May 31st, Capt. Dixon came on board, and said everything horrible, made me stand on the deck and look where poor Mr Boyd's[22] dead body lay, and boasted of various murders. A fellow came opposite to me, drew his Pistol from his Girdle, and with the look of a Demon seemed to enjoy my terror. Mrs Dixon came and said if I had any papers that showed I was a *Protestant* I must destroy them, as a party were coming that wou'd destroy her and her Ship if they found a Protestant in it. On this I unlocked my box of papers and they tied them all round with large coal and sank them in the Sea. Another boat now came. One Man seemed more humane than the rest; I took him aside and offered him my purse if he wou'd get us safe on Shore. He said 'Yes', spoke to a friend of his, and instantly made us get into his boat. Elizabeth brought my writing box. No one said we did ill or well. Mrs Dixon asked, 'Wou'd I take my Trunks?' I had sufficient presence of mind to say 'No', that I thought them much safer with her. This, and a most curious liking that Isabella took to her, I believe got us out of the Ship alive. The Child cried at parting with her, and clung round her.

We rowed off; I had no place to go to, and the Streets were as thick of armed Men firing random Shots as Leaves on a Tree, for that was the Boatman's Similie. One of them considered and asked me if I knew any Catholic. I named Mrs Talbot.[23] He brought me [by] a back way from the water to her house. It was all shut up and deserted, and we got again into the boat. I sat not caring what they did with me, when to my amaze, I was asked if I knew Doctor Jacob.[24] I said 'Yes'.

'Then we will take you to him, for his is a safe house'.

They landed me opposite his door, and most kindly was I received by all his family. Do not, however, suppose I was for an instant either in peace or

---

22 John Boyd, see Chapter One, note 18.   23 The identity of Mrs Talbot is not clear, but she may have been connected with the Talbots of Castle Talbot, one of the few Catholic gentry families in Co. Wexford. William Talbot had married as his second wife Anne, daughter of Robert Woodcock of Killown on 24 Aug. 1796 (see 'Talbot of Castle Talbot', *Burke's Landed Gentry of Ireland* [1912], 682).   24 Dr Ebenezer Jacob was the third son of John Jacob of Rathdowney by his wife Sarah, daughter of Ebenezer Radford of Brideswell. He was born about 1738, studied medicine at Glasgow, and became a surgeon in the Army. In 1764, he had married Elizabeth, daughter of Laurence O'Toole by his wife Mary Talbot, a Catholic gentry family, and had fifteen children. He was founder of the Co. Infirmary in 1770 and had commanded the Wexford Yeoman Infantry, which was left behind when the regular Army forces evacuated the town (see Freemen, 327; Hay, 147). A political liberal with pro-Catholic sympathies, he was not only shielded from harm by the rebels, who regarded him highly on account of his medical skill, but was elected mayor of the town during the time of the Wexford Republic. Brownrigg's assessment of him is favourable, although that of Jane Adams is highly critical (see Jane Adams, Chapter 8). Jacob was reinstated as Mayor of Wexford by loyalist forces. Musgrave notes that the house where Mrs Brownrigg stayed was actually that of Nicholas Hatchel, Dr Jacob's son-in-law (Musgrave, 422; David Goodall, 'Hatchell of Co. Wexford', *Irish Genealogist* 4 [Nov. 1972]: 469–470).

safety. The Hall etc. was full of Ruffians, and in 10 minutes after they brought faggots to set fire to the house. Some of the more humanity dissuaded them.

I had now been from Saturday night the 27th without Sleep or food, for I can hardly say I eat once and only drunk some tea from Mrs Dixon. You have read in what manner my time passed, and can scarcely wonder that my Senses partly forsook me. It was, however, only partly, for I perfectly recollect all that passed. I think I may say I was more guided by the enthusiasm of *Despair* than Insanity. I took Isabella by the hand, and went directly to Bagenal Harvey. He did not know me, which was only what I expected, covered as I was with Coal Ashes, and convulsed by Misery. I told my name, reminded him of his acquaintance with John, and *desired* (for I felt too much indignation to *intreat*), that he wou'd protect me and my children. He spoke with great kindness, seemed greatly struck by the misery he must have felt he had caused, and gave me the paper I sent to you, at the same time saying he had no *real* command, and that they were a Set of *Savages* exceeding all description. I asked, 'When is this to end?'

His answer I can never forget. 'Probably not *for some time*, for Government will not now send a force till they send a *proper one*'. He seemed so perfectly sensible that he had no authority that his protection gave me little comfort. He said he must try and get the people out of the town to form Camps or it wou'd be destroyed in a few hours. It seems Mr John Hay[25] harangued the Mob, intreating them to burn the Town, and of course all of us that were in it. Shortly after the Rebels consented to go to Camp. I saw thousands beyond my ideas of reckoning depart, [with] many Priests as Leaders. Often the people stopped, knelt down, wiped the Ground, and crossed themselves, then set up their hideous Yells and followed their Priest. The day passed looking at and listening to them. Shots fired every instant, and small parties searching the house as they pleased, drinking and sending other friends to follow their example.

Next day, June 1st, just passed in the same way. John Ricards came to me with tears, lamented my situation and his own fate in being obliged to join the Rebels, who with great difficulty spared his life or admitted him, as they knew from his not knowing their Signs that he never had been an United Irishman. He insisted on my taking *eight* Guineas. When I refused [he] laid it on a table and swore he never wou'd touch it, that he owed me more than he cou'd ever repay, and wou'd willingly lay down his life if it could be of use to me. He told me, I am sure with *real* horror, how the *Protestants* were spoke against, but he trusted the Women and Children wou'd be spared. I took his money and felt more pleasure in sending him Gen. Leake's[26] Protection when the army came than in anything that I met

25 See Chapter One, note 36. 26 Gen. Gerard Lake (1744–1808) was commander-in-chief

with. I trust I shall yet be able to repay his attachment still more fully. In the evening Doctor Caulfield came to see me. Poor Ricards had gone to tell him where I was, etc., etc. Caulfield[27] was very kind, and gave me an ample Protection, but like Harvey, declared he had no Influence, and added that he was cautioned in the Street coming, to beware how he protected Protestants. He said, 'The People cou'd not be described, that in reality the Devil was roaming at large amongst them. That their power cou'd never hold. That they w[oul]d make it a religious War which w[oul]d ruin them. That Government was strong and must conquer, and that this rebellion had been hatching for the last four years'. I think he might have given Government notice of it.

June 2d. – This day we sat in expectation of our speedy release. Nothing was talked of by the Mob in our hearing but the *punishing* of the Protestants, and Mrs Lehunte[28] and *many many* others went to the Chapel, renounced their Religion, were *christened* (for it seems we are not Christians), and were marched in Procession through the town. Flanagan, the Boatman who brought me on shore, came to intreat I wou'd go. Various were his reasons. He assured me I was *happy in my sufferings*, as they wou'd compel me to save my precious soul, which must else be eternally lost. I answered him with great civility and *thanks*, but he saw I wou'd not go, and at last took his leave intreating me to consent to come then *with him*, and with great emphasis to beware of being the last to go to Mass. Elizabeth was by and enraged at my *mildness*, 'how I cou'd patiently bear such a fellow's daring to speak to me, that they might kill her, and so she supposed they would, but never should they get her into a Chapel alive'.

of the British forces in Ireland during May and June of 1798; he was responsible for the British victory at Vinegar Hill on 21 June, and later marched into Wexford, putting to death those rebels found with arms. He is also notorious for the so-called Daguery of Ulster, and his men were widely despised for their lack of discipline (see *Dictionary of National Biography*, 11:411–415). **27** Dr James Caulfield, Roman Catholic bishop of Ferns, deplored the excesses of the Rebellion and remained loyal to the crown. He opposed radicalism in his Diocese, preferring instead a gradual thaw in establishment attitudes (see James Caulfield, *Reply of Right Revd Dr Caulfield, Roman Catholic Bishop and of the Roman Catholic Clergy of Wexford to the Misrepresentations of Sir Richard Musgrave, bart.* [Dublin, 1801] in Whelan, 'Role of the Catholic Priest in the 1798 Rebellion in Co. Wexford', 297–8). For a thorough account of Caulfield and his role in the Catholic church of the 1790s, see Dáire Keogh, *The French Disease: The Catholic Church and Radicalism in Ireland, 1790–1800* (Blackrock, Co. Dublin: Four Courts Press, 1993). **28** Probably Alicia Mary Corry, wife of Col. George Le Hunte of Artamont, see Chapter One, note 39. Her temporary conversion in 1798 was among the most prominent of the Protestant community (see Whelan, 'The Religious Factor in the 1798 Rebellion in Co. Wexford', 76). Charles Jackson notes that Mrs Le Hunte was turned out of her house by her housekeeper, who told her that 'she had a good deal of impudence to expect it' (Charles Jackson, *A Narrative of the Sufferings and Escapes of Charles Jackson, late Resident of Wexford ...* [4th edition, 1802], 29). She later moved with her husband to Wales.

From this time to the 20th of June, a day ever to be remembered with singular horror, we passed in misery and agitation. On the 2d of June, from fear that our filth might be too offensive, I sent Flanagan to the ship for my trunks. None of us had changed any of our dress from the 28th of May. They would not give them without an order from Mr Harvey. I put my Arm under a Rebel's who offered it (I think he was a bricklayer), and walked through the streets crowded with armed villains firing incessantly (sincerely I wished some shot might hit me) till I arrived at Mrs Lett's,[29] where Centinals were placed, colours flying, and all proper dignity observed. The Centinels stopped me, so I asked for Mr Harvey. He immediately came out and took me into a parlour, where sat Keugh and Fitzgerald,[30] with various papers on a Green Table before them. I intreated Mr Harvey to allow some boat or Ship to take me away. He promised in a couple of days to *try* and get one. Mr Keugh was all condescension, made me sit down, but *wondered* much why I shou'd wish to leave a place where I was in perfect safety. Fitzgerald never spoke, but gave me a most ferocious look which I did not care one pin about. After some conversation, principally Mr Harvey's describing all the fatigue he suffered and the present difficulty of procuring bread for The People who were demanding it most clamourously at the Door, he wrote an order for my trunks and I departed. So ended my visit to *The Council. My Trunks* were then sent, but the locks all broken, and (except a few things at the bottom of one trunk), totally empty. Fortunately there came Linen enough to make us clean. I set about undressing, and before I could dress again had Rebel men in my room.

June the 3*d*. – They made three Protestants shoot a man of the name of Murphy[31] in The Bull Ring. They wou'd not kill him themselves because he was a Catholic, but he cou'd not be pardoned as he had given information against Dixon, *a Priest*, who was transported in consequence. The Rebels told the Men who shot Murphy that they shou'd also suffer. However, they sent them back to jail. One of them was butchered on the Bridge the 20th of June. Murphy had been Servant to Mr Edwards,[32] who

29 Mary (Moore) Lett was the daughter of James Moore of Milne Hill, Co. Cavan and was a cousin of Bagenal Harvey; she married Stephen Lett of Newcastle, a United Irishman (see Ranson, 'A '98 Diary', 47). 30 Matthew Keugh and Edward Fitzgerald, rebel leaders. See Chapter One, notes 7, 26. 31 Francis Murphy of Kilscoran, a gardener for the estate of Cadwallader Edwards of Ballyhire, was listed among the prisoners in the Wexford gaol (Musgrave, 806). His public execution was ordered by Thomas Dixon in revenge for the testimony Murphy gave against Dixon's cousin, Fr Thomas Dixon (Whelan, 'The Catholic Priest in the 1798 Rebellion', 303). Taylor states that the executioners were Middleton Robson and Richard Julian, both gaugers; and Robert Pigott, a Surveyor of Excise (Taylor, 98). The three held unpopular occupations and were probably conservatives, having held their positions through the political patronage of Lord Ely. The Bull Ring, where the execution took place, was a square in the central part of Wexford town. 32 Cadwallader Edwards of Ballyhire, eldest son of Cadwallader Edwards and his wife Anne Bunbury, was

had retreated with the army to Duncannon. Not having him in their power they showed their good intentions towards him by tearing his mother's house to atoms and destroying all her property. She and her daughters had luckily escaped to Wales. *Two* Ships only were loyal and went off; she by chance was on board one of them.

From the 3rd to the 10th I recollect nothing particular, every day was equally miserable and passed in the same Manner, our doors open, Rebels ever coming in and walking all over the House, some Civil, some not, no one ever knowing whether they wou'd murder or not before they departed. The Rebel Troops paraded twice a day on the Quay opposite our door. They had fiddles, Drums, and Fifes. They were pleased to call it a parade. It was in reality a *regular tumult*, every one gave his advice and opinion. One said, 'I will go and take Ross', another, 'I will take Newtownbarry'.

Henry John listened one day with great attention and said, 'Dear Mama, are they every one *kings?*'

At this time the John Street Corps of *300* Men was commanded by Monaghan,[33] a Derry boy. He had the most truly ferocious countenance I ever beheld. Henry John asked whether it was God Almighty that put *that face* on him. The Corps afterwards displaced him (they all changed officers as they pleased), and he went away to the camp at Oulart with *General* Fitzgerald.

About the 10th I was told that a Mr Masterson, a Catholic, was to sail in a Ship which had been taken by the Rebels a few days before and to proceed for England. I wrote to Mr Keugh (as Harvey was absent) for permission to go. He came, and in the most plausible manner gave his consent, sent orders to the Committee appointed to give out provisions to supply me with Sea Store, and assured me he wou'd take care that I shou'd have most comfortable accomodations and sail next day at 10 o'clock. This was the hardest Trial God was pleased to give me. My hopes of deliverance were great, but next day came and I heard nothing of Mr Keugh or of the Ship sailing. I could see *it* from the windows, and to make my Story short, was left to find out at my leisure that I would not be liberated from my Prison; for Mr Keugh never had the humanity even to break it to me. I did not see him for several days. When he came he said *The Committee* could

admitted to Trinity College, 20 May 1736. He served as Mayor of Wexford in 1780. In 1763 he married Elizabeth, daughter of Richard Donovan of Clonmore (see Freemen, 120).
33 Richard Monaghan, alias Dick Monk, of John Street, Wexford, was a United Irish leader in that town and had been a prominent leader in the movement for Catholic rights in the 1790s. During the Rebellion, he commanded what was termed the 'John's Street Corps' and later set himself up magisterially in Wexford jailyard where, to the awe of his town companions, he interrogated yeoman prisoners to determine if they were United Irishmen (see Furlong, *Fr John Murphy of Boolavogue*, 92). Dickson gives evidence of humanity and asserts that he was responsible for helping to stop the massacre on Wexford Bridge (see Dickson, 208–210). He was later shot dead near Bunclody by a group of yeomen.

not permit *my* Departure – a member of the Committee was *really* a friend of mine, and never, I am sure, was it brought before them.

For several days I never wished to go out, but was desired to do so by Mr Keugh. 'Why should we confine ourselves? Surely we could have no Fears or Distrust?' I went to see Mrs Ogle, Mrs Boyd, and Lady Anne Hore, and Mrs Richards.[34] Few ventured to any of those I have named, and truly miserable was their situation.

June the 14th Capt. Dixon and his Wife rode into town carrying a small Fire Screen from Col. Lehunte's country house. Unfortunately it was decorated with *orange* Paper. Dixon stopt on the Quay [and] spoke to the Sailors with his usual violence. All I cou'd hear was, 'You see, we were all to be massacred'. He rode into town, and as soon as the Sailors collected their arms they followed him. There was a most dreadful Tumult. Poor Col. Lehunte dragged from his Lodging, fired at, struck, and many Pike Men attempted to stab him. How he escaped is hard to say. Some leading Rebels interfered, and *The People* determined at last on putting him *regularly* to Death next day, so consented to his being lodged in jail. He only received one or two slight wounds, which considering his situation, was truly wonderful. The Rioting continued all night. Dixon and his Wife made out that the Fire Screen was *The Orange Standard*; and that all the figures on it pointed out various methods of *torturing* Roman Catholics. At another time, or if their views had been different, the interpretations of the Charades etc. wou'd have been truly laughable. As to the Figures, Hope on *her* anchor was a Sailor tied and left to die on a *red hot* anchor, so all the Wexford Sailors were to have perished. A Heathen Goddess in buskins was transformed by their Bigotry into Saint Patrick with a *new* kind of torture applied to his legs, and showed clearly how all true believers in *him* were to perish. The Babes in the Wood were the Roman Catholic Children turned out to Starve, the *birds* to pick their eyes out.[35]

34 Mrs Ogle was Elizabeth Moore, daughter of William Moore of Tinraheen and wife of the Hon. George Ogle of Bellevue; she died 11 Aug. 1807, aged 65, and is buried at Ballycanew (see Freemen, 451). Mrs Boyd was Elizabeth Hore, daughter of Col. Walter Hore of Harperstown by his wife Anne (Stopford); she married Capt. James Boyd, Captain of the Wexford Yeoman Corps (Ibid., 112). Lady Anne Hore was Anne Stopford, daughter of James Stopford, first earl of Courtown, who, in 1758, married Walter Hore of Harperstown (see 'Hore of Harperstown,' *Burke's Landed Gentry* [1850], 593). Mrs Richards is perhaps Martha, daughter of Col. George Rawson of Belmont, Co. Wicklow, wife of Solomon Richards of Solsborough, Co. Wexford, commander of the Enniscorthy Yeoman Cavalry and a positive neutral (see 'Richards of Solsborough' in *Burke's Landed Gentry of Ireland* [1912], 589). 35 The Revd Robert Leech of Drumlane noted that Mrs Dixon, 'a tall fine-looking woman, had been previously outraged by one of the soldiers and this seems to have been the cause of their fury and revenge' (see Leech's letter in *The People*, 13 Aug. 1898). The killing of Mrs Dixon's brother-in-law at Artramont was also a factor. Le Hunte's survival was almost miraculous. Ordered to be taken to the prison-ship, 'he fortunately happened to be in the gaol, where he eluded their search in the corner of a cell.

It was hard on the Poor *Red breasts*, whose humanity I never before heard any doubt of, but I suppose they had turned Protestants. In the course of the evening one set of Rioters bust into the council room and nearly killed Keugh, his crime was being an Orange Man. The Catholic members of the Committee rescued him. They were *all* Catholics, for Keugh had embraced that Religion, and always went at the head of the men to Chapel, so did all other leaders and soldiers that joined the Rebels, but the latter never forgot who had once been Protestants and treated them accordingly. I have heard some say 'All their *Policy* and their christening shan't save them'. and latterly it was avowed that no Protestant shou'd live much less command them.

About 9 o'clock the 14th, a Party of Sailors, about 20 armed, came to our house. Their Leaders called out, 'Some go and secure the back of the House and now my Lads get ready your pieces and seize every person you meet'.

Our Terror was dreadful. Isabella was in Bed rather delirious, and heard some one speak of this party. I was obliged to lie down by her and wait their appearance. They brought candles in to help them in their search, as they said, for arms, ran their swords under the beds, etc. At last one said, 'We won't have any *blood*'. I never can forget how delightful I thought those words. They told us a long history of Col. Lehunte's crimes, his dreadful *screen*, etc., drank some Whiskey and departed.

[On] the 17th and 18th of June small Parties of Horse appeared on parade. They were called foraging parties, but in reality were sent out to watch the Progress of the Army. Of its approach we had not an Idea, were told that the Rebels were every where successful, and that Dublin and all the Northern towns were theirs. The Rebels cheered on Parade for taking Ross the day after they had been defeated there, and Mr Keugh came in to tell us of the victory. He said, '*Ma'am*, there are 500 Soldiers lying *dead, dead!*' The common people *really* thought every thing was their own. Their Priests and Leaders dare not undeceive them. Recollect this, and it will account for their different line of conduct. The latter knew a day of reckoning was at hand, and as far as they cou'd do it without *danger* to their own lives would, I believed, have saved ours. But the former, certain of success, threw off all disguise and showed themselves in their true colours. Never till then had I any Idea of what Wickedness the human heart is capable when deprived of all restraint, or still worse, given up to Bigotry and the grossest superstition.

Their mistake, and the delay occasioned by it, very fortunately saved his life, as the express arrived, and the alarm took place in the mean time' (Musgrave, 457). Edward Hay and Matthew Keugh were instrumental in saving him from the mob (see Hay, 263).

Some anecdotes of this Superstition I must give you. My acquaintance, Mrs Dixon's Sister, told me, enveighing most desperately against the soldiers that they had *dared* to fire on the Holy Man (Roche the Priest),[36] but that as soon as the balls *touched* him they fell as soft as feathers, adding, for I fancy she doubted *my Faith*, 'I saw them Myself'. Unfortunately, this holy man forgot any Preservative against Hemp, and was hanged on Wexford Bridge the 23rd of June.

Murphy, a Priest,[37] was killed at the battle of Arklow, but my Rebel acquaintance informed me that the Army took him alive, tortured him cruelly, and spent an entire day endeavouring to burn his *right hand*, but no, *that* they could not, the Holy Man's hand wou'd not burn. Ask one of these *Holy* Men to save a Friend's life; they were all benevolence, but alas! had no Power, their influence had long ceased over the minds of the People. So they go on, and so they will ever go on, whilst God for the just punishment of our sins suffers such a Religion to Exist. The Rebel *Leaders* said they fought for Liberty, Emancipation, and Reform, their Soldiers that they fought for Religion, to *punish* the Protestants, and to save their own lives, as *We* were certainly to have massacred all of them on Whitsun Tuesday. This I was assured their Priests had preached to them. One night on our Steps a man lamented much the hard life he had led, and said he was much happier in his own Cabin. 'So we were', said another, 'but consider your Religion'.

'I never will be *backward* for my religion', was his answer.

On the 19th of June one of the Protestant Maid Servants came in with a countenance impossible to describe, Joy and Terror were so equally blended. She had been in a Shop where Keugh was, when a man galloped into town covered with Sweat and Blood. Mr Keugh called out, 'Sir, why are you from your Camp?' The man gave an account of the Destruction of Lacken Camp that morning by the Army from Ross, whom he represented as close at his horse's heels. All the People wished to hear him and general confusion ensued. Mr Keugh called him a Liar and sent him to Jail, but every one believed the Story he told. This was the Crisis I had long looked for, and went trembling to Pray. The Drums beat to arms. Mr Keugh made a Speech on Parade which I cou'd not hear, the Tumult was so great; but about 200 men armed with musquets stepped from the Ranks and formed a separate body. Women came with Holy Water, sprinkled and crossed the men. I must here inform you of the merits of holy water. Whoever had used it *and* possessed *Faith* were invulnerable. Those that escaped unhurt from battle were preserved by it, those that fell perished from want of *Faith in it*. Let matters end as they wou'd, the efficacy of Holy Water was never doubted.

---

36 Fr Philip Roche, see Chapter One, note 38.   37 Fr Michael Murphy, see Chapter One, note 40.

To proceed with my history. The Gun Men marched off headed by Mr Gray.[38] Mr Edward Hay[39] was on Parade, and when it was over, mounted his horse and galloped over the Bridge, so did Capt. Dixon and his wife, [the latter] dressed in my riding Habit. In the evening one of the Committee came to tell us that the Army were approaching and English Frigates [were] off the coast. No one cou'd feel pleasure, for we were all certain we shou'd not live to see them conquer. I sat up the entire night at an open window listening to every sound. Often I had done so before, and never had undressed except to change my Linen from the 27th of May.

At dawn of day, Wednesday June the 20th, I saw a Rebel Troop coming over the Bridge headed by Capt. Dixon and carrying a *Black* Flag with a White Cross and some white Letters. It was a very small party, but they only came to reconnoitre. In about an hour the Wexford men who had marched with Mr Gray the day before returned to Parade. They had been all night at the Three Rocks and in another hour marched out of town (as I afterwards knew) to fight the Army at Goff's Bridge. They were accompanied by a large body of Pike Men. The town was now remarkably quiet, and some began to entertain hopes, as the Wexford People talked of sending letters from Lord Kingsborough to the Army and offering to surrender. Capt. Dixon returned with a very large Troop; I heard Mr E. Hay came with them, but I did not see him. The apparent Ferocity of this Troop surpassed (if possible) all we had seen, but their actions will speak for them. I have been near a week endeavouring to write the account of their Execrable Barbarity, and can hardly now prevail on myself to undertake it. Yet I think I ought for *my own* sake; if ever you think me unjust to the Catholics or hard-hearted towards them, remember what follows, and you will not condemn *me*.

The day went miserably on. Threats both by words and looks were bestowed on us. I sat as usual at the Window and cou'd see the Frigates off the Coast. Capt. Dixon had made various proposals to the People in the course of the day, all tending to the same end, our destruction, which the

38 Nicholas Gray of Whitefort, Co. Wexford and Athy, Co. Kildare, was a Protestant attorney and United Irishman, who served as secretary to the Rebel Council and aide-de-camp to Bagenal Harvey at the battle of Ross (see Freemen, 319; Cloney, 155). In 1795, he had married Elinor, second daughter of Henry Hughes of Ballytrent, also a United Irishman. Gray was a member of a divided family, his brothers both remaining loyal. He emigrated to America before 1809 and settled at Natchez, Mississippi, where he died before 1819. For the thorough study of this family, see David Goodall, 'A Divided Family in 1798: The Grays of Whitefort and Jamestown', *J. of the Wexford Historical Society* 15 (1994–5): 52–66.   39 Edward Hay, the eldest son of Harvey Hay of Ballinkeele and brother of John Hay, was later the author of a popular history of the Rebellion (*History of the Irish Insurrection of 1798* [Boston: Patrick Donahoe, n.d.]). He belonged to the civilian wing of the United Irishmen, not the military, and his intercession on behalf of some prisoners during the Rebellion led in 1799 to his acquittal of high treason (Dickson, 217–218).

Committee and Townspeople wished to prevent as they had no hopes of defeating the Army; Policy might have *partly* influenced their conduct, but I really don't think at any time the towns-people appeared inclined to Cruelty.

About three Capt. Dixon came on the Quay calling out, 'To the Jail!' He was followed up the Custom House Lane by numbers. They returned after some time calling out, 'To the Bridge!' I thought some alarm induced them to leave the town and sat eagerly watching till I beheld – yes, I absolutely saw a poor fellow beg for his life and then most barbarously murdered. To give a minute account of this hellish Scene is beyond my Strength, nor cou'd any one desire to hear it. No Savages ever put their prisoners to more deliberate Torture as I *heard* but indeed did not *look* at them, but I saw a boat go to the Prison Ship and bring my friends and acquaintances (who on landing passed by our Door) to Torture and Death. I saw the horrid wretches kneel down on the quay, lift up their hands seeming to pray with the greatest Devotion, then rise and join (or take the place of) other murderers. Their yells of delight at the sufferings of their victims will ever, I believe, sound in my ears. To describe what we all suffered wou'd be impossible. I never shed a Tear, but felt all over in the most violent *bodily Pain*. My darling Isabella's feelings were dreadful. I intreated her not to disturb [herself], but to let me pray if I cou'd; still she would lament *my* being killed. At last I assured her I w[oul]d make the Pike Men kill *her* before *me*; this quieted her at once. Shortly after she left the room and returned with a cheerful look. 'Dear Mama, grow better, I have prayed to God to make the Pike Men not kill *you* and to make the bad men Good, and I am sure He heard me'. After the army came she reminded me of this and said, 'You see, Mama, God did hear me'.

The murderers went on with their execrable work and put to death in all (from the most accurate account I cou'd afterwards get) *ninety-three* people. Some few out of the Prison Ship they *acquitted*, that is, spared till the next day at the earnest intreaties of some of the Rebel Leaders. One man when acquitted said, 'Well I suppose I may go home to my wife now?'

'No Sir', says Capt. Dixon, 'go to your prison, your being acquitted now is no reason [why] you shou'd not be tried again'.

We only expected Life till the prisons and ship were emptied, when an express came in the town to say the army were marching against Vinegar Hill camp, and that if they did not reinforce it immediately all was lost. The town priests *then*, and not till *then*, made their appearance on the bridge and carried back to Jail 19 prisoners; one priest told me *he* could have saved all the lives that were lost if he had heard of the massacre. It was wonderful, indeed, how he cou'd avoid hearing of it. The leader of *the* murderers called to his men in these words which I distinctly heard, 'Come my lads, we will go now and blessed be God we have sent some of their souls to Hell'.

They went off really as if they had been performing a praiseworthy and religious action. Capt. and Mrs Dixon followed on horseback, their horses wou'd not go over the place where the Blood lay on the bridge, but started back. They alighted and led their horses, she carefully holding up her habit to keep it clean. I think she *must* have felt some disagreeable sensations at that moment. It was said she desired the murderers not to waste their ammunition on the prisoners but to give them plenty of pikes. So alas, they did.

Late this evening Mr R,[40] a Catholic and late one of the Committee for Provisions, came to see us. He was like ourselves half dead with horror, and declared he had intreated the priests to come down with their crucifixes and prevent the massacre, which they refused to do. We told him how Father Broe[41] said he had saved 19 Prisoners. This Mr R denied, as it was the express only that saved them. He told us the black flag meant that every one of that party had taken the *Black Test Oath*. We had often heard of that, but wished for a particular account of it. He declared he never knew of it till that week. It seems there are three or four oaths for United Irishmen which they take according to their rank and *merits*. The Black Test is the last. It devotes all Protestants, men, women and children to death in the most solemn manner, as it has been published in the papers I need not copy it here. A man came into a shop where Mr R was and asked another to give him the Black Test. This was refused, and the person he asked left the shop, on which the man who wanted to take the oath said, 'That fellow shall be one of the first I will kill, but as to the oath I don't care, for such a one can give it, and I will go to him for it'. Mr R gave us intelligence of the success of the army at Goff's Bridge and endeavoured to persuade us we were then safe, as the people of the town were all fully determined not to oppose the army, and the country people wou'd be employed at Vinegar Hill.

I cou'd not indulge any hope, spent another night at the window, and saw Capt. Dixon, his troop and the *black* flag, return to town in the morning. We all then gave ourselves up, though we cou'd see the frigates and hear their guns battering Rosslare Ford at the entrance of the harbour. Mr Keugh's brother, a very infirm old man, was so much shocked at the massacre, the state of affairs and the part his brother had taken in the rebellion, that he shot himself. Mr Keugh himself came in a wretched state

---

40 Musgrave identifies him as Pat Redmond, 'a man of humanity, who filled his situation with reluctance' (Musgrave, 463).   41 Fr John Broe (1737–1803), a native of Wexford town, was educated at Prague and was one of six Franciscan friars in Wexford during the Rebellion (see Kevin Whelan, Catholic Priests of Co. Wexford, unpublished manuscript in possession of the author). Musgrave recounts Broe's humanitarian gesture in attempting to christen Protestants on the prison ship in Wexford Harbour in order to shield them from the massacre on the bridge (Musgrave, 472).

of mind to Doctor Jacob and requested he (as a man of known loyalty) would go with a message from Lord Kingsbro' to the Army. Doctor Jacob said he wou'd. The few rebel soldiers that remained in town were called together and spoken to by Keugh and Carty.[42] They agreed readily to surrendering the town, and also appointed Lord Kingsbro' to command it till the arrival of the Army. Most fortunately they changed their mind as to Doctor Jacob and wou'd not let him leave the town, where he had been kept the entire month attending their sick men. Luckily for him they all knew his medical skill and took good care of him for their own sakes.

Mr Harman[43] of the N. Cork Militia was sent in his place accompanied by Mr Frayne,[44] a rebel chief, who shot the poor young man about a mile from the town. The runaways from Goff's Bridge and several from Vinegar Hill poured into the town vowing vengeance against every one. Protestants to be sure were first, but the towns-people and all the advisers of a surrender were equally threatened. The sailors of Wexford took an oath to defend Lord Kingsboro's life, and did fire several shots on the Mob from his lodgings. The great anxiety to kill his Lordship *first* was, I believe, one cause of our escape, for the mob wasted much time in endeavouring to get him.

About 4 o'clock Mr R and Doctor Jacob came in. They had been fired at in the street. Doctor Jacob was as composed as I am *now*, but I really never saw such firmness of mind as he possessed on all occasions. Mr R said the *general massacre* was just going to begin, that he came to try to save

42 Robert Carthy or Carty of Birchgrove, Ballyhogue, near Enniscorthy, was a wealthy Catholic middleman and with his brother Dennis took a leading role in United Irish movement in Co. Wexford. During the Rebellion, he challenged Keugh over the latter's governorship of Wexford during the Republic and at one time engaged him in a fistfight. He was among those leaders who approached General Moore with peace terms (see Dickson, 81; Cloney, 63; Wheeler, 155). He later fled to France and there befriended Robert Emmet (see Helen Landreth, *The Pursuit of Robert Emmet* [New York: Whittlesey House, 1948] 156; see also Marianne Elliott, *Partners in Revolution: The United Irishmen and France* [New Haven, CT: Yale Univ. Press, 1982], 317). Landreth recounts his arrest in London in 1803 and his extradition to Ireland, where he gave evidence against a number of revolutionaries (Landreth, 362–3, 369). 43 Thomas Harman, ensign of the North Cork Militia, was sent as a messenger by Lord Kingsborough to General Moore with terms for the surrender of Wexford, but he was intercepted by a rebel force led by Fr John Murphy, who ordered his aide-de-camp Whelan to shoot him (Musgrave, 467). His widow Esther later claimed compensation (see 'Widows and Orphans,' n.p.). 44 Edward Frayne or Fraine, tanner and United Irishman, was born about 1774, the son of Patrick Frayne, grocer and spirits dealer of John Street, Wexford (see Freemen, 315; also David Goodall, 'Frayne of Co. Wexford', *Irish Genealogist* 4 [Nov., 1970]:214). Musgrave called him 'a man of some opulence, and who was supposed to gain 300 [pounds] a year as a tanner' (Musgrave, 427). Kavanagh states that the Fraynes were 'a very respectable family' who 'kept a shop in John Street, Wexford, and did a thriving business' (Kavanagh, 324–5). On the orders of Thomas Dixon, he served as Officer of the Guard and compelled Charles Jackson, Jonas Gurley, and Kinnieth Matthews to shoot Joseph Murphy, threatening immediate death if they refused (Ibid.; Taylor, 100). Frayne was executed at Wexford on 26 June, 1798, aged twenty-four (Ibid., App. 160). His house still stands in Wexford and has been restored as a guesthouse.

us, or rather to share our fate, for he feared we cou'd not escape. However, he had got a boat with men he thought he cou'd rely on at the end of our house, that we must try to get in, stand the fire of the rebels from the quay and in passing under the bridge, and if we got clear throw ourselves on the mercy of the gun boats. This was truly desperate. I walked up stairs and went to a window. The rebels were settling themselves as before on the bridge, and sending a boat to the Prison Ship, when, conceive my astonishment, I saw them all begin to run. I flew down stairs, doubting my senses, to tell Doctor Jacob. He came to the window. It was no illusion. Run they did in such confusion that I am amazed numbers were not trampled to death. A general cry, 'The army are come, they are in the town!' explained their flight.

Wretches out of the infirmary in their shirts ran in an incredible short space of time. The streets were almost clear; about fifty armed rebels rushed into our house, tore out their green cockades, threw their arms under the beds, and hoped to escape by being found under Doctor Jacob's Roof. He put on his regimentals and went into the Street. A villain that was running off turned and fired at him, he wiped Doctor Jacob, then took another pistol and said, 'If I must die, I will die like a cock', and shot [at] him. This is what I heard, but as I never asked Doctor Jacob myself, cannot be sure of the concluding part. Bostick Jacob,[45] a young boy, saw the villain fire at his father from a window. Mr Percival the Sheriff[46] galloped on the quay to our door, said 'here we are and 12,000 Soldiers with us', or something to that purpose.

Imagine *if you can* our feelings, exclamations and conduct. I never can forget the expression of Elizabeth's countenance as she came down Stairs to shake my hands. The boat that was sent to bring the prisoners to torture and death brought them to Liberty and rapture. Several came to us; one (Mr Milward)[47] had been with us ten days before they put him in prison. No kind of *decorum* was observed, nothing but *kissing* and embracing. Most of the men cried violently. I wish that dear General Moore cou'd have seen us. He in reality was two miles off and there were only *12*

---

45 Bostick Radford Jacob was the son of Ebenezer Jacob and was named for his uncle, a Lieutenant in the 21st Foot (see Freemen, 327). **46** Edward Perceval of Barntown (1763–1809), son of John Perceval and his wife Martha (Martin), married Mary, daughter of Robert Woodcock of Killowen. He was Deputy Governor of Co. Wexford in 1793, High Sheriff in 1798, and a strong conservative (*Burke's Landed Gentry of Ireland* [1904], 479). **47** Capt. Henry Milward of Ballyharaghan was the son of Henry Milward and Elizabeth, daughter of Henry Archer (see Freemen, 333). In 1794, he married Barbara Morgan (*Ferns M.L.*). Milward had been a surveyor and hence owed his office to the political patronage of the conservative Lord Ely. He was captured whilst hiding at Hatchel's house and narrowly escaped execution on Wexford Bridge through the intercession of Esmond Kyan (Musgrave, 425–6). In 1799, he claimed losses that included 'a Mare, Cloaths [and] Pistols' (Claimants, cccxciii).

Horsemen in the town, but no one knew that till next day. Romantic as it sounds, I saw above five thousand men fly from *one* horseman.

It was supposed above 4000 fled from the *Faith* end of Wexford. They took all the cannon with them and Sir Charles Asgill[48] afterwards [gave] a good account of them. My *bridge* acquaintance and those under the command of Fitzgerald, Roche, and Perry[49] have since spread misery and destruction through the co. of Wexford and Wicklow. We never heard with certainty what became of Dixon, none of us saw him go over the bridge, and as he is a very large man and rode a tall white horse, he could hardly have escaped the observation of more than 12 of us who were all particularly anxious to see *him* depart.

I think it was about nine o'clock when Gen. Moore's army *really* arrived and that we were in *safety* after 26 days and nights of the most exquisite misery. Not one hour or even moment of Ease had I experienced from Monday May the 28th. How indeed cou'd I, at the mercy of thousands of ruffians who might at any time they pleased do whatever they pleased without fear of punishment or even censure! The prospect of immediate death is horrible (as I can tell) but that was little to the horrors every *woman* must have dreaded.

I have mentioned that only 12 men were in Wexford for an hour [when the] great body of rebels fled. Their names I shall add to this. They were coming on with General Moore's army when they saw the flames of two Houses near the Green Walks, for the long intended scheme of burning the town had actually begun. Mr Boyd,[50] as I have been told, went up to

---

48 Sir Charles Asgill (1763?–1823) served in the American Revolutionary War and was present at the surrender of Yorktown. Named staff brigadier in 1797, he later rose to become Colonel of the 46th Foot. In 1798, he became a Major-General and served as Commanding Officer in Queen's and Kilkenny (*Dictionary of National Biography*, 1:631). He led the attack on Borris during the rebellion. His men were undisciplined and widely disliked.   49 Anthony Perry of Inch was the only son of Anthony Perry, cardmaker, of Dublin. He resided at Perrymount, near Inch, and married Eliza Ford of Ballyfad, Co. Down. He was a Protestant but had formerly been a Roman Catholic. A first lieutenant in the Coolgreany Yeomanry, he held liberal views and in 1792 helped organize a United Irish society in Gorey. Upon resigning his post, he was captured by the North Cork Militia on 24 May 1798, pitchcapped, and tortured for information, which led to the subsequent arrests of Harvey, Fitzgerald, and Colclough (see Dickson, 43–7). Later released, he fought bravely in the insurrection, was acclaimed a rebel general and developed a battle tactic of yelling at the top of his voice to confuse his enemy in battle. He was subsequently captured at Clonbullogue, Co. Offaly and executed at Edenderry on 12 Jul. 1798 (see Furlong, *Fr John Murphy*, 43–4, 70, 94, 165).   50 See Chapter One, note 20. James Boyd, magistrate, M.P., and captain of the Wexford Yeoman Calvary, was the son of Highgate Boyd and his wife Amy (Phillips). He married Elizabeth, daughter of Col. Walter Hore of Harperstown (*Freemen*, 112; 'Boyd of Rosslare', *Burke's Landed Gentry* [1850], 130). In 1798, his name circulated through the co. on a list of four magistrates, including also Hawtrey White, Archibald Jacob, and Hunter Gowan, as being 'particularly obnoxious to the people on account of their brutal conduct ... ' (Dickson, 87). When Wexford fell, Boyd was among the

the General and requested permission to ride on and rescue his wife or perish with her. Permission was given, and 11 others joined him. The consequences of their desperate gallantry I have already told. Never should I have written this but for them; *half* an hour would probably have decided *all* our fates and certainly mine and those in the house with me. We could hardly have escaped in Mr R's Boat, and being in the first house on the quay, of course, would have been first butchered. Our situation on the arrival of our deliverers you have heard. Mrs Boyd told me she and Lady Anne Hore were sitting expecting the entrance of their murderers [when they] heard a gallop up Street and stopt at their door. They went to the window and *saw Mr Boyd*. Is it not amazing that no one lost their senses from joy? Several had done so from terror.

Names of our 12 Deliverers: Mr Boyd, one of the proscribed; Mr Percival; Mr Joseph Sutton;[51] Mr Archer Bayly; Mr John Byrne;[52] a *Roman Catholic*; Mr Hughes;[53] Mr Stedman;[54] Mr Archibald Jacob,[55] Proscribed; Mr John Tench;[56] Mr Boyd's *servant*;[57] Mr Irwin;[58] Mr John Waddy.[59]

---

first to flee. Failing to escape by sea, he rode to Barrystown to the house of his friend, Richard Newton King, and there, with his companions, obtained a boat to cross the Pass of Scar to Duncannon (Ibid., 88). His house on George's Street in Wexford was burned, and he later claimed losses of more than £1564, but received nothing (Claimants, cccxxix). **51** Joseph Sutton was a member of the Wexford Yeoman Cavalry (see Musgrave, 469), but his identity is otherwise obscure. He was not a claimant in 1799. **52** John Byrne was a loyal Roman Catholic and a merchant in Wexford. **53** William Hughes, merchant, was a lieutenant in the Wexford Infantry (see O Snodaigh, 37). Musgrave calls him 'a respectable inhabitant of Wexford, of the protestant religion, and a rigid loyalist [who] generously entertained in his house some of the wives of the officers of the North Cork regiment, after their husbands had retreated' (Musgrave, 469). He testified later on behalf of Bagenal Harvey's humane character during the Rebellion (Freemen, 326). Possibly it was he who married Margaret Archer in 1780 (*Ferns M.L.*). **54** John Stetham was a corporal and a tanner in Wexford (see Musgrave, 469). He married Margaret Goodison in 1792 (*Ferns M.L.*). In 1799, he claimed losses of 'Hides, Skins [and] Cloaths' (Claimants, ccccxxv). **55** Archibald Hamilton Jacob of Templeshannon was a magistrate, a middleman on the Portsmouth estate, and an Orangeman. He descended from the Jacobs of Tipperary and was not closely related to the liberal Jacobs of Wexford. In 1791, he married Elizabeth Francis (*Ferns M.L.*). Archie Jacob served as Captain of the Vinegar Hill Rangers, one of Co. Wexford's most brutal yeomanry corps, famous for its use of the triangle in flogging and torturing Catholics (see O Snodaigh, 37; Madden, 4:431). Together with Boyd, Gowan, and White, he was 'adjudged guilty of cruelty and oppression' by the rebels and therefore much despised (Dickson, 126; see also 87–8; Hay, 119–20). In 1799, he gave testimony against Thomas Cloney at his trial (Cloney, 262–3). Later that year he claimed losses of more than £1,956, including 'House, Beds, Furniture, Cloaths, Fire arms, Cattle, [and] Corn' and received over £529 (Claimants, ccclxxvii). **56** John Tench was probably the son of Samuel Tench of Spa Well, Co. Wexford, who married Margaret, daughter of Highgate Boyd in 1796 (*Ferns M.L.*; see also Goodall, 458–9). Thus he was a brother-in-law of Capt. James Boyd. A conservative, he became sub-sheriff in 1799 but nonetheless attempted to assist Cloney in his defense (see Cloney, 127–8). **57** Musgrave identifies him as William McCabe (Musgrave, 469). **58** Christopher Irwin or Irwine, permanent sergeant of the troop, followed these men on foot, since his horse had been shot (Musgrave, 469). He married Elizabeth Learned in 1799 (*Ferns M.L.*). **59** Probably John Waddy, hatter, of Dublin, who

Copy of Bagenal Harvey's Pass given to me in Wexford May 31st 1798:

> Permit Mrs Brownrigg, her two young Children and Servant, to pass free. They are strangers unprotected and have no connection with publick affairs. B. B. Harvey.

Copy of Protection from J. Caulfield, the Titular Bishop:

> Having long known the Bearer, Widow of the late Commissioner John Brownrigg to be a most benevolent Gentlewoman and universally esteemed, I now in the name of Humanity and in the name of Jesus Christ recommend her to the Protection and good offices of every Christian that she may not be injured in her person, property, or children. Given in Wexford, June 1st, 1798.
>
> James Caulfield.

ACCOUNT OF WEXFORD REBELS FROM MY OWN KNOWLEDGE AND BELIEF

Mr Matthew Keugh was originally a *fifer* in the same regiment with Gen. Johnson, and I heard the general recollect it when he sat as one of the court martial who condemned him. By some means Keugh procured an ensigncy and then a lieutenancy, came to Wexford with his regiment, where he contracted a *very* particular friendship with a gentleman and *lady* of that town, sold out and made a *visit* to them of *several years*.[60] Some family misfortunes obliged Mr Keugh's host to leave the kingdom. The *lady* also went amongst her friends, and he had an abode to seek for. An excellent one he procured by prevailing on a widow (Mrs Grogan), who was possessed of very considerable property to marry him contrary to the advice and intreaties of all her friends, who did not visit or speak to her for some time after. However, Keugh, who was really a man of abilities and most gentlemanlike in both appearance and manners, conquered their dislike so as to live on very friendly terms with all her family, and on most intimate once with B. Harvey, who was a near relation of Mrs Keugh. The gentlemen of the country all disliked and shunned him, and he was ever reckoned a dangerous and disaffected man.

---

claimed losses in Wexford in 1799 (Claimants, ccccxxxi). He married Frances Finn in 1795 (*Ferns M.L.*). Waddy may have been related to Dr Richard Waddy of Clougheast Castle, famous for identifying Harvey at the time of his arrest and for dropping a portcullis on top of Fr John Byrne (see Chapter Two, note 15). Musgrave does not include John Waddy as one of this party, but he does include Marcus Doyle and Abraham Howlin, neither of whom Mrs Brownrigg mentions (Musgrave, 469).   **60** Mrs Brownrigg insults Keugh twice, first

I saw him frequently during *his reign*. His *manners* were humane and plausible, but he never acted up to his professions. He told us one evening he would protect Lord Kingsborough and keep him in his house if he lost his life by it, and the next morning we heard of Lord Kingsborough's removal to a poor ale house in the town. Keugh took great delight in reading the various letters that were found in plundered houses and the robbed mails, and went to Mrs C's to read out to her and *23* others a letter from a nephew of hers, giving an account of a very delicate and distressing affair which had occurred relative to a sister of his, and which *till then* had really been kept a secret from every one. Keugh's defence was amazingly able, several of his court martial shed tears, and he had no doubt of a pardon to the last moment of his life. He walked from the jail to the gallows and bowed to some ladies he saw at a window with a composed and cheerful countenance. At the gallows he made a speech, again declaring (what was the substance of his defence) that he never knew anything of the united business till the rebels were in possession of Wexford, and was then forced into it to save his life; this he said in such a solemn manner, and with such an appearance of truth, that Gen. Moore[61] was induced to speak to the guard to defer his execution, and went off to Gen. Lake to solicit his pardon, but Gen. Lake was in possession of *letters* that proved he had carried on the plan for *five years* and had been one of the most active agents in Ireland for the cause. He objected much to the rope, said it was too slight for his weight, and made them get another, which on Gen. Moore's return he found, poor wretch, strong enough.

Edward Fitzgerald's[62] father was a farmer that lived about 7 miles from Wexford on the Oulart road. His mother was a sister of Hays of Ballenkeale.[63] Old Fitzgerald made a very tolerable property by farms, malt houses and selling horses. He is dead some years. The young man is, as I am told, both weak and stupid. He was a lieutenant in Col. Lehunte's Cavalry, and the intimate friend from childhood of Mr Edward Turner,[64] who was so barbarously murdered without his ever interfering to save him. Mr Fitzgerald declared during the rebellion to a lady I knew that he wou'd be thankful to any one [who] wou'd shoot him, his life was so miserable and his power so uncertain.

by calling him a fifer (a lowly miltary rank), and implying that he had had an affair after his marriage to Grace (Thornton) Grogan, widow of Lawrence Grogan.   61 Moore was regarded as a moderate by the rebels, in part because of his well-disciplined men. Lake had taken a more hard-line view in suppressing the Rebellion and wanted the executions to set a public example.   62 See Chapter One, note 7.   63 A reference to the Hay family of Ballinkeele, a wealthy family of Catholic gentry and middleman, to which the rebels Edward and John Hay belonged (see Chapter One, note 36; Chapter Four, note 39; see also Whelan, 'Catholic Community in Eighteenth-Century Co. Wexford', 132–3). Both were thus first cousins of Fitzgerald.   64 Edward Turner was a magistrate at Newfort and a moderate, who was 'positively' neutral toward the Catholic cause in Co. Wexford (Whelan, 'Politicisation in

Gen. Edward Roche[65] was a farmer and lived on Col. Hatton's estate at a place called Garrylough, near Ferrybank. He was a Sergeant in Le Hunte's Cavalry, and commanded the Rebels from some days in Le Hunte's uniform. He married a Miss Dixon, sister to Capt. Dixon[66] and cousin to the priest that was sent off for transportation by the Wexford gentlemen before the rebellion.

[Here Mrs Brownrigg's account ends. A letter from her daughter, Isabella, written from Bath to her uncle in Ireland, tells of her mother's death in December, 1804.]

13 December 1804
Bath, 21, Brock Street.

My dearest Uncle,

Aunt Mary has no doubt informed you of the melancholy event which has happened, and which I am sure gave you great concern. My dear mother often desired me not to repine when I lost her. I am determined in every particular to follow all her wishes, though I shall find none harder than this one. I try to hide my sorrow as much as possible, but I never could meet with such a misfortune. I have, however, many consolations. I know that she died without the least pain, and that she was spared the only pang she often said death would have for her, parting with me and John. Now, indeed, her children may see the advantage of not putting off repentance to a death bed, but that she often said she had no faith in. For five days before she died she was in a stupor and quite delirious. She always knew me, and never saw me without kissing me. The last kiss I had from her was about half an hour before she died. Oh! how her sweet face was altered, and how plainly death was written on it. She was quite easy but could not speak.

My dear uncle, how I wish you would come over as soon as you can. It would be such a comfort to me to see you. I have often been told by my dear mother that I should always live with you when she was gone. Aunt Mary says that Mama told her a year ago that I should live with her. The last letter I wrote you was by her directions, and you know in that she

Co. Wexford and the Origins of the 1798 Rebellion', 162). He may be identical to the Edward Turner who married Penelope Hatchell in 1794 (*Ferns M.L.*). Turner's house was among the first attacked by rebels on May 26 on account of its store of arms (see Gahan, 22). Turner escaped unharmed and rode to Wexford to warn the garrison that the rebels had taken up arms. He was responsible for setting on fire several Irish cabins at Oulart on the day of the battle there in an attempt to lure the rebels from their strongpoint on the hill (Cleary, 'Battle of Oulart Hill', 88). He was later imprisoned by the rebels in Wexford and executed on the bridge on Dixon's orders. **65** See Chapter One, note 18. **66** See note 17.

made me mention living with you. However, a letter that there is for you will settle all that, and all I wish at present is that you would come here.

Henry John came here on Monday morning. He was very much affected indeed. Without any partiality I think there cannot live a sweeter tempered or better disposed boy than he is. He minds every word his aunt says to him, which is what few boys of his age would do. He intends writing you very soon.

Col. Hardy came here on Monday night and has been as kind and goodnatured as possible. Good bye my dearest Uncle, give my best and most affectionate Love to my Aunt and dear Anne, and believe me to be your very affectionate and attached Niece,

ISABELLA W. BROWNRIGG.

5

BARBARA LETT

Barbara Lett née Lett of Killaligan, Enniscorthy, Co. Wexford, was born in 1777, the eldest child of William Daniel of Fortview, Co. Wexford, by his first wife, whose identity has not been determined.[1] Her father served as Surveyor of Excise in Enniscorthy, a civil service position that he undoubtedly held through Lord Ely's patronage, thus suggesting his alliance with the conservatives. He was among the Protestant prisoners piked to death on Wexford Bridge, 20 June 1798.[2]

In 1794, Barbara married Newton Lett, son of Joshua Lett of Killaligan. The Letts were Anglicans and were large tenant farmers. Hence, they were just below the professional-middleman social rank of Mrs Brownrigg, and perhaps for this reason were treated with less deference, both by many of the rebels they encountered and by the British. More intriguing is the fact that the extended Lett family was divided in its sympathies in 1798. Newton Lett remained loyal, but his brother Stephen Lett of Newcastle, Tilliken (whose wife was a niece of Bagenal Harvey), was a United Irishman. Stephen's son James played a prominent role on the rebel side at the battle of Ross. Newton's father, Joshua Lett, had remained neutral, but his friendship with rebel Thomas Cloney led him to testify on Cloney's behalf at his trial. These liberal connections resulted in Newton's claim for compensation being rejected in 1799, despite his own loyalty and the destruction of his house and farm.[3]

---

1 See Joseph Ranson's introduction, 'A 1798 Diary by Mrs Barbara Newton Lett, Killaligan, Enniscorthy', *The Past* 5 (1949):117–118. Ranson suggests that Mrs Daniel was a Peare (possibly related to the Peares of Kilmallock), since Barbara mentions an Uncle Peare in her account. 2 William Daniel of Fortview was born in 1754, and married for the first time at the age of twenty-two in 1776. In 1789, while serving as Surveyor of Excise in Enniscorthy (a post that reflects his political conservatism), he seized a quantity of smuggled wine in a raid at New Ross (*Wexford Herald* quoted in *The People*, 20 Feb. 1932). Three years later, in September 1792, he joined other residents of Enniscorthy in signing a petition to request the appointment of a resident municipal magistrate (Hore, 6:564). Following the death of his first wife, he married (2) Sarah Hughes in 1789 (*Ferns M.L.* 7a:134). By her he had five children, the eldest of whom was seven in 1798. Daniel's tombstone in St Selskar churchyard, Wexford, bears the inscription: 'Sacred to the Memory of William Daniel, one of the unfortunate ninety-eight who suffered on Wexford Bridge, 20th June 1798, aged 44 years. Father, forgive them, for they know not what they do' (Cantwell, *Memorials of the Dead*, vol. 6 [East Wexford], 275). His widow survived until 1830 and was buried beside him. 3 Newton Lett claimed losses in 1799, including 'Houses, Cattle, Corn, [and] Rent' totally

Little is known of Barbara's life following the rebellion. In 1859 at the age of eighty-two, she wrote the following narrative of her experience, and, not surprising, she used it to express the bitterness she felt at her family's mistreatment. She recalled many details of the rebellion, including the names of rebel participants and her own specific movements during May and June, 1798. With any account written so long after the event, however, there is always the possibility of exaggeration. Yet the account has importance not only because it reflects a 'large farmer' loyalist perspective of the rebellion, but also because it provides some balance. Unlike the other Protestant writers, Barbara often casts the conquering British in a negative light, declaring that the army was guilty of excess in firing at loyalist Protestants rushing to welcome them and in challenging the loyalty of others who were dispossessed and wearing ragged clothing. Barbara died at Killaligan on 5 November 1867, aged 91, and was buried at Kilmallock.[4]

The original manuscript of Mrs Lett's narrative is housed in the National Library of Ireland. It was acquired in December, 1942 from a Mr O'Toole. Earlier in 1940, it was in the possession of a Miss Meyers of Millpark, Enniscorthy, a descendant of the writer. It consists of seventy unnumbered pages, written in a fine, legible hand, but without punctuation or paragraphs. The first page has suffered some tearing, with the result that the opening paragraph is lost. It was previously published with annotations (and some errors) in 1949.[5]

THE ACCOUNT

To narrate the suffering and persecutions which I endured during the Rebellion of 1798 would call forth the energies of a youthful mind, but even at this late period of life, when aided by a sketch drawn up [at] that period, and which had for more than half a century dropped dead from my pen, the narration is now taken up with avidity in order to recount to posterity scenes of death and suffering wholly unknown to the present generation. I shall, therefore, commence the little narrative by recording the first circumstance which was attended with serious alarm [manuscript torn] [ ]th, who lived on our [estate?] ...

more than £614; the claim was disallowed (Claimants, ccclxxxvii; see also Dickson, 70). 4 Her tombstone reads: 'Sacred to the Memory of/Barbara Lett, widow of Newton Lett/of Killigan [*sic*] in this co. who departed/this life on the 5th of November 1867 aged 91/in the sure and certain hope of the Resurrection/to eternal life through our Lord Jesus Christ' (Cantwell, *Memorials of the Dead*, vol. 6 [East Wexford], 250). 5 National Library of Ireland, Mss. 4472–3. See also J. F. Ainsworth, 'Report on the Lett Diary of the 1798 Rising in Co. Wexford', *National Library Report on Private Collections*, no. 221.

Captain Jacob[6] and some of his corps seized [him] for this offence. He denied the charge with vehemence at first, but when one of his accusers drew forth a rope from under his arm and threatened to hang the delinquent, he called aloud for mercy and immediately pointed to the spot where these dreadful weapons were concealed. This horrid creature dined every day with our servants and was a person whom we never should have suspected as the author or maker of these deadly weapons. He was tried for the offence and transported for life.

On Saturday, 26th of May ... [manuscript torn] with horror on that eventful [manuscript torn] rebellion blazing forth in co[unty Wexford]. [We were] told that a great body of armed rebels were assembled quite near us. We were so panic-struck at the aspect of affairs that we determined upon leaving Killaligan and taking refuge in the town of Enniscorthy, where we should consider ourselves safe under the protection of the military, with whom we were badly provided and consisted of the North Cork Militia, who were badly disciplined,[7] and a few corps of yeomanry but newly raised though of heroic courage.

We left Killaligan early on Sunday morning and took refuge at Mr Stephen Lett's.[8] Church Service was suspended on that day, it being Whit Sunday. About 12 o'clock the town was thrown into the greatest commotion by expresses arriving very rapidly which called forth the vigorous exertions of yeomen cavalry, who were severe sufferers in this dreadful conflict. Little rest could be experienced through the whole of Sunday night; their patrols were so incessant that we were every minute at the windows hailing the guards, who demanded a countersign from all who approached them. Next day, an eventful one, dawned upon us with accumulated horrors peculiar to that time. Every moment accounts arrived of murders committed, of houses burned, of property destroyed. As near as I can recollect, about the hour of 2 o'clock the rebels attacked the town in a great body, which was but feebly defended, our country being engaged in a war with France at that time, and our yeomen cavalry being unable to defend themselves from the murderous pike, which did greater execution than the carbine or sword.

6 Archibald Hamilton Jacob, captain of the Enniscorthy Yeoman Cavalry, later renamed the Vinegar Hill Rangers. See Chapter Four, note 55. 7 As a Protestant loyalist, Barbara's admission here that the North Corks were badly disciplined is significant. Introduced at the behest of George Ogle and led by Lord Kingsborough, two national figures of the Orange order, the corps brought a measure of brutality to Co. Wexford in the spring of 1798 that it had not seen previously. The corps introduced the pitchcap and had a reputation for raping young women (see Whelan, 'Reinterpreting the 1798 Rebellion in Co. Wexford', 20–2). 8 Stephen Lett of Newcastle, Tilliken, son of Joshua Lett of Killaligan and brother of Newton Lett, was a United Irishman with close ties by marriage to the family of Bagenal Harvey. Lett worked as a cabinet-maker in Enniscorthy, and briefly offered shelter to Revd Samuel Heydon before the latter's murder (Musgrave, 726).

Soon after the first charge, Mr Wilm Pounder[9] of Cooladine was borne in between two men into Mr Lett's, desperately wounded in the back, by the pike. He begged of me to bind up his wounds, to stop the effusion of blood, a distressing task which I readily undertook, and directing him to be placed on a bed, with difficulty removed his military jacket, then tearing up a pillow case, with the assistance of Mrs Daily, swathed him tightly round the waist, then gave him a glass of water and next removed his boots and stockings.

Just as I had performed this last sad office, our retreating army, overpowered by numbers, called loudly to women and children to follow them. Of course, I left my poor wounded patient weltering in his blood, and in quick succession followed our defeated troops whom, it was said, were put to flight by the dastardly conduct of Captain Snow,[10] who commanded the North Cork Regiment. Be that as it might have been, I felt more terrified at the plight with which we were enveloped than by the myriads of rebels who poured in upon us. They had set fire to every quarter of the town, and it was well known that the disaffected inhabitants assisted in adding to the general conflagration in order to defeat the army.

I had not proceeded far till my progress was arrested by a burning broom which fell from the top of a house in flames. The lane we were passing through was under the influence of the devouring element and, almost unconscious of whither I was going, I turned aside from the flames and entered Mr Brett's[11] house, which stood at the foot of Castle hill. I was

9 William Pounder of Cooladine (no relation to the Pounden family of Daphne) married Elizabeth Masterson in 1787 (*Ferns M.L.*). He was a First Lieutenant in Solomon Richards's Enniscorthy Yeoman Cavalry, a moderate corps in contrast to Jacob's Vinegar Hill Rangers. In a letter to Thomas Cloney dated 18 Jan. 1826, he wrote: 'I was severely wounded at the first battle of Enniscorthy, on the 28th of May, in consequence of which I was made a prisoner, and immediately after a violent faction conspired against my life, and brought the most unfounded and malicious charges against me. I applied to you, and you wrote immediately in the strongest manner to your friends in Enniscorthy, who could devize no plan of saving my life, except to summon a jury of twelve men, amongst whom they called as many friends as they could. The trumpeter of our corps was my principal prosecutor, his evidence was, however, disbelieved, and I was honourably acquitted. To the exertions of yourself and your friends I owe the protection of my life ... ' (see Cloney, 102). In 1799, as 'William Pounder of Enniscorthy, lieutenant', he claimed losses of 'Furniture, Corn [and] Cloaths' in 1799. Joseph Pounder of 'Coolydine' was also a claimant (see Claimants, ccccvii).
10 William Snowe, Captain of the North Cork Militia, played a prominent role in the defense of Enniscorthy on May 28, 1798. His troops seized the bridge connecting the town with the neighbouring hamlets of Templeshannon and Drumgold. When the town was overrun by the rebel army, he retreated to Wexford, and subsequently to Duncannon (see Dickson,, 71, 73, 87; Musgrave, 328, 331). In 1799, he claimed losses at Enniscorthy, including 'Cloaths, Plate and Bedsteads' (Claimants, ccccxxi). Following the Rebellion, he was accused of abandoning the loyalists of Enniscorthy, prompting him to pen a defence of his experiences (see William Snowe, *Statement of Transactions at Enniscorthy* [Bray, Ireland: Privately published, 1801]). 11 James Brett of Enniscorthy, surveyor and likely conservative, is included on a list of prisoners in Musgrave) Musgrave, 802). He survived

soon joined by numbers who followed me, and too soon a h[o]rde of ruffians entered the parlour and demanded from Mrs Brett everything her house contained.

As I passed into another apartment, I met Mr Hayden, Rector of Ferns, and his lady.[12] The dear old man did not long survive the events of that dreadful day. He was soon dispatched with many other victims. He addressed me with all the benignity of a truly pious divine. As I was weeping bitterly, he strove to console me, and as he was speaking I was addressed by a person named Williams, who offered to protect me. Williams was implicated in the Rebellion before the general outbreak. He was taken on suspicion, but admitted to bail, through the interference of Mr Stephen Lett of Enniscorthy, who considered him innocent of the offence with which he was accused. He now stood foremost in the ranks on this occasion and kindly offered to protect me and any friend I wished to bring with me. He gave me to understand that his influence was unrivaled. I therefore directed his attention to Mr and Mrs Hayden, and we walked up to Mr Lett's without meeting any interruption.

When [we] arrived there, we found the door closed & all the inmates flown. A dead rebel lay on his face under the parlour window. Williams said, 'I shall raise the window, and do you let us in at the Hall door.' I did so, stepping over the dead body of an enemy, & admitted those who had shuddered at the idea of remaining without. Williams said he should go in search of Mr Lett, to whom he owed such an extent of obligation. He returned after a short space and told me that a dead yeoman lay on his face in the yard. He asked me to go with him, as he feared it might be one of Mr Lett's sons. Pounder, whom I had left bleeding in bed, recurred to my mind. I said, 'Do not ask me; I could not bear the sight. It is Pounder whom they have dragged down and murdered, and take me hence.'

We again entered the street, leaving our Revd friend & his lady after us. They felt such horror at again meeting the multitude who were turning in upon us. We were but a short time parted from them when a monster

the bridge massacre and in 1799 claimed losses of 'Furniture, Cloaths, Cows, Potatoes and Meadow' totalling over £176, of which he recovered £88 (Claimants, cccxxix).   **12** Revd Samuel Heydon was born in 1726, son of Revd John Heydon, Prebendary of Clone and Rector of Leskinfere. He entered Trinity College Dublin in 1742 at the age of 16, and received his B.A. in 1746 and M.A. in 1749. He was ordained a deacon in 1751 and a priest two years later. He served as Prebendary of Toombe (Camolin) from 1767 to 1781, was Vicar of Carne, 1792–8, and Rector of Ferns, where he served at the time of his murder at Enniscorthy, 28 May 1798 (see Leslie, 59). He was disliked by the rebels, because he served as a clerical middleman, a collector of tithes, and was active in local politics. In 1769, he had married Catherine, second daughter of Alderman Robert Donovan of Bride Street, Dublin, and was therefore part of the liberal gentry Donovans of Ballymore, Co. Wexford (a Protestant family with Gaelic origins). Her brother Peter was a lawyer in Dublin and a member of the Dublin Society of United Irishmen. Her deposition was published in Musgrave (725–8).

named Bigan,[13] a butcher, rushed upon Mr Hayden and dispatched him with many wounds from the pike, in [the] presence of Susan Lett who with bitter sorrow recounted this awful tragedy. His remains lay on the steps of Mr Lett's Hall door until devoured by pigs. Thus fell the Rev'd Samuel Hayden, Rector of Ferns, whose many virtues will be mentioned as long as memory can record. Benevolence like his, the piety and excellent qualities of this truly good Divine will be mentioned as a loss which time has not since repaired. Surely the dark ages of heathenism could not record more dreadful acts of cruelty.

My protector Williams[14] was leading me through an infuriated rabble, when a ruffian snapped a pistol at me with deadly intent, declaring at the same time that every female who was connected with the Orange System should fall. A struggle ensued between him and my friend in which Williams was successful, having wrested the pistol from my unknown enemy.

I pressed on through myriads of the enemy during this conflict, terrified and breathless from terror, not knowing whither to turn or from what hand to receive a mortal blow. I was soon joined by my friend, who brought in his hand the pistol which he had wrested from my enemy as a trophy of victory just achieved. Through smoke and fire he led me on through an infuriated mob who were mad from a desire to rob and murder. They were smashing the windows of every house, bursting open every door and clamouring for the victimized inhabitants. Williams also took Mrs Johnson under his protection. The events at that time threw us together for some days, & indeed we were a mutual comfort & support to each other. Mrs Johnson was sister to Mrs Tom Lett.[15] Her husband, General Johnson, was at that time a captain in the army and with his Regim't in the West Indies.

Just as we had reached the Duffry Gate the first field which met our view presented a scene of horror which I could not bring myself to look upon. The mangled remains of Mr John Pounden[16] of Daphne lay there, I was told, in a state of nudity, surrounded by his murderers who were yelling fearfully and exulting in the barbarous act. Mr Pounden was a person of exemplary character, kind-hearted, humane, and benevolent, indulgent to his tenantry and possessed of every virtue which constitutes the sincere Christian. But the good and virtuous were the victims of our

13 James Beaghan, a butcher, was tried for Heydon's murder and executed on Vinegar Hill, 24 Aug. 1799. His confession was reprinted in Musgrave (733–4).   14 The identity of Williams is unclear; he was a Catholic and the brother of George Williams, mentioned later in the account.   15 Probably a reference to Thomas Lett of Templeshannon, whose wife's name is not known. Cloney mentions being 'treacherously and violently assaulted by a ferocious Yeoman' while leaving Lett's house (see Cloney, 104).   16 Col. John Pounden of Daphne and Ballywalter, commanded the Enniscorthy Yeomanry and was killed in the defense of that town. See the Introduction to Chapter Six.

blood thirsty enemies. One ruffian insisted upon my entering the field and having a nearer view of their victim that I might feel aware of what every member of the orange institution might expect.

Williams, who possessed unbounded influence with them, would not allow any constraint to be used and therefore he hurried on in hopes of getting us quietly to his own house where, he said, we might remain in safety. When we had passed this dreadful scene, he placed us in a cart, and as we proceeded we were attacked by a set of ruffians who arrested our progress and demanded an explanation from Williams, who endeavoured to calm their rage against us. They uttered a furious yell and threatened to take the life of any man who would protect the orange party, and thus saying one of them rushed upon the unoffending horse that drew the cart and stabbed him with the pike. The animal plunged wildly, flinging the inmates of the cart into the ditch. My infant narrowly escaped with [his] life, and Mrs Johnson's face was frightfully contused. They let us escape & vented their rage upon the horse, which they perforated with many pikes.

After a long and fatiguing walk we reached Williams' about 9 o'clolk [*sic*] at night. We were kindly received by his wife, who seemed shocked at the part her husband had taken. She assured me she was in total ignorance of the change in his principles, she being strictly loyal, and she very much deplored the part he had taken. When we had been there about a day or two, Mrs Johnson's trusty maidservant sought her out, and came to induce her to return to her lodgings, which were undisturbed. Her abode was at a Quaker's in Slaney Street. These quiet people were not injured by the rebel party. Mrs Johnson had two sons by a former marriage. They were fine boys and her fears for them were greatly excited, but they were too young to give rise to suspicion in the enemy. She used every entreaty to induce me to accompany her, making the most earnest professions of kindness and declaring she would share the last morsel with me, but so great was my horror of the town that no argument could prevail on me to enter Enniscorthy. After Mr Johnson and the young Bruisters had left, Mrs Williams suggested that our better plan would be to send for the priest. She said if we were christened by him, they would no longer look upon us as heretics. In this she was mistaken, for after submitting to this form, our enemy were not less cruel.

I should not omit to mention the kind and humane conduct of Father Doyle[17] who obligingly said he was ready to perform any office that might

17 Fr James Doyle, parish priest of Davidstown, was born in 1752 at Raheen (Adamstown) and lived with the Dunne family at Coolamurry. As with most parish priests in Co. Wexford, he felt little sympathy for the rebellion, expressing both his frustration with his lack of influence over the people and his hope that the army would restore order. This attitude contrasted with the curates, who were younger and generally more radical. He died in 1825 (see Whelan, 'The Catholic Priest in the 1798 Rebellion', 310–12).

contribute to our safety. He supposed we were actuated by fear to make this proposal to him. We might rest assured that this Beautiful Island would not long remain in the hands of the Rebels, to use his own words, 'King George would soon send an army to defeat them'. But in this matter the priest was mistaken, for a supine Government left us three weeks and three days in the hands of a merciless rabble & then poured in an army large enough in these times to take Sebastapol, hired troops who were as merciless as the rebels they came to subdue, who fired indiscriminately upon unoffending women and killed the suffering loyalists who escaped the other party. Mrs Pounden was killed by a random shot which was intended for the Reverend J[oshua] Nunn, Rector of Enniscorthy. They both rushed forward with delight to hail the conquerors when Mrs Pounden[18] received her death-blow from those whom she considered her deliverers. She was the mother to Mr John Pounden, who was killed on the 28th by the rebels. Mr John Stringer,[19] an attorney, who was concealed during that time by a friend named Devereux, rushed forth to meet his deliverers, was fired on and killed in a moment. Such were the dangers with which we were surrounded on every side.

The day after we were visited by the kind priest, a mob surrounded Williams' house and demanded his cousin, whom they said he was hiding & to whom he conveyed food every night at a silent hour. Their rage against George[20] was so great that they set fire to a knock of furze bushes in order to destroy him. One of them, more humane than the rest, actually discovered him & desiring him to lie close, he would not betray him, then turning to his companions, assured them that George Williams was not there, so took them off in pursuit of other victims, and George made a fortunate escape to the Fort of Duncannon, the resort of our straggling Loyalists.

George's wife next became the victim of their persecuting spirit. They returned soon after and demanded this poor unoffending woman, who lay hiding upon an obscure loft. They said she must be produced, and one ruffian ascended a ladder which led to her retreat and actually dragged her down by one foot, then hauling her into the yard, threw her on a dung hill.

18 Jane Maria, daughter of the Revd Joshua Nunn of Whitechurch, married Patrick Pounden of Daphne in 1761 (*Ferns M.L.*) and was the mother of John Pounden of Ballywalter and Joshua Pounden of Enniscorthy. See the introduction to Chapter Six. 19 John Stringer, attorney, married Martha Gethings in 1793 (*Ferns M.L.*). Martha survived him and from Dublin claimed losses in 1799 of a 'House, Furniture, Cloathes, [and] Accounts' (Claimants, ccccxxv). In 1799, she testified to Cloney's good character (Cloney, 256–7). Joseph was possibly related to claimants Joseph Stringer, a Dublin apothecary, and Richard Stringer, a carpenter of Gorey. A Mr Stringer of Enniscorthy was cast overboard by rebels but swam to shore (Musgrave, 420). 20 The identity of George Williams is unclear. George Williams, farmer, of Enniscorthy, was a claimant in 1799, but was probably not the same man (Claimants, ccccxxxix).

This courageous woman when she found she had nothing to expect but cruel treatment, called forth resolution that might have graced an Amazon. She raised herself up and assured them in a determined tone that a time was approaching & not far distant when another King William should release us from the lands of our enemies. Strange to say, they did not resent this language from her, but went off for that time, saying they would visit her again, & she escaped to a kind family of Quakers near Wexford, who suffered her to remain till her husband returned to protect her.

My husband, who shared in the perils of the 28th, retreated with the Army to Wexford, not able to learn what was become of me, determined to return to Enniscorthy in search of me. He therefore made application to Bagnal Harvey, who held a high command in the Rebel army, for protection, which he readily obtained and which, joined to the influence of James Lett,[21] his nephew, brought him safely to Williams.

Williams every day attended the camp on Vinegar Hill and returned at night to his family, shocked and shuddering at the scenes of wholesale murders which he daily witnessed; innocent, unoffending persons for whom he could not utter a word that might obtain mercy or pardon. One of his day labourers was in constant attendance at the camp, and every night returned laden with plunder. He would frequently display various articles of clothing which were taken from the murdered remains of his victims. You may judge what my sufferings were when called upon to behold the garments of persons who were well known to me, and he would frequently boast of having killed persons whom I afterwards met in the land of the living.

Thus we went on for the course of a fortnight, every night hearing of the daily murders committed on Vinegar Hill & broken in upon by strange rebels, who came to record to their captain the wonderful feats achieved by them. Our NewtownBarry Cavalry were a distinguished corps. They kept the enemy at bay & oft-times pursued them in view of their camp. The rebels frequently came to Williams to boast of the defence they made against this gallant corps.

Williams told us one day with seeming concern that he could no longer harbour us. He was losing his influence with the rebel army in consequence of our being so long at his house, so in order to secure his authority he and his wife took themselves off and did not return till we had left. Hence, we perceived how perishable a virtue is friendship. It was true we had no claim on these people. We were discarded after the period by people who should have protected us, but the human heart was divested of all kindly feelings. Self-preservation was the ruling passion, and the nearest relatives were opposed to each other and espoused different causes. My husband said we

21 James Lett, the son of Stephen Lett (see Chapter One, note 28).

must seek protection in another quarter, everything in our house being destroyed, the windows and doors broken, and everything made a wreck. Our cattle were also taken off and never recovered. We therefore left Williams and bent our course across the country, and after a long and fatiguing walk of some miles, reached the door of our neighbour, George Hore[22] of Moyne, from whom we met the kindest protection.

The day after our sojourn there I was told by a servant that two persons on horseback wanted to see me. With fear & trembling, I approached them and discovered friends in the garb of rebel chiefs. One was Jacob West, a poet and artist, though of humble birth, and the other, Fenelon,[23] from whom when a child I had received lessons in drawing. This person stood high in authority and could dispense life and death at a nod. He had been in Wexford from whence he brought Orangemen to Vinegar Hill to be murdered next day. This murderer, Fenelon, came to me with professions of friendship and protection. He brought me a letter from my dear father, whom he had seen in jail, a letter fraught with spiritual consolation, for great was his resignation under affliction. I told Fenelon how much I wished to be with my father, and consulted him as to the manner I should be able to go to Wexford. He advised me to apply to Captain Barker[24] for a protection, who might also direct me to the care of some proper person to take charge of me. He also assured me that if my father were at Enniscorthy and under his protection, no one should injure him.

Encouraged by Fenelon's advice, I set out for Enniscorthy, attended by an humble friend who promised to conduct me into the presence of this august legislator. As soon as I had reached town, I met Barker marching in triumph at the head of a rebel band armed with pikes. I addressed him with great courtesy, told him how much I wished to go to Wexford to see my father, and begged him to give me a written permission to conduct me thereto. This he most obligingly promised to do. I then complained of the harsh measures we had met from the united army. They had made a wreck of our house and driven off our cattle. He assured me it was not by order of the committee that we had been so treated. It was a difficult matter to keep order amongst a disorganized mob, amongst whom he regretted he had taken command. He desired me to meet him in the course of an hour at the committee where he would give me the desired protection.

22 George Hore of Moyne resided at Milehouse, and a road from this house led to the Duffrey Gate at Enniscorthy (Dickson, 70). He belonged to one of the very few Catholic middlemen families on the Portsmouth estate. According to Ranson, Hore's son John, who married Mary Furlong of Scoby, was shot carrying a flag of truce at the battle of Ross (Ranson, 147).   23 Martin Fenlon was a school teacher, and according to Musgrave, was a 'fine young man of pleasing manners and genteel appearance' (Musgrave, 347). He was executed at Wexford with Roche, Keugh, and John Kelly of Killanne, on 25 June 1798. He should be distinguished from William Fenlon, nailor, executed on 12 September 1799 (Gordon, App., 9).   24 Capt. William Barker (see Chapter Three, note 12).

Barker was a gentleman by profession and education. He was a retired officer from the French service. The laws at that time precluded Roman Catholics from serving in the British army. He was a person of polished exterior & possessed all the urbanity so peculiar to the French people. He was a native of Waterford and nearly allied to Mr Wheeler of Mill Park, with whom he spent much time & was esteemed in good society. I heard after this period he received a musket ball in the arm and suffered amputation, and at the winding up of events he was captured & brought to trial & his life made amenable to the injured laws.

I waited on Barker at the appointed time & found it most difficult to get through the dense crowd that surrounded the gate which led to our wise and learned legislators. A very kind person whom I did not know addressed me & asked if I were Mrs Newton Lett, to which inquiry I answered in the affirmative. He took my hand & said he would conduct me through the crowd who were assembling in front of the gate, where our committee were holding council for the wise government of the Kingdom. Barker very kindly wrote me the desired protection, dated 'the 1st Year of Liberty'. He desired me to travel in company with Mrs Brett,[25] to whom he had also granted a protection & whose husband was a prisoner on board the prison ship in the Harbour of Wexford.

We therefore set out together, riding behind two trusted persons & secure in Barker's passport. We arrived about 7 o'clock in the evening in Wexford without meeting any interruption by the way. The sight of my father's beautiful house at Fortview, tattered & rifled of everything it contained, greatly afflicted me. We alighted from our horses and walked on a little, Mrs Brett not knowing to whom she could apply to be taken to her husband. I met my stepmother[26] about West Gate. She had been with my father, to whom she had taken some refreshment. She uttered a faint scream at sight of me & the next moment clasped me in her arms. 'Come', she exclaimed, 'and see your dear father. I have this moment left him; he was speaking of you. It will delight him to see you. I could give him no information about you. But come, you shall be messenger yourself'.

Hence, we walked on to the jail where we had some difficulty in obtaining an interview with our poor captive. One of the guards said, 'You have been here just now, we cannot be troubled so often'. With some entreaty we prevailed and our dear prisoner was called from his cell. My feelings at sight of a parent I loved with such filial affection cannot at this distant period be described, to see him imprisoned, plundered & surrounded by a

25 The identity of Mrs Brett, wife of James Brett of Enniscorthy, remains unknown. James Brett's name does not appear among the marriage bonds for the Diocese of Ferns, indicating that the couple was perhaps married by banns. See note 11 for further reference to her husband, who undoubtedly had conservative ties. 26 Sarah Hughes married William Daniel as his second wife in 1789 (*Ferns M.L.*).

set of demons who seemed to mock our grief. I sunk into his arms in an agony of sorrow, & it was some time ere I could give utterance to my feelings. He threw his arms affectionately around me & bursting into tears, exclaimed, 'Thou dearest pledge of my first affection, since thou art spared, I'll never more repine. I'm happy, though a beggar and a captive, since I now behold you'.[27]

'My beloved father', was all I could utter.

'Do not afflict me, my darling', he said. 'Be more composed. Place your confidence in that Being Who alone is able to protect us. His arm is not shortened by our afflictions, and His darling attribute is mercy'.

The sergeant on guard seemed softened by our sorrows. He spoke kindly to me, endeavoured to soothe me by saying my father was in no danger, and I should see him again in the morning. Consoled by these assurances, we parted for the night.

On our return from the gaol we met Mrs Lett[28] & her daughters. She was the widow of my husband's eldest brother, Stephen Lett of Newcastle. As this lady was near allied to Bagenal Harvey, she thought it necessary to adopt his principles and to scorn every loyal member of her husband's family. I met her and her daughters. They were decked in green, the rebel uniform. They appeared gay and cheerful. I addressed her in supplicating language, told her briefly of my distressed situation, & craved a bed for the night. She turned from me with contempt, saying that her principles were so publickly known, she was surprised how I could make such a request. Her character which she so highly valued had suffered materially with the united gentlemen, in consequence of the number of persons crowding her doors for protection, but in order to rid herself of such intruders she had taken a voluntary oath to them not to admit any persons but friends to the cause. She asked me why I left my own house, as she was sure I had nothing to fear from such a noble enemy, people who were ground down by oppressing laws & were now struggling in the cause of freedom. She

---

27 Revd William Gurley, a Wexford silversmith and Methodist minister, was imprisoned in an adjoining cell with William Daniel. He recalled that Daniel, with Robert Pigott and Richard Julian, came to his cell door. 'As they came near, several cried, 'O, Mr Gurley, pray for us!' 'Pray for yourselves', said I. 'O, we can't', replied they. 'What', said I, 'is the matter now?' 'Don't you hear', said they, 'the shouting? Five or six hundred sailors are trying to get in to murder us all!' I then called one of the prisoners, who was not religious, to pray, but he was so terrified he could not. So I bade them kneel down. But O, the situation we were in! Such weeping I never saw before … I observed that he [Daniel] prayed very fervently' (Revd L. B. Gurley, *Memoir of Revd William Gurley* [Cincinnati: Methodist Book Concern, 1850], 120). 28 See Chapter Four, note 29. Mary Moore, wife of Stephen Lett, a United Irishman, was the daughter of James Moore of Milne Hill, Co. Cavan, by his wife Mary, daughter of the Revd William Harvey, Rector of Mulrankin and Prebendary of Edermine by his first wife, Susanna, daughter of John Harvey of Killiane Castle (*Burke's Landed Gentry of Ireland* [1912], 299–300; Leslie, 72; Ranson, 148). Her mother was a cousin of Beauchamp Bagenal Harvey, who was the son of Francis Harvey of Bargy Castle.

wished me good-night and joined her daughters who waited at a distance, and left me prey to bitter reflections. Previous to that time a most friendly intercourse subsisted between us & after my marriage, her daughter Dolly, afterwards Mrs Burrows, spent three months at my house. But now that the flag of rebellion waved from her windows, on which was wrought murder without sin, her beautiful daughters were designated the rebel angels. They spurned me as a reptile not worthy of a place in existence. My mother, perceiving how greatly I was disappointed at their unkind treatment, sought to reconcile me by saying I should have the bed allotted to her and her children. It was a pallet stretched on the boards of an upper room at Mr W____.

I never felt so thankful as that night when I lay down. I knew that my dear father was living, that I should see him again next morning, and it was the first night for a fortnight that I had stretched my weary limbs on a bed or taken off my clothes. The town of Wexford bore a more orderly aspect than the locality I had left. Whilst at Williams' we were frequently broken in upon thro' the night & obliged to listen to acts of chivalry performed by the rebels upon our suffering yeomen, whom they would say they put to flight with the murderous pike. Our NewtownBarry Cavalry were a most distinguished corps for their undaunted courage. They ably defended their little town and put their enemies to flight with great loss. Dismayed and defeated, they would flock in great crowds to Williams' to tell the fatal news & often when suffering great loss, they would boast of being the victors.

Early next morning I awoke from sleep very much refreshed & comforted at the idea of seeing my father. Many obstacles had arisen since the evening before. The guard had been relieved & the person then in command would not allow us the privilege of seeing our prisoner. He said he dare not call him to us without the consent of the sergeant, an indulgence which I flattered myself would be easily obtained, but to my great surprise and disappointment, the person who now appeared was morose and unfeeling. He asked my business in an angry tone, said he supposed I was a spy from Enniscorthy. He was determined to cut off all communication between his prisoners and their orange confederates. 'I am no spy', I exclaimed. 'I only crave the trifling indulgence of seeing my father. What harm can arise from an interview that may be witnessed by everyone present?'

One person more humane than the rest called to the turn-key in an imperative tone and ordered him to call down Daniel, that he would hold himself responsible for the consequences, which could not affect the cause they were embarked in. My father was accordingly called down. His countenance wore a placid resignation that was pleasing to behold. That brutal sergeant held a sword between us to impede our meeting. The person who so kindly interfered ordered him to give no further opposition to a meeting so harmless. 'My dear father', said I, 'perhaps this is the last time I shall see you. God only knows whether we shall be allowed to meet again'. With tears of sorrow I expressed these words.

'Do not afflict yourself, my beloved child', he said. 'We are all in the hands of a merciful God, without Whose permission a sparrow cannot fall to earth. I am thoroughly resigned to his divine will and as happy as man can be in captivity. We shall meet again, I hope, in happier regions where no disturbance can have place'. Our tormentor, eager to separate us, said he would no longer hearken to such nonsense. I then supplicated a lock of my father's hair, which I obtained through the interposition of my unknown friend.

That morning I intended returning to Enniscorthy, and the idea of seeing my father for the last time greatly afflicted me, so great was the struggle between filial affection and maternal tenderness. I had left my baby in the care of Mrs Pierson, who was nursing a child of her own, and kindly took charge of mine. I found it impossible to tear myself from the gloomy prison which contained the object most dear to my affections. I therefore remained in Wexford until Tuesday following, which was the 19th of June, and by some means saw my father twice every day when supplying his frugal meals, which consisted of bread and milk. Through the interference of some kind friend, I was able to see him twice every day, altho' the wretches who surrounded the gaol were heartless, unfeeling monsters who always mocked our grief. Yet some individual, by speaking a kind word, obtained this melancholy indulgence for me.

As I was returning from jail, I met Mrs Cooper[29] of George's Street; her husband and his father were at liberty, & although much censured & suspected for enjoying this privilege,[30] I am convinced they were truly good men. They were attorneys by profession, they made every exertion in their power to serve their suffering friends. Mrs Cooper kindly invited me to her house. Whenever I wished for the society of a sympathising friend she would ask the opinion of those that were enjoying their liberty. When I entered the parlour, several persons sat around a table on which wine and glasses were placed. They appeared in earnest conversation when I entered the room, which ceased for a moment but was soon resumed by Cooper, who was strongly recommending a friend of his, an object of mercy, to the kind consideration of Capt. Rossiter,[31] who appeared a person of

---

29 Eleanor Cooper married Henry Cooper in 1770 (*Ferns M.L.*). He was attorney at law, Commissioner for taking affidavits in the Exchequer, coroner, and clerk of the peace (*General Directory of the Kingdom of Ireland, 1788* (section on Wexford printed in the *Irish Genealogist*, 3:413). Goodall adds that he was appointed town clerk in 1770 and that his house was resorted to by both loyalists and rebels during the rebellion (Freemen, 116). His relationship to Samuel Cooper, a lawyer and United Irishman in Wexford, is not known. 30 The word 'liberty' is crossed out in the original manuscript. 31 Ignatius and John Rossiter of Grange were United Irish leaders and members of the committee in charge of

considerable influence in the rebel army. Cooper's friend was Mr Grey[32] of Whitefort, who, I think, was a member of the Yeomen cavalry. He was so obnoxious to the rebels that he lay concealed under a bed in Cooper's house. At the same time, his brother, Nick Grey,[33] wore the rebel uniform and was an active and noisy commander, shouting and yelling fearfully with his wicked companions. Such were the state of affairs in these perilous times that fond brothers took opposite sides and were cruelly opposed to each other. A third brother, Tom Grey,[34] was a captain in the Wexford regiment of militia. Hence arose great opposition in families. Some were considered worthy of a portion of the claims adjudged to suffering Loyalists, while others were branded with ignominy and disgrace.[35]

Cooper used every argument & remonstrance to soften the resentment of Rossiter, who seemed an implacable foe to his friend. He begged & implored to be allowed to bring Grey into his presence which, after much entreaty, he was allowed to do. When Grey entered the parlour, I may with truth aver that such an object of misery I had not seen up to that time. His hair stood on end like the quills upon the fretted porcupine; his clothes which were black were covered with feathers, & horror & despair depicted in his countenance. Cooper said, 'Give your hand to Captain Rossiter', but the supplicating hand was rejected with scorn and contempt. Rossiter said, 'I shall not take your hand, but in consideration of your brother's services, I shall not injure you, but every lover of that freedom which has just dawned upon us must heartily despise you'.

The events passed on in lively conversation upon the general success which crowned the united army, & sorry am I to add to this little narrative that a brother of a colonel in the British army was most energetic in supporting the justice of their claims. I, of course, was silent upon these subjects of interest, tho' I must say great was my surprise.

I received much kind attention from Mrs Cooper, & many other friends who were undisturbed, also invited my stepmother, who was considered an

---

the Wexford jail (see Musgrave, 462).   **32** Joseph Gray was a member of Ogle's Loyal Blues, one of the most Orange of the co'.s yeomanry corps. The son of Nicholas Gray of Whitefort, he married Bell Crozier in 1792 (Freemen, 319; see also Goodall, 'A Divided Family in 1798: The Grays of Whitefort and Jamestown', 52–66). He moved later to Jamestown, where he built a house that was visited by Thomas Atkinson in 1814. Atkinson called him 'a good and honest man', and in enjoying the view from the top of his lawn, asked him 'whether he was in possession of his reasoning faculties when he built his neat little house in yonder hole at the bottom of all this beauty' (Atkinson, *The Irish Tourist* [1814], 508–9).   **33** Nicholas Gray of Wexford (see Chapter Four, note 38).   **34** Thomas Gray married Joyce Sophia Bennett, widow, daughter of Joseph White of Whitefort. He was a captain in the Wexford Militia in 1798 and later paymaster to the Wicklow Militia in 1828 (Freemen, 319).   **35** Of the three brothers, only Joseph Gray appears on the list of claimants, showing losses of 'House, Furniture, Cattle, Hay, [and] Fire-arms' totalling over £437, of which he received £125.

object of great pity. Our best friends were afraid to show us any kindness. Doctors were allowed to live. My father's house was convenient to an hospital, and Dr Jacob,[36] who was the infirmary doctor, was appointed to attend their sick & wounded.

A heart-rending sight was displayed at the bridge, which was a scene of carnage throughout. Four dead bodies were tied there to the frames; from the arms they were suspended and remaining floating on the water during the whole time; one of them, the nearest in view, was the remains of Capt'n Dalton.[37] I think he fought at Enniscorthy with the defeated army and retreated to Wexford with them when put to flight. I did not hear how he fell, whether by pike or gun, but I had a heart-rending sight to witness when passing that way. The remains of poor Captain Dalton were to be seen floating upon the water; George Sparrow[38] of Enniscorthy was placed next to him. The other two I do not recollect; perhaps I did not know them.

About this time the most awful event which ever appeared in any country or at any period of time, took place. I mean the burning of Scullabogue Barn, filled with Protestants of every description. Ben Lett[39] of Kilgibbon was one of the victims thrust in there. He was a lad about fifteen or sixteen years old at that time, but by the enterprising and persevering courage of his sister, he escaped the dreadful fate of those who suffered. She threw herself prostrate before a priest, whose name was Shally,[40] and declared she would never rise until he was free. She was promised him next morning, but she clung more closely to the priest, declaring she would never rise till her brother was set free. The priest could not resist her entreaties: he gave an order to have him given to his

---

36 Dr Ebenezer Jacob (see Chapter Four, note 24).   37 David Dalton, a gauger and hence almost certainly a conservative, served as a Private in the Orange Enniscorthy Yeoman Cavalry under the command of Archie Jacob, though he is called 'captain' by Mrs Lett (see the claim of Mary Dalton in 'Widows and Orphans', n.p.). He was executed at Wexford (Musgrave, 736). His widow Mary of Enniscorthy claimed losses in 1799, including 'Cloaths, Furnitiure, Books and Provisions' (Claimants, cccxliii).   38 George Sparrow married Mary Burt in 1797 (*Ferns M.L.*). He was undoubtedly related to the Sparrows of Back Street, Enniscorthy, who were victuallers (see Chapter Three, note 9). His widow Mary was a claimant on the list of widows and orphans in 1800 ('Widows and Orphans', n.p.). She may have been the Mary Sparrow, widow, of Garryrickard, who claimed losses at her residence of 'Cloaths, Furniture and Provision' (Claimants, ccccxxi).   39 The Letts of Kilgibbon were cousins of the Letts of Killaligan and were leaders of the Orange party in Co. Wexford (see Whelan, 'Religious Factor in the 1798 Rebellion', 69). Benjamin Lett was one of three sons of William Lett; with his brothers Nicholas and John he decked the bridles of their horses in orange and blue ribbon, and attended meetings at an Orange lodge in Enniscorthy. William Lett of Kilgibbon claimed losses in 1799 that included 'Cattle, Corn, Furniture and Cloaths' (Claimants, ccclxxxvii).   40 Fr John Shallow was a native of Park (Old Ross) and served as parish priest of Newbawn, Co. Wexford, from 1795 to 1817. Like other parish priests, he remained opposed to the United Irish, likening their philosophy to French atheistic revolutionary principles. Once when he refused to hear a rebel's confession,

sister, and thus escaped the cruel tortures inflicted on those innocent victims of Scullabogue Barn. These melancholy events I learned from Miss Lett,[41] who was afterwards married to Mr Boxwell of Linseystown.

One day when returning from the gaol, I saw a servant, whom I knew was a Protestant, standing in the door of a very obscure house. She was living in the service of Mr King[42] of Macmine Castle, who was my husband's cousin. I enquired if she could give me any information of her master's family. She said, 'They are hiding in this house'. She took me upstairs, and opening a door desired me to go in. Mr King was sitting on a feather bed which laid on the floor, without bedclothes of any description. He stood up to receive me, & Mrs King soon entered the room, which was destitute of furniture. Our feelings were mutual at meeting. Our hearts were full to overflowing and tears of bitter anguish flowed from our eyes. I said to Mr King, 'I have seen your mother, and she is safely lodged with Mrs Warren at Enniscorthy. She begged me, if possible, to see you and to let you know at my return how you were and with whom you were stopping'.

he was told 'Hell would be his bed, he was worse than any Orangeman and he would pay for it' (Quoted from Shallow's affidavit in J. Caulfield, *The Reply of Right Revd Dr Caulfield, Roman Catholic Bishop and of the Roman Catholic Clergy of Wexford to the Misrepresentations of Sir Richard Musgrave, Bart.* [Dublin, 1801], cited in Whelan, 'The Catholic Priest in the 1798 Rebellion', 311). Shallow attempted as a humanitarian gesture to save several Protestants at Scullabogue. Nevertheless, he was falsely accused with complicity in the burning, but was later acquitted on the testimony of several Protestants (see Gordon, 146–7). He died in 1831. **41** Elizabeth Lett married Samuel Boxwell of Linziestown in 1801 (*Ferns M.L.*). Samuel was the son of Samuel Boxwell of Sarshill and his wife Mary, daughter of Revd Ambrose Harvey of Bargy (see 'Boxwell of Butlerstown', *Burke's Landed Gentry of Ireland* [1958], 104). **42** Richard Newton King of Macmine Castle was probably the son of the Revd Jeremiah King, a freeman of Wexford in 1776 (see Freemen, 329). Musgrave calls him a magistrate and recounts his narrow escape from the rebels while concealed in the Hatchel house in Wexford: 'One Herring [John Herron], a rebel captain, in the course of making domiciliary visits in quest of orangemen, entered Mr Hatchel's house with a drawn sword, at the head of an armed band of rebels. On finding Mr [Henry] Milward, he conveyed him to prison; but first informed Mr Hatchel's family, that he would burn the house, if they concealed any more orangemen. On this Mr King, who happened to be in the only room which they did not search, declared that no person should suffer on his account. He therefore retreated backwards to another house at some distance, and in doing so, was obliged to scale some walls, and to wade through a small stream, much swollen with the tide. He lay concealed some days in a wretched out-office, and was supplied with food by Mrs Jacob. His wife, though she lodged near him, would not venture to approach him, lest the place of his retreat should be discovered. At length, the rebels who were active and incessant in their researches, discovered and committed him. These two gentlemen were on the point of being massacred the twentieth of June, on the bridge of Wexford, when Mr Esmond Kyan, a rebel chieftan, saved their lives, by telling the rebel bloodhounds, that the king's troops must finally succeed, and that they would take ample vengeance of them for putting so many protestants to death in cold blood … ' (Musgrave, 425–6). In 1799, he gave a deposition against Thomas Cloney (Cloney, 271). He also claimed losses of 'Cattle, Wine, Furniture, Cloaths [and] Crop' (Claimants, ccclxxxv).

'Tell her', he said, 'that daily murders are committed here; we know not how long we may remain undiscovered'.

He then asked for my husband. I told him he was safe under [Bagenal] Harvey's protection. 'But', I added, 'they have my dear father in gaol'.

After many painful reflections upon both sides upon the state of affairs, I left them. Their abode was near the Barracks, the gaol at that time being in that direction, and the house occupied by the Kings being of the meanest description, it proved a fortunate asylum to them as they escaped detection.

On Tuesday, the 19th of June, I was sent for to return to my husband & children, who were stopping at Hore's,[43] who were our kindest friends in this time of suffering. I found I could no longer stop where filial love and duty invited me. My husband and children had the first claim on my affection, yet my aching heart clung more closely to my father. I told him at our last meeting the necessity there was for my return. He seemed shocked at the idea of parting me & made me promise to return to Wexford with my children, to which I partly consented & left him for the last time.

When I parted from him, he lingered at the door as long as he was allowed to remain, sure something boded that we should meet no more. When I reached a turn in the street, I looked behind – a last look. I saw him riveted to the spot, regarding me with a look of parental solicitude. I was absorbed in bitter anguish, not knowing what to decide upon. I was roused from my reverie by the approach of Mr Rob't Carty,[44] who was a person of some respectability who possessed unbounded influence with the rebel army. I was acquainted with him previous to this time and flattered myself that I should have met some degree of kindness from him, but greatly indeed I had deceived myself. I begged of him to allow me to travel in company with him to Enniscorthy, as I should feel safe under his protection. To this request he made a bow of consent, but before we reached Ferry Carrig he gave spurs to his horse & dashed off at a hasty pace, leaving me to my fate.

The trusty person who had charge of me endeavoured to quiet my fears by repeated assurances that he would take me to Hore's in safety, which promize he fully verified, although several times by the way he was hooted at and sometimes threatened for lending assistance to the orange party. He diverted them by saying I was returning home to see provisions supplied to them, to which office I was appointed by the committee. They said sportingly it was well I had got such an honourable office as to wait on them that were fighting in the cause of freedom & the rights of the people. I should now wait on those who were too long oppressed, but better days

---

43 George Hore of Moyne (see note 22).   44 See Chapter Four, note 42.

had now dawned upon them. All this was amusing & readily consented to by me.

I arrived at Enniscorthy about 8 o'clock in the evening. On Castle Hill I met a fellow-sufferer whose life was spared because he played the violin & amused his enemies with party tunes. It was Henry Minchen,[45] whose brother was shot before his face, and he was compelled to play every tune they demanded. I met him holding his violin in his hand and walking without shoes; our hearts were too full to give utterance to words; we gazed on each other and burst into tears. They were tears of bitter, heart-rending sorrow. Poor Henry would have rather played his dear brother's funeral requiem than play Party tunes demanded by the enemy. Every feeling was sacraficed [*sic*] to self-preservation at that time. We dare not express sorrow for our dearest friend. I walked on to Mrs Warren's, whose house escaped. She, living a widow, had neither husband nor son to take part in these broils. She also rented her house from a Roman Catholic. Hence she escaped undisturbed & gave refuge to many respectable persons. Mrs Newton, Mrs King's mother, stopt there during the three weeks & 3 days of suffering. Mrs Hatton,[46] whose husband was murdered on the first day of the outbreak, she also found an asylum with her kind neighbour.

My friend who brought me thus far, whose name was Leary, advised me to stop with my friends for that night, it being too late to proceed to Hore's, and it was rumoured that we were hemmed in by a powerful army, which would soon attack Vinegar Hill and put our enemies to flight. Agreeable to the advice Leary had given me, I stopped the night at Mrs Warren's, & next morning at 4 o'clock my trusty guide called me up and begged me, if I valued my life, to flee from the town, which would soon be attacked, that we should retire by the most private way to Hore's. We therefore hastily proceeded hither by the most retired way, carefully avoiding the road. When [we] arrived there they fully confirmed the happy news which Leary had heard at Enniscorthy. My husband said our deliverance was at hand and suggested that we might be safer in our own house than with

45 Henry Minchin was probably the son of William Minchin, carpenter and builder, of Church St, Enniscorthy by his wife Margaret Hawkins, whom he married in 1756 (*Ferns M.L.*; see Freemen, 333). Henry's brother, Jacob Minchin, was captured on 28 May 1798 and imprisoned in the windmill on Vinegar Hill. James Beaghan described Jacob as one of 'the sons of old Minchin the carpenter', and confessed to having him executed (Musgrave, 734, 747). Nothing is known of Henry Minchin subsequent to the Rebellion, except that he gave a deposition on behalf of Cloney in 1799, crediting Cloney with giving him protection (Cloney, 257). Henry Minchin was not among the claimants of 1799, as were Mary and William Minchin of Enniscorthy and John Hawkins Minchin of Ballycourcymore, Henry's brother (Claimants, cccxciii).   46 Mary, wife of Henry Hatton of St Mary's, portrieve of Enniscorthy, appears in Musgrave, asserting that her husband was murdered on Vinegar Hill, which was also affirmed by their daughter, Jane Hatton of Hollywood, who added that he was murdered 'sooner than change his religion' (Musgrave, 744; see also Freemen, 323).

our friends. We therefore set out for Killaligan, accompanied by Hore & his sister. They drove all their cattle upon our deserted[47] fields. It was confidently thought that retaliation would be visited upon them. We passed a sleepless night, not having a bed to lie down on.

Next morning the booming of cannon awoke us to a sense of our situation of heartfelt gratitude to the Almighty for the prospect of deliverance to our desolated country. Cannon was placed on Cherry Orchard Rock, and such deliberate aim was taken from Vinegar Hill that the Royal Cannon was dismounted. Val Gill[48] was the engineer that conducted the Rebel guns. They had four cannon playing on our army, but a powerful force soon put them to flight. How fondly did I anticipate my next meeting with my father upon the explosion of every cannon. When I saw the tree of liberty fall on Vinegar hill, how did my heart dilate with pleasare [*sic*]; how different, I thought, shall our next meeting be to our last farewell. I shall see him established in his own house and surrounded by a happy family. We are now, thank heaven, set free from the yoke of popish persecution & again a free people. Alas, I little thought my father had for ever done with transitory things.

About 3 o'clock that evening we saw two soldiers approach our house. One of them came into ask some refreshments, and after some conversation he strongly advised us to go to Enniscorthy and place ourselves under the protection of Military friends who might protect us, as the soldiers were ordered to shoot every man who appeared in plain clothes. They could give no quarter, as they were told that every loyal man had to be murdered. This soldier was a private from the Donegal Militia. We used every argument to induce him to accompany us to town, but this he declined, saying he should join his regiment who were encamped at Daphne. We then agreed to set out for Enniscorthy, in consequence of the soldier's advice, which seemed so essential to our safety.

My husband urged me to remain after him while he & Hore would seek protection from the Army. Fortunately for them, I was opposed to this measure and finally determined to go with them & share their fate. We accordingly set out together for Enniscorthy, and never saw a human being from the time we left Killaligan till we arrived at Duffry Gate. A dreary gloom seemed to surround us. Nature seemed appalled at such a scene as broke in upon our view. Upon entering town, we were interrupted by a military guard, one of whom seized my husband with the one hand & with

---

47 'Denuded' is crossed out.　48 Valentine Gill was a surveyor, whose well-known map of Co. Wexford was published in 1812. A loyalist in 1798, he was compelled under duress by the rebel army to position the rebel cannons against the English army. In 1799, he gave testimony in 1799 against Cloney, who was accused of the murder of John Gill, Valentine's brother, on Vinegar Hill (Cloney, 266–7).

the other he drew his bayonet, swearing vehemently that he should die that moment for a croppy villain. In vain I pleaded that we were suffering loyalists, who were plundered and persecuted by the Rebels and had flown to them for protection. The irritated warrior [*sic*], steady to his purpose & deaf to my remonstrance, cast a furious look upon me & desired his comrade to dispatch the other croppy, meaning Hore. The rebels, who showed no mercy, should meet none from them. He again seized his victim with deadly intent.

Terrified beyond description & breathless with horror, I looked wildly around me and at that moment beheld two young officers approaching on horseback. I flew to them for succour in that moment of peril & briefly told them our danger & cast myself on their humanity for mercy & protection. One of them seemed to regard me with an eye of pity & politely alighting from his horse, asked in what manner he could be of service to me. He desired the soldiers to give up their prisoners, whose case he should investigate. Hore stood trembling with terror, & my husband seemed conscious of the danger of his situation. Our gallant deliverer, with that humanity which ever distinguishes the truly brave, rescued the poor delinquents from the hands of the enraged soldiers, then turning to me asked whither he should conduct me. With heartfelt gratitude for such timely deliverance, I begged of him to take me to Capt'n Nuttle's,[49] where I expected to meet Military friends, Mrs Nuttle's brother being an officer of rank in the army who, before he sheathed his sword, sought his sister, and her house, under the protection of Colonel Freeman, became the refuge of the suffering loyalists.

Therefore, to Capt'n Nuttle's we proceeded and soon entered upon scenes of death and desolation so terrible that I know not how to describe it. Livid bodies covered with ghastly wounds, over which we were frequently obliged to step; human bodies charred I could not tell from what cause. The smell was so overpowering I was affected with the sensation of sickly horror and often on the point of fainting. My gallant deliverer supported me with a protecting arm, which brought me & my company safely to Capt'n Nuttle's door, then asking if he could render me any further service, mounted a horse, richly caparisoned, & rode off.

We were soon surrounded by innumerable friends & acquaintances, similarly situated, who received us with demonstrations of delight. I could not for some time return their congratulations, so great was my excitement, so many horrors crowded upon my recollection, exhausted in body & mind from such a tide of overwhelming events, that I could not for some time give utterance to the joy I felt at once more beholding many whom I

---

49 Captain Nuttle remains unidentified. He was perhaps related to the Nuttall family of Co. Wicklow (see 'Nuttall of Tittour', *Burke's Landed Gentry of Ireland* [1912], 517).

thought were dead. When I had regained a little composure, I recognized an old friend and acquaintance in Capt'n Mellifont[50] of the 4th Dragoons. He had been quartered at Enniscorthy some years previous. He expressed great pleasure at seeing us in safety and got a protection for our house, whither he advised us not to return for that night, nor again expose ourselves to the insults of the soldiers.

Capt'n Nuttle's house was so crowded from the numbers who flocked there for protection, that I proposed going to Mrs Warren's, whose house was undisturbed through every vicissitude. Therefore, protected by an officer of a yeoman corps, Mr Murphy[51] of Aulartlee, we proceeded without any interruption to our unwavering friend. We had not been there many minutes when the house was entered by a guard of soldiers, who came to demand the two croppies who had but just entered & who now stood in imminent danger. Mrs Warren said that Colonel Bligh[52] of the Dublin Militia had just taken possession of her drawingroom, a circumstance which made her very happy, as his interference might be the means of saving the lives of my husband & my friend, who now looked like men fated to die instantly.

I flew to this stranger, to whom I recounted briefly my state of distress & from whom I implored protection. Colonel Bligh had been thrown from his horse on a rock on Vinegar Hill when charging the enemy. His face was very much contused, and when I entered the room he was washing the blood off his forehead & temples. Breathless, I implored his mercy at his hands for loyal sufferers, and disdainfully he looked upon me. He could not be persuaded that a loyal man had escaped the fury of the enemy. Contemptuously he said, 'You will now pull down your crosses and clap up Dundas, but I shall know how to deal with such hypocrites'. His prejudice seemed so implacable that I fortunately placed in his hand the letter which my dear father had sent me by Fenelon. He read it with attention & walked out of the room, as if to show it to the officers who stood outside. He soon returned; his countenance bore a kinder aspect. He said he had released my husband and Hore, who were prisoners in the hands of the soldiers, and then wrote a protection for my house, signed 'Edward Bligh'.

When this flurry had subsided, a pleasing scene came on. I had the happiness of meeting many friends and relatives whom I thought were

---

50 Captain Mellifont is unidentified. This surname is unusual in Co. Wexford. There were several Mellefonts listed among the 18th-century marriage bonds of Dublin.   51 Possibly Francis Murphy, a first lieutenant in the Scarawalsh Infantry, a Protestant of Gaelic ancestry (see O Snodaigh, 36). Oulartleigh was a townland in the parish of Ballyhuskard.   52 Col. Edward Bligh of the Dublin Militia remains unidentified. His name does not appear among the indexed Dublin marriage marriage bonds. Perhaps Mrs Lett confuses his name for Lt-Col. Blyth of Dublin, mentioned in Gen. Lake's letter to Lord Castlereagh, 21 Jun. 1798, as one from whom he received able assistance (Musgrave, 813).

numbered with the dead. My Uncle Peare[53] and his son, who were members of a highly distinguished corps of cavalry, met me with delight. They had fought the rebels in every quarter, and now, crowned with victory, met us with delight. When the first effusions of joy had a little subsided, we fixed upon sitting up all night, there not being beds to accomodate so many, and indeed but few houses which had escaped the devouring elements; so little accomodation was to be had in the town, we fixed upon sitting up and reciting to each other the various sufferings endured through that time of persecution.

Next morning my husband and Hore went in search of our cattle which had been plundered by the rebels, and I stopped at Mrs Warren's, anxiously awaiting the result of affairs at Wexford. Our enemies met such a final defeat at Vinegar Hill that they passively yielded to the royal army, who treated them with great clemency, leaving them a passage for retreat when they were put to flight. The most atrocious murderers put up the orange lily, retreated to Wexford, where they stepped on shipboard and were quietly wafted across the Atlantic and in America spent the remainder of their bloodstained lives, free and secure from detection.

About 3 o'clock that day we saw one of the Enniscorthy cavalry on horseback, surrounded by a number of women to whom he seemed to communicate something of importance. I stepped forward to enquire the cause, and soon heard a melancholy tale which nearly deprived me of life and motion. He had just returned from Wexford and was giving an account of the dreadful massacre committed on thr bridge the day before. Hope and fear alternatively took possession of me. I could not summon up resolution to enquire for my father. I begged of Mrs Warren to ask if he had escaped, but judge of my despair when Stacy[54] said he was piked to death. To describe my feelings upon this heart-rending occasion I shall not attempt. Suffice it to say my kind friend used every entreaty to soothe my sorrow, which was overwhelming; then sinking into a state of languor and stupor not easily described.[55]

---

53 Ranson speculates that this may be a clue to the identity of Barbara Lett's mother, suggesting that she may have been a member of the Peares of Kilmallock (Ranson, 118). Humphrey Pear of Killenaugh claimed losses in 1799, including a 'House, Furniture [and] Cattle', while Mary Peare of Kilmallock, widow, lost 'Cattle, Corn and Provision' (Claimants, cccci). Elizabeth Pear married William Good in 1754 (*Ferns M.L.*), and Good is mentioned later in Mrs Lett's account. 54 The identity of this Stacy is uncertain. Edward Stacey, farmer, of Tomgara, was a claimant, whose deposition appears in Musgrave (Musgrave, 729–30; Claimants, ccccxxiii). Benjamin Stacey and George Stacey were both killed on Vinegar Hill, and Elizabeth Stacy, widow of Benjamin, a Private in the Enniscorthy Yeoman Cavalry, claimed losses in 1800 ('Widows and Orphans', n.p.). 55 Gurley writes that in searching for the body of his brother Jonas, another victim of June 20, he discovered the body of William Daniel: 'I saw, partly in the water, the body of Mr M'Daniels [*sic*], the same that called on me so earnestly to pray for him in the jail. I had his body put in the

I was roused from this lethargy by a general cry of 'the rebels are coming again, they are pouring in upon us to attack a defenceless town', the military being gone on to Wexford. I tottered up to the door & from thence I saw a number of commissary carts drawn up in the street. The guard that had charge of them would proceed no further without a more secure number to protect the provisions. The town was thrown into the greatest state of excitement. An immediate attack was expected and all was despair. Such a succession of overwhelming events crowded so rapidly upon my sinking mind that the impulse of the moment led me to return to my own house. With this object in view, I walked through a crowd of women & soon met several whom I knew, the wives of our Yeomen who, like me, were wending their way to the country in order to avoid the commotion which prevailed in town in consequence of a report which had no foundation. Hence I returned to the country with these humble women who, a short time before, entered the town decked with orange lilies, the insignia of their order, which they now hastily removed upon hearing the rebels were returning to destroy them.[56]

When I returned to Killaligan [torn] with bitter anguish & unavailing sorrow at the accounts of the dreadful massacre on the bridge of Wexford, I gave way to sorrow bordering on despair. I had many companions in affliction. There were few who had not lost their dearest friends & relations. I prevailed on my husband next morning to take me to Wexford, that I might mingle my sorrow with my father's family, so consoling did I consider to mourn with those who felt an equal share of affliction with myself. Too soon, alas, I heard the fatal truth of this bloody act. 95 victims perished on that fatal day and their bodies cast into the Slaney, whose waters ran crimson with Protestant blood. An humble man named Parslow[57] from Enniscorthy, a shoemaker, stood by my father's side when the first murderous attack was made on him. Parslow slipped among the murderers and so escaped to describe the horrors of this bloody day. This awful event occurred a few days after the burning of Scullabogue barn.

coffin I took for my brother, and sent word to his wife, who sent and had him buried' (Gurley, 195). Elsewhere in the book, Gurley notes that he found Daniel's body 'on a place called the Cat's [Kaat's] Strand, without a particle of raiment, except a black velvet stock about his neck' (Ibid., 121).   56 Here Barbara makes an important reference to women of the Orange order during the Rebellion, about whom little is known. Clearly, she disassociates herself from what she terms 'their order' and with her husband was probably more moderate in their political outlook.   57 Musgrave shows Robert and Eben 'Parsley' on the list of prisoners in the Wexford gaol, but neither are shown to have been piked (Musgrave, 807). 'Parsley' is a vernacular pronunciation for Parslow, which, in turn, may be a variation of Paslow (see Freemen, 451–2; Goodall lists Henry Paslow of Ballyhaddock and John Paslow of Ballylurkin among the Freemen of Wexford in 1776). Ann Parslow of Adamstown, widow, and Robert Parslow of Adamstown, Yeoman, were claimants, as was Esther Parslow, widow, of Enniscorthy (Claimants, cccci).

Could anything be more atrocious or barbaric than the cruelties inflicted at that time on innocent and inoffending persons? O pray we never experience such cruelties again. May we never more fall into the hands of our neighbours, who are more barbarous than any foreign enemy.

To describe my first interview with my stepmother after this awful event cannot well be done justice to. She uttered a piercing shriek at the sight of me, which I responded to by a burst of sorrow from an aching heart. When we were quite exhausted by giving way to unavailing cries of bitter distress, we were called to order by a kind message from our hostess who sent us word that we should quit her house. She could no longer be annoyed by our cries. Little was said on our part. We walked into the street, not knowing whither to direct our steps, and surrounded by my father's 5 children who were of tender years, the eldest being but seven years old.

We had not gone far until we met Mr Charles Parsons,[58] who was a member of the Wexford Cavalry. My mother exclaimed: 'O, Mr Parsons. Behold me, widowed, houseless, and penniless; my cries and sorrows have hardened the hearts of those who in pity should have ministered to my distress. I have been ordered to seek another asylum'.

'My dear madam', he said, 'come to my house though ill-suited for your reception, Mrs Eustace[59] & Mrs Parsons having escaped to Dublin before the outbreak. Come with me where everything shall be done for your accomodation. I am ordered off with an express which I hold in my hand, & so limited for time that I can only stop for a moment to give directions to have you made comfortable. I hope at my return to find you here more composed and resigned. This is a season of bitter trial to us all. I know not how soon I may cut off now, setting off on a dangerous enterprise.'

Poor Parsons' words were prophetic. We never saw him more. He was fired at through a hedge and killed on the spot at a place called Tubbernur [*sic*], as he proceeded with his dispatch, and left his amiable young widow, to whom he had been married three or four months, to mourn his loss, which she did through the remainder of her life. Parsons was the son of a clergyman. He came to Wexford about a year before the rebellion. He taught the sabre exercise to all the yeomen cavalry, and was a general favourite with all who knew him.

I stopt for some days in Wexford & saw the miserable authors of all this carnage leading to execution, and almost the next minute beheld the reeking heads dropping crimson gore (upon the point of a pike) stuck up over the courthouse. The human heart was turned to stone at that time.

58 Charles Parsons of the Wexford Yeoman Cavalry was killed at Tubberneering in June 1798. He had married Henrietta Hughes the year before (*Ferns M.L.*; see Musgrave, 745).
59 Possibly Susanna Hewett, who married John Eustace of Wexford in 1784 (see Freemen, 121).

Unmoved I gazed upon these horrid spectacles. My great revenge had stomach for them all. These unfortunate men who nearly lost their influence with the rebels before their lives paid the just penalty due to their crimes, stood high in society, possessed estates which at that time were confiscated, & were considered good landlords & benevolent members of society. Thus, untimely and unpitied they fell almost as soon as the victims whom their murderous band led to the bridge. The four heads which were suspended over the courthouse were Bagnal Harvey's, Grogan's of Johnstown Castle, Capt'n Koagh's [Keugh's], who was a retired officer from the British Service, and an humble person named Kelly[60] from Killanne.

Capt'n Koagh [Keugh] was brother-in-law to Stephen Reynolds,[61] who was shot on Vinegar Hill & whose remains lie under a tombstone in Monart Cottage Lawn. Reynolds was truly a good man, kind-hearted and benevolent & indulgent to his tenants & dependents, a sincere Christian & devoted to the management of his land with the most persevering industry. He was neither an orangeman nor a yeoman, nor did he enter into any party broils. Yet with all these perfections of head and heart, he was torn from the bed to which he clung, for he held the bedpost firmly to resist them, & from which he was torn with brutal violence & thrown into a cart and taken to Vinegar Hill, & in the presence of Mrs Reynolds, deprived of life. O what were her feelings when she saw her beloved husband shot before her face & then thrown into the cart in which they were both conveyed there. They allowed her the privilege of taking his remains with her, and, with the assistance of a faithful servant maid they dug his grave and, according to his own directions, placed him in that spot where he shall remain until the last solemn trumpet shall call his murderers to judgment.

The faithful Peggy who assisted to make his grave was a Protestant. Perhaps her family suffered from the persecuting spirit of the enemy while they were killing poor Reynolds. They rifled the house of everything it contained. They carried off the clock, and made Mrs Reynolds wind it when the occasion required. The first interview I had with her after this awful event shall long be remembered by me. She said, 'Come with me and see where I have laid my dear Stephen.' I may add what bitter tears watered that spot hallowed by her sorrow. Her misery was sacred and could not be alleviated.

60 John Kelly of Killanne had played a prominent role at the battle of Ross, during which he had been wounded (Madden, 4:493). Before his head was displayed, it was kicked by soldiers along the quay in Wexford, allegedly near where Kelly's sister resided.   61 Stephen Reynolds of Monart married Catherine Bennett in 1774 (*Ferns M.L.*). He was shot on Vinegar Hill and buried at Monart. His widow claimed losses in 1799 of 'Cloaths, Cattle, Furniture [and] Plate" (Claimants, cccxi). Musgrave states that the husband of Catherine Reynolds of Monart was 'murdered at Enniscorthy' (Musgrave, 746). Stephen Reynolds is called the 'brother-in-law' of Matthew Keugh, but his precise relationship is not known.

It is now time I should mention my deserted patient, Pounder of Cooladine, whom I left bleeding & to appearance, mortally wounded. When he heard a retreat sounded, he raised himself up in bed & with great difficulty replaced his boots and stockings. An humble & humane friend took him under his care unperceived & concealed him on the roof of a house, where the eaves of the two houses met. The channel in the middle received our poor wounded Cavalry soldier and there, behold, without medicine or medical attendant, his wounds festered [and] gangrened. But a merciful providence led him through the valley of death and restored him to an affectionate family with whom he lived many years after this period. He always called me his deliverer. When first I saw him, after the restoration of law and order, great was my surprise for I thought he had been murdered at Mr Stephen Lett's, whose house had been burned soon after Pounder had been taken away. I asked myself 'Can this be his ghost risen from the dead to accuse his murderers?' His gratitude for the trifling service I had rendered him could only be equalled by my amazement at seeing him risen from the dead.

In narrating events connected with this melancholy period, I omitted one very striking passage which I shall now mention, tho' out of place. When the rebels were taking their victims to the bridge to be murdered, my father addressed Miss Good,[62] as he passed her door; she was looking out at her shop door, not knowing what was going forward. He said, 'Matty, behold me for the last time. They are going to murder me – and pray [for] me.' She turned into her parlour & falling on her knees, with uplifted hands, implored her heavenly father to have mercy on them who were fated to die. She seemed so long absorbed in fervent prayer, that her sisters endeavoured to restore her to herself, but poor Matty had suffered such a shock that she never recovered the wound it inflicted. Her intellect became impaired and her mind wandered so wildly that after much suffering on the part of her family from the various caprices of the complaint, they were obliged to remove her to an asylum, where she spent her remaining days, constantly calling on her dear Mr Daniel, whom she thought was continually hovering about her. My stepmother called at Swifts Hospital to see her after her removal there. She knew her perfectly well & conversed rationally for some time. She said my father's last look, his last words to her dwelt continually on her mind and could never be erased from her recollection. The Misses Good kept a grocer's shop near

---

62 Martha 'Matty' Good was perhaps the daughter of William Good, 'many years an eminent innkeeper', who died 22 Feb. 1789 (*Wexford Herald* cited in Freemen, 317). She may have been a cousin of Barbara Lett through her mother, as William Good married Elizabeth Pear in 1754 (*Ferns M.L.*). Among the claimants of 1799 is Hannah Good 'and company', grocers, of Wexford, who suffered losses at their residence and at Roes Park (Claimants, ccclxiii).

the Bull Ring. They were well connected & very much respected in Wexford. At their house Capt'n Jacob's[63] wife and son were concealed during the rebellion. I met them there and felt aware how great danger they stood in if discovered. During my stop at Williams' I heard every day vengeance pronounced against Capt'n Jacob. Various cruelties were to have been inflicted upon him if discovered. Fortunately, he took refuge in the fort of Duncannon with his valiant corps, and many years survived this awful period.

Thus ends a melancholy & faithful narrative of my sufferings during the rebellion of 1798, at which period I numbered 21 years, had been married four years previous to that time, and am now 82 years.

63 See Chapter 4, note 55. The name of Jacob's wife and son are not known.

6

ALICIA POUNDEN

Alicia, wife of John Pounden of Daphne, was born on 7 April 1772 at Ballywalter, a townland in the parish of Donaghmore, Co. Wexford. She was the only daughter of John Colley of Ballywalter and his second wife, Frances (Boyle). The origin of this Colley family remains in dispute. Simon L. M. de Montfort states that her father was the son of Thomas Colley of Balcarrack, Co. Wexford; yet David Goodall makes an excellent case for John being the probable son of William Colley of Ballywalter, who left a diocesan will at Ferns dated 1719.[1] John Colley was a prominent member of northern Co. Wexford's gentry and was among the freemen of Wexford who met to vote in 1776. Following the death of his first wife Alice on 23 May 1770, he married in June, 1771 the sixteen-year-old Frances Boyle. In an effort to improve the story, *Walker's Hibernian Magazine* had reported erroneously that he was aged eighty and his wife's name was 'Bolland'. When Colley died on 6 April 1777 at age seventy-six, daughter Alicia was his only child and the exclusive heir of the Ballywalter estate.

In 1786, Alicia married John Pounden of Daphne, parish of Monart, Co. Wexford. John's grandfather, an immigrant from Liege, France, had settled in Co. Wexford after 1734 and had voted in the election of 1753, though his right to do so was later challenged because of his Catholic parentage.[2] John's father, Patrick Pounden, married Jane Nunn, daughter of the Revd Joshua Nunn, rector of Whitechurch, Co. Wexford. The Nunns were a wealthy, liberal gentry family that was not disturbed during the Rebellion. Pounden's uncle owned a house in Enniscorthy that was used as a hospital during the attack on that town.

Pounden moved to Ballywalter upon his marriage, though the couple owned several estates in Co. Wexford where they maintained residences. They had six children: Mary, John Colley, Jane Marie, Revd Patrick, Fanny, and Joshua. As magistrates, he and his brother Joshua showed kindness to their Catholic tenants and allied themselves with the liberals on Catholic issues, a fact which sometimes made them a target of Orange

---

1 See Simon L. M. de Montfort's introduction, 'Mrs Pounden's Experiences During the 1798 Rising in Co. Wexford', *Irish Ancestor* 8 (1976):4. See also Freemen, 116. 2 See Freemen, 116; see also 'Pounden of Ballywalter House', *Burke's Landed Gentry of Ireland* (1912), 572.

propaganda.[3] Both men had also served in Solomon Richards' Enniscorthy Yeoman Cavalry, a unit known for its moderation in contrast to the notorious Vinegar Hill Rangers of Archie Jacob. John and Joshua fought with their corps in the defense of Enniscorthy on 28 May 1798, but were overwhelmed in the rebel attack. John fell in the fighting, and his body was stripped and desecrated by the rebel army.[4]

In 1799, Alicia submitted a claim for losses at her residence at Daphne, Tomduff and Sweet Farm, totalling £761, of which she recovered only £211. The losses included 'Cattle, Provisions, Wine, House, Meadow, Barley, and Furniture'.[5] She continued to reside in Co. Wexford and died at Ballywalter on 16 December 1861, aged eighty-nine years.

Written as a sketch for her grandchildren, the location of the original narrative is not presently known. A typescript version exists in the Public Record Office of Northern Ireland, and a variant was published in 1976.[6] Like Elizabeth Richards' diary, it reflects the views of a liberal gentry family in 1798, but like Jane Barber's narrative, it also records the conditions of Protestants in the wake of the battle of Enniscorthy, where liberals and conservatives alike suffered significant losses.

THE ACCOUNT

In this transitory life where every day evinces the uncertainty of our stay here, I would wish while time is allowed me to address some lines to my dear children, with the view of assisting them in bearing the innumerable trials and disappointments they may meet in this world.

The best plan I can pursue is to give a small sketch of my own life, which has been marked with the most trying events, but I have with humanity acknowledged the necessity of attaching my mind and thoughts to a better World, and at the same time learned in whatsoever state I am in, therewith to be content.

I was born with the brightest prospects. My Father, a most estimable character, was highly esteemed in the part of the country where he resided. He was married to a woman older than himself, whose unpleasing temper

---

3 See Whelan, 'Politicisation in Co. Wexford and the Origins of the 1798 Rebellion', 162.
4 For a description of John Pounden's death and the subsequent desecration of his body, see Chapter Five, 'Barbara Lett', note 14. 5 Claimants, ccccv. 6 A note in the *Irish Ancestor* 8 states that an original version of the manuscript was owned in 1976 by Miss Davida Beatty, a descendant of Mrs Pounden. This published version differs in a number of slight ways from a typescript in the Public Record Office of Northern Ireland (Manuscript T.720). The reason for this variation cannot be explained; one of the two versions appears to have been edited. Reprinted here is the previously published version; significant variations found in the typescript are added in brackets.

he bore with the most unwearied patience to her last moments. In some years after her heath he married my Mother, who by the goodness of her disposition atoned for the reverse of the former.

About a year after their marriage I was born. My Father was 72 years old at the time. He often said he did not wish to caress me too much for fear of attracting his mind too much from the Lord. He only lived till I was five years old, leaving me heiress to a property worth at least £15,000.

About the age of ten years, I was sent to Mrs Weekes' School, considered the best in Dublin. The example and precepts of this excellent teacher improved those principles instilled in my Mother. I was very unhealthy most of the time allotted to my education. I was beginning to grow strong and healthy, when I was removed to the country for vacation. My Mother was alone, living in a remote part of the country, and she delayed from one month to another sending me to school again.

Being on a visit about 12 miles from our residence, I met your Father, a young man 21 years old, possessed of extensive information and every accomplishment and engaging manner, calculated to attach any female. You may imagine how pleasing the attention and profession of affection from such a person, must be to a young mind which never felt even esteem for any man. I confess I never made the slightest objection to his proposals of marriage, for my heart informed me I could never feel another attachment.

My Mother, having a perfect knowledge of his character, was too wise to make my extreme youth an excuse for rejecting a match so suitable in every respect. When I think of the uninterrupted happiness in which we lived, I am sometimes inclined to think it was a dream, but it was a delightful reality which lasted 12 years, the first four of which I had no children, but during the last 8 years, had one child each year, two of whom died at 3 months old.

We had arrived at what I considered the highest summit of earthly happiness, blessed with children, fortune, increasing affection, at the same time beloved and respected by our neighbours of every description, when that dreadful spirit of rebellion diffused itself into the minds of the Roman Catholics, and shame to say some who were not of that profession joined in the bloodthirsty business, and at a time when they were taking the oath of allegiance to the King. It was only to lull the minds of the loyal inhabitants, and while hundreds were coming to your father saying he was milder than other magistrates, an express came from Enniscorthy to let him know that the town was surrounded by rebels. He did not lose a moment in going.

The State I was in cannot easily be imagined. I had a dreadful foreboding, which was too truly verified. The rebels, however, did not come that night. The inhabitants of the town and neighbourhood as well as the few military were under arms. The next morning, May 28th 1798, I was blessed with a sight of my beloved husband, who came to hurry me and my little infants to Enniscorthy, thinking we should be more safe there. I can never forget what I felt at leaving my sweet home. I told darling John we were like Adam and Eve driven out of Paradise.

Ah! never did I return to it till a widow and a beggar, for on Whitsun Monday the rebels did indeed come and were but too successful; they had more than 1000 men for every twenty of the loyalist party. My dearest John was amongst the first who fell and after about 3 hours engagement, the town was surrendered, the ammunition being all expended.

Most of the people fled to Wexford, some to Duncannon; the town of Enniscorthy was taken by those Butchers. I with my poor little children and their nurses got on the Wexford road through fields by the Slaney side, thinking myself fortunate to be able to get my little family out of so dreadful a place, not having an idea of my loss till I got to Wexford (a kind person having taken us part of the way in his car).

But what pen can do justice to my feelings when I heard the dreadful certainty of your Father's death? How much did I accuse myself for leaving Enniscorthy without a certainty of him, though my staying would have been to no purpose.

I walked most of the way with one of the young babes on my back, and when I arrived at the door of my Mother's house, and learned the extent of my misery, I fell into the hall, and was only preserved from being hurt by the kind friends who came to meet me; thence I was tenderly conveyed to bed. The children's maids were most attentive and were enabled to bring them all without accident, but we were not suffered to remain long in this place in quiet.

An alarm was raised that the rebels were coming into Wexford and everyone, who could go, was advised to get on a vessel that night. The following day we all went on board a vessel; I was so exhausted, I lay down on the ribs of the vessel (which was only a small one for conveying coals or timber), till roused by the crying of my children.

My anxiety about you had the good effect of recalling me to exertion; I assisted in tacking up some old linen my Mother had brought with her to change you, and felt a little relieved when I saw you clean and comfortable. We remained in the ship till Thursday, when parties of the Rebels went out in boats and took all the men prisoners, but told the females they should not be injured in honour of the Virgin Mary.

My first wish was to return to Enniscorthy, fearing that the body of my beloved husband might be exposed to insults. Accordingly I lost no time in setting off; and on arriving there had the melancholy satisfaction to find that John McGuire [McGuise], a tenant of ours, had the humanity to procure a coffin and had him interred in the Church-yard.

At Enniscorthy I did not know where to go, Mr Nunn's[7] house being made an hospital for wounded Rebels, his Glebe burned. I with my poor little babes stopped at McGuire's House that night; the following morning I thought the Rebels, who came in, looked particularly wicked at McGuire, and hinted something of his harbouring Heretics, which determined me not to remain another night. I then went out and found your Father's Uncle, Mr Nunn, and his sister, your Grandmother Pounden,[8] at the Priests' House (the house belonged to Mr Nunn). What a meeting!

The Priests of Enniscorthy, not taking part in the Rebellion, were afraid to remain in Enniscorthy, and Mr Nunn, being ill and confined to his bed, some of his parishioners came to him, and saying 'he had always been so easy with his Parishioners [about the tithe] they would do all in their power to prevent his being injured, which would happen, if he remained in his own house', carried him across the street to the above house [which belonged to him], where they [he with his sister (your grandmother)] remained during the Rebellion. He and his family were scarcely removed from his house [glebe], till it was converted into a hospital for wounded Rebels.

When I found those dear relatives, you may imagine what a sorrowful meeting we had. I found shelter there for some days, but even that we were not allowed to enjoy; women constantly coming in, and abusing us for filling up the Priests' house, and calling us Orange people.

In short, everything combined to make our stay there so dreadful that, in a kind of forlorn hope, I went to beg an asylum in my house at Daphne, which was rather reluctantly granted; however, that was no time for ceremony; the Town being set on fire, at every entrance the number of cattle etc. that were burned and people killed, made the atmosphere so offensive, and even affected the taste and smell of the water to such an excess, any place was preferable. The house and offices were full of Rebels, but I was glad to get in on any terms, as I always endeavoured to submit without repining to the Will of the Almighty.

7 Revd Joshua Nunn III, the uncle of John Pounden, was born in 1732, the son of Revd Joshua Nunn II, Prebendary of Coulstuffe, and his wife Mary Hodginkinson, widow (Leslie, 64, 150). He belonged to one of Co. Wexford's wealthiest landed families. Entering Trinity College Dublin in 1750, he received his B.A. in 1754, served as Rector of Killanne, 1766–74, and was a resident of Castle Ellis in 1778. A political liberal, he remained neutral in 1798, was widely respected for his humanity, and was not harmed by the rebels (Whelan, 'Religious Factor in the 1798 Rebellion', 75). In 1799, he reported losses of furniture, houses, cattle, and plate, totalling over £2,600 (Claimants, cccxcix). He died on 22 Apr. 1802.
8 Jane Nunn, daughter of Revd Joshua Nunn II and wife Mary (Hodginkinson), and sister of Revd Joshua Nunn III of Enniscorthy, married Patrick Pounden of Daphne and was the mother of Col. John Pounden and Col. Joshua Pounden. Barbara Lett states that she was fired upon and killed by British troops in Enniscorthy, who mistook her for a rebel when she rushed out to greet them (see Chapter Five, note 18).

[About a fortnight after we were rescued from our perilous position by the arrival of a powerful Army. Everyone has heard of the 'battle of Vinegar Hill' so that I need not refer to it – but I had still another trial to endure on that day. Your grandmother Pounden came to the door to endeavour to save any attack on the Priest's house – a cannon ball from a great distance killed her on the spot.]

I had a kind nurse, who came and took most of my little children; the eldest boy John Colley I kept with me; he and his dear Father were so mutually attached I felt a greater degree of pity for him. The first day when walking out to Daphne[9] I had him by the hand, a shot was fired. I don't know whether by accident or design the ball rolled quite close to us, but did no injury.

When I arrived at my once happy home, the servants made my room as comfortable as in their power, but there was a family who took up their abode there, who professed great kindness, but who I found most annoying – they were so dirty in their habits. The first night I went, they had a dance and fiddle, the sounds of which were most distressing to me; the servants said it was cruel, just as the poor Mistress had come, but the women of the before mentioned family said: – 'if she does not like it, we will turn her out;' indeed these were amongst the few instances where any incivility was offered, as the numerous persons who were assembled at my place during the Rebellion, were particularly respectful and said that no one would ever have [wilfully] injured Mr Pounden, if he had not been killed in the battle.

I began to think that the Rebels would keep possession of the Parts of the Country they occupied for ever, when a strange Man came into the place where I was, and implored a bit of any kind of food. He said: 'I have been going with them ever since it began, and have worn out my clothes and shoes without being better, but a great deal worse'. He then said they had been beaten at a battle at Arklow, one in Borris and one at Ross, which was the most severe of all. And they were soon beginning to find that, let the result be what it would, the poor would be poor still.

This was the first hope of any change. A few days after a Shopkeeper from Enniscorthy, who was a favourer of the Rebels, came in the middle of the night, saying in a deep sepulchral voice: – 'Get up, get up, the Enemy's at hand'. Upon which, the numerous persons, who were placed to guard the House, were off in a few minutes.

I must observe there was a proclamation written in very large characters put up in the Hall, just opposite the door, to the following effect: – 'As this House and Demesne have been surrendered for the use of the Republic, it

9 Daphne Castle was a large, Gothic structure, with a circular main block and two wings, each with bays. The house fell into ruins and was demolished in the 1960s (see 'Daphne Castle' in Walsh, *100 Wexford Country Houses*, 46).

is requested, that no person will do any injury'. Signed Father Murphy,[10] Father Roche,[11] Father Kearns,[12] Thos. Clancy, Col.; Morgan Byrne,[13] Capt.; Dan Flaherty, Capt.; with a long list of other signatures, which I do not recollect.

On the 20th of June, the Ross Road provided a most brilliant appearance; as far as the eye could extend from Daphne was crowded with troops of every description, cannon, ammunition, sumpter carts, and all things necessary for 4 or 5000 men. When they arrived the Pioneers pulled down sufficient of the demesne wall to allow them to march in with all their artillery, cavalry, etc. From the situation of the lawn nothing could exceed the magnificent appearance of such an array, when they formed into the most exact order on the ground, and at the same time such a contrast to the dirty ragged creatures we had been accustomed to for the last three weeks.

By the way, when the rebels were going to fight the battle of Vinegar Hill, they left two sheep roasting in the court at Daphne for their refreshment after the battle, but the Hessians came and ate them instead.[14]

[Daphene House being built in the Castle style] the two Gothic entrance gates were soon guarded by two of Hompuck's Hessians,[15] who showed the greatest humanity to me and my children. My dear little John was so gratified by their kindness and stopped a great part of the day with them.

The Army, on sending out reconnoitring parties, met members of Rebels running to offer them battle, but they drove them back and did not engage till the following day, when two armies of 4000 each marched from opposite directions, so that on 21st June they all surrounded Vinegar Hill, and had the opportunity of killing every one of them. But Humanity triumphed and the orders were issued 'to disperse but not kill'. There was an opening left to them, and not more than 2000 were slain in the Battle.

When the Army marched off the next day, it is impossible to describe the desolate appearance of everything around. The numbers of men,

---

10 Fr John Murphy of Boolavogue (see Chapter Two, note 7).   11 Fr Philip Roche (see Chapter One, note 38).   12 Fr Mogue Kearns was born at Kiltealy on the Blackstairs Mountains in Co. Wexford. He was a large man and because of his strength, he was well-known as a hurler. He was ordained to the priesthood in 1785 and sent to a mission on the Kildare-Meath border. Here he developed an association with the Defenders, which led to his suspension by Bishop Delaney. He returned to Co. Wexford, but was denied a parish by Bishop Caulfield, who later claimed that Kearns was 'notorious for drinking and fighting' (Caulfield-Troy Correspondence, Troy Papers). He became involved with several rural pursuits, including grouse shooting, and befriended Fr John Murphy. He joined the Rebellion at its beginning and played a prominent role at the battle of Enniscorthy. After retreating to Kildare in June, he was later arrested with Anthony Perry and executed at Edenderry, 12 Jul. 1798.   13 See Chapter Three, note 16.   14 This paragraph does not appear in the PRONI version.   15 Hompesch's German Hessians (see Chapter Two, notes 23, 26).

Horses, cannon, that had been on the Lawn for two days completely burnt up the grass; then the Demesne wall thrown down in several places, but above all the complete absence of every person except a couple of female servants, rendered it utterly cheerless, and as Wexford was not out of the Rebel Possession, I went with my little family to my Mother's [house], where I remained about six months, during which time I added another son to my Stock, who from the agitations and perils I endured, was afflicted with severe fits.

Your Uncle[16] came for me, and I with my two eldest children accompanied him to his House in Dublin, where his attention and that of his wife was most kindly extended towards us.

And I have been most wonderfully enabled to bear the various trials to which I have been exposed. I mention these few circumstances of my life to shew that with a firm reliance on Divine Providence, we are enabled to bear, what the very idea of would be worse than death, assuredly believing that all things work together for our good, and that had I remained in the uninterrupted state of happiness, I might have been too much attached to this world to wish for a better.[17]

16 Col. Joshua Pounden (see Chapter Three, note 5).   17 A note at the end of the PRONI version states: 'Extracts from the Life of Mrs Alicia Pounden, copied by the widow of her grandson the late John Colley Pounden of Ballywalter, son of the Revd. Patrick Pounden, rector of Westport & who died at Ballywalter Dec. 1861 in full assurance of everlasting life through the merits of the Saviour she loved & served.'

7

MRS 'M'

'Mrs M' is a pseudonym given to an anonymous writer, whose account is cited in the appendix of Sir Richard Musgrave's *Memoirs of the Different Rebellions in Ireland*. Musgrave gives no clue as to her identity, except to say that she was a 'respectable gentlewoman, who remained the entire night of Monday, the twenty-eighth of May, 1798, in Ringwood'. The initial M was, according to Musgrave, 'not really the initial letter of her name, which I conceal, lest it might expose her to rebel vengeance'. The account describes the conditions at the estate of William Bennett at Bormount, near Enniscorthy, Co. Wexford, as well as the rebel camp at Vinegar Hill before the British assault. It is obviously part of a much-longer narrative, which apparently does not survive.

THE ACCOUNT

Mr Bennett,[1] of Birmount, lay concealed in the wood that night. Next morning, about seven o'clock, when we were almost sinking with cold and hunger, he kindly invited us to his house, which lay close to the river Slaney, at the opposite side of it. Having gone there, about seven o'clock in the evening, a woman came to us, trembling with fear, and said, 'That the the rebels were approaching in all directions to burn the house, and to murder us'. Mr Bennett hid himself in his garden. We were advised to get some green boughs, as the emblem of rebellion, and to go out to meet them; and having accordingly done so, they desired us not to be frightened, as they never injured women; and they asked us if we were christians (meaning Roman Catholics,) and very fortunately we told them we were. They informed us, that they had just killed Mr Edward White[2] of Roxana, and his son, who lived near Vinegar-hill, having, as they said, searched his house for arms and Orangemen. Having found Mr M in the garden, they

1 William Bennett of Bormount, the son of Parsons Bennett, was an extensive landholder and a liberal (see Freemen, 111). He was admitted Freeman of Enniscorthy on 29 Sep. 1782. In 1799, he claimed losses, including 'Cattle, [a] Saddle and Fire Arms', for which he received nothing (Claimants, cccxxiii).　2 Musgrave states in his appendix that Edward White senior, and Edward White junior, both of St John's, Roxana, were murdered at home (Musgrave, 753). Edward Sr. married Elizabeth Hardy in 1763 (*Ferns M.L.*).

presented their firelocks, and were on the point of shooting him; but said they must suspend his execution till their officer, who was absent, arrived. They took him off, mounted behind one of them; when they galloped off speedily to Vinegar-hill camp, and procured him a protection from father John Murphy, who was then commander in chief there.

On Thursday I went to Vinegar-hill, in hopes of getting a protection from father Philip Roche,[3] a rebel chieftain, and in our way thither, we saw the bodies of Mr White and his son, lying dead and naked in the lawn before his house; for the rebels would not suffer them to be buried.

In our way to Enniscorthy, we saw twelve dead bodies lying on the road; and on entering the town, we were filled with horror at beholding a great number of them in the streets.

The camp at Vinegar-hill presented a dreadful scene of confusion and uproar. A number of female rebels, more vehement than the male, were marching out to meet the army from Newtown-barry. This was a large body which father Roche led from Vinegar-hill to the attack of that town, which took place the first of June. Great numbers of women were in the camp. Some men were employed in killing cattle, and in boiling them in pieces in large copper brewing pans; others were drinking, cursing, and swearing; many of them were playing on various musical instruments, which they had acquired by plunder in the adjacent protestant houses; and this procured a most disagreeable and barbarous dissonance.

At last I met father Roche in Enniscorthy, and he gave me a protection, not only for Mr M, but one for Mr Bennett's house, in the following words, which was posted up in the hall: 'No man to molest this house, or its inhabitants, on pain of death!'

However, next day, a rebel guard came to Mr Bennett's, and compelled him and Mr M to go before the parish priest of Bree, in order to send them to the attack on Ross; but Mr Devereux,[4] a rebel captain, on seeing Roche's protection discharged him; and soon after father John Sutton[5] of Enniscorthy, and a Mr William Barker,[6] a rebel general, gave them protections, and certified that they had been tried by a court-martial and acquitted.

We then repaired to Mr Joshua Lett's,[7] a mile beyond Enniscorthy, where we stayed some days. During our residence there, we daily saw great

3 See Chapter One, note 38. 4 Walter Devereux of Ballybrittas, a rebel captain, was executed at Cork in November, 1798 (see Dickson, 109, 120, 170; Cloney, 41). 5 Fr John Sutton served as curate of Enniscorthy from 1789 to 1801. He remained bitterly opposed to the Rebellion, and according to Thomas Handcock, attempted to offer protection to as many Protestants as he could (Handcock, 125). He went to Vinegar Hill with Fr Michael Lacy in an effort to gain the release of some Protestant prisoners (Whelan, 'Catholic Priest in the 1798 Rebellion', 310). He was the sole witness against James Beaghan in the murder of the Revd Samuel Heydon, which led to Beaghan's conviction and execution (Ibid., 311). As a result, he was ostracized until his death in 1832. 6 See Chapter Three, note 12. 7 Joshua Lett of Killaligan was the father of Stephen Lett and Newton Lett (see p. 106). He was

crowds of rebels, who often boasted of the number of protestants they had put to death, and even in what manner they had piked them. They said that Cork and Limerick had capitulated to them; that Dublin was surrounded by forty thousand United Irishmen; that the whole kingdom would soon be in their possession; and that there should be no other religion but the Roman Catholic. They compelled us to go to mass, which we did to preserve our lives.

At last, the rebels, having discovered that Mr M was concealed in Mr Joshua Lett's house, threatened to demolish it, unless he was instantly dismissed. As Mr Lett was obliged to comply with this mandate, we repaired to Mr Fitzhenry's[8] of Ballymacus, about five miles off. In our way thither, we met many parties of rebels, who would have put Mr M to death, but for the priest's protection; for which they showed the utmost respect. This shows the great influence of the sacerdotal order, and how easily they might have prevented the massacres of protestants.

We were there but a few hours, when a rebel guard arrived, and carried us back to Enniscorthy, where Mr M was put into a guard-house, containing about a dozen unfortunate protestants, who were shot or piked next day in the camp. I was then desired to apply to one of their officers, named Morgan Byrne,[9] whom I found sitting in their committee-room, at a long table, with many books and papers before him. Father Kearns[10] was at the head of the table, round which all the members of the committee sat. On representing my situation, and that of Mr M, Mr Patrick Sutton,[11] who was a general among them, said he would do his utmost to serve Mr M. and me; and Mr Morgan Byrne said he 'would spare his life, provided he would join and fight with them; but on no other condition'.

Unheard-of barbarities were committed at Enniscorthy, Vinegar-hill, and in all the adjacent country, before the rebels were subdued and driven from them. The pikemen would often show us their pikes all stained with blood, and boast of having murdered our friends and neighbours.

---

described by Thomas Cloney as 'a most particular friend of my father's and mine, and, although a Protestant, [went] with great composure to hear mass' (Cloney, 52). In 1799, he testified at Cloney's trial on his behalf (Ibid., 273). His claim for losses of 'Cattle, Crop, [and] Furniture' was rejected, probably because of this friendship (Claimants, ccclxxxvii). 8 William Fitzhenry of Ballymackessy, gentleman, was admitted Freeman of Enniscorthy on 24 June 1774 (Hore, 6:543). He belonged to a family of Catholic middlemen (see Whelan, 'Catholic Community in Eighteenth Century Co. Wexford', 138). William's son Jeremiah was active among the exiled United Irishmen in France (see Elliott, *Partners in Revolution*, 335, 550–2). 9 See Chapter Three, note 16. 10 Fr Mogue Kearns (see Chapter Six, note 11). 11 Patrick Sutton, maltster, and his brother Matthew, an attorney, were among the most prominent Catholics of Enniscorthy (see Cullen, 297). As a general in the United army, Patrick Sutton attempted to bring to task those rebels 'committing outrages on the wives and daughters of several persons' and ordered his officers to bring those found guilty to the camp at Vinegar Hill (Musgrave, 344).

8

JANE ADAMS

Jane Adams née Owen of Summerseat, Wexford, was born about 1753, probably in Dublin. Like Mrs Brownrigg, she belonged to the professional middleman class, a rank just above the large farmer status of the Letts, but below that of the landed gentry. On 9 January 1773, she married the Reverend Tobias Adams in Dublin, possibly at St Michan's or St Catherine's.[1] Adams served at the time as vicar of Templebodan and Clondulane in Co. Cork, where he and Jane had three children: a son Charles, who served in the army and later became a clergyman; and two daughters: Letitia and Susan, born ten years apart. The latter was a youth at the time of the rebellion. Some time before 1798, for unknown reasons, Jane became estranged from her husband and moved with her daughters to her father's house at Summerseat, a few miles south of Wexford. Her date of death is unknown, but she was apparently still living in 1823, when the following narrative was first published.

The best-known member of Jane's family was her brother, the Reverend Roger Owen, who became Prebendary of Tombe in Co. Wexford. As a clerical magistrate and an outsider, he was much-despised for his conservative views and his advocacy of pitchcapping Irish convicts. Out of revenge, the United army at Gorey took him prisoner in 1798, pitchcapped him, and then suspended him outside the top story window of the market-house there. The experience drove him to the point of insanity. However, the persistent intervention of his sister with United army officials led them to release Owen into her custody and thus spared his almost certain death on Wexford Bridge.

Completed some time after 1801, Jane Adams's account may have been based, at least in part, on a narrative written at the time of the rebellion, apparently as part of a lengthy letter to a friend. As with Mrs Brownrigg's

---

1 See James Leslie, 'Biographical Succession List of the Clergy of Dublin Diocese', (Typescript, Representative Church Body Library, Dublin), 340; see also W. Maziere Brady, *Clerical and Parochial Records of Cork, Cloyne, and Ross* (London: Longman, Green, 1863), 2:16. Tobias Adams was the son of Robert Adams of Dublin. He was educated by a Revd Mr Ball, entered Trinity College in 1762, and was licenced as a curate in 1767. He served as curate of St Michan's, Dublin, 1769–71, until obtaining the degree of A.M. Afterwards, he was vicar of Templebodan (Cloyne), 1771–96; vicar of Clondulane, 1772–96; vicar of Ahern and rector of Bretway, 1796–1805. He died in 1805 and was buried at Cloyne Cathedral, 23 Jan. 1805.

account, it reflects the attitudes of her class, but what is more surprising, it is not excessively bigoted. Indeed, despite the conservative views of her brother, Jane appears to have treated her Catholic neighbours with humanity, writing letters of protection, befriending the local parish priest, inviting a hungry woman to dinner, and offering aid to refugees. In this light, Jane's narrative has particular historical importance, not only for illustrating the differences in attitudes toward Catholics within some Protestant families and possibly between men and women, but also documenting the kindnesses and humanity sometimes shown by United army soldiers in contrast to some rebel women.

This narrative first appeared in print in 1823, when it was included in T. Crofton Croker's *Researches in the South of Ireland*.[2] Croker noted that the account 'was written without any view to publication, and was transmitted to me by its amiable writer, to whom many thanks are due for the kind and friendly manner in which she granted me permission to insert it in this work'. Well-known for having bowdlerized his edition of Joseph Holt's work, Croker also took some liberties with this narrative, changing the original sentence structure in many instances, eliminating some clauses, modifying grammar, and inserting short clauses of his own.[3] Published here for the first time is the original, unaltered version from the British Library. It is not apparently written in Jane's hand, but was copied by an unknown third party. A few lengthy passages from the Croker version are included here and appear in brackets, since it remains unclear whether they were written by Croker or added later by Jane Adams.

THE ACCOUNT

Summerseat, Co. Wexford
May, 1798

My dear friend,

I fear we are in a most alarming situation. We have just had dreadful accounts from Naas – the rebels have defeated and killed Captain Swayne,[4]

---

2 T. Crofton Croker, *Researches in the South of Ireland*, 2nd ed. (Shannon, Ireland: Irish University Press, 1969), 347–385. The original manuscript, reprinted here, is housed in the British Library as Ms. 21,142. It contains 63 pages and was acquired in 1855 from C. Hamilton, a dealer, who purchased it from Croker's estate.   3 See Joseph Holt, *Memoirs of Joseph Holt: General of the Irish Rebels*, ed. by T. Crofton Croker (London: H. Colburn, 1838). See also Ruan Donnell and Bob Reece, 'A Clean Beast: Crofton Croker's Fairy Tale of General Holt', *Eighteenth Century Ireland* 7 (1992):7–42.   4 Captain Swayne of Youghall, an Orangeman, headed the City of Cork Militia and was described by Pakenham as 'a zealous Protestant' (Pakenham, 113). He walked into a local chapel and threatened Catholics to surrender their arms, adding that 'If you don't have it done, I'll pour boiling lead down your throat' (Swayne quoted in William Farrell, *Carlow in '98: The Autobiography of William*

of Youghall. Nancy Owen[5] writes me word that there are hundreds giving up arms and pikes, but that the country wears an almost alarming appearance. My Father laughs at the idea of danger; but I strongly suspect we are surrounded by rebels and spies. Yesterday, rather a genteel looking young man came up the lawn to me, and said he wished much to have the pleasure of instructing a few young ladies in geography &c. &c., and hoped I would allow him to put down my name. I told him my daughters were too young, and that I did not think he was likely to get any one in the neighbourhood. This day, as I was walking in the shrubbery that looks into the road, on hearing a number of horses, I looked out and saw this very same young man under an escort taking to jail on information sent to Mr Boyd[6] from government! There was found about him a plan of all our houses, the names and numbers in each, and the Pamphlet of 'Paine's Age of Reason'. Mrs Harvey,[7] our near neighbour, has got a guard to sleep at Killeen Castle;[8] we supped with her last night, and there was an express sent for the gentleman who commanded the party. – My father remains incredulous!

Whit-Sunday May. – Just returned from church. In our way there, we met the Wexford Cavalry escorting Mr Cogely[9] and Mr Bagnal Harvey to jail; they are both gentlemen of good fortune in this barony. What a task for Captain Boyd! men in whose houses he was in the habits of intimacy. Where will all this end? I want my father to come to Dublin, but he seems determined neither to see or hear that. While at church Mr Bevan[10] hurried over the communion Service and told us he was not without his fears that we should be surrounded by Rebels while at the communion table! I am told the whole country is up. Mr Bevan saw the Smiths openly

Farrell of Carlow, ed. by Roger McHugh [Dublin: Browne and Nolan, 1949], 224). He was killed in his room at Naas by a party of four rebels, who later burned his body in a barrel of tar.   **5** Anne, daughter of Loftus Cliffe of Bellevue, New Ross by his wife Anne Hore, was born 2 Feb. 1764. She married Revd Roger Owen, brother of Jane (Owen) Adams, on 1 May 1783 (Leslie, 96; 'Cliffe of Bellevue', *Burke's Landed Gentry of Ireland* [1912], 116). She was evidently nicknamed 'Nancy' and was termed as such in Roger Owen's letter (see later). She died on 23 Feb. 1844, aged 80, and is buried beside her husband at Camolin (Cantwell, *Memorials of the Dead*, vol. 5 [North Wexford], 176).   **6** Captain James Boyd of the Wexford Yeoman Calvary (see Chapter Four, note 50).   **7** Dorothy, daughter of Loftus Cliffe and his wife Anne Hore, and sister of Anne (Cliffe) Owen, was born 2 Jan. 1756. She married, in 1772 (*Ferns M.L.*), John Harvey of Killiane Castle, High Sheriff of Wexford (see 'Cliffe of Bellevue', *Burke's Landed Gentry of Ireland* [1912], 116; see also *Wexford Gentry*, 74). **8** Killiane Castle, the seat of the Harvey family.   **9** John Henry Colclough (see Chapter One, note 7).   **10** Revd Richard Bevan was born in 1759 in Co. Cavan. He entered Trinity College Dublin in 1775, receiving his B.A. in 1779 and his doctorate in 1781. He was curate of Killinick, 1781–1798, and vicar and later rector of Carne, 1798 to 1842. He married Charlotte, daughter of William Mussenden of Larchfield, Co. Down and had several children. He died at Carne, 23 May 1842 aged eighty-three, and was buried in the Carne churchyard (Leslie, 126; Cantwell, *Memorials of the Dead*, vol. 7 [South-east], 289). His tombstone states that he was curate of Killinick under Revd Benjamin Adams, who is not otherwise identified.

at work making pikes as he rode to church, though Whit-Sunday. In my way home we met Mrs Percival's[11] carriage, the coachman driving furiously would scarcely wait to tell us that he had left some of the children in Wexford, and that he was returning for his Mistress and the rest; that an express had arrived in Wexford saying there were seven thousand rebels within 3 miles of the Town. I will continue to write & collect all for to-morrow's Post. Mr Percival & many others are getting off to England, caring little for accomodation if they can get any kind of boat. This is truly alarming. Mr Perceval is high sheriff! The North Cork are sent for, & all the Yeomen & Cavalry to rout the rebels. In vain do I implore my father even to come to Wexford.

Whit-Sunday Evening. Every moment becomes more frightful. An account has just arrived to say the North Cork are all put to death by the Rebels in an engagement. The unfortunate Soldiers' wives are screaming through the streets of Wexford & that every creature that appears is put under arms. The thatch is stripped off the houses in the suburbs of the town, that Enniscorthy is burnt & the inhabitants are pouring into Wexford! Women of fortune, half-dressed, some without shoes or stockings, with their children on their backs & in their arms, many without a stitch but their under petticoats, endeavouring in this state to get on board ship. There never was a more dreadful scene that Wexford at this moment exhibits. I am assured that but four out of the North Cork have escaped the fury of the Rebels. One hundred have been put to death! Major Lombard,[12] whom I think you knew, has fallen. I am told the post cannot proceed, the roads to Dublin are all occupied with Rebels. Captain Boyd has sent for the 13th Regiment to Waterford. Thank heaven I wrote to poor Mr Adams[13] and Letty Kynaston yesterday. What dreadful anxiety they must be in!

Whit-Monday. – A report to day that the 13th are taken prisoners by the Rebel army, and that Mr Coguely and Mr B. Harvey have been sent to the Rebel camp to compromise with its leaders – a compromise with Rebels seems strange to me! So far I had written last Tuesday – what I have suffered since I cannot describe. On Wednesday the Army and all the Loyalists fled. We saw them on the hill to the left of our house. Can you believe it? My father[14] still perseveres in making light of it; ordered his

11 Mary, daughter of Robert Woodcock of Killowen and widow of Ralph Evans, married, on 31 Oct. 1788, Edward Perceval of Barntown (1763–1809), High Sheriff of Co. Wexford in 1798 and an Ogle partisan (see Chapter Four, note 46). She died 8 Nov. 1803 (see 'Perceval of Barntown', Burke's *Landed Gentry of Ireland* [1912], 558).   12 Major Thomas Lombard (see Chapter Four, note 14).   13 A reference to her husband, Revd Tobias Adams, rector of Bretway, Co. Cork. The nature of their relationship is unclear. They appear to have been estranged from one another as husband and wife, but still corresponded occasionally. 14 The identity of Jane's father, Mr Owen, remains unclear. The family was perhaps related to Rowland Owen, a wine merchant of 24 Moore Street, Dublin, and a Freeman of Wexford

horses, and would have rode into the Town, but for some ladies that were flying from it, who assured him the Rebels were in full possession!

Whilst he was away, I had his bed & what things of value I could collect, sent on a car to the strand, where Hayes, our gardener, went to procure a boat. We fortunately had a good deal of cold meat, which with a basket of wine & a small cask of brandy, I sent off in the hope of prevailing on my Father to leave the house & try to get on board ship. We saw several vessels lying-to. My strong desire to get to England enabled me to be a little preemptory to my Father when he returned. Poor man! he seemed quite subdued and thunderstruck! We got into a boat & many of the peasantry, strangers to me, forced their way into it. When we got off a little, we found it impossible to get to a ship & were advised by our gardener who rowed us, with another of our servants (neither of whom had ever rowed before,) to make for an Island a few miles of us & at least remain there till we could get some further intelligence of affairs in Wexford.

Whilst debating on this subject we saw a boat sailing towards us full of men with green boughs in their hats, and a white handkerchief displayed as a Rebel flag. They soon got up to us, and said if we would go home and turn Christians, we should be safe enough. This speech conveyed enough; I thought I should have fainted, but was soon roused by their vociferations to put back – to return – that all was peace and liberty – that they had chaired Dr Jacob[15] – that he was *their* Mayor. I begged, however, to prefer the liberty of the island till the first fury of the Mob abated & my Father consented, but a Mr and Mrs Woodcock,[16] who were with us, said they would return.

We soon landed at our Island, and there I found many of the peasantry who had made their escape at the early part of the day. We had brought plenty of cold provisions with us, and as those poor people had contrived to light a fire, and were boiling their potatoes, which they seemed most heartily to enjoy, but alas we were not so well off. The servant who had a Basket of Bread & wine was knocked down in his way to the boat & I had

in 1776. He left a prerogative will in Dublin dated 1785 (see Freemen, 451).   15 Dr Ebenezer Jacob, Wexford mayor and Captain of the Wexford Yeoman Infantry (see Chapter Four, note 24). The reference to Jacob being 'chaired' reflects the induction ceremony to the mayor's office, whereby he was carried through the streets in a chair. Because of his liberal politics, Jacob remained unpopular with many. Jane's depiction of him as a rebel collaborator differs markedly from Mrs Brownrigg's impression of benevolent benefactor.   16 The identities of Mr and Mrs Woodcock are unknown (see note 8). They were not among the claimants of 1799. Goodall states that the Woodcocks 'were a well-known, mainly Quaker, family in co. Wexford at this time' (Freemen, 463). Robert Woodcock of Killowen, banker, was presumably the son of Robert of Killowen, who left a diocesan will in Ferns dated 1776 (Ibid., see also C. M. Tenison, 'The Private Bankers of Cork and the South of Ireland', *Cork Historical Journal* 2 [1893]:137). He was admitted a Freeman of Enniscorthy in 1769 (Hore, vi:542). William Woodcock of Lambstown voted with the Freemen of Wexford in 1776.

neither for my Father. Night was now approaching; where to place his bed was my next object: there was scarcely a bush on the Island. But a friendly thorn tree enabled me to throw a temporary curtain over his bed, which he went into thanking God with as much devotion as if lying down in his best bedchamber. I put my two dear children at one side of him and sat at the other to keep the clothes over him. I was soon roused from every thought but present danger. I heard the dashing of oars and a whispering among the people. I had hoped we were in security at least till morning, as they all told me no one could land till the tide was full in; but what was my horror when the oars ceased, and, by the dim light, I saw a man walking towards me. I jumped up, he seized me by my arm. I could scarcely breathe with terror, when poor Hayes said, 'Don't be afraid Madam! It is I – happy am I that you are here; it was scarcely night when a party of rebels came to the House[17] & fired several shots over the hall door, insisted on admittance, went up to all the bed-rooms in search of arms and said if I concealed an Orangeman they would have my life. They then swore me into their gang & brought me to give them up every thing they wished to take. They carried away all the bacon pigs, broke open the cellar door & took the wine & rum away. Such a wreck as they have made of the place, Madam, they had six carts with them. It is dreadful, Madam! I could scarcely prevail on them to let me remain after them'.

You may think how happy I felt at this temporary escape, tho' almost the moment before I had reproached myself when looking at my dear Father asleep on the *ground*. I begged our faithful Hayes to return & try to save what he could & come for us in the morning. I saw the impossibility of remaining where there was no shelter of any kind.

'I will, Madam, but' –

'What, Hayes? Speak out!'

'Why, Madam, they did say, they would come in the morning and burn the House!'

He then pointed to many distant fires. I really felt as if my head would burst in considering what was best to be done. At length I determined on his returning, making him promise to come early as he could. My father did not awaken till six in the morning; his two companions kept pace with him and slept all night. I told him of Hayes's having been with me & that I expected his return every moment; that I feared we could do nothing but go back to Summerseat, if it had not shared the same fate of several houses in the country.

All chance of getting a vessel to take us to Wales was over: some of the unfortunate people who thought themselves happy in making their escape

---

17 Dickson states that Summerseat has since been renamed Somerset House and is located three miles south of Wexford town (Dickson, 44, 224). It is still standing and privately owned.

were brought back to Wexford & delivered up to the Rebels. The large and respectable family of Killane Castle would have been put into the common jail *only* had there been room for them. They were put into an old House with a guard placed over them, & the first sight they saw in the Bull-square (a square so-called in Wexford) were kitchen tables & carpenters at work on them making pike handles. Mrs Cliffe[18] since told me that the captain's wife came on deck a little after they had got on board, with a brace of pistols in the belt of her gown, swaggered up & down the deck saying she hoped to be up to her knees in Protestant blood before night!.[19]

But to return to our own distresses. My father bore my intelligence astonishingly and agreed to return the moment Hayes came for us. The poor fellow lost no time when the tide answered, & he brought us word that the house was not burned nor had any one returned to it.

We got once more into the boat. When we reached near enough the shore to discern objects, we discovered hundreds of rebels, and on a nearer view, saw they were all armed. I begged Hayes to turn back to the Island and must here acknowledge it was my impious hope that the boat might upset & end all our cares together. I had soon reason to adore that Providence I had dared for a moment to distrust. They called out to us to land! Almost petrified with horror, I looked at my poor Father & then at my children, expecting the moment we landed we should be put to death. Hayes endeavoured to quiet my fears, with a countenance full of horror as my own: but what was my surprise when the moment I got out of the boat, a man came up & shook hands with me & desired me not to be frightened; that he was Captain Butler,[20] & would protect me as long as he could; that he would order a serjeant's guard home with me.

'I know you very well; I was coachman to Mrs Percival, and you were very kind to me the last day she went to see you; you ordered me a good draft of porter'.

He then turned round to choose our guard. They were all contending for rank, were all wielding pistols & blunderbusses in the most vociferous manner. I expected every moment the contents would be lodged in our heads from accident if not design. They at length fixed on the guard to attend us home; one calling himself *captain*; another that he was *head* Lieutenant; and in mock procession they marched towards Summerseat

18 Anne, daughter of William Hore of Harperstown, married in 1755 (*Ferns M.L.*) Col. Loftus Cliffe. She died in March, 1814, aged eighty-three, leaving one son, Lt.-Gen Walter Cliffe, and three daughters: Dorothy, wife of John Harvey of Killiane Castle; Barbara, wife of John Stanford of Born, Co. Cavan; and Anne, wife of Revd Roger Owen ('Cliffe of Bellevue', *Burke's Landed Gentry of Ireland* [1912], 116. 19 Probably a reference to Margery, wife of Capt. Thomas Dixon (see Chapter Four, note 20). This depiction of Mrs Dixon affirms Mrs Brownrigg's description. 20 Possibly Lawrence Butler, a rebel captain in Co. Wexford (see Whelan, 'The Religious Factor in the 1798 Rebellion in Co. Wexford', 72).

with us; but before we were half way, I found myself unable to proceed & begged to stop at my neighbour's, Mrs Woodcock's, who had at first accompanied us part of the way to the Island. When we were near her house they left us to join a party they saw at a distance.

When we arrived at Mr Woodcock's, we found them all in the greatest consternation & dismay; they had been up all night at the mercy of several parties of the rebels, who came repeatedly, insisting on examining every part of the House & possessing themselves of everything they chose to take. The moments Mrs Woodcock had to herself she employed in hiding flour, and any thing she could collect in the way of food. She had some in the chimneys and roof of the house. Many of the rebels had threatened her with a Pistol at her breast that if she had arms or Orangemen concealed, she should pay for it with her life.

While she was tremblingly recounting this to me, we saw a party our guard left us for, approaching towards the house with carts. Mr W went out immediately to meet them: they obliged him again to open all his barns and offices (he was a respectable farmer, and a quaker,) out of which they filled their carts with flour, potatoes, &c., &c. But not content with this, they insisted on coming into the house; & after searching the lower part they crowded up stairs, where Mrs W, her family, with my poor dear father and children, were waiting in terror their departure. On hearing them, I actually pushed my father and children behind a bed, but by the time the rebels reached the room, I pulled them out again, fearing had they found them hiding, it would have made them more desperate.

I stood before them & again *my friend Captain Butler*, came up to me and said no harm should happen to me, and begged I would tell his mistress that as long as he was Captain, he would protect her house; he believed she had got to England, but he did not know what was become of his master, the high Sheriff; however he was done with that now. The party examined every drawer, press & chest in the house; and one of them said on going away, 'I would take care of the next party, they are coming to burn all your Houses'. With what horror did we hear them. We looked at each other & literally without the power of utterance for several minutes. At length I said any thing was better than to be burned to death, & we had better collect what we could & return to the Island, at least for a short time, till the Fury of the day was over. I helped Mrs W to collect as much as we could take with us; and though our own house was within a few fields distance, I was afraid to venture for anything belonging to us.

With some difficulty we again got on board our boat. We nearly reached the Island, but the tide was not near enough in for us to land; and while we were watching with impatience the covering of every rock or pebble, as we lay on our oars, we discovered a boat which seemed to make fast towards us. It soon got near, & we perceived the men were all armed. Dearest

Susan, unconscious of danger, amused us all by her innocent & enter-taining conversation; – never was such a child; she really appeared more delightful than ever, and I do believe exerted herself to rouse us all from the stupor we were thrown into.

At length the boat came close up to us & asked what we were doing there. Hayes answered that we were going to the Island as soon as we could land. They called out, in a voice, 'Go back, go back; if you don't we will sink you. We want the Island to put cattle on for our camp'. Remonstrance was in vain, – 'Go home said they or to jail – take your choice'.

We were obliged again to turn towards home where with horror we got in about four hours. There we found every thing in the utmost confusion; all the servants had departed, but one faithful Creature, who welcomed us with tears of joy that we had returned to her. She had determined to stay till the last moment, but lamented she had been of so little use. She told me the beds had been taken & several of them opened, the feathers thrown about the yard, to enable them to carry off the clothes & curtains &c. &c with the greater expedition. I observed my beautiful geraniums were all broken to pieces. When Alley said, 'Oh Madam, I wish you had nothing else to be sorry for: they have taken your beautiful guitar, and thumped Miss Susan's piano that I was afraid they would break it to pieces; desired I would get them a rope to tye it on a car, but every strap and rope had been taken & to this I owe the safety of the dear child's piano'.

[What to do for beds I knew not; but so soon as it was known that we were returned, one of the rebels, who had lived near Summerseat, came to me and said, 'Madam, I have four of your beds; God forbid you should sleep without one; I will bring them to you when it's dark: I took them off a cart at the cross-road, and swore I would let no one take them, till I heard you were *entirely* gone'. Poor honest creature! He brought them as he promised.][21]

In constant dread did we live, Parties riding up to the House at all hours, & taking their seat in the drawing room, *sans ceremonie*, till the second of June, when my faithful Alley burst into the room where I was; she was pale as death.

'What's the matter, Alley?'

'Oh, my dear mistress, I wish I had died the first day I saw you'.

She continued sobbing and clasping me to her, and was a length of time before she could bring herself to tell me there was a party coming to take us to jail. I dropped upon the floor, & the first knowledge I had of any thing for some time was seeing my Father and children hanging over me, and hearing them thank God my colour was returning. I jumped up, with

---

21 This paragraph does not appear in the original version. Whether Jane Adams added it to another version of the manuscript, or whether Croker invented it, remains unclear.

a confused idea of what Alley had told me; said I was a little sick and would go into the air.

In a few moments I saw a large party ride into the lawn: I hurried into the House to prepare my dear Father for what he would soon hear from those people. I assumed as much composure as I was capable of and told him I feared the party riding up to the House were coming to take him to jail, but that no power should separate us; I would go with him and take my children.

He calmly said, 'Was it that made you faint, my dear?' Then standing up, he put his hand upon his throat, and said, 'I am ready for them, but surprised the army are not sent to us. God's will be done'.

I walked about the House in a state of distraction. My poor children behaved with the utmost propriety, doing every thing to assist me & hiding their own fears to keep up my spirits, which were much subdued by this fresh shock. In a few minutes a party of fifty men, armed with blunderbusses and pistols, arrived and made their way to the room in which my father was. I found him with a large Prayer Book in his hand reading the prayer for the universal Catholic church: this had little effect on them, and remonstrances had less.

One of them said to me, 'Mr Owen has been favoured more than any gentleman in the Barony: you should have sent for the priest long ago' and wickedly added that our saviour's prophecy was now fulfilling when he said, 'the first shall be the last, and the last shall be first;' that *we* had been *first* long enough. This shocked me & confirmed the opinion that it was a religious business & that they came for my father to put him to death.

Fearing that he may be put into a dungeon without food he could eat, I had all the eggs I could get boiled hard, and some Cheese cut rapped up in separate papers, concealed them about me, and slipped some into his coat pockets. I asked one of the guards if the intended to murder my dear father & said if that be your intention, I implore you to put us all to death this moment & let me have the comfort of knowing that he and my children are at peace before you shoot me.

They said, 'You had better not repeat that, for we might do it if we chose; there is no one to punish us. We may do as we please'.

'Come, come', they continued, 'there is no use in delaying, take him we will'.

I then said it was impossible, the carriage-horses have been taken & our coachman, there is no possible conveyance for my Father. They answered, 'Oh, we'll get a cart for him, and you are young enough to walk'.

Another of them objected to my coming; but I said, with some warmth, I hope if any of them had a father & children, they could not have the heart to separate me from mine. This seemed to make an impression, & a few of them went in search of a cart, [the rest took my darling Susan into all the rooms, desiring her to be a good child, and shew them where the guns were.][22] & in their absence I went to Alley and told her if she heard that we were to be murdered, to come immediately to Wexford, as I had thirty guineas sewed up round my waist, and that I wished her to get it as a reward for her compassionate feeling toward us.

Almost choked with tears, she said, 'Oh! my dear mistress, if you had allowed the priest to christian you all, it would not have come to this'. She was the only one amongst us who had the relief of tears. She sobbed aloud & when they brought the Cart to the door for my dear father, she insisted on their allowing her to put a feather bed into it – with which desire, after some consultation, they complied.

Never shall I forget the sensation I felt on seeing my dearest venerable father taken by the arm to be placed in his own Cart to be sent into jail! I put my two little girls with him, and assuming as much cheerfulness as I could, said, 'Well, Sir, the poor Pope had not the Comfort of a Child and grandchildren to travel with him to prison'.[23]

I walked by his side till we came near Wexford, when they suddenly stopped, and all collected together, stood for some time whispering. My terror of a jail was such I hoped they were consulting about putting us to death, & at once ridding us of all the horrors we had to contend with. One of them at length came forward, & with the greatest air of importance, said, 'You have no right as prisoners to wear these green boughs; take them out of your Hats'. I forgot to mention that, previous to our leaving Summerseat, they ornamented our heads with green boughs. So, after taking from us this honorable badge, they proceeded with us to jail.

On our arrival there, the person who opened the Door said to me, 'You must not go in'.

'Not go in? Not go in with my father? No one shall prevent me'.

They instantly put their pikes across me: I implored them not to separate me from my father: one of them gave me a push and said there is no room for women.

I turned round almost distracted, & seeing a person amongst the crowd who had the appearance of a gentleman, I implored him not to suffer those fellows to prevent my going with my father into the jail, that he was extremely ill, and never had been separated from me: 'I would not leave him for worlds – my children too! Do, dear Sir, let me share his fate – let us at least be together'.

He seemed much affected, and said, 'Certainly, Madam, you shall go in', & after taking my poor father and children out of the Cart, he handed

22 This sentence is not in the original version, and it suggests Croker added it for dramatic effect.   23 A note in the manuscript reads: 'The Pope was at this time prisoner with the French.'

me in after them, and with the utmost concern of countenance, lamented the shocking place he was leading us to.

It was a small front room, and so crowded that there was not room to sit nor indeed a Chair. I begged permission to get the feather Bed that was on the Cart, which request was complied with, and just as I was putting it into a corner to lay my poor father on it, a gentleman came up to me & lamented very much seeing us in such a situation. This gentleman was priest of our parish. He apologised for never having waited on Mr Owen and myself. Since our residence in his parish he had heard much of both & again expressed his concern at the place he saw first seeing us in. I said I had hoped my father's age would have screened him; that he was not a magistrate, nor had he any thing to do with public affairs; that he was extremely ill, & what to do I knew not that the crowd in the room was enough to kill him. Fortunately, the panes of glass were all broken outside the prison bars. He very kindly told me he would do what he could, and at the same time beckoned to the young gentleman who had already evinced so much compassion for me. The priest whispered to him for some time and in about an hour returned with a pass from General Keogh,[24] directed to all United-men & desiring they would suffer Mr Owen and family to return to Summerseat as prisoners and to protect his property.

We were immediately liberated. My father asked if any fees were to be paid, and upon being told there was not, he begged of the gentleman who had taken so much trouble to accept of the few guineas he had in his hand, which he politely, tho' positively, refused. He took care of us to the door, where there was a guard of fifty to guard us home. Upon enquiring for our humble vehicle, we were told that Dr Jacob had ordered it to the Camp with flour for the Army: this was the *second* act of *kindness* to us. When we were in jail, he was on horseback near the window: I called out to him, and holding a guinea between my fingers, said, Dr Jacob, my father has not had any Bread since the rebels have had possession of the town. He answered me with the utmost *sang froid*, saying he could get me none, he was on suffrage himself.

We were very anxiously enquiring for Mrs Harvey and Family. While making the enquiry at the door we saw two carts filled with prisoners, & on their coming close we discovered her, her mother, her four daughters, the nurse, and her infant son and heir packed into two small carts, guarded by a strong party of pike men. She begged to stop a moment to speak to us, & while I was telling her I knew not how to get my poor father home, as the cart he was brought on had been taken, one of her guard, a young gentleman, got off a small poney he was riding & most kindly said he would walk with pleasure to accomodate that fine old gentleman. He went up to my poor

24 Matthew Keugh (see Chapter One, note 26).

dear father & begged to help him in his poney, which he assured her was perfectly quiet.

Mrs Harvey had a pass similar to ours & had only just been released from imprisonment, tho' not in the common jail, it being too full to receive her. When we got a short way from Wexford we met above two thousand Rebels drawn up, ready to march to the battle of Ross. Overcome with fatigue, I sat down on a heap of stones, and seeing a girl run quickly past with something in her apron, it occurred to me it might be bread. I called to her and begged she would let me have a crown's worth: she replied, there was not a bit to be had. I lifted up my eyes and said, 'It would have been more charitable to put us to death than starve us'.

In an instant one of the rebels broke from the ranks and threw a large lump of bread and cheese into my lap, and with the utmost compassion of countenance begged of me to take it. I had just time to return it to him & was trying to slip some money into his hand, when he darted from me with a significant look & appeared frightened lest he had been observed. He rejected the money & I have never since heard of this noble creature. How unlike Dr Jacob's conduct, to whose activity for the rebel camp were we deprived of our Cart & a valuable carriage horse that had cost my father above forty guineas about three months before.

When we returned home we met our faithful Alley at the lawn gate & all the rest of the servants who had not been ordered to the camp; their joy at seeing us appeared indeed unfeigned. Alley did all in her power to keep up my spirits; and when I impressed my fears that we should be all starved, reminded me that we had a good garden, plenty of vegetables, fruit, and abundance of milk, eggs, and some young pigs; and that she was sure God Almighty would send us enough and never let us want.

As we passed on to the house, I met a most respectable farmer, who lived near us & was surprised at seeing a pike in his hand; on asking him the reason, he looked fearfully about, and finding that our guard had left us at the gate, he told me that he had endeavoured to escape, but was seized, and *sworn*; that they had plundered his house and barns, and he feared Mrs Parkes [Parker] (his wife) was at that moment without food. 'It is owing to my infirmity', said he, 'I am appointed to guard this place, and see that you do not attempt your escape: they found me too feeble for any thing else'.

When I parted from Mr P, I went into a little garden in the shrubbery that Hayes had made for dear Susan, and here I sat embracing and rejecting hope by turns, till I was roused from reflection by a number of persons walking quickly past. I stood on a garden-seat, and saw them all make it into the hall-door. I instantly followed, trembling at every step; but before I reached the door, I distinctly saw them entering into in the drawing-room with lights, passing and repassing. I hurried on, and after entreating my father to remain with the children in the breakfast room, I went up to them.

On entering the room I was accosted by a hideous, fierce-looking man, who was half-drunk; there were above twenty of them armed with pikes. I saw at the end of the room a most gigantic looking woman, with a hat and feathers, a muslin gown richly trimmed with lace, and a cloak of the same She was tossing over the music books. On approaching nearer she turned round and I found that this strange-looking figure was a man dressed in woman's clothes, no doubt some of the plunder of the day, and very valuable it was, being deep and fashionable Brussels [lace]. The man standing near him had a brace of pistols in his belt and a blunderbuss: he took hold of me, and said, 'I want a book I saw here yesterday – it was a great big one, and the cover will serve me for a saddle'.

I begged, most *quietly*, he would take any thing he wanted; upon which he lifted up a folio editon of the History of London, with fine engravings of the different buildings, which dear Susan had been copying. Recollecting that she had been in the Habit of putting each copy in the leaf she was drawing from, I requested he would allow me to shake the book, upon doing which you can scarcely believe that with some of her drawings there fell on the floor a copy of 'Croppies Lie Down'. I snatched it up, and put it in my pocket unperceived. This was a popular song. Can I ever sufficiently thank my God? I have since been assured that an entire family lost their lives by a similar circumstance. One of the rebels found this song on a drawing-room table, and they were all so outrageous, they put the family to death. I believe this is recorded in Sir Richard Musgrave's account of the rebellion.[25]

One of the party came up to me, and said, 'It was I that took your big fiddle, or *Jar*, as the maid called it: we cannot make music *in it*, but we will come for you soon; we are to go a great way off to-morrow'.

The next day a large party rode up to the door and called for me: I frightened almost to fainting, thinking it was this man that had encouraged them to come and take me to the camp. Poor faithful Alley intreated them not to make a noise, that her master was in bed & ill, but they would not be dissuaded from their purpose, and insisted on having me *out*. When I came to them, they desired I would get breakfast directly. I assured them there was no provision of any kind in the house; it having been taken the night we escaped to the Island. They then said, 'Well, give us the whiskey, till we drink success!'

Upon my producing a bottle of what we had brought from the Island with us, one of the men advanced, and desired I would drink some myself; that they had got an order not to take any thing from *us* without us previously tasting it; upon which another advanced, and said, he would

25 Jane's reference here to Musgrave indicates that the work was written or embellished after 1801. It may have been based on an earlier narrative written contemporarily with the rebellion.

take the first glass himself, that the gentlewoman was above any such works.

It instantly occurred to me that should this man to be taken ill or any of the party, they might come and revenge it on me; I therefore thanked the man & calling for a glass of water I put some whiskey in it & took a sup myself, and gave a little to each of the children. They were then satisfied, and, after finishing the bottle, they rode off.

I then began to consider what I should do for my poor father's breakfast; a morsel of bread or flour I had not, nor could I get to buy. I sent to our neighbour Mrs Woodcock to beg she would give me a little of either for him. She told the servant she had none, but desired I would contrive to go over to her. She lived within two fields of us – I went directly – and on her seeing me, she, with an air of mystery, beckoned me into a House closet from a loft over which she pulled down a small pillow case of flour, telling me that was all she had. She hid in different places & did not like to acknowledge, even to my servants, that she had any lest her house might again be searched. Delighted with my prize of a few pounds of flour, I hurried home, and made it into biscuits for my poor father, my children and I happy at having potatoes. To me, I never felt hunger but was continually sipping milk and water to cool my lips, which were actually parched: I do believe I was in a fever the whole time.

My father's usual habit was, immediately after breakfast, to inquire into the state of the larder. On this day he said, 'I suppose we have nothing to eat for dinner! – What can we have?' I was shocked and said I would consult with Alley, wo told me she knew of nothing but a roasting pig, if she had any one to kill it. After some difficulty we were able to get Hayes, to whom I told my distress. He was a handy creature and said he would prepare it as well as he could for the spit. I then thought of the farmer's wife, a most respectable woman, whose husband was one of the guard to our place; I sent to request she would come and partake of the pig at four o'clock. She was much delighted, and when dinner was over, expressed her thanks to me for having given her the first quiet meal she had eaten since the commencement of the Rebellion.

She told me every thing her husband possessed the rebels had taken; with a pistol to her breast, desired her to confess if there were any Orangemen in her House or in the Neighbourhood; that the terror she was in the night we fled was not to be described; that every moment the rebels broke in & behaved in the most vociferous manner. She expressed her fears to me that her Husband had been forced to a Battle they expected at Ross & that she did not think he could live to go half the way.

Next day Hayes came to me & after hestitating some time, begged I would not ask Mrs Parkes [Parker] again; that it was talked of much at the Cross (the rendezvous of the Rebels) that they said we could not forget old times; that we could not live without company; but that they would shew us we had no right to make use of any thing without leave. A few days after, when I wanted him to kill a pig of eight months old (a few of which were the only food we could get), he said it was as much as his life was worth to touch them without leave of the Committee, but he would try & come at night. He did so and hid it in a cellar and put loose stones about the door to prevent their examining it. He told me they were coming for the cows, but one of the Rebels, whose name he mentioned (I had ordered milk to constantly [*sic*] his wife, having a family of young Children), and this poor fellow said while he had life he would protect the Cowes & every thing belonging to me & the Master (meaning my dear Father).

I shall ever have reason to love the poor Irish for the many proofs of *heart* they have shown during this distracted season; particularly as they were persuaded into a belief that they were all to possess the different estates of the gentlemen of the country; & that they were only to draw lots for their possessions. [One day a large party of rebels rode through the meadow of the lawn; the priest, whom I have before mentioned, was sitting with my father; he went out to expostulate with them for spoiling the meadow, and one of them said, 'Faith, we ought to take care of it, for we don't know whose *turn* it will come to, to have it for himself'.][26]

My father continued very low and ill. I had not a drop of wine for him or kind of nourishment for him. Poor Hayes, who saw my agonizing distress about him, brought me a bottle of wine from the rebel camp – never was I more overjoyed. I do believe it saved his life; it at least was a comfort he had not had since our escape to the Island.

All this time we were very uneasy about my Brother and his large family, his living being near Enniscorthy, & of course they must be in the midst of the rebellion. The first question every time Hayes came from their rebel camp was, 'Have you heard my Brother's[27] family?'

---

26 This passage is not in the original version.   27 Revd Roger Carmichael Owen was born in 1756. He entered Trinity College Dublin in 1772, receiving his B.A. in 1777. He was prebendary of Tombe from 1781 until his death in 1844, and Rector of Kiltennel from 1804 to 1835 (see Leslie, 96). Owen was also a land agent and a clerical magistrate at Tombe, two factors which made him widely disliked by local Irish. Miles Byrne writes that Hawtrey White, Solomon Richards, and Owen 'were all notorious for their cruelty and persecuting spirit, the latter particularly so, putting on pitch caps and exercising other torments' (Byrne, I:33). For this reason, Owen was arrested by the rebels and himself pitchcapped, and then displayed for public view, suspended halfway outside the top story window of the market house in Gorey, high enough so that pikes could not reach him (see Byrne, 1:150; Furlong, *Fr John Murphy of Boolavogue*, 111–112; see also Musgrave, 438; Taylor, 125, 176–180). Byrne added, 'I often had difficulty in preventing the others, who had suffered so much at his hands, from tearing him to pieces' (Byrne, 1:33). When he was later taken down, he appeared to be insane. At his own request, he was released to the custody of a group of rebel guards, who escorted the barefoot and pitchcapped prisoner to Wexford for trial.

One night I was obliged to repeat the question, & on looking at Hayes, I evidently saw his countenance marked with the deepest concern, he appeared not to like to answer my question. I felt terrified & desired he would not keep me in suspense – I guessed all! They are all murdered, I suppose.

'No, Madam, not so bad; but Mr Owen has been taken prisoner at the head of his parishioners. He was brought into the rebel camp, and from thence marched into the jail of Gorey; & indeed, Madam, I am afraid he is a little *light* in his head'.

At once it flashed into my head that the strong sense of his situation, his wife, who was near being confined, and his eight Children, had deprived him of his senses. This so completely shocked me, I was overpowered. I fell against a Table & was some time before I could utter. Every thing I had suffered felt light compared to the horror of his Malady. What was to become of his family? When I could collect my thoughts I charged Hayes to keep this dreadful intelligence from my dear Father & the children. How often did I thank Heaven that my mother had not lived to come to the county of Wexford, where she had planned so much happiness for herself

The question of Owen's state of mind following this incident has prompted a variety of opinion. Clearly, his sister judged him to be insane. However, Byrne believed that he feigned insanity in order to escape persecution, noting that 'he played his part very well … Perceiving some young girls amongst those whom curiosity brought to see the prisoners, he offered his services to marry any of them who wished to be joined in wedlock to their lovers. A young man and a young girl being very near us, he advanced and put their hands together, and instantly began the ceremony of marriage, when the young girl screamed and ran away, which caused much laughter and seemingly amused all present' (Byrne 1:150) This view is shared more recently by Nicholas Furlong, who states that Owen, during his torture, asked to see Fr Francis Kavanagh, parish priest of Camolin, who, horrified by Owen's predicament, demanded his immediate release. 'Owen's wits sharpened as he realized that Owen released was Owen lynched. He firmly refused Kavanagh's offer and insisted on being brought as a prisoner under guard to Wexford jail. Still wearing the cone pitchcap, he was led on foot down the long hot road to Wexford under escort' (Furlong, 120).

Another view of Owen is provided by some of his fellow prisoners. Gurley recalled: 'One day the Revd Mr Owen … was brought into our cell. He looked wildly; his hair was shorn off, and his head daubed over with a coat of tar or pitch. When he came near me he said, "O! Mr Gurley, I want you to make me a pair of gold boot buckles, as I am to go hunting in a day or two, perhaps to-morrow". I replied, 'Very well, sir, furnish me the gold, and if I have time you shall have them!' Poor man! he was deranged, and no wonder. He was torn from the bosom of his family … ' (Gurley, 129–130). T. Acres Ogle's view differs slightly: 'The poor gentleman, through the fatigue of the long march and pain of his head, was nearly out of his senses when he arrived; but shortly after, owing to the kindness of the gaol officials, he was relieved from his sufferings and properly clothed. This prisoner was a most pious and beneficent Divine, and from the day after his arrival he preached and read prayers to us every day. The prisoners might be seen generally gathered round him, for he always had some cheering words of consolation or laughable anecdote to tell us, to keep up our spirits' (T. Acres Ogle, *The Irish Militia Officer* [Dublin: The Author, 1873], 98).

Owen survived the Rebellion and died on 23 Sep. 1843, aged 87. He lies buried in the churchyard at Camolin (Cantwell, *Memorials of the Dead*, vol. 5 [North Wexford], 176).

and Family. What blind creatures are we! How often did I wish my poor father quietly laid by her, expecting as I did that he would be murdered before my eyes. Oh, how impious it is to despair! Hayes added they were irritated against him, because he laid hands on a priest, & that it was with difficulty he could prevent them coming to Summerseat to revenge it on his Master & family, but his own opinion was that all they said about the priest was only to excuse themselves for using him so ill 'because he is a clergyman'.

He begged of me not to suffer his Master to go out on the road, as there was a party coming to put him again in jail on account of Mr Owen.[28] I asked where my Brother was, & what was become of his family. He assured me he did not know. My fears that it had been put to death were soon relieved: in about an hour after this information, I received an open note written in his hand, but in such an agitated manner I could scarcely read it; it ran thus:

> Dear Jenny, I never was merrier or happier in my life. Nancy, the children and money are gone off I know not where. Come see me – bring some vegetables and cucumbers. Wexford Jail.

It was eight in the evening when I received this note. I called for Hayes to consult about what was to be done. He was gone to the Camp; it was too late to attempt to go that night, but I determined on going early next morning. How to frame an excuse for my absence to my poor father I knew not; and to tell him I *dared* not venture; indeed my fears were that I should be seized on & put into the jail, with this intended victim of their ferocity. It is impossible to give an idea of all the ills I foreboded for myself, Father, and Children, but all was overcome by the hope of saving him & humbly trusting in the protection of heaven I was on the point of setting out, when Hayes returned from the Camp.

I told him where I was going. He started and said, 'I beg, Madam, you'll not be so mad – it is but 5 o'clock – the roads are crowded relieving guard, and if they know you are going to take part with Mr Owen, you will bring trouble on yourself and my master. He is hated by the people & boasted of being an Orangeman, & if you would be too much troubled by hearing it, he is quite out of his senses, & it was that that saved his life for he was dancing thro' the streets of Wexford & singing out that he was an Orangeman & feared no one. They were taking him to jail, & indeed he was every way in a bad condition; I would have put my own coat and hat on him but for fear of my life, for there were two hundred guarding him'.

---

28 The Croker version states here that the rebels were 'so exasperated against Mr Owen for avowing himself an Orangeman that he [Hayes] heard them talk of coming again to send his master to jail'.

Instead of poor Hayes's zeal for me awakening my fears, it more strongly determined me to risk every thing to try & get him to Summerseat, & I told him nothing could dissuade me from my purpose. He entreated me again not to go, for he [Mr Owen] was to be tried by the Committee at 12 o'clock. This only added wings to my impatience; I lost not a moment, thought every pebble impeded my speed. Dearest little Susan cried so violently at my leaving her I turned back and brought her with me; my poor Letitia (who, you know, is 9 years older) I left to take care of my father, and I own when I kissed her at the door I thought it was for the last time.

When I got to Wexford (a distance of near 3 miles, which I was obliged to walk, having neither coachman or horses left me) I knew not to whom I could apply to get me into the jail. The streets exhibited the most frightful appearance – the Church was shut up tho' on Sunday – a ragged boy beating the Drum belonging to the unfortunate North Cork Militia – thousands of pike men marching in the middle of the street – not a female was in it but myself and child. Terrified at this, I involuntarily stopped – stood motionless, till I observed myself the object of universal attention & heard one of them say, 'She is a spy!'

'Who the devil is she?' another said, & a third,

'She would make a good wife for the camp'.

Had I seen one amongst the Hundreds that passed me that had the slightest look of a gentleman, I would have implored his protection for myself & Child; but they were all drunken, ill-looking fellows. In this distress I saw with joy, at the opposite side of the street, our friendly priest who had got us liberated from jail; I called to him to cross over to me, being afraid to break through the multitude that were marching; but, to my utter amazement, tho' he evidently saw me, he turned his head & walked forward faster than the rebels marched, to avoid me. In this dilemma it occurred to me that if I walked up & down before the jail I possibly might see the object of my anxiety as he was likely to be in the room we had so lately occupied. But I soon found this impossible, the crowds of pike men passing and repassing prevented my getting near; & they looked so horridly at me & pushed me about so savagely, I was afraid to speak, or make any inquiry. Seeing the impossibility of effecting my purpose, I returned to Summerseat.

There I found my poor father very ill and unable to get up. Such were the scenes that presented themselves to my imagination, I should have rejoiced at seeing him sinking into a quiet *natural* Death. I told him the confusion I found Wexford in prevented my seeing my Brother, but that I hoped to be more fortunate tomorrow. He violently opposed my going. I told Alley of my disappointment about the priest & begged her to try & get him to come to me, as I wanted much to speak to him. When she returned from his House, I saw that she wished to say something that she hesitated about; I begged she would speak openly to me & ask'd her would the priest come to me?

'Yes, Madam, but don't be angry, Madam'.

I assured her I believed her perfectly in my interest & could not be angry with any thing so faithful a creature might say.

'Well, Madam – if you would allow Father O'Connor[29] to christen my master, the young ladies, & yourself, it might be the saving of you'.

I quickly answered he may do any thing if he will assist me in getting my Brother out of jail.

The priest promised to meet me at a Mrs Moore's in Wexford, an old lady of my acquaintance who had been overlooked in the hurry, and, I believe, was the only individual not visited by the Rebels. Delighted at the prospect of accomplishing my wishes, I again set out with my dear companion Susan without having closed my eyes or lain on a bed since the night before; but I felt as if nothing had power to tire me, tho' I could not eat a bit, & my thirst was not to be satisfied. When I had reached the distance of half a mile, I heard some one running violently after me, & on stealing a look round, frightened at every footstep, I perceived it was Alley, who had followed me with a message from the priest to request should I see him in the street not to appear to know him, that he found he was obliged most unwillingly to refund his promise as it would ruin him in the eyes of *the people*. This frightened me so much, I questioned myself, was it not temerity to proceed. But I soon rejected the idea, and trusting in that Almighty Power that had hitherto spared me, I told Alley nothing should deter me, were I only to gratify my poor brother by seeing me. But I own I was not without my fears that I was only exposing myself & child to the fury of the mob, & perhaps the unfortunate object of my anxiety to their greater vengeance by my interference. I felt, however, a something in me which impelled me forward, spite of all the dangers that fancy had conjured up.

When I got to Wexford, I was much as ever at a loss to whom to apply for admittance to the jail. I saw immense numbers of rebels, running in great confusion & heard one of them say, 'Make haste to parade, Gen'l Keogh is gone'.

It immediately occurred to me to follow at a distance & that this *general* might be of a superior order to those common, ill-dressed men, who passed in such numbers I thought they would never cease. At length they all got into an immense field, where Gen'l Keogh paraded them for above

29 Possibly Fr Roderick O'Connor, parish priest of Rathmacnee. He was born about 1739 and served as parish priest from 1782 until his death on 2 Apr. 1807 (see W. H. Grattan Flood, *History of the Diocese of Ferns* [Waterford: Downey & Co., 1916], 172).

an hour; all which time I stood at a distance, under the most parching sun I ever felt; tho' my blood ran cold at times to see their numerous pikes & knowing intention of them.

When the parade broke up, I took the opportunity of addressing Mr Keogh. He was dressed in full uniform, green and gold, with a cocked hat trimmed with gold Lace. He strove to avoid me, but I courageously called to him and stop a moment. I told him in a few words as possible the situation of my brother [and presented him a letter, which he refused to take.] He knew it well, lamented it, but that he had no longer the charge of the prisoners – that department, he said, had been taken from him, that Mr Kearney had the care of them at present (this Gen'l Keogh had been a Captain in the King's army for years & was hanged when the army came to our relief.)

I then made enquiries about Mr Kearney's[30] residence & immediately went to him. In him I met a man of great humanity, tho' a rank rebel. He was much affected at my account of my Brother's situation. When I told him he was married and had eight children depending on him, he turned to a Cradle, in which there was a beautiful infant of his own asleep. He said, 'Innocent creature, you are happily ignorant of the state your father is in & the fears around you'. I believe at this time they were fearful of not succeeding in their cause. His tears rolled down his cheeks. 'This child's mother', he said, 'fled from France in the revolution there, it will be hard if the same fate attends her here'.

I scarcely listen'd to him, I was so impatient to see my poor brother; but he went on talking & said, 'I suppose you know the park near Dublin, it is full of Rebel encampments; that they suffer no provision into the city, their army possessing themselves of every thing that come near it; they have the canals and have stopped the entrance of the shipping'.

This unexpected intelligence was a new source of wretchedness to me; if my dear friends in Dublin were in such danger, I cared little for my own safety, tho' I hoped the account was exaggerated. I endeavoured to interest him about my brother & promised most solemnly if he should get out of prison, even for a few days, I would myself watch him & be answerable with *my life* that he should be forthcoming if sent for. I begged he would allow me to see him, with which he complied & walked with me to the jail; he desired me to go to the front window & he would have him brought there, which was all he could do; but advised me to come next day & he would endeavour to interest the Committee in his favor. He said he would

---

30 William Kearney of Abbey Street, Wexford, was a Catholic and a civilian United Irishman in charge of the Wexford gaol (see Whelan's discussion of his radicalism in 'Reinterpreting the 1798 Rebellion in Co. Wexford', 13–24). He served on the Directory of Eight and acted an assistant to Keugh (see Dickson, 89). Musgrave states that he served as a Colonel in the Merchants' Corps (Musgrave, 193).

himself give him the vegetables and cold meat I had brought in a napkin. He then took his leave, & I with difficulty made my way to the window. The panes of glass were fortunately in the state they were when I left that dreadful abode; this enabled me to look in.

I soon saw some person hurrying towards me held by two men, from whom he was endeavouring to force forward. Oh! Shall I ever forget the sight! He almost flew when he saw me, stretched out his burning hand through the bars, and endeavoured to force out to kiss dear Susan. He had on him an old flannel waistcoat, neither shoes or stockings; his beard an inch long; his hair cut close to his head, the rebels had put a pitch plaster, which he had torn off. I was obliged to hold the bars of the window to prevent my falling. I reached him a leaf of cherries & some cucumbers, which he devoured.

'Don't be afraid, Jenny! I have sent an express this day to Lord Castlereagh and the Bishop of Ferns. I shall desire one of them to buy a harp for dear Susan. How is my friend, Jemmy Boyd?' (Mr Boyd had been an active magistrate, had a corps, with which he was obliged to fly the day the rebels entered Wexford.)

The moment they heard my brother inquire for Mr Boyd, I had twenty pikes raised over my head, I believe with the intention to put me to death; till one less savage than the rest restrained them. I assured them I knew nothing of Mr Boyd, nor had I seen him since I came to Summerseat.

My brother, not knowing what they were saying, called aloud to me, 'Jenny, Jenny, my dear, tell me have you seen my friend Haydon?'[31] (Mr Haydon was a venerable clergyman in the diocese of Ferns, and my brother's most particular friend. Report said that his own butler assisted in his murder, having first turned him and Mrs Haydon out of their house. They fled on foot to Enniscorthy, where Mr Haydon was inhumanly butchered by Mrs Haydon's side.) He paused & repeated, 'Haydon, Haydon!' His face became quite convulsed, & when he could utter, he said, 'Excellent man! These villains have murdered him'.

Then clasping his hands together, he looked up and said, 'Oh God, the dead body of thy servant have they given to the fowls of the air, & the flesh of thy saints to the beasts of the land! Oh, let the vengeance of thy servants' blood that is shed be openly showed upon the heather in thy sight. Oh let the sorrowful sighing of the prisoners come before thee!'

He was agitated beyond description; he said he must go and read prayers for the poor people up stairs. I could bear his madness no longer; I endeavoured to restrain my feelings before him, but finding it no longer possible, I walked from the window and went into the first door I found open. There I burst into the most frightful fit of screaming, which I had

31 Revd Samuel Heydon (see Chapter Five, note 12).

not power to stop, & instead of being relieved, it agitated me to such a degree I was wholly deprived of the use of my limbs for near an hour.

When I could look round, I found I was in a common ale house; four women were sitting in a corner of the room at breakfast, all this time unmoved, though my darling Susan repeatedly begged of them to give her mama a glass of water; but to the disgrace of *our sex*, she called in vain, till two men came into the house and rendered me every assistance in their power, brought me water, and one of them turned most angrily to *Judy* (his wife I suppose) for not asking the Lady to take a Cup of tea. I continued so ill, I dreaded being obliged to remain in this House, but in about an hour the numbness of my limbs abated, and I crept as far as Mrs Moore's, where I got hartshorn and water, which relieved me so much that I was soon able to walk about the room; & at length a violent flood of tears relieved me more than medicine could. I told her my poor brother's situation, & she kindly promised to send him tea & bread.

When able, I returned to Mr Kearney's, who kindly assured me he would himself take him his breakfast. Shocked at the little I had effected compared to the risks I had ran, I again reluctantly turned my steps towards home. It was by this time 6 in the Evening, and I was wretched at the uneasiness I knew my father and Letitia must suffer at my being so much longer away than they expected. Overcome with fatigue, the heat of the day & violent agitation I had gone through, I sat down about a mile from town, on a small bridge over a rivulet. I remained almost petrified with horror at our situation, when I saw a number of pikemen coming towards me. I started up, and my first sensation was to hide my darling Child under the arch; but they came too quickly towards me to to do any thing but stand.

They saw terror in my countenance, & humanely, & in a voice, desired me not to fear. One of the men knew me, tho' I had not the most remote knowledge of him. They all advised me not to venture so far from home lest I might meet Strangers to me. I trembled so violently I could scarcely walk & was obliged to take hold of one of their arms to enable me to proceed, which the man perceiving, desired me to be of good heart, he would take care of me: 'No one shall harm you, ma'am, & if you wish it, we'll try & sleep turn about at Summerseat'. There was an honesty of manner in those poor-deluded fellows that precluded doubt or suspicion. I thanked them & gratefully accepted a service offered with such humane warmth. They left me safe at home & promised to return at night.

How to tell my dear father the melancholy state I left my brother in I knew not; nor could I bring myself to tell him the complete bondage we were in. How often did I thank God that the Bishop of Ferns had not ordained Charles, because he could not swear of a proper age. Had the Bishop complied with my Father's request, he was to have had the Curacy of Ross & would of course have been put to death early in the Rebellion, which the curate of it was, & tho' they kept us as much as they could in the dark about their proceedings, it was plain they wished to annihilate all the Protestant clergy. They continued to behave with great kindness to me. Many of them, perfect strangers, used to come at night, & after looking mysteriously about, put down by me a bottle of wine and lump of bread for my poor dear Father.

Tho' at the same time some of them were quite abusive to my faithful Alley, who they found one day smoothing some muslin handkerchiefs, and asked her did she think herself still my servant, & that she ought to make me change places with her – she had the *right* to command me. [This shewed how impressed they were with the idea that they were really to *change places*, as they said, and all to become gentlemen.] She, excellent creature, burst into tears & said she would die first. He was the man who had the presumption to quote our Saviour's words, 'The first shall be the last & the last shall be first'.

At night the men who took care of me home were true to their promise; four of them came to sleep at Summerseat, & I felt such confidence in their protection, I, for the first time since the rebellion, went into bed, where I slept most soundly till 4 o'clock in the morning; when I was awoke by the galloping of Horses up the approach, which was succeeded by a violent knocking at the hall door. I was terrified lest it should be some more dreadful account of my poor Brother. I flew down stairs & impatiently asked what was the matter, entreating them not to awaken my father with their noise. They swore violently & called for the men who were in the House – saying they should be punished & sent to Vinegar Hill for leaving their posts. I ran at once to their rooms, so terrified was I lest their compassion for me might lead them to the revenge of those men. I actually assisted them in looking for their Cloaths & putting them on, totally unmindful of my own want of dress.

Soon as I was a little recovered from this scene of terror & confusion, I prepared for my third walk to Wexford. Alley offered to walk there with me & said she never was afraid to let me go before. I forgot to mention that when the priest called on me, I told him she had expressed the greatest anxiety that we should all be christened by him. He answered, 'Madam, that is between you and your God; I should be sorry to influence any one, tho' many have come to me for that purpose'.

I gave him great credit for his answer to me & said He could have but a bad opinion of any one who could so suddenly & thro' fear change their religion. My not doing so was the reason. My faithful servant trembled for my safety. I was, however, afraid to leave my father and Letitia, without her protection, & again set out with my little companion Susan at 6 in the morning to brave all danger and the hope of getting my Brother from the jail, & this interesting creature's sensible conversations cheered me, & I safely arrived at Mr Kearney's without any interruption. What was my disappointment when Mr Kearney told me he could give no answer till the next day. But when this humane man saw my extreme agitation & that I feared when tomorrow came it would be tomorrow still, he kindly said he would go out for a little & try to a *certainty* what I had to depend on.

I sat in fearful expectation at his house for above an hour, when he returned with a positive assurance to me that the next day my Brother should be sent to Summerseat, but under a strong guard, & that I must be answerable with my life for his safe keeping – desired I would not let him out of my sight, for if he escaped it might prove fatal to myself and family, & that I must give my solemn assurance I would give him up if sent for by the Committee, that a few days was the extent of the leave he had procured for him.

I was too happy at getting him even for that short time, not to promise every thing required of me. His mind was so very much disturbed, I dreaded his not quietly submitting to a guard with him, & when a great distance from town, I returned to Mr Kearney's to request he would allow our coachman to be one of the guard; which he kindly promised, & it proved a great comfort to him, as he kept him in conversation about us.

The moment I could get from home I set out to meet him; and tho' I had previously to his coming had him shaved & had sent him a suit of my father's clothes, I had forgot a Hat; & when I met him he looked such an object, I dreaded my Father's seeing him. The clothes, much too large, were hanging on him; his head still bleeding & exposed to the sun. This was a tacit reproach to my forgetfulness. With some difficulty I prevailed on him to allow me to tie my veil around his head. He walked so fast, the guard told me they could scarcely keep up with him. We met my poor father at the lower gate impatiently looking out for us. You may suppose how much he was shocked at seeing him, for in a moment he betrayed the state of his mind. He talked incoherently & took off his coat before the guard to shew the wounds those rascals, as he said, had given him. My father, conceiving it was the men who were with him, turned on them with great indignation & began to call them to account for their barbarity, when he perceived his Old Coach Man. This added to his horror, but I complained to him that those men had only come from Wexford & that I had got Matthew by special favour to be one of the guards who were to remain with him at Summerseat.

Matthew gave me a pass which was given for protection & will paste it on this paper:

Let Mr Owen pass to Summerseat, & remain there a prisoner.
June 19, 1798.
Will. Kearney.

He could give no account of Mrs Owen or his children; but they had got off, he knew not where.

While we were sitting at Dinner, I was called out of the room, & on looking towards the yard, I perceived a large party of pikemen, & Alley, walking in a state of distraction, talking to them. I went into the yard and asked the occasion of it. 'Oh my dear mistress! I knew what trouble you would bring on yourself and my master: my mother has sent for me; they say, unless you give up Mr Owen to them, the House will be burned this night'.

All this time the rebels were consulting together at the coach house gate. I implored her to be quiet – she was in fits of tears & quite hysterical. I went over to the men. They called out, 'Produce Mr Owen, or we will tear the House down'.

I endeavoured to excite their compassion by assuring them he was quite out of his senses; that if he was with me a few days it would calm him, & he might then be able to give an account of anything he had done to cause this violence. They said he had owned himself an Orangeman & have him they would. I then took Mr Kearney's pass from my pocket & read it to them; after which I said with a resolution I am at this moment amazed at: 'At your peril lay a finger on him!'

Never can I forget their look of amazement, & as if with one consent, they literally marched out of the yard, muttering, 'this night the house shall be burn'd'.

On my return to the dining parlour, I found my father & Brother in such deep conversation they had not missed me. Again Alley made her appearance at the Door & beckoned to me. The men who left the yard met her mother & told her to send for her daughter, swearing a great oath that this night the House would be burned, as I would not give up the Orange man that was in it. She implored me not to sacrifice her master and the young ladies; but when she found me determined, she desired the people who were bringing down her trunk to take it away & tell her mother she had not the heart to leave me. I did all I c'd to make her go to her mother, but it was to no purpose.

I found it very difficult to keep my Brother quiet; he talked incessantly, told me he never loved Nancy so well as when she dressed her boys in Orange ribbons, & sent them to fight those villains; but he did not know where they now were. He also said the first Bed he had lain on was the Bed I had left for him in jail, which that humane man, Mr Kearney, had settled for him on the floor in one of the rooms. He repeatedly said, I don't know where the boys are, but I sent them to their mother. (The eldest of them was not more than 13.)

We could not depend on any thing he said; but [he] recollected that Mrs Cliffe & Mrs Harvey, his wife's mother & sister, lived at Killean Castle &

insisted on going to see them. I told him I was under a solemn promises not to let him leave the House; but he flew from me & said he would go & spoke very harshly to me, reproaching me for my cowardice, out he would go. I was obliged to send Matthew and one of the other guards after him, who with difficulty overtook him & brought him back. I then got our faithful Matthew to go and tell Mrs Cliffe and Harvey come & see him as he would certainly be again put into jail if he was seen on the road. They ventured across the fields & never was there any thing more difficult than the interview. Mrs Cliffe enquired for her daughter & grandchildren & getting none but incoherent answers from him that left them in the most wretched suspense as to their fate. When they left us, I tried to prevail on him to go to bed; he did not appear in the least fatigued, & it was near one before I could prevail on him to consent. The guard insisted on staying in the room. He soon fell into a disturbed sleep, distinctly quoting several lines from Shakespeare & other Authors, one or two I recollect: 'Come, let's away to prison' & 'This tempest would not give me leave to ponder'. 'Take physic, pomp'.

In this manner he went on the whole of the time I was in the room, which indeed I scarcely left but to examine now & then if there were combustible matter left about the house to put their threats in execution. Though his sleep was so disturbed, I had the comfort to see the next day he appeared much more composed & very much refreshed.

I was standing talking to him by his bed-side, when I saw a large party galloping towards the house. I shut his shutters & begged he'd try to sleep more & that I w'd come again to him. I dreaded his seeing the party & that he would expose himself to them. I got downstairs quick as I could & almost flew to stop their coming to the House. They were about half way & as this party was composed mostly of gentlemen, they stopped directly on my entreating them not to disturb my Brother as he had just fallen asleep. They said two of them would alight & walk the House, but they *must* go to search for Mr Boyd. I assured them in the most solemn manner that Mr Boyd never had been inside our doors since we came to Summerseat. They politely bowed & ordered the party to turn round. They then went to Killean Castle to Mrs Harvey's, & she has since told me they searched every wardrobe & even an empty hogshead; [but this may be accounted for, as Mr Boyd was married to a near-relation of Mrs Harvey.][32]

My Brother remained in bed till dinner time. Soon as he came down, he insisted on going to dine with Mrs Harvey. I entreated him not to do so & caught hold of his arm, which he wrested from me and leap'd over the

---

32 James Boyd married Elizabeth, daughter of Col. Walter Hore of Harperstown (see Chapter Four, note 50). Anne Hore (who married Loftus Cliffe and was the mother of Dorothy Harvey) was the daughter of William Hore of Harperstown and the sister of Col. Walter Hore (see 'Hore of Harperstown', *Burke's Landed Gentry* [1850], 592).

ditch. I was obliged to send the guard after him, who soon brought him back; he was extremely angry with me for my silliness as he called it. Poor fellow! He little knew the risk I run, and the danger we were all exposed to in having a Protestant clergyman & an avowed Orangeman in the House. Nothing saved him but the insane State they all saw him in, & this I think does honor to poor Paddy's feelings, ferocious as they were in some instances.

We were under great uneasiness about our faithful Hayes; he had been four days absent, & we feared he had been killed. At ten o'clock at night there came into the House two horrid-looking fellows; they told me they were come for Mr Owen – he must go to jail! Whilst I was remonstrating with them, there rushed in five or six, calling the guard that had been left to watch my Brother. I intreated them to leave Matthew with me, but the men who came for them said, 'We are all too little – the road must be doubly guarded'. Had I understood him, it would have given me some comfort, for I have since heard they had that night received intelligence that the King's army were making towards the Town. They then had not time to seize my poor Brother, & he most providentially escaped for that night, & it was under the providence of God the means of saving his life, tho' the next day they brought a written order for him.

I detained them as long as I could, much against his will. He had no fear; he vowed he would go with them. Mr Kearney sent me an assurance nothing should happen [to] him. I delayed the guard long as I could on different pretences till 6 soldiers took him. I walked with him nearly half way to Wexford. It was getting late, & I returned home almost distracted, fearing I had taken a last leave of him. To the delay and the providence of God does he owe his life, for while on the road a party went to the jail to take the prisoners to the Bridge to put them to Death.

Mr Owen, the protestant clergyman, was the first they call'd for; not finding him, they took out seventy-five prisoners & were taking them to the Bridge in the opposite direction to the road my Brother was on. Mr Kearney (most humanely & may God for ever bless him for it) went to meet him, told the guard he would take care of their prisoner & pointed to them to follow the crowd. Can I ever cease to be thankful to God! To the delay I owe his life, for had he been ten minutes sooner, nothing could have saved him. He must have shared the fate of those unfortunate victims, the murder of whom must ever be a disgrace the Country. They went on murdering the prisoners with the most barbarous ferocity till a priest (whose name I forget)[33] went on his knees to them to desist, that surely they had blood enough for that night. A Mr Cox,[34] receiving the most

33 A reference to Fr John Corrin, who interceded on behalf of the prisoners on Wexford Bridge (see Chapter One, note 21).   34 William Allen Cox of Coolcliff was Captain of the

dreadful pike wounds, made an effort & leapt the bridge; they then fired at him till he sunk. At this time we were fortunately ignorant of all that was going on at Wexford, but I had determined to go there next day & get my Brother back.

About nine o'clock that night I found the Servants in the greatest confusion & consternation, messages coming back & forward to them every moment. As soon as the day appeared, I observed a large ship outside the Harbour & saw the Rebels galloping with great fury back and forwards towards the coast. We began to hope that this vessel had brought troops to our assistance; but the Rebels gave out it was their *friends*, the French, that were coming to them. They knew nothing to a certainty till a boat was sent out to them. I kept watching at the dining room window & plainly saw them firing from the vessel & at last the boat was brought to its side. This was a boat the Rebels had sent out to their *friends* the French, but they were soon made prisoners, & this confirmed our hopes that there were troops on board. But even this hope was accompanied with fear; the shores and Hills were crowded with pikemen, & we were in terror for our troops landing amongst such a furious set.

I was preparing to go to Wexford in spite of all remonstrance, when our faithful Hayes made his appearance after an absence of some days. He looked miserably & scarcely able to walk. Susan flew to him, leapt into his arms, kissed him, and burst into tears. He was scarcely able to hold her. He was greatly attached to her, & the day before he went away he seemed very melancholy. She ask'd him what ailed him & [if] the rebels had ordered him to kill her. He started up and took hold of the sword that was lying by him and broke it to pieces, most solemnly saying that he never would lift his arm but in his own defence, & turning towards her, said, 'Kill you, my dear child! God forbid I should live to see the day that any one would attempt it – if they did, it should be through my heart, while it's in me to protect you'.

This honest creature, I am certain, had heard of the intention of putting all Protestants to death and his fears were that he might be ordered to be one of the executioners. You cannot wonder at the dear child's delight at poor Hayes's return; indeed we were all happy at seeing him and anxious to do everything in our power for him. The poor creature was so overpowered with gratitude at our attending on him, he said he was made amends for all his sufferings. He shewed us his hat perforated with two

Taghmon Yeoman Cavalry (O Snodaigh, 37). He had endeavoured to make his escape in a small boat on the Bannow in the hope of reaching the sea, 'but he was so beset by pikemen, that he was under the necessity of landing in the midst of a horde of those savages … He then took to his boat, and was soon after seized by the pikemen at the Scar-pass of Barrystown, and conveyed to Wexford, where he suffered on the bridge' (Musgrave, 395).

balls while he was lying concealed in a ditch during the heaviest cannonading he ever heard; [he told us] that the man that was with him was
shot dead through the Head – that never was such a fight -the dead were
lying in heaps, & that there could not be less than ten miles of the road
cover'd with the King's troops. This was joyful news to us, but my unhap-
piness & suspense about my Brother made me fearful of indulging hope.

He concluded his history by saying, 'What could we expect, Madam!
The generals (that is, the priests who are generals, Madam) told them not
to fear, for as fast as the red hot balls were fired on the rebels, *they* would
catch them in their hands & that they had not power to hurt them. There
were many among them that believed it; but I am sure I saw hundreds
dropping before my eyes as fast as the balls were fired from the cannon'.

Tho' this account was dreadful, yet it gave us an assurance that the
Army were coming to our relief; my terror lest the jail should be set fire to
by the rebels, made me so wretched I insisted on going to Wexford; & just
as I was ready to set out, our friendly priest, whom I have before mentioned, rode up to the House in great agitation, saying, 'The King's troops
have taken possession of Wexford without firing a shot'.

I instantly asked was the jail safe? He looked shock'd. 'Pray, for God's
sake tell me, can you tell me any thing of my Brother?'

He s'd, 'I hope he's safe; but there were dreadful doings on the Bridge
last night'.

I ran out of the room, calling for my hat & Hayes, & while standing in
the hall I heard a horse gallop furiously to the Door, & in a moment my
dear Brother had me in his arms. He was so much agitated, & indeed we
were all in such a state of surprise, joy and gratitude to Heaven for our
deliverance that we were some time incapable of saying any thing but
'Praise be to God; Oh God, make us thankful!'

Never can I forget the sensations of that moment. In a little time we saw
the rebels flying in all directions; at night one of them came to me with his
wife and six children & implored me to give them protection – that he
must fly – that his cabin was be burned, & that she had brought her
blankets with her. He was in such distraction I promised I would let her
sleep in the coach House. They all fancied they were to be burned in their
cabins.

When I ordered potatoes & milk for the wretched children (the only
food in my possession), who really looked starved, the poor woman
prepared her bed with such confidence in me as produced a most
pleasurable feeling. Removed so suddenly from the terrors of my own
situation, I could hardly believe it was in my *power* to give protection to any
one, but after leaving her and turning into the yard, I found it crowded
with men, women, and Children, who implored me to give them shelter
anywhere about the House. They were really in a distracted state, being

sure they were all to be shot. I did every thing in my power to quiet them & assured them I would write to the commanding officer in the morning, & that mean time I would have cards nailed on all the cabins within reach of me to certify their good conduct and refer them to Summerseat for a further account of those who behaved well. This appeased the poor deluded creatures, who were most of them forced into this dreadful business.

As night approached, all the Back offices and yard became crowded with rebels, imploring protection for themselves, wives & Children. They besought liberty to lie on the walks of the garden, such of them as could not elsewhere find room. Every office & bit of ground near the house was crowded with them, & when the proclamation was issued next day [for their pardon on returning to their allegiance], they thought it was only to delude them into the Town to be shot. Many gave up their pikes & arms to my father. Two days after the Army came to our relief, a young priest begged to speak to me – he was disguised in the dress of a peasant. After entreating secrecy, he told me who he was and begged I would give him permission to administer the Sacrament to a young man I had given protection to – that he was in a desperate state with a ball in his arm & that all who were found wounded were ordered to be shot without trial, & there were soldiers sent thro' the country to search for them. In vain I endeavoured to convince him that the King's free pardon would be given to all those who gave up their arms & returned to their allegiance.

This poor young man was so very ill, I had him in one of the spare rooms, where I brought the priest to him & left them together. He remained above an hour, where he had performed his last office. I went to the young man & begged he would allow me send for Dr Johnson,[35] who would extract the Ball from the arm & that he would get well directly. He appeared in great torture, but all I could say he would not consent, so sure was he that were it found out he would be shot. Whilst I was endeavouring to give him confidence in the proclamation & saying every thing I c'd think of to compose him, a person desired to speak to me whom I found was this lad's mother. I desired she should be shewn up stairs & really dreaded the affecting scene I thought must have ensued; but she strutted into the room with the greatest affrontery & turned to him more with an air of command than tenderness & said, 'What signifies your arm, if you suffer death it is in *the good cause* – your Saviour suffered for you'.

---

35 John Johnston, M.D., was listed as living on Main Street in Wexford in 1788 (*General Directory for the Kingdom of Ireland*, 413). He was a liberal, like Ebenezer Jacob, and was closely alligned politically with Harvey. Possibly he was identical to the John Johnston who married Elizabeth Hatton in 1778, the Hattons being another liberal family (*Ferns M.L.*). In 1799, he claimed losses for 'Furniture, Cloaths, Wine [and] Horses' totalling £430, of which he received £141 (Claimants, ccclxxix).

I was shocked at her countenance, but assured her he was in no danger, except from his wound, & urged her to let me send for Dr Johnson, which she refused very bluntly & desired her son to take her arm and come home, that 'all was not over with us yet'. This horrid woman frightened me so much that I most gladly saw her departure, tho' I offered to keep her son till he was better able to return to his wretched cabbin.

When I found myself at liberty again to ask a friend to dine, I wrote to our friendly priest & told him how happy my father & I would be to see him at Dinner, & that he should have a bed. He wrote to say he was afraid to stir out of his House without a protection, & that it would extremely oblige him if we could procure him one. I wrote in my father's name to the commanding officer, stated his humane conduct & was happy at immediately getting a protection, which I sent him. This was great delight to us all. He lost no time in coming, & after dinner dearest Susan and I sang him the [Sicilian] Hymn to the Virgin, which he said had more power to compose him than he could imagine it possible for him to give, & you may think how great our delight was, not only at affording him such gratification, but that we were once more able to sing together. It is impossible to describe this angelic creature's feelings – if her lot be not fortunate it will be a short life to her, for she is all soul & heart, a treasure to me, tho' I have trembled for them & often wished them any where but here.

Next morning I received a Letter from the Mayor, & to my great surprise on looking at it, I found it was Charles'[36] handwriting. 'Twas dated from Ross. It expressed his joy, his gratitude to Heaven in the most lively terms, to find that we had escaped, that he had been within 9 miles of us a few nights before, & tho' his mind was tortured with suspense, he dared not advance to inquire our fate.

I knew not whether to rejoice or grieve at this intelligence, for tho' we were at that moment under the protection of the Army, reports were such as continually to keep up our fears. The messenger who brought my letter also brought an order from the high Sheriff to my father, desiring he would have all the pike handles cut into pieces of a foot long before an hour. This made me very unhappy – the idea that Charles might be called into the field of battle against his own countrymen was shocking to me, and I heartily wished him back at Jersey. The Reg't he was in was ordered from thence in consequence of the state of Ireland. This was an additional

---

36 Charles Robert Adams was ordained a deacon, 12 Sep. 1802, and a priest, 24 Aug. 1803, both at Cloyne, Co. Cork, where his father had served as rector. He was licenced on 1 Apr. 1804 to the curacy of Dungourney, and on 8 Jun. 1814 to Aghada. Between 1837 and 1844, he held the curacy of Carrigdownane. On 15 Jul. 1829, he married Constance Buckmartin at St Mary, Shandon; they had two sons, Benjamin Hallowell and Thomas Carpenter. Adams was buried in Cloyne Cathedral, 31 Jan. 1844 (see Brady, *Clerical and Parochial Records of Cork, Cloyne and Ross*, 86–7).

weight upon my mind. [The order from the Sheriff made me fear we were not so secure as we at first hoped: and the speech which the woman made when I was trying to give comfort about her son, nearly confirmed me in this opinion.]

Soon as I could get a messenger to venture on the road, I sent most anxiously to enquire for a Mrs Bevan,[37] whose husband was our Parish Clergyman & had been very active amongst the Peasantry previous to the rebellion breaking out, & the morning the loyalists fled, he was in Wexford & obliged to get off to England, leaving Mrs Bevan with her infants, but it was really impossible for him to return to her, as the road leading to his place was crowded with rebels. Mrs Bevan gladly accepted my invitation & brought her children. Her eldest son, a lovely child of 8 years old, affected me extremely by asking me (whenever he got me alone) where his Papa was and was I sure the Rebels had not killed him. Poor Mrs B's eyes filled with tears whenever she looked at her children. She began to despair, as I had a letter from Wales, and his name was not mentioned.

The day after she came to us, Mr Harvey and Mr Colclough (pro-nounced Cokely) were taken prisoners on an island called the Saltees. She received a letter from the former [*sic*], requesting she would come immediately to Wexford to give evidence for him. She complied with his desire, tho' she had nothing to communicate that could serve him. He and Mr Harvey were condemned and hanged. When she returned from the court, she was in the most violent agitation, describing to me to awful scene she had been witness to. I prevailed on her to come into the shrubbery for air.

Just as we got into it we heard the lawn gate open. She gave a scream I can never forget and dropt on her knees. 'It's Bevan, it's Bevan. My God, my God have you restored him!'

She was *powerless*, but he soon reached her with his two youngest children clinging to him. Never did I see a group, whose countenances could have given a finer hint of genuine feeling to the pencil of an artist. The mixture of happiness and gratitude to God I must ever remember, and the contrast of the children's playful countenances I can do but little justice to. It was indeed most truly affecting.

After shaking him warmly by the hand, I turned from them into the shrubbery. I thought such a meeting should be sacred! I partook silently of their happiness and did not despair, but a merciful God might yet have such joy in store for me, when his protecting arm might be pleased to

---

37 Charlotte, daughter of William Mussenden of Larchfield, Co. Down, married Revd Richard Bevan on 20 Nov. 1790 (Leslie, 126). They had several children, including Revd Richard, who became Curate of Carne in 1823; William, who entered Trinity College Dublin in 1809, aged 18; and Frances, baptized 27 Aug. 1797 (Carne Parish Register).

restore me to you and all my beloved friends. His account to us was that on Wednesday morning, the day the rebels took possession of Wexford, he intended as usual to ride about his Parish and harrangue the peasantry, tho' he despaired of doing any good; he had the day before perceived such sulkiness about them. Upon riding to his own forge, he saw his smith openly at work making pikes, and a heap of them piled up in the corner of the forge. He galloped off to Wexford to give information of this outrage, when to his utter astonishment he found the town evacuated by the Loyalists and army, and all the Loyalists endeavouring to get on board ship. To return thro' the country alone would have been certain death. He saw the Rebels in all direction making towards the town and was obliged to choose the heart-breaking alternative of leaving his wife and children in a remote part of the country where his house was, or deprive them of him for ever by braving a mob determined on the destruction of every clergyman they could get at.

The Sunday after his return, Mr B read prayers in our drawing-room; all the neighbouring protestants attended, & never I suppose did a congregation offer up their prayers with more devotion or gratitude to the Almighty power, who granted us the happiness of again meeting to acknowledge his great mercies. But tho' we were surrounded by the King's encampments, I perceived a murmuring that a Protestant clergyman was again allowed to do his duty. They did not speak out, but discontent and disappointment was visible, and I believe they were far from giving up hopes that the day (to use their own language) would yet be their own. Many of them openly said so, with the King's pardon in their pockets.

The Sunday following we once more ventured to Mr Bevan's Church (which is quite in a remote corner of the barony), but not without fear and trembling I own, tho' he disdained the offer of a guard of soldiers during service. His confidence was too forcibly felt in that divine providence which had so miraculously restored him to his family and preserved them in the midst of such peril. Poor Mrs B had suffered a vast deal, but we were too happy to allow ourselves to talk of the past. It was several days since I had heard from Charles, and I grew very apprehensive for his safety, as there were constant accounts of marauding parties doing great mischief in the country, which was by no means quiet.

After we returned from Church, I mentioned my alarm to Mr B, who did all he could to quiet my fears, but I thought there was mystery in every one's countenance. We were just going to sit down to dinner when he called me out of the room, saying, 'Now don't be alarmed. I have good news for you. I will show you a person you are not a little ancious about'. Notwithstanding his kind precaution, I was near dropping on the stairs when he assured me Charles was safe but afraid to make a sudden appearance. Think of my joy at seeing this dear fellow, after all the parts he had been in, and my misery about him. He was completely accoutred – a brace of pistols in his bosom & four more in his belt and holsters, with a broad sword. Sir C. Asgill[38] gave him 3 days leave and indeed he rode from Kilkenny at such a risk I would gladly have dispensed with the gratification of seeing him, but his impatience to see us was not to be longer retrained.

When all the family were in bed but myself and him, I could not resist the desire I had of *showing him* to my poor rebel friends that I was hiding. I made above above twenty of them come into where he was sitting after dinner and drink his health. He poured out a large glass of whiskey and water, and reaching out his hand to them, said, 'Come my lads, won't you drink the King's health?'

And in a voice they answered, 'Yes faith and your's too'. Then looking at his uniform, sneered and said, 'Our liberty dress is not quite so grand [as] even the best of them. We had nothing but our own ould clothes'. He recollected several of them that he had seen on Lackin Hill, and they said they knew the dress the moment they saw him. How were matters changed! A week before this how I should have trembled to see him surrounded with Rebels.

He staid with us but a day and a half. When he was gone I felt very differently at Summerseat. My confidence fled with him. The reports kept us in a continual state of alarm, and when the post failed coming in (which it frequently did) we framed the worst, and thought all our miseries were to be renewed. I was most anxious to get to Dublin, but it was impossible to travel in safety, and as our carriage horses had never been returned, I proposed to my Father to go by sea. He consented to it after a fortnight resisting my entreaties. Every one who could get a passage in the wretched traders were hurrying off. We took our passage, and I brought a bed for my Father, there not being any accomodation for passengers, but when I look'd at him and my children and felt that I was bringing them in safety to Dublin, every thing appeared delightfully. But my happiness was soon to be clouded. The pilot was drunk and struck us on the bar at Wexford. It was impossible to get off until the next tide. We had 3 officers and 12 men of the Queen's regiment, and some gentlemen and Ladies on board, all of whom except the soldiers determined on taking the boat and remaining in Wexford for the tide. I declined proposing to my Father to be of the party, lest I should find it difficult to get him back, as I feared the disappointment might determine him to run all risk and go by land.

Soon as the boat was out of sight, the pilot came on deck and in the most daring manner said swearing most horridly, 'You are one of the passengers, d—n me if you shan't suffer for not giving me a crown when

38 See Chapter Four, note 48. Asgill was commander of the 46th Foot, known for its lack of discipline and brutality in suppressing the Rebellion.

you came on board, & I struck the vessel on purpose to be revenged of you all'.

He was quite drunk. There was no person near me but my dear Susan. My father and Letitia had fallen asleep at the other end of the vessel on the bed I had arranged for him. This horrid fellow continued swearing and talking in a most horrid manner. I looked at the soldiers and desired them to protect me from him. They immediately desired him to hold his tongue or they would throw him over. This gave me courage and I loudly called to know where the Captain of the vessel was. The Pilot said, 'Captain indeed, he has no power while I am on board and he would do as he pleased'.

I then desired one of the soldiers to call loudly for the Captain, and in a moment or two an ill-looking fellow came up, evidently drunk and his eyes half shut. He had been asleep. A great deal of abuse on both sides insued, and I felt more dead than alive. The noise woke my Father as I dreaded, and he was angry with me for having influenced him to come into such a vessel. At length the dispute ended, and this fellow was prevailed on to lye down.

In some time I joyfully perceived the boat coming from Wexford with the passengers. Soon as they came on board, I told them of the Pilot's conduct and that he had said he would strike us again and keep us in the Harbour as long as he liked, upon which a Mr Stringer,[39] an Enniscorthy gentleman, declared the Captain should not take in the boat, that he would go back to Wexford and complain to the commanding officer, and that he would not return without a Mr Grey, a respectable man, a protestant Pilot. The Captain remonstrated, but Mr S was steady. He with two gentlemen went for the Pilot he mentioned, and I requested one of the officers would stay on board to protect us from farther insult. This Mr Turner of the Queen's Regt politely offered to do, and to this charming young man, I am sure under God, we owe our lives.

In a few hours the gentlemen returned with the Pilot they had sought for. He soon took us safe over the bar and returned to Wexford. We had a fine evening and a fair wind, but at the fall of the tide between one and two o'clock and dark for the time of year, we were struck upon a rock! This threw us all into great consternation. Mr Stringer, a gentleman who had suffered materially at Enniscorthy, increased our alarm by declaring aloud that the Captain did it designedly. In a moment the deck was all confusion. Think how I was shocked when the three officers came and whispered me to hide their swords under my great coat and to stand near the Hold, as they must all go and try to work the ship off the rock, and desired me to

39 Joseph Stringer of Enniscorthy and later Dublin, apothecary, claimed losses at Enniscorthy totalling £774, including medicines, bank notes and clothes, of which he received only £191 (Claimants, ccccxxv). He was probably related to John Stringer, whose widow Martha claimed more than £1,672 in losses, including a house, furniture, clothing, and accounts (Ibid.).

call to them should any of the men belonging to the vessel approach me, as they suspected they had arms on board; that we were just under Glascarick Hill, the rendezvous of the retreating rebels and that the Captain had brought us there to give us up to their fury.

Mr Turner insisted on getting out the long boat and put six of his men to work the windlass, and swore he would shoot the first man that put his hand to a rope without his orders. I heard Mr Stringer whisper him to beware of their slipping the cable. He was scarcely in the boat when he called out to know who the rascal was who had slipped the cable, and desired they would put out another, as he would go on board and lash everyone belonging to the ship. All this time it was thumping violently against the rocks. I gave myself up to despair, reproaching myself for bringing my dear Father against his will. I was unconscious that I was saying a word, till my attention was called off by my angelic Susan's saying, 'Oh dear Mamma, don't be afraid – did not God Almighty save us from the rebels'. Such piety in so young a creature not 11 years old was indeed a lesson to me.

Mr Turner remained near an hour rowing round the ship in hope of disengaging it. He then came on board and said it was in vain till the tide came in. He did all in his power to quiet our fears, assuring us the night was so calm we were in no danger. Every thump the vessel gave filled me with horror, and every noise made me fear the rebels were coming out in boats for us. In no period of the rebellion were my feelings, sufferings equal to those of this night. I do think I should have lost my senses but for the compassionate attention of Mr Turner. My self reproach was not bearable. Had I not forced my dear Father into this danger, I would have submitted with resignation. The passengers wanted to have the corn thrown over, particularly Mr Stringer, who could not give up the idea that the Captain drove us purposely on the rocks to put us into the hands of the rebels and that he deserved the loss of his cargo. Mr Turner, full of humanity, remonstrated and said it was private property and might ruin the owner, that the Captain was only conveying it to Dublin. He assured us we were safe, that the tide was coming in fast and desired us to observe how seldom the vessel thumped comparatively. It is impossible to say too much of this charming young man, who, in the few hours of my acquaintance with him, displayed steadiness, bravery, activity, and humanity. I could not help telling him, I envied the Mother who had such a son to boast of.

The vessel continued violently agitated for several hours, during which time hope and despair alternately took possession of me, but my most powerful feeling was reproach. Indeed, my dear child's religious reflection made me blush at one moment doubting the mercy of that Providence, which had so recently brought us through such perils. I felt at times thankful that my dear Father and children had been spared the more painful death of being murdered by the rebels, and if the ship could not be saved, we were likely not one of us to be doubtful of the other's fate. At length the joyful cry, 'She's off! she's off!' I was too much overwhelmed with gratitude to know what was going on. I was almost stupified. At length they made me sensible that we were sailing with a fair wind and that a few hours would bring us to Dublin. We arrived without further obstacle.

We found carriages on the quay, into one of which we joyfully got, and indeed our sensations are not to be described. We looked at each other without being able to utter a word, till going thro' York Street I saw my beloved dear Doctor Hartigan's[40] carriage at the door of some patient. I begged my Father to allow me to go into it, and that he and the children could drive to his house, the place of our destination. He consented, and into his carriage I went, my heart jumping at every sound. At length the hall door opened, and the footman opened the carriage door for his master. But what was my dear Willy's surprise when I threw my arms about him.

The coachman was ordered home, and I continued embracing Willy without being able to utter, until he saw a gentleman nodding and laughing. Till that moment we neither of us recollected the extraordinary exhibition we were making. He drew the string and beckoned to the gentleman and told him I was the dear relation he had heard him so often lament as in the hands of the rebels, and of whom he had believed had been murdered. We soon arrived at his house and were received with such joy by Mrs Hartigan, poor Mr Adams,[41] and a party of my friends that words cannot describe the joy of that moment. I pray God I may never loose sight of the mercy shown my family and myself. I have written every circumstance just as they occurred, and really the incidents followed exactly as I have stated them, tho' were you reading a novel you would say they were previously arranged. Tho' this is merely a narrative of facts which chiefly concerned ourselves and gives little of the general features of the rebellion, I know they will be interesting to you, my dear friend, who suffered so much about us when our fate was doubtful.

As ever affectionately yours

Jane Adams

August, 1798[42]

40 William Hartigan, apothecary, was admitted a Freeman of Dublin, Midsummer, 1777 ('Alphabetized List of the Freemen of the City of Dublin', *Irish Ancestor* 15 [1983]:59). 41 This was the Revd Tobias Adams, Jane's estranged husband, who at the time was rector of Bretway, Co. Cork. 42 The British Library copy bears no date. At the bottom is the following note: 'Mrs Adams, I believe, speaks of her son Charles; in this in the former part of it, it is her brother Charles [*sic*]; her son was in some regt and is now Curate to the Bishop of Cloyne, lives at Ahada Glebe. Mrs Adams has sent the original pass to be sent to you; it is enclosed in this.'

9

MARY LEADBEATER

One of the most articulate female voices of eighteenth century Ireland was Mary Leadbeater née Shackleton. An avid diarist, she left a vivid, detailed account of her life from childhood to old age, together with a lengthy commentary on her times that included her experiences in 1798. Born on 1 December 1758 at Ballitore in the county of Kildare, Mary was the daughter of Richard Shackleton and his second wife, Elizabeth Carleton. The Shackletons were prominent members locally of the Society of Friends. Mary's grandfather, Abraham Shackleton, 'a learned and good man',[1] was a native of Yorkshire, who arrived in Ireland in 1720 as a private tutor for the families of John Duckett of Duckett's Grove and William Cooper of Cooper's Hill in Co. Carlow.[2] He returned briefly to England and married Margaret Wilkinson of Skipton, Yorkshire, but by March, 1726, he had decided to settle in Ireland permanently and establish a boarding school in the village of Ballitore. The school soon attracted the children of many prominent Irish families, and its alumni included Edmund Burke, James Napper Tandy, and Paul Cullen (later Cardinal Cullen, Primate of Ireland).

When Abraham retired as headmaster in 1756, he was succeeded by son Richard, who maintained the school's tradition of excellence. By 1766, the school 'consisted of fifty and sometimes sixty boarders besides day scholars', including several French and two Norwegians.[3] Richard was married twice. Following the death of his first wife Elizabeth (Fuller) in 1754, he married his second wife, Elizabeth (Carleton), on 17 October 1755. Together they had four children. When Richard died in 1792, he was eulogized by the Carlow Monthly Meeting as 'a kind, affectionate husband, a tender and careful father, a good neighbour, liberal and generous, especially exemplary in anything relating to the wants of our Society'.[4]

Reared in her parents' devout Quaker household in Ballitore, Mary received an extensive, liberal education. Her faith provided her with an

---

1 'A Memoir of Mary Leadbeater', in *The Leadbeater Papers* [London: Bell and Daldy, 1862], 1:1. 2 Frank Taafe, 'Some Ballitore Shackletons', *Carloviana* 36 (1988/89):22. 3 Mary Leadbeater, 'Annals of Ballitore', in *The Leadbeater Papers*, 2 vols (London: Bell and Daldy, 1862), 1:42–3. 4 The Minutes of the Carlow Monthly Meeting cited in Taafe, 23.

altruistic view of her neighbours that greatly influenced much of her later writing. To a certain extent, her views found further encouragement in the idealistic, egalitarian writings of the Enlightenment, though, as her biographer Kevin O'Neill has stated, she and her fellow Quakers 'could never accept that human reason could stand alone, apart or especially in contradiction to Divine Truth'.[5]

In 1791, Mary took as her husband William Leadbeater, a former pupil of the Shackleton School who converted to the Society of Friends at the time of their marriage. He farmed a tract of land at Ballitore and resided there until his death in 1827. Mary kept the local post office. Together they had two children: Elizabeth and Jane, the latter of whom died in a fiery accident in 1798, for which Mary would later blame herself.

Mary did not remain isolated in Ballitore. Throughout most of her adult life, she maintained a wide correspondence that included Edmund Burke, George Crabbe, Sir Joshua Reynolds, Maria Edgeworth, and Mrs Melusina Trench. She saved all of her papers and appeared grief-stricken when two of her letters from Burke disappeared during a robbery of her house in 1798. Keenly interested in social reform and equality, she wrote several books, including *Extracts and Original Anecdotes* for the *Improvement of Youth* in 1794 and a book of poetry in 1808. But it was her *Cottage Dialogues of the Irish Peasantry* in 1813, published in several series, for which she is best known. The *Dialogues* were directed toward the Irish peasantry and intended as a means of giving moral instruction for the improvement their living conditions. Four more books were to follow, including *The Landlord's Friend*, also published in 1813, *Tales for Cottagers* in 1814, *Cottage Biography* in 1822, and her last book, *The Pedlars*, in 1824. She died two years later in 1826.

The most important of Mary's work is her private journal, which she kept from 1766 to 1826. In it, she chronicled events in her beloved Ballitore and included the only known female narrative of the rebellion in Co. Kildare, from which the following extract is taken. The journal was later given the title, 'Annals of Ballitore' and was first published in 1862 with some of her letters in *The Leadbeater Papers*.[6]

Mary's role in the years leading up to the rebellion is a complex one. She has been called a 'peaceful rebel', and indeed one could argue against including her account in this collection of loyal and neutral women's narratives, for she was not entirely a neutral observer. Her biographer O'Neill observes that she was 'a peaceful revolutionary ... she was an advocate of radical equality in Irish society'. It was only her 'equally

5 Kevin O'Neill, 'Mary Shackleton Leadbeater: Peaceful Rebel', Keogh and Furlong, eds. *The Women of 1798*, 144.   6 The editor wishes to acknowledge the kind assistance of Dr Kevin O'Neill of Boston College, whose forthcoming biography of Mary and edition of the Leadbeater papers is expected to be the definitive work.

radical commitment to peace' that prevented her active support of the rebellion in more traditional ways.[7] Though she provided moral and logistical support to United Irish organizer Malachi Delany, she and her family were nonetheless the victims of rebels who broke into their home to rob them. Like the account of Dinah Goff, Mary's pacifist views reveal her disdain for the excesses committed by all sides and her horror at the sufferings of fellow townspeople and Quakers. In the end, like the Goffs, she embraced the return of order while clinging to her idealism.

THE ACCOUNT

This year, which in its progress was clouded with so many horrors, opened upon me more delightfully than any former year had done; for on the morning of its first day my beloved husband's life, which for fourteen days was suspended in a very doubtful scale, rose up with hope, and the crisis of a dangerous fever was past. It was like escaping from a prison-house, from torture, and from darkness, to breathe the free air, to shake off the painful shackles, and to gaze upon the sun, when this inestimable favour was granted. In this time of deep trial I received all the comfort and aid which friendship and sympathy could bestow. My husband *was to live*. When that was the case, all means co-operated to that end. The interest caused by the danger of one so much loved and respected was exceeding and extensive, and among our immediate neighbours it was intense. It was touching to see one of his labourers, who would not be denied the privilege of seeing him, as he believed for the last time, approach his bed, take his fevered hand, and weeping, exclaim, 'Oh, my dear master!' Even the great mastiff housedog came pattering up stairs, laid his head on the bed, and looked long and wistfully, with almost human affection in his eyes, at his master. It was delightful when we could meet our friends at our fireside again, and receive their unaffected salutation, with smiles and tears which welcomed us once more to health and happiness.

The attack on Willowbrook alarmed Robert Bayley,[8] who fled from Ballitore with his handsome wife in a fright, declaring that every man,

---

7 O'Neill, 'Mary Shackleton Leadbeater', 162.   8 Robert Bayley of Willowbrook was probably a Quaker. Although his house was burned, he does not appear as a claimant in Co. Kildare. Bayley was an heir to the Strettell family, who founded the original Quaker colony at Ballitore, which made him owner, in fee, of the principal part of the village. His house was called 'Ballitore House'. He married Kitty Yates or Yeates of Moone, undoubtedly a relative of Richard Yeates of Moone. Betsy Shackleton called Kitty 'the handsomest woman in the world' and related a story that before marrying her, Bayley had courted a lady who later married John Stratford, earl of Aldborough. 'There is a tradition that the rivals and their lovely brides happening to meet at a ball, Bayley, who could not pronounce th, addressed Stratford as follows: "Well, Jack, which of us has got *de* best of *de* bargain?"' (Betsy

woman, and child in the village were 'United Irishmen'. Now and then a person was missed, and this misfortune was unfeelingly accounted for by saying that 'Brownie had eaten them'. These mysterious disappearances were horrible, and no certainty of the fate of those victims of party rage was ever obtained. A time had come when nothing but what was honest, and fair, and 'above board' could stand the test. Amongst other precautions, the names of the inhabitants were posted on the doors of each house, and the authorities had liberty to enter at any hour, night or day, to see whether they were within or not. This appeared a necessary precaution, yet it exposed the quiet of families to be sadly broken in upon.

Houses were now searched for fire-arms, proving the wisdom of our friends in banishing all such weapons from theirs. Notices were put up demanding the arms taken by the 'United men' to be restored, on pain of allowing the military to live at free quarters; for many nightly incursions had been made by these robbers to plunder houses of whatever arms they contained. A detachment of the King's Co. militia was at this time sent here from Athy, where Sandford Palmer,[9] an old Ballitore boy, was stationed as their captain. The men were very well liked; perhaps it was for that reason they were so soon removed, the villagers escorting them on their way with tears and lamentations; and when my husband, from his fields, saw them departing, he sent his workmen to join the procession. Perhaps these painful feelings sprung from an unconscious presentiment, for it those men had remained here, Ballitore might have escaped its subsequent distresses. They were replaced by the Tyrone militia, mostly comprised of professed orangemen, wearing the ribbon of their party.

Hitherto the soldiers were quartered in our houses but found themselves in provisions; the threat respecting free quarters was now put into execution; foraging parties went into the country, shops and private houses were searched for whisky, which was ordered to be spilled; and seditious papers were sought for.[10] On the day of this search I was not at home, else I suppose I should have opened my desk in the security of conscious

Shackleton, *Ballitore and Its Inhabitants Seventy Years Ago* [Dublin: Richard D. Webb, 1862], 3). The Bayleys owned a parrot which Miss Shackleton, in her youth, always longed to see. 9 The roll of the Shackleton school lists Robert Sandford Palmer among the students in 1778 (*Leadbeater Papers*, App., xiv). It is unclear whether he was related to the Palmers of Rahan, Co. Kildare (see 'Palmer of Rahan', *Burke's Landed Gentry of Ireland* [1912], 550). 10 An anonymous Friend in Ballitore, almost certainly Abraham Shackleton, kept a journal that affirmed Mrs Leadbeater's account, asserting that these actions were part of a series of coercive measures designed to frighten the public into obedience. There was a gradation of punishment: 'First, putting soldiers on private houses, -Secondly, allowing them free quarters there, so that many poor people left their beds to the soldiers and lay upon straw, – Thirdly, burning their houses, on intimation of disaffection, or proof of concealed arms, – Fourthly, whipping, which was conducted with such severity, that many said they would prefer to be shot at once than be thus tortured to death ... ' (Abraham Shackleton quoted anonymously in Hancock, *Principles of Peace*, 108).

innocence, quite forgetting that I had thrown into it one of the squibs then privately circulated, which in very tolerable poetry avowed disloyal sentiments. I started at the danger it was so near bringing upon us, and thankfully flung it into the fire. Account was taken of the stock and provisions in the village, that none should be sent away; and six cwt. of bacon which was being sent to Dublin by one of the villagers was seized by the yeomen. Robert Bayley was pursued because he attempted to take away one of his own horses; his horse was captured, and himself made a prisoner. Ephraim Boake's[11] house was plundered, and he very narrowly escaped personal injury.

These attacks on the most loyal people amongst us were not to be borne. Some of the inhabitants went to Colonel Colin Campbell,[12] who commanded the district, and got protections which stopped further depredations upon them, and procured the restoration of their property. Colonel Campbell was willing to grant protections to all peaceable people, but none of the Friends applied for them, some doubt being entertained of its being consistent with our principles to apply for armed protection. We were thus exposed to the imputation of being disaffected, and the provision we had for our families was rudely taken out of our houses for the yeomen. This was an unpleasant sight to the soldiers who were with us on free quarters, and they hid our bacon for us and for themselves.

11 Ephraim Boake of Boakefield, near Ballitore, was born about 1724 and was perhaps the son of Thomas Boake, who, with Abraham Shackleton, was a witness to the will of Henry Fuller of Ballitore on 23 Dec. 1740 (P. Beryl Eustace and Olive C. Goodbody, *Quaker Records Dublin, Abstracts of Wills* [Dublin: Stationery Office, 1957], 41). He died by drowning in the summer of 1800. Hancock describes him as 'an aged neighbour, long since deceased, who had united his endeavours with those of Abraham Shackleton and his friends, first to moderate, and then to protect the misguided people' (Hancock, 119). Mrs Leadbeater wrote of his death: 'one fine morning Ephriam walked down to his sheep-pond, near to the house, with the intention of washing his head there, as he had often done before. It was no wonder that his limbs, stiffened with age, should fail as he stooped to the fatal water, and occasion the lamented catastrophe which closed his long life' ('Annals of Ballitore', 273). He appears to have had several children: a daughter, Jane Thomas, who attempted to revive him at his death, and perhaps sons Thomas and Ephraim, who are listed as students at the Shackleton school in 1776 (Ibid., 274, App. xiv).   12 Colin Campbell was born in 1754, the second son of John Campbell of the Citadel and deputy keeper of the Great Seal of Scotland. He entered the 71st Regiment as an ensign in 1771, and was promoted to lieutenant in 1774. Accompanying the 71st to America, he was promoted to captain in 1778 and, while stationed there, married Mary, daughter of Col. Guy Johnstone on New York. His regiment was ordered to Nova Scotia in 1786, and later to the West Indies during the war with France. After being promoted to lieutenant-colonel in 1795, Campbell was dispatched to Ireland, and in 1798 became a colonel. He was present at Vinegar Hill and the defeat of the French at Ballynahinch. He remained in Ireland till 1803. In 1805 was made a major-general, and in 1811 he was appointed lieutenant governor of Gibraltar. He died in 1814. (See *Dictionary of National Biography* 3:801–2. Several of his letters are reprinted in Hancock, 116–17.)

Great waste was committed, and unchecked robbery. One hundred cars loaded with hay, potatoes, oats, etc. led by the poor owners, and guarded by soldiers, who were in one day marched into Ballitore. Colonel Keatinge[13] urged his yeomen to take with a sparing hand; to remember that this was the 'scarce season', when the new food was not yet come in and the old was nearly exhausted, and not to bring famine upon the country. But he spoke to deaf ears, for pity seemed banished from the martial bosom. One exception I must record; one of those men quartered upon us refused to partake of the plunder upon which so many of his comrades riotously feasted, and appeared much dejected – yet he, as well as another of a very opposite cast of mind, fell by the insurgents when the burst came. Threats were multiplied, and the military poured in one day, so as to terrify the scared inhabitants with the prospect of army and yeomanry. Public notice was given that the nightly patrol should be withdrawn, to give opportunity for returning the arms of which the 'United men' had possessed themselves, and that if not returned within a stated time, the whole neighbourhood should be burnt.

Colonel Keatinge went in person to the chapel, and with tears and fervent entreaties besought the misguided people to comply with these conditions: but he entreated in vain; so when he saw that even his influence could not avail to preserve them, he and his lady left the country. They left their dear Narraghmore – left it never to return, and their loss has never ceased to be felt and deplored. A large quantity of arms was left as directed, but broken into pieces, and thus rendered useless. The clouds gathered darker and darker in our political horizon though nothing could be sweeter, calmer, or brighter than our vernal sky and balmy gales. In the midst of these tumults a dear friend of ours died; we could not lament a tranquil escape to a world of eternal rest. My mind felt wearied with what

---

13 Col. Maurice Keatinge of Narraghmore, Co. Kildare, a liberal, commanded the East Narraghmore Cavalry in 1797 and 1798, which included both Catholics and Protestants (see Oliver Snoddy, 'The Volunteers, Militia, Yeomanry and Orangemen of Co. Kildare in the 18th Century', *J. of the Co. Kildare Archaeological Society* 15 [1971]: 47; see also L.M. Cullen, 'Politics and Rebellion: Wicklow in the 1790s', in Ken Hannigan and William Nolan (eds), *Wicklow History and Society*, [Dublin: Geography Publications, 1994], 469). Taafe describes him as 'a well-meaning and honourable man [who] spent time and energy in encouraging the local Catholics to remain loyal to the Crown. His efforts were in vain as even the encouragement of this respected member of the community could not persuade the long suffering Catholics to forget decades of poverty and intolerance' (Frank Taafe, 'Athy in the Years of the Rebellion, 1798–1803', unpublished manuscript). Musgrave calls Keatinge 'a most active and intelligent officer, who raised sixty yeoman cavalry and twenty infantry to preserve the peace' (Musgrave, 254). In 1799, he claimed the loss of a house worth £400 (Claimants, ccxiv). This fact is confirmed by an unknown diarist in Hancock, who stated that 'Narraghmore House, the new unfinished mansion of Maurice Keatinge [was] ... (with the assistance of fire) demolished' (Hancock, 119). The Revd Cadog Keatinge of Narraghmore, Dean of Clogher and also a claimant, was probably a relative.

appeared to me oppressive in the melancholy state of the times – rule and mis-rule fighting with each other, and the country torn to pieces with the strife.

To the Tyrone militia were now added the Suffolk fencibles; and the Ancient Britons, dressed in blue with much silver lace – a very pretty dress – came from Athy, seized the smiths' tools to prevent them from making pikes, and made prisoners of the smiths themselves. I could not see without emotion poor Owen Finn and his brother, hand-cuffed and weeping, as they walked after the car containing those implements of industry which had enabled them to provide comfortably for the family. Several of these were whipped publicly to extort confessions about the pikes. The torture was excessive, and the victims were long in recovering; and in almost every case it was applied fruitlessly. Guards were placed at every entrance to the village, to prevent people from entering or leaving it. The village once so peaceful exhibited a scene of tumult and dismay, and the air rang with the shrieks of the sufferers and the lamentations of those who beheld them suffer. These violent measures caused a great many pikes to be brought in: the street was lined with those who came to deliver up the instruments of death.

A party of military from Naas entered Ballitore, and took prisoners twelve of our neighbours, whom they removed to Naas gaol. Most of the villagers stood outside their doors to see them depart. They looked composed for the most part, though followed by their weeping wives and children. One child, with his cries of 'O father, father!' excited great compassion. Six yeomen were taken prisoners to Dunlavin. I was walking in our garden when they passed on a car, with their coats turned inside out, and one of their guards, a mere boy, cried out to me in a tone of insulting jocularity. We, who did not understand this case, were only qualified to see one side, and, though we forbore audibly expressing our disapprobaton, our looks betrayed the depression of our minds. This excited jealousy of us: how ill-founded! For who could expect us to rejoice at the misery and degradation of our fellow-creatures and neighbours, or even to behold them unmoved? These unfortunate yeomen were shot! There was too much exultation in the military; they were not aware, perhaps, how deeply an insult is felt and resented, and that an injury is sometimes more easily pardoned.[14]

---

14 The condemned yeomen, Andrew Ryan, Matthew Farrell, and two Duffy brothers, were Catholics and members of the liberal corps of Morley Saunders of Saundersgrove. As such, they were widely suspected by conservatives of being rebel sympathizers, although there was no evidence offered for their condemnation (see Cullen, 'Politics and Rebellion: Wicklow in the 1790s', 466–9; Pakenham, *The Year of Liberty*, 135–6). Suspicious of their loyalty, Saunders ordered their execution on the green of Dunlavin, 26 May 1798. The incident was immortalized in the popular ballad, 'Dunlavin Green' (see Georges-Denis Zimmermann,

The morning of the 24th of the Fifth-month (May) orders came for the soldiers quartered here to march to Naas. A report was circulated that Naas gaol had been broken open, that Dublin was in arms, and so forth. All was uncertainty, except that something serious had happened, as the mail-coach had been stopped. The insurrection was to begin in Dublin, and the mail-coach not being suffered to leave the city was the signal for the general revolt. This purpose being defeated by the vigilance of government; the mail-coach had got to Naas before it was stopped, yet its detention there persuaded the people that the day was there own. They threw off the appearance of loyalty, and rose in avowed rebellion. In the morning the Suffolk fencibles first marched out, nine men remaining to guard their baggage at the Mill, which was their barrack. The Tyrone militia followed, taking their baggage with them. All was hurry and confusion in the village. Several who had kept out of sight now appeared dressed in green, that colour so dear to United Irishmen, and proportionally abhorred by the loyal. The Suffolks went by the high road, the Tyrones through Narraghmore. As they marched out, a young woman privately and with tears told their lieutenant her apprehensions that their enemies lay in ambush in Narraghmore wood. He was therefore prepared to meet them, and sad havoc ensued; many on both sides fell, particularly among the undisciplined multitude. The court-house at Narraghmore was attacked, and many met their death there. We heard the reports of firearms, and every hour the alarm increased.[15]

Dr Johnson[16] had been sent for to Narraghmore to dress wounds; the rabble despoiled him of his horse and case of instruments, and sent him back jaded and worn out. About three o'clock in the afternoon John Dunne and many others came as far as the bridge with pikes, and Dr Johnston turned them back; but not long after two or three hundred men armed with pikes, knives, and pitchforks, and bearing sticks with green rags fluttering from them, came in at the western side, headed by Malachi Delany on a white horse, and took possession of the town; Dr Johnson, as representative of the yeomanry-guard, having capitulated on condition of persons and property being safe. I saw from an upper window a crowd coming towards our kitchen-door; I went down and found many armed

Songs of Irish Rebellion: Political Street Ballads and Rebel Songs, 1780–1900 [Dublin: Allen Figgis, 1967], 140–1). **15** Musgrave writes of the ambush: 'At the end of the bog road near the turnpike, they were attacked and surrounded by the three thousand rebels from Narraghmore, on whom they kept up a brisk fire, for near half an hour. The rebels having perceived his [Lt. Eadie's] approach, placed a number of wool packs on cars, which happened accidently to be passing by; and some of their marksmen concealed behind them, fired and killed seven of the Suffolk fencibles, and then retreated to their main body. But the major pursued, and obtained ample revenge; for in a short time, two hundred rebels lay dead, and many more were wounded' (Musgrave, 257–8). **16** Dr Francis Johnson is described as a 'surgeon' (Musgrave, 258).

men, who desired to have refreshments, especially drink. I brought them milk, and was cutting a loaf of bread when a little elderly man, called 'the Canny', took it kindly out of my hand and divided it himself, saying 'Be decent, boys, be decent'. Encouraged by having found a friend, I ventured to tell them that so many armed men in the room frightened me. The warriors condescended to my fears. 'We'll be out in a shot', they replied, and in a minute the kitchen was empty.

Daniel Horan, a young farmer from the Long Avenue, was standing in our yard – a fine looking fellow. I had observed a dark cloud upon his countenance when, a few days before, he was requesting a protection from the officers; that cloud was now gone, and joy and animation played on every feature, unaccompanied by any expression of malignity. A party of insurgents, as they went to the mill, met some of the wives of the soldiers stationed there, whom they sent back to tell their husbands that if they surrendered they should not be injured. But the women, instead of delivering the message, ran shrieking to announce the approach of the rebels, and the soldiers prepared to stand on the defensive; but, when they saw such a multitude, fled. In the pursuit over Max's-hill a soldier turned, fired, and shot Paddy Dempsey[17] dead. They were soon overpowered, and their lives were spared only on condition that he who killed the insurgent should be pointed out; with this hard alternative his comrades reluctantly replied, and the soldier soon lay dead beside his victim. Another of the soldiers was killed by a shot from the Mill-field, which reached him about the middle of the avenue, and his remains are buried in the ditch just by the spot where he fell. Most of the others were wounded, but I believe none mortally.

Malachi Delany[18] exerted himself to prevent bloodshed, and showed as much humanity as courage. He had thrown off no mask, for he never wore

17 Paddy Dempsey lived in Ballitore in a house on a row of houses near Bill Lennon and Betty Malone. Betsy Shackleton wrote: 'I have little to say of Paddy Dempsey. He was shot in the mill-field by the Suffolk Fencibles who guarded the Mill House, which was a barrack in 1798. His wife, Poll Dempsey, survived him many years. She was a baker, and when unable to bake on a large scale, she made pickelets and carried them about the village. Her son Christy is now a man of considerable consequence at the sign of The Three Birds and the Sheaf of Wheat' (Shackleton, 51–2).   18 Malachi Delany was among the principal United Irish organizers in Kildare and a confidant of Mary Leadbeater (O'Neill, 'Mary Shackleton Leadbeater', 155). He was thought by Miles Byrne to have been a native of the Kerry mountains, but according to Madden was the son of a landed proprietor in Co. Wicklow (Madden quoted in Thomas Addis Emmet, *Memoir of Thomas Addis and Robert Emmet* [New York: Emmet Press, 1915], 2:39). He had studied in France and at the Irish College, and 'was considered a young man of talent and an accomplished scholar' (Byrne, *Memoirs*, 2:284). He had served as an officer in the Austrian army prior to becoming a rebel leader in Co. Kildare, where he distributed copies of Thomas Paine's *Rights of Man* (Landreth, *Pursuit of Robert Emmet*, 85). He later became a close friend and associate of Robert Emmet and after 1798 took an active role in France in attempting to raise money for the Irish cause (Elliott, *Partners in Revolution*, 275–6, 344). In the spring of 1803, he was

one, and he proved himself to be a generous enemy. A great number of strange faces surrounded us, and a message brought to me to request any thing of a green colour. I told them we could not join any party.

'What! not the strongest?' enquired one of the strangers.

'None at all' – and though our parlour tables were covered with green cloth, they urged their request no further.

Richard Yeates,[19] son to Squire Yeates of Moone, was brought in as a prisoner, his yeomanry coat turned. A private of the yeomanry corps to which he belonged was also brought into our parlour, where my husband and I sat at tea. He was an old man; we made him sit down to tea, and invited his captors, but they declined; one of them went to the table and helped himself to bread and butter, looked at himself in the mirror, and remarked it was 'war time'. The prisoner, with tears trickling down his cheeks, spoke sadly of his seven children; his guards strove to console him by telling him that 'he was an honest Roman, and should not be hurt'. Presently we heard a shot, and those strangers immediately said they 'supposed Richard Yeates was shot'. This was really the case. He was taken into a house, and despite of his own entreaties, the endeavours of many others to save him, and even the efforts of Priest Cullen,[20] who begged the

arrested in Dublin and charged with murder, but the charges were mysteriously dropped. Then in September, 1803, he was arrested again, this time on a charge of high treason, but was discharged four months later on the orders of William Wickham. Some have suspected him of being an informant against Emmet and his associates, but these assertions have not been substantiated (Landreth, 119, 361–2; Emmet, 2:113). In 1825, he is believed to have supplied biographical information about Emmet to Thomas Furlong, who published a series of articles on Emmet in the *London and Dublin Magazine* (Emmet, 2:273). He died reputedly at Drumcondra after this date. **19** Lt. Richard Yeates of Moone was born about 1773, and was a school-fellow of Patrick O'Kelly of Kilcoo, who later wrote that Yeates, 'having fallen into the hands of the people was mercilessly put to death by Captain Murphy ... From his having been a school fellow of ... the author he has cause to say that the inoffensive, modest and gentlemanly habits of Richard Yeates have raised in him a sincere regret for his unfortunate and untimely end' (Patrick O'Kelly, *History of the Rebellion of 1798* [Dublin, 1842], 65; see also Peadar Mac Suibhne, *Kildare in 1798* [Naas, Ireland: Leinster Leader Ltd., 1978], 9). Yeates had been a pupil at the Shackleton's school in July, 1787 (*Leadbeater Papers*, App., 1:xvi). **20** Fr Michael Cullen was parish priest of Ballitore in 1798. He seems to have been divided in his sympathies between rebels and loyalists. Musgrave writes that Cullen was compelled to give his blessing to a crowd of rebels after their defeat by Lt. Eadie (Musgrave, 256). When Campbell offered terms for the surrender of Ballitore to Abraham Shackleton, Cullen was undecided about what course of action to take. Shackleton wrote: 'I took [Campbell's letter] to the priest, who lodged in town, and who appeared all the day of wavering counsels, sometimes, *before us*, persuading the people to surrender, and at other times, *apart*, harranguing them to opposite measures; here was another mischief that attended the deluded people' (Abraham Shackleton quoted anonymously in Hancock, 118). Later, when Campbell's men sought revenge against the town, Cullen fled to the garden at Boakefield and hid in the shrubbery. In 1803, he became parish priest of Narraghmore, where he served until 1827 (Very Revd Joseph J. Young, *Parish of Narraghmore* [Naas, Ireland: Leinster Leader, 1957], 7). He was the uncle of Paul Cardinal Cullen, born at

life of the young man on his knees, – he was murdered, being piked and shot! That day his father had been requested, I suppose by one who knew what was intended, not to let his son leave the house; but he could not prevent him – he would join the corps. His brother-in-law, Norcott D'Esterre, narrowly escaped being taken a prisoner at the same time.[21]

The insurgents at length left, first placing cars of the bridge as a barricade against the army. They took two of our horses. We saw several houses on fire northwards, and, while standing gazing at them outside our door, bullets whizzed by our ears, and warned us to go in for safety. There had been an engagement on the Bog-road between the army and the insurgents; the latter were worsted, and Malachi Delany, finding his efforts to rally them were in vain, fled along with them. The soldiers retreating to Athy had fired at random those shots which we had heard, and almost felt, and by which a poor woman was killed and her daughter's arm broken. They had also set the houses on fire; and one serjeant, one might think impelled by his fate, came into the village with a baggage car. It was thought he must have been in liquor, for had he his reason he could not have thus exposed himself to his enemies at the height of their rage. He had just gone to bed in his lodgings when those enemies rushed in, and quickly put an end to his life.

The insurgents now returned from the Bog-road, and, having increased to an immense multitude, went to Castledermot late in the evening. We laid our beds on the floor lest bullets should enter our windows to our destruction, and got some disturbed sleep. All became quiet, and in the morning messages came to us from our neighbours to tell us they were living. This was indeed good news, for we dreaded that many who attacked Castledermot were repulsed by yeomanry who fired at them from the windows. The crowd dispersed, and did not assemble here in such numbers again.

As my friend and I walked out to see a sick neighbour, we looked with fearful anxiety over a wall inside of which we saw lying the youthful form of the murdered Richard Yeates. There he had been thrown after his death, his clothes undisturbed, but his bosom all bloody. For many days after I thought my food tasted of blood, and at night I was frequently awakened by my feelings of horror, and stretched forth my hand to feel if my husband was safe at my side.

All the horses which could be got were taken by the insurgents. A man came to me with a drawn sword in his hand, demanding my own mare. I

Prospect, Co. Kildare in 1803 (Mac Suibhne, 9; Young, 45). **21** Musgrave gives a similar account: 'The rebels, after their defeat by lieutenant Eadie, retreated to Ballytore [*sic*], where they gained reinforcement of many thousands … Then, headed by Redmond Murphy, and Malachi Delany, two rebel leaders, they broke into a house where lieutenant Yeates, the son of a respectable magistrate of the neighbourhood, was prisoner, butchered his body in a most curel manner, and threw it into the streets to be devoured by pigs' (Musgrave, 256–7).

told him that one of the Tyrone officers had borrowed her, and fortunately another man who knew me bore testimony to my veracity, so that I was left unharmed. When I saw how the fine horses were abused and galloped without mercy by the insurgents, I rejoiced that my Nell was not in their hands.

A man afterwards came, with a horse-pistol in his hand, to take my husband. My brother[22] had been previously taken, together with some of his guests. They were all to be brought to the camp in the hollow side of the hill at the east, and when the soldiers came, they should be placed, the insurgents said, in the front of the battle, to stop a bullet if they would not fire one.[23] This man, not finding my husband below, and thinking he was concealed, ran upstairs where our little children were in bed, with the huge pistol in his hand, swearing horribly that he would send the contents of it through his head if he did not go with him. I stood at the door, less terrified than I could have expected, and asked a young man who had accompanied the other if they meant to kill us. 'To kill you?' he repeated, in a tone of expressive surprise and sorrow at such a supposition. At length he prevailed on his angry companion to go away, threatening as he went, that if the Quakers did not take up arms their houses should be in flames, 'as Mr Bayley's was'. I was sorry for the destruction of the Hall, but soon found that, though it had been attempted, the fire had been put out before much damage had been done. My husband, having been visiting his mother, was not found, and did not know he had been sought for. Many came to us weeping and trembling for their friends; and to the doctor, who, having much influence with the people, exerted it to do them good. We could do nothing.

The cars laden with goods from Dublin, which the carriers were bringing to our shipkeepers, were plundered, and a barricade made of them across the road leading down to the village. The insurgents talked boldly of forming

22 Abraham Shackleton of Fuller's Court and Griese Bank, Co. Kildare was the son of Richard Shackleton by his first wife, Elizabeth, daughter of Henry Fuller of Fuller's Court. He was therefore a half-brother of Mary Leadbeater. He was born 8 Dec. 1752 and died 2 Aug. 1818. He married, on 23 Mar. 1779, Lydia, daughter of Ebenezer Mellor of Manchester by his wife Margaret, daughter of John Abraham of Swarthmoor Hall, Lancashire. They had nine children. *Burke's Peerage* (1975), 2411. It was probably Abraham Shackleton's account that appears anonymously in Hancock's *Principles of Peace*, 106–126.
23 Abraham Shackleton wrote: 'So they took me out, and two honest men with me ... and said that we should stand in front of the battle, if we would not fight, we should stop a bullet. They took us beyond a bridge, to the side of the road; our people following us with their eyes, and tender affection ... They said that I could not be spared from home, and from the care of so many of the poor, who had taken sanctuary in my house ... I told the men that, as to myself, I felt quite undisturbed, and I had no real displeasure against them, who did it ignorantly; that they might put be to death, as I was in their hands; but they would never persuade me to use any act of violence against my fellow men. At length they were persuaded to liberate us' (Shackleton quoted anonymously in Hancock, 112–13).

a camp on the Curragh. All who were missing were reported to have fallen in the ambush in the wood, or in the encounter at the Bog-road. At both places many did fall. The wife of one of my brother's labourers was told that he lay dead in the wood; she hastened thither; but when she reached the spot, she found the face so disfigured with wounds that she could not recognize it. She examined the linen – it was not his; even this melancholy satisfaction was denied her. But what a satisfaction was in store for her! She met her husband alive and well, and brought him in triumph to the house of their master, whose young daughter, who had participated in the anguish of the supposed widow, now shared her joy with all the vivid warmth of her ardent nature. This young creature, still a child, was endued with uncommon courage and prudence in this time of trial. Her bodily powers were exerted in paying attention to her father's numerous guests; for over a hundred people sought refuge under his roof; and the strength of her mind seemed to invigorate all around her. A soldier lay ill of a fever in a house in the garden. It would have been death to him if his asylum were known to the insurgents; so she carefully attended to all his wants herself. Such was Betsy Shackleton.[24]

Everyone seemed to think that safety and security were to be found in my brother's house.[25] Thither the insurgents brought their prisoners, and thither, also, their own wounded and suffering comrades. It was an awful sight to behold in that large parlour such a mingled assembly of throbbing, anxious hearts – my brother's own family, silent tears rolling down their faces, the wives of the loyal officers, the wives of the soldiers, the wives and daughters of the insurgents, the numerous guests, the prisoners, the trembling women – all dreading to see the door open, lest some new distress, some fresh announcement of horrors should enter. It was awful; but every scene was now awful, and we knew not what a day might bring forth.

All our houses were thronged with people seeking refreshment and repose, and threatening to take possession for the purpose of firing on the soldiery when they should come. Ours seemed peculiarly adapted for such a purpose, being a corner house, and in a central situation; so, believing its destruction was inevitable, I packed up in a small trunk such portable articles as I esteemed of most value, amongst which were some of my dear

24 Elizabeth 'Betsy' Shackleton, daughter of Abraham Shackleton and wife Lydia (Mellor) of Ballitore and niece of Mrs Leadbeater, was born on 23 Mar. 1783 and died unmarried on 9 Mar. 1843. She was the author of *Ballitore and Its Inhabitants Seventy Years Ago*, published posthumously in 1862. In the preface of this work, the editor of this work described his recollections of her 'lively manners, expressive countenance, dark hair, dark eyes, fresh complexion, and sweet smile, her sympathizing disposition, and energetic and industrious habits ... she was ever doing or contriving some good thing' (See the anonymous Preface in ibid., xii).

friends' letters, and made packages of clothes for my husband, myself, and the little ones. I wore two pair of pockets, wishing to preserve as much as I could; though in my heart I had not much fear of an engagement, believing that the spirit which had animated the insurgents had evaporated.

Young girls dressed in white, with green ribbons and carrying pikes, accompanied the insurgents. They had patrols and a countersign, but it was long before they could decide upon the password. At length they fixed upon the word, 'Scourges'. Sentinels were placed in various parts of the village. One day, as I went to my brother's, a sentinel called to a man who walked with me not to advance on pain of being shot. The sentinel was my former friend, 'The Canny'. I approached him and asked would he shoot me if I proceeded. 'Shoot you!' exclaimed he, taking my hand and kissing it, adding a eulogium on the Quakers. I told him it would be well if they were all of our way of thinking, for then there would be no such work as the present. I thought I could comprehend 'the Canny's' incoherent answer, 'Aye, but you know our Saviour – the scourges, oh! the scourges!' With little exception, we were kindly treated, and the females amongst us were frequently encouraged to dismiss our fears, with hearty shakes of the hand, and assurances that they would 'burn those who would burn us'. We began to be familiarized with these dangers; and added our entreaties to the representations of our men that they should give up their arms, and resign the project which threatened them with destruction.

They had been mistaken as to their prospect of success. Dublin was safe, and at Naas and Kilcullen great slaughter of the insurgents had been made, though on Kilcullen-green many of the military had also fallen. An attack in the night had been made on Carlow, which was repulsed with slaughter, almost to massacre. A row of cabins in which numbers of the defeated insurgents had taken shelter were set on fire, and the inmates burned to death. No quarter was given, – no mercy shown; and most of those who had escaped, burning with disappointment, rage, and revenge, joined the Wexford party. John Bewley,[26] a man endued with wisdom, courage, and benevolence, exerted them all in behalf of the deluded

25 Musgrave affirms that the widows of two soldiers of the Suffolk Fencibles were lodged under rebel guard at the house of Abraham Shackleton (Musgrave, 257). Shackleton himself added that 'our poor neighbours, fearing pillage of property, now began to flock to our house; so, as my school was small, we had room to accomodate about one hundred persons, men, women, and children; who, day and night, collected up and down in our houses. The school-house, a large room, was given up to them; so that, what with the people seeking an asylum, and the men under arms, we had very little quiet, or scarcely any thing we could call our own' (Shackleton (anonymous) in Hancock, 111). Among the widows were Anne Gore and Anne Hemet, 'the latter a Jersey woman', along with a Col. Wolseley (Ibid.). 26 John Bewley's identity is uncertain, though undoubtedly he was related to the famed Quaker Bewley family. He is mentioned by initials in the account written by an anonymous Quaker (probably Abraham Shackleton) as being an intermediary between Col. Campbell and the rebels, but his efforts failed (see the account in Hancock, 116–122).

people, along with my husband and brother; and as he was not exposed to the suspicion which attached to an inhabitant, he treated with Colonel Campbell on their behalf. The Colonel was willing to make favourable terms with the insurgents, most of whom were willing to come in to him, but a few still held out, and amongst these was a priest.[27] John Bewley proposed to take another message to Colonel Campbell; the people at length consented; but so much time had been lost meanwhile that Colonel Campbell's terms were now less favourable. Six hostages were demanded to be sent before an appointed time, to guarantee the surrender of the arms before the noon of the next day. They could not decide upon the hostages, the hour passed by, and the fate of Ballitore was sealed!

We believed the hostages had been sent, for we perceived the people had begun to weary of ill-doing; and a stranger, who begged some refreshment wistfully, asked me when there would be peace. We got our beds replaced upon their steads, and sank into that quiet repose which for some nights we had not known, little imagining what the morrow was to bring forth. This eventful morrow was the 27th of Fifth-month (May). At three o'clock in the morning the intelligence that the army was near roused us from our beds. We saw the glitter of arms through the dust which the horses of the 9th Dragoons made, galloping along the high road from Carlow. We heard the shots repeatedly fired. We saw the military descend the hill, cross the bridge, and halt before our house, where some dismounted and entered, and asked for milk and water. As I handed it, I trembled; my spirits, which had risen superior to the danger till now, fell; the dragoon perceived my emotion, and kindly told me I need not fear, that they came to protect us, adding, 'It is well you were not all murdered!' Thus assured, I recovered my composure. I should not have recovered it so easily had I known that my brother and his friends had walked forth to meet the troops, who were commanded by Major Dennis. John Bewley, holding up a paper from Colonel Campbell, said, 'We are prisoners!'

'It is well for you', said the Major, 'that you are prisoners, else I should have shot you, every man.'[28]

27 A member of Campbell's staff wrote on 26 May 1798 that if 'the deluded people of that place … will lay down their arms of every kind, in front of the moat at Ardskull, this afternoon at six o'clock, and retire half a mile in the rear of it, Colonel Campbell will send out a party … to receive the arms, to prevent their falling into the hands of the disaffected. It gives the Colonel much pleasure to find, that the people have at last found out their error, and that they have been imposed on by designing men … and he will, in the mean time, afford them every protection in his power. Their compliance with this proposal will save much blood, as they must now be convinced, from their late attacks on the outposts, how impossible it is to make any impression on a well disciplined army' (member of Colin Campbell's staff quoted in Hancock, 116). 28 Abraham Shackleton gave a similar version of this story: 'As the army from Carlow, consisting of horse and foot, moved slowly down the hill, I proposed to J[ohn] B[ewley], that he and I should go forth to meet them; which we did, also the Phelps's and Samuel Eves, then with us. The commanding officer, Major

Then raising himself in his stirrups, he revoked the orders given to his men, to fire upon every man in coloured clothes. Oh, rash and cruel orders, which exposed to such danger lives of such value, which if thus sacrificed no regrets could have restored! Nothing can justify such commands.[29]

I thought the bitterness of death was passed, but the work was not yet begun. Colonel Campbell's men, who had impatiently rested on their arms several hours, marched out of Athy. They took Narraghmore in their way, and directed their mistaken rage against the newly erected house of Colonel Keatinge, planting cannon to destroy the dwelling which so much worth had inhabited. They mortally wounded John Carroll, cousin to the Colonel. This party of soldiers entered Ballitore exhausted by rage and fatigue; they brought cannon. Cannon in Ballitore! The horse and foot had now met. Colonel Campbell was here in person and many other officers. The insurgents had fled on the first alarm, the peaceable inhabitants remained. The trumpet was sounded, – and the peaceable inhabitants were delivered up for two hours to the unbridled license of a furious soldiery! How shall I continue the fearful narrative?

My mind never could arrange the transactions which were crowded into those two hours. Every house in the Burrow was in flames; a row of houses opposite to the School was also set on fire; none others were burnt immediately in the village, but a great many windows were broken, and when I heard this crash I thought it was cannon. We saw soldiers bending under loads of plunder. Captain Palmer came in to see me, and was truly solicitous about us, and insisted on giving us 'a protection'. Soldiers came in for milk; some of their countenances were pale with anger, and they grinned at me, calling me names which I had never heard before. They said I had poisoned the milk which I gave them, and desired me to drink some, which I did with much indignation. Others were civil, and one enquired if we had any United Irishmen in the house. I told them we had. In that fearful time the least equivocation, the least deception appeared to me to

Dennis, rode on to meet us with a pistol in his hand, and stopping near us, asked, who commanded in the town? He was answered by J[ohn] B[ewley] that 'the town had been for these few days in the hands of the Insurgents, but as to us', said he, 'we are only passengers'. 'It happened well for you, gentlemen', said he, 'that it is so, or I should have shot you, every man'. (It appears that he had previously given orders to shoot every man in coloured clothes.)' (Shackleton quoted anonymously in Hancock, 120). 29 Shackleton explained that Campbell gave the order to burn the town that night, when the hostages he expected to be delivered did not appear: 'Col. Campbell, not finding the hostages sent as he desired, marched his army in the night to patrole the country, and came down from Narraghmore on us, about five or six o'clock, bringing fire and desolation wherever they came. The houses were generally burned, and many of the people shot, I suppose, almost all who appeared, whether guilty or not of the crime of *disaffection*' (Shackleton quoted anonymously in Hancock, 121). Shackleton's house was spared, because the soldiers recognized some friends among the refugees at the house.

be fraught with danger. The soldier continued his inquiry – 'Had they plundered us?'

'No, except of eating and drinking'.

'On free quarters', he replied, smiled, and went away.

A fine-looking man, a soldier, came in, in an extravagent passion; neither his rage nor my terror could prevent me from observing that this man was strikingly handsome; he asked me the same question in the same terms – and I made the same answer. He cursed me with great bitterness, and raising his musket presented it to my breast. I desired him not to shoot me. It seemed as if he had the will, but not the power to do so. He turned from me, dashed pans and jugs off the kitchen table with his musket, and shattered the kitchen window. Terrified almost out of my wits, I ran out of the house, followed by several women almost as frightened as myself. When I fled, my fears gained strength, and I believed my enemy was pursuing; I thought of throwing myself into the river at the foot of the garden, thinking the bullet could not hurt me in the water. One of our servants ran into the street to call for help. William Richardson and Charles Coote,[30] who kindly sat on their horses outside our windows, came in and turned the ruffian out of the house.

That danger passed, I beheld from the back window of our parlour the dark red flames of Gavin's house[31] and others rising above the green of the trees. At the same time a fat tobacconist from Carlow lolled upon one of our chairs, and talked boastingly of the exploits performed by the military whom he had accompanied; how they had shot several, adding, 'We burned one fellow in a barrel'. I never in my life felt disgust so strongly; it even overpowered the horror due to the deed, which had actually been committed. The stupid cruelty of a man in civil life, which urged him voluntarily and without necessity to leave his home and bear a part in such scenes, was far more revolting than the fiery wrath of a soldier.

While Captain Palmer was with me, a soldier who had been previously quartered at my mother's came to him, to beg leave to go see 'the old mistress'. My dear mother,[32] who was now in the stage of second childhood,

---

30 Charles Coote was enrolled in the Shackleton school in 1778 (*Leadbeater Papers*, vol. 1, App. xv).   31 According to Elizabeth Shackleton, Johnny Gavin was a shoemaker. 'The front of his house was adorned with a splendid sign, on which was painted a gentleman with a bright blue coat drawing on a boot. Johnny was a strange-looking man, who strutted about with a conceited air. His daughter was a belle, and his father a degenerate Friend' (Shackleton, *Ballitore and Its Inhabitants*, 25–25).   32 Elizabeth Carleton married Richard Shackleton as his second wife on 17 Oct. 1755. She died on 23 Mar. 1804 at Ballitore after a period of increasing senility. Mrs Leadbeater wrote of her mother: 'Our beloved and venerable parent glided from us by degrees almost imperceptible. She was reduced to a state of helpless infancy. Still the serentiy of innocence gilded her setting day … ' (Leadbeater, 'Annals of Ballitore', 1:295). Betsy Shackleton wrote: 'My grandmother, although of a more sedate and orderly disposition, was also much beloved by her friends and neighbours, and, though so

in her unconsciousness of what was passing had lost the timidity of her nature, mingled and conversed freely in her simplicity with all parties, and was treated by all with the greatest respect and tenderness; for, amid the darkness of the tumult, some rays of light gleamed forth, some countenances expressed humanity and a weariness of the work of death.

I must be an egotist in these relations, for I can scarcely describe anything but what I saw and heard. I scarce had the guidance even of my own movements. Sometimes I found myself with my children, whom I had shut up in a back room; again I was below, enquiring for my husband. Our old gardener was discovered lying in the shrubbery, and the instrument of death which was aimed at his defenseless breast was arrested by his daughter, who, rushing forward, begged that her life might be taken instead. The soldier spared both, but poor Polly was ever after subject to fits, which reduced her to a deplorable situation, and by which she eventually lost her life, being seized with one as she crossed a stream. A carpenter in the village took his goods into the grave-yard, and hid himself and his family there. But in vain – this solemn retreat was violated, their goods were plundered, and the poor old man was murdered in wanton cruelty.

Owen Finn, the smith who had been imprisoned and liberated, felt himself secure because of his late acquittal, and could not be prevailed upon to conceal himself or leave his house. Alas! he was mistaken in expecting that rage reeking with blood would stop to discriminate. Owen was dragged out of his cottage; his pleadings were not listened to; his cottage, where industry had assembled many comforts, was pillaged and then set on fire. His wife ran through the crowd, to assure herself of her husband's safety. She beheld his bleeding and dead body: she threw herself with her infant upon the corpse, while those who had wrought her misery assaulted her with abusive language, and threatened to kill her also. 'And I wished', said she, 'that they would kill me!'

Tom Duffy, called 'the Fairy', had come from Dublin that morning to the house of his sister, whose husband was a yeoman, and had fallen in the battle of Kilcullen. The widow, though antagonized with sorrow, found some little comfort in assuring herself and her children of protection by reason of her husband having suffered on the side of the government. Her grief was mingled with astonishment heightened to frenzy when she found she had deceived herself. Her brother, poor Fairy Tom, was murdered; her son was murdered; her servant-boy was murdered; her house was plundered; her little daughter, on seeing her brother's dead body, fell into fits which caused her death; and her own reason gave way. Such are the horrors of civil war.

different from her husband, was quite a companion to him. She had a sensible and well-cultivated mind, a great knowledge of history, and a good taste in general reading; and, above all, they were closely united in religious fellowship' (Shackleton, 67).

Our poor Doctor Johnson had suffered much from fatigue and anxiety during those days of terror; he ate and slept but little; and on the 26th, coming into Mary and Anne Doyle's, he declared his firm belief that he should fall by one party or the other, adding he did not care how soon. They wanted him to lie down and get a little rest, but his agitated mind would not permit him to take any. Next morning he was made a prisoner, not endeavouring to conceal himself. I saw him walking in his yeomanry dress with a crowd of soldiers, and thought he was in friendship with them. I did not know that they pressed the ends of their muskets on his feet as he walked, and, by thus tormenting him, showed how little mercy he had to expect from them. The crowd stopped before Mary and Anne Doyle's[33] shop; the tumult was loud; I believe they called it a court martial. An officer asked my husband had the doctor been at the battle of Narraghmore. He assured him he had not. Charles Coote stood by him, and begged to have him taken to the colonel. What his friends said was disregarded. Some young men, prisoners, passed by; Doctor Johnson appealed to them, but they passed on in silence. He was alone and unarmed, and I believe had never raised his hand to injure any one. Captain Sandys, who afterwards lost his life at Vinegar Hill, took the doctor's part in this business. So many swords and bayonets, and at length a musket, could not be long in taking the life of an unarmed man.[34]

A short time before the end, a soldier came into our parlour, and, with a kind of bitter smile, told me they were going to hang the doctor. I said I hoped not, and went up to my children, trembling. One of our servants entered the room, and said the doctor was shot. I started up and contradicted her; just then the trumpet sounded a retreat. The window near my bedside had for some time caused me a dread which I could not account for, save by having heard of persons being shot through windows. But to this window I now went mechanically, and saw stretched before it, lying on his back, the friend I had known from childhood – my neighbour,

33 Abraham Shackleton described Mary Doyle 'an old nurse' and recalled that she interceded for his release after being taken prisoner by the rebels (Shackleton in Hancock, 112). 34 It would appear that Francis Johnson was was executed for having surrendered Ballitore to the rebels without bloodshed and for attending the rebel wounded. Musgrave asserts that he was executed for having been seen leading the rebels, a charge which seems to have been a fabrication by the army: 'When the general [Campbell] entered Ballytore [sic], he found it deserted by every male, except Mr Francis Johnson, a surgeon; and as some of the Tyrone regiment had repeatedly seen him commanding the rebels, the sight of him kindled such indignation in them, that one of them bayoneted him through the breast, on which he fell. He rose again, laid his hand on his wound, and strongly, and with many oaths asserted his innocence. Several of the soldiers cried out, that they had frequently seen him at the head of the rebels – an opening was made – five of the Suffolk fencibles presented their muskets at him; when he found that all subterfuge was vain, he exclaimed. "Since I must die, guilty as I am, the Lord have mercy on me!" and he was instantly sent into eternity' (Musgrave, 259).

my physician. His arms were extended; there was a large wound in the lower part of his face; and his once graceful form and intelligent countenance were disfigured with more than the horrors of death. I took but one look; I cried aloud; and Anne Doyle led me away. We went to the back apartments; the glass of the windows was hot from the reflection of the burning houses, but I looked on them with a stupid composure. My only thought was, is my husband safe? Had not our dwelling and offices been slated, we should have been probably houseless, for the unchecked flames rose in dreadful spires, and the crash of falling roofs caused a terrific sound. The morning was balmy, beautiful, and mild; bounteous Nature smiled sweetly upon us, rich with the treasures of a benign Creator. The unbridled passions of man alone deformed the scene!

Captain Palmer, naturally good-hearted, was peculiarly desirous to preserve everybody and everything in the vale he loved so well. He learned the doctor's danger, and hastened from Athy to save him; but he came, alas! too late – too late for that purpose, but in time to rescue another who was in those hands reeking with blood, and ready to take his life, as, speechless with terror, he stood beholding the sad spectacle. Priest Cullen, justly apprehensive for his life, had applied to my brother for one of his coats wherewith to disguise himself, but dared not wait to put it on. He ran to Boakefield, and hid in one of the clumps of trees in the lawn, while several officers were refreshing themselves in the parlour, and soldiers were scattered about the house, who seemed to thirst for his blood.[35]

After the trumpet had sounded a retreat, a soldier shot one of our pigs, for which he was tied to a car and lashed. Oh! how shocking that seemed to me! Commanded to take the precious human life – punished for taking that of a brute! The progress of the army on the way they now went was impeded by trees purposely felled by the insurgents a day or two before. Some of the soldiers availed themselves of this delay to return to Ballitore, and renew the work of plunder. This alarmed Charles Coote on our account, as he justly feared the protections previously granted would not again avail. The soldiers were overloaded with their spoils, and had to throw some away. A paper was discovered in a work-bag, containing a list of names which roused suspicion. Charles Coote, on the watch, claimed to look at the paper, and quickly convinced the soldiers that their suspicions were unfounded; yet his heart was wrung in secret, for this paper, in my handwriting, contained the charades and rebuses with which we had amused ourselves on one of our past happy evenings, with a list of explanations. He feared lest those who had returned might plunder and

---

35 Abraham Shackleton agreed with this version: 'The priest now fled to Ephraim Boake's, and hid in the garden; but, thinking that place unsafe, he lay down in one of the clumps before Ephraim's door, and waited there till the bitterness of death was past' (Shackleton in Hancock, 119–20).

murder us; and the anguish of such an apprehension was quickened by the contrast with the convivial hour. Thus Homer heightens our interest in the fate of Hector, by pointing him to our view as flying from his destroyer by those fountains,

> 'Where Trojan dames, ere yet alarmed by Greece,
> Washed their fair garments in the days of peace'.

Now the blast was over – all was silent and sad. Our houseless tenants were sheltered under our roof; we sat down with Mary and Anne, the closed window concealing our dead friend from us. Mary, pale as death, shook the table on which she leaned with her excessive trembling; and when Anne saw the body carried along and thrown over the little wall at the corner where the elm tree once stood, her cry of grief was heart-piercing; while I sate [sic] like a stone. The report of the soldiers intending to return made his neighbours afraid to shelter in their houses those dear remains. Here they were carefully watched, for the swine, snuffing blood, were waiting to make a horrid repast. For several months there was no sale for bacon cured in Ireland, from the well-founded dread of the hogs having fed upon the flesh of men.

The first use we made of our minds' returning strength was to visit Maria Johnson. She knew not that her husband was in the hands of his enemies, nor that they were his enemies, until one of the Tyrone militia came raging into the house, boasting that the doctor was shot, and calling for his wife that he might cut her head off. She sank down upon her knees in a state that baffles description; her sister was little better, and the lamentations of the children touched even the hearts of the soldiers – so that instead of doing farther injury they endeavoured to soothe their distress. I saw those mourners looking so sweet, so innocent, so sorrowful that I could not bear it, but hastened into the garden; thither their servant followed me to consult what should be done with her master's body. We concluded on having him buried in our graveyard without loss of time, in whatever clothes were left upon him, for alas! even his corpse was plundered. This needful conversation calmed my feelings, and I was able to return and sit with the widow.

There was no motive for consolation to be urged in this dreadful calamity; we could only weep abundantly with her. It was a comfort to us that she could weep. No harsher expression escaped her lips than, 'Ah, it was a cruel enemy!' Her little Eliza[36] sprang into the room, threw her arms

---

36 Eliza Johnson is not otherwise identified. She should be distinguished from Eliza Leadbeater, 'a great pet in the house'. 'It is said that she could read a few words at three years old, and I believe she read fluently at four' (Betsy Shackleton, 65).

about her mother's neck, and, in a tone which bespoke the anguish of her young heart, exclaimed, 'What shall we do for my poor father?' He was one of the tenderest of fathers, as well as of husbands; his little daughters were his pride and delight, and his family, including his siter-in-law, loved him with reciprocal affection. I caught myself saying, 'Why are these things permitted?' And I thought that if the murderer were to see what I then saw, his conscience would compel him to cry out, 'My punishment is greater than I can bear'.

On the 29th, people ventured to seek for their friends, and to bury their dead. Whether it was that having so many companions in misfortune lightened the load, whether they considered those that had fallen as martyrs, or whether

'Vengeance, deep brooding o'er the slain,
Had locked the source of softer woe'.

There did not appear so much lamentation as one might have expected. The ruins of cars lay in some of the ditches at the entrance into Ballitore, and in another ditch lay the scull of the poor youth who had been burnt in the barrel where he had sought refuge.

I saw moving along under the arching trees a few persons, chiefly women, bearing an empty coffin. I joined them in silence, and met in the grave-yard my husband and two or three more, about to open the grave in which the poor doctor was laid, and at his widow's desire to re-inter him in a coffin. I saw the earth being removed; I wished yet dreaded to see the body. A shroud was wanted; I hastened back to Mary and Anne's for it; we hastily made it, till a boy met us who had been sent to fetch it; therefore the body had been washed, wrapped in its shroud, and laid in the coffin before we got there. I experienced strange and contradictory feelings while I stood at the grave-yard door, wishing yet fearing to enter; Mary and Anne confessed to similar sensations, but we all regretted our irresolution when we heard the coffin lid screwed down. My husband, when he saw how it disturbed me, regretted that he had hastened to prevent our seeing so sad a sight, though the remains were little altered by having lain three days in the earth. The bloody waistcoat lay near, and the sight of it renewed our emotions of horror.

Timolin was attacked after Ballitore, and several houses in its suburbs burnt. Conway, a Protestant, was protected, or rather spared by one party of soldiers, but was cut down by another, and his house shared the fate of the other dwellings. The Dublin road for nearly four miles north of Ballitore exhibited a scene of desolation, few houses having escaped there; and about Narraghmore and Crookstown the same destruction was apparent. The street of Ballitore was strewed with broken glass and earthenware, ground by the trampling of feet. We looked around at our altered village, and were ready to wonder that we yet lived. 'Surely the wrath of man shall praise Thee, the remainder of wrath wilt Thou restrain'. We were sensible that a preserving Providence had restrained that wrath which threatened general destruction.

Hostages having been sent, the insurgents prepared to deliver up their arms on the 30th. A little boy was the herald, who with a bit of white paper stuck in his hat to announce his office, and secure his person, passed safely between the opposite parties, and we respected the little fellow for his courage. The appointed spot for meeting was about half way between this and Athy, and there the insurgents were informed that those who had assembled on the Curragh for a similar purpose, had been, I suppose by some unfortunate mistake, fallen upon by a party commanded by Sir James Duff, and put to the sword. Terrified by this intelligence, many returned at full speed; but by my brother's and Ephraim Boake's exertions, representations, and offers to accompany them, they were prevailed upon to go back and conclude this disastrous business, by delivering up their arms, and obtaining pardon for their offenses against government, though not for those committed against the laws of their country. Ephraim Boake was a wise old man; he was truly loyal to his king, but he did not think loyalty incompatible with mercy. 'Those who do not like this government', he was wont to say, 'let them go and live under another; but while they are protected by this, let them not disturb it'.

The prisoners had gone away under the protection of the army – some of the soldiers leaving money to relieve the present distresses of the poor. Indeed many characters were now developed; the sordid, the carnal, the selfish had gained opportunity of gratification; while brighter through the surrounding gloom beamed the candid, the liberal, the benevolent mind, and Captain Chenery and Captain Palmer will long be remembered in Ballitore.

That pretty cottage built by poor Dr Johnson, to which he had brought his bride, was now a blackened ruin. Many families sheltered themselves under hedges, or wherever they could thrust their heads; and some poor women brought forth their babes under these sorrowful circumstances. Yet the houseless wretches expressed thankfulness that their lives were spared, and a long period of remarkably fine weather was granted, as well as uncommon health, for we rarely heard of any sickness except that caused by wounds, and previously Ballitore had seldom passed through a summer without being visited by fever amongst the poor. Great was the terror in which the army were held. A soldier was an unwelcome sight, unconscious that the time was not far distant when they should be most welcome. And this dread was not without cause; we frequently saw the blaze of burning houses on the surrounding hills, and several men were shot by the military when going about their lawful business; so that people were afraid to cut their turf, save their hay and corn, or even to sleep in their own abodes.

When the corn had shot into ear, three months after her poor husband's death, Dolly Finn went to her little farm to look at her crop. She was alone, she entered among the black walls of her ruined cottage, her heart was oppressed with horror and grief, and she vented her anguish in tears and groans of despair, lamenting her deplorable condition. A soldier was passing at the time; he heard the sound of sorrow, and through the aperture which had once been a window he saw a lovely woman, whose appearance inspired his depraved heart with sentiments very different from compassion. He alighted from his horse, and having questioned her closely, he showed her his pistols, and then attempted to seize her. She ran out of the walls, shrieking, believing his intent was to render her still more wretched; he followed, and compelled her to walk beside him. The trembling widow looked around and cried aloud for succour, in vain; the high-road was now solitary, war and terror had depopulated it. Some persons who had taken shelter in a deserted stable, at length came out, when her enemy immediately assuming the character of a friend advised her not to frequent those ruins again, and departed. Her alarm was such that for a long time she feared to walk anywhere alone, and her fancy pictured every furze bush to be a soldier!

The garrisoned town of Athy was thronged with those who were afraid to remain in the country – yet where was safety? Even in this garrison a man from Narraghmore was shot by a soldier – accidentally, they said.

When we went to the monthly meeting of Carlow we saw marks of dismay on all sides, especially in the pale and immoveable countenances of two women sitting before an open window. An attack from the insurgents was said to be expected that night, and yeomen hurried to and fro with weapons in their hands. The state of the times engrossed all conversation, till we longed to shut our ears from hearing of blood; and we scarcely dared to utter humane sentiments, the tide ran so strongly against those who had put the inhabitants in such jeopardy. All our friends rejoiced over us, as beings delivered from the jaws of danger and death.

We hastened back to Ballitore, where, once more, all wore the appearance of peace and security; where we walked out in the delightful evenings, unmolested by those counter-signs which had been so constantly called for during the last three months – undisturbed by the sight of licensed or unlicensed instruments of destruction – feeling for one another with that tender melancholy affection peculiar to fellow-sufferers. But all sensations of cheerfulness had fled, and our spirits wore a covering of sadness which forbade our enjoyment of the beauties of Nature. A retrospect of past events presented itself almost continually to the mind; and surely this state of humiliation was intended for our refinement by Him who afflicts us not willingly.

Though the storm had spent its fury here, it raged elsewhere with redoubled violence. The reports from the county of Wexford were terrible – the hard-fought battle of Ross, the camp on Vinegar-hill, the horrible burning of the barn at Scullabogue, the slaughter on Wexford-bridge, and the dreadful retaliations. O how does the flame of party burn up all on which it seizes! Do men forget that their common Father is a God of love, a God of mercy? Or must we say,

> 'There is no flesh in man's obdurate heart,
> It does not feel for man!'

Some who had been witnesses to those shocks could palliate a little the excesses of the misguided multitude. They said the burning of the barn at Scullabogue was not the work of the whole body, but abhorred by them, and was done by a party maddened after the defeat of Ross. Women and children were spared, and Quakers in general escaped; but woe to the oppressor of the poor, the hard landlord, the severe master, or him who was looked upon as an enemy!

John Jeffers[37] of Narraghmore, returning from Kilcullen to Athy was way-laid near the ruins of his own house, which had been burned by the insurgents, and shot dead. His mother-in-law was within hearing of the shot; she got assistance to take away the body, and although most probably in the midst of enemies, was treated with kindness and compassion. Soon after this event three or four of our neighbours, young men, were made prisoners and suffered death in Athy. One young officer of dragoons on his return to Dublin from Vinegar-hill was heard to boast that he had cut off several croppies' heads; perhaps he might not be quite so brave in the day of battle. Most of our neighbours who had been prisoners at Naas, now returned and came joyfully to see us. They had been acquitted after a confinement of nine weeks. One however still remained behind. I was requested to write to Captain Chenery on his behalf; I did so, and the captain sent my note into the court where it was to be decided whether Pat Lyons should remain a prisoner or return home a free man. When it was perceived that the note came from a female, it was treated with contempt; 'Women did not care what they said, and it was from a woman'. On further

---

37 John Jefferies, permanent yeoman sergeant of the Narraghmore Yeomen Corps, was described by Abraham Shackleton as 'a staunch man to the constitution', whose property was destroyed after a rebel captain was arrested at Narraghmore by the Tyrone Militia under the command of Lt. Eadie (Shackleton in Hancock, 110). Musgrave writes that 'John Jefferies of Narraghmore, who escaped on the day they burned his house, having gone to that village from Athy, to look after such part of his property as might have remained, was murdered at two o'clock in the day' (Musgrave, 259). His widow Mary was among those who fled to Athy for safety.

inspection they observed the date; 'Quakers tell truth, and it was from a Quaker' – and accordingly Pat was liberated.

Martial law continued to be observed in Athy; Hugh Cullen, of Prospect, was made a prisoner, and carried from his fields to encounter this formidable power. Ephraim Boake saw the threatened destruction of his neighbour, the industrious father of a large family, whom he did not believe to have been guilty of any violence. Ephraim's body and mind were not rendered inactive by age. He went to Dublin and exerted his influence with his friend Agar, Archbishop of Cashel, by whose means he obtained an order to stop proceedings by court martial, from Lord Castlereagh,[38] whose brother, Colonel Stewart,[39] commanded in Athy and that district. His messenger hastened from Dublin on his errand of mercy; the uplifted sword was stayed, and though long detained a prisoner, Hugh Cullen was not irrevocably torn from his family. His brother Paul, a fine young man, had been condemned by a court martial a little while before. His poor father attended the trial; when he returned the family anxiously enquired, 'What news?'

'Good news', replied the parent, sadly. 'My child is to die, and he is willing to die!'

Late one evening, as we leaned over the bridge, we saw a gentleman and lady watering their horses at the river, attended by servants fully armed. They wore mourning habits, and though young and newly married, looked very serious and sorrowful. Their chastened appearance, their armed servants, the stillness of the air scarcely broken by a sound, rendered the scene very impressive. We very rarely saw any of the gentry; when we did, they were generally dressed in deep black; for what family had not lost a member? Mourning was the language, mourning was the dress of the country.

Some of Ephraim Boake's relatives who resided at Baltinglass, fearing an attack upon that town, sought safety under his roof. But that night a party came to Boakefield, demanding arms. They were told there were none; they wanted the family to swear to this, but did not insist on it; and on being refused admittance said they would not break the door. They

---

38 The Rt. Hon. Robert Stewart was born in 1769; he was elevated to the peerage of Ireland as Baron Londonderry in 1789 and in 1795 was created Viscount Castlereagh. As a conservative, he was hated in Ireland, especially by Presbyterians in Ulster, and brought to trial many whom he implicated as rebels (see A.T.Q. Stewart, *The Summer Soldiers: the 1798 Rebellion in Antrim and Down* [Belfast: Blackstaff, 1995], 22–6). The following year he became earl of Londonderry, and in 1816 he was named marquess of Londonderry. He was one of the architects of the Act of Union in 1801 and became one of the original representative peers of Ireland, elected after the passage of the act. He committed suicide on 8 Apr. 1821 (*Burke's Peerage* [1975], 1642; *Dictionary of National Biography*, 18:1233–1245).   39 Alexander Stewart of Ards, who commanded an army at Athy, was born 26 Mar. 1746 and died in August 1831 (see *Burke's Peerage* [1975], 1642).

asked for whiskey and a newspaper. This was in Sixth-month (June), and was the beginning of our troubles in this way. It did not make much impression on our minds, but our pensive tranquility was not long to last. About two months after this, in the dead of the night, a demand for wine was made at my mother's door, by persons who represented themselves as travellers, and excused themselves by reason of the inclemency of the weather. They asked for two bottles, which were handed to them from a window, and on going away they said, 'Not one word of this in the morning'.

In the Eighth-month (August) we heard of the French having landed at Killala, but in so small a force as not to cause any great alarm. It proved, however, that an able general was necessary to stop their progress, joined as they were by many of the country people. This able general was found in the good Cornwallis, who succeeded Lord Camden in the government of Ireland, and who held out the olive-branch, and sheathed the avenging sword wherever it was possible. He discouraged the distinctions of party, and when the Lord Mayor of Dublin appeared before him, wearing an orange cockade, he enquired the meaning of it, and on being told it was a badge of loyalty, said, 'I did not know till now that the first magistrate was suspected'. When he overheard some of his officers disputing about a bed, on their march to meet the French, it is reported of this gallant veteran that he said, 'Gentlemen, any of you are welcome to my bed; a little clean straw behind the door will satisfy me.'

At our fair it was pleasant to see so many people alive, and to behold the joy with which they greeted one another. Soldiers moved amongst them to prevent unlawful confabulations, and a reformation soon ensued at those places, by the people being dispersed early, and not permitted to assemble in drinking, and as a matter of course in fighting parties.

The days were now shortening. Another demand for wine in a larger quantity, and enforced in a more peremptory manner than before, was made at my mother's; and on the same night a person climbed over the rails of my brother's yard, and unbolted the gate for others, seeking more wine. This was the only attack made on my brother, and his subsequent escapes were suprising and unexpected to the family. The mail-coach was burnt; horses were taken out of the fields; and one beautiful moonlight night a desperate band plundered several houses about Narraghmore. Glassealy House was burned to the ground. The master of this mansion, T.J. Rawson,[40] and his family were fortunately in Athy. He had been very active in bringing the disaffected to punishment, and was consequently obnoxious to them, and exposed to their resentment.

---

40 Thomas James Rawson of Athy was captain of the Loyal Athy Infantry (Snoddy, 47). He was also a hardline magistrate and Orangeman, who brought to Athy the dreaded triangles used in flogging. In January 1798, before the Rebellion broke out, Rawson sent an address to

Alas! these banditti did not stop at plundering and destroying property. That fine night was obscured by murder – a murder which brought upon the country a greater stain than any other act had done. Hannah Manders, a Protestant, who held a farm and was well liked by her neighbours, with her sister, her nephew, and a maid-servant, were all murdered.[41] Another servant snatched up a little child, whose father had fallen at the time of the rising, and who was sheltered and protected there by the kind-hearted mistress, and ran away to conceal herself and it. They lay hidden in a lime-kiln, and the little creature, though quite awake, kept a profound silence, while the poor servant trembled lest it should cry out. The farm-house, late the seat of peace and plenty and benevolence, was burned to the ground. This savage deed caused general horror and detestation. It was thought that some incautious words which the servant had uttered after a visit from the marauders might have been the cause of this cruel act; but nothing could extenuate the crime.

Not long after this, the depredations seriously began at Ballitore. Those whose offenses had debarred them from the privilege of protections were outcasts from society, and had no apparent means of subsistence save by rapine. They sheltered themselves in the Co. Wicklow mountains, and from thence made nightly excursions for food, money and clothes, levying their 'black mail' on the timid and peaceful, while the lengthening nights favoured their designs. Holt who was their general was said to be a brave and merciful man. Their first visit to Ballitore as avowed robbers was to Mary and Anne Doyle. My husband and I had spent the evening with Maria Johnson. We returned impressed with that tender feeling of compassion and sympathy which the sense of her injuries created; while the silence of the night and the gloom of the trees mingled awe with our regret. It was early in the Tenth-month (October). The clock was about striking ten when we called at Mary and Anne's door, being accustomed

all of the Catholic chapels in the vicinity of Narraghmore in which he urged loyalty and promised leniency if they surrendered their arms. Musgrave writes that Rawson's house was destroyed at the same time as Hannah Manders's, 'and in one hour destroyed the production of twenty-five years of active industry' (Musgrave, 260). He claimed losses in 1799 including 'House, Furniture, Sheep, [and] Wines' totalling more than £1,241 (Claimants, ccxxi).
41 The murder of Hannah Manders took place on 24 December 1798. Musgrave offers a sensationalized account of the murder, stating that 'a party of rebels, most of them from the Wicklow mountains, and under the command of Matthew Kenna and Redmond Murphy ... set fire to the house of Mrs Hannah Manders, close to Glassealy, and murdered her, her two sisters, and Mr John Anderson her nephew, all protestants, and a servant woman of the Romish persuasion, and threw their bodies into the flames, in which they were reduced to ashes ... A Roman catholic servant, who was in Mrs Manders's house, was suffered to pass unmolested; but Mr Anderson, attempting to follow him, was shot ... In a short time later, captain Rawson had one Whelan, an assassin, better known by the nick-name Black Top, apprehended, for the murder of the Manders family; and he was tried before a court-martial at Carlow' (Musgrave, 280).

never to pass without calling on these dear friends, particularly now that we lived at the Retreat,[42] for the protection of my mother. Four men were lurking near the door, and entered when it was opened for us. We saw that they were armed. My husband went to alarm the neighbours, and get assistance; for one unarmed man could do nothing. They would not let him return, for which I felt thankful, as single-handed he could only expect to be sacrificed, and he could get no assistance. I remained with my friends, saw them robbed of their money and goods, and a pistol presented to Mary's breast, though I thought I saw the man uncock it first. He was of her own name, Doyle, a very handsome man, and affected to speak broken English. One fellow stood at the shop-door, repeatedly calling as to some one without, 'All's well;' sometimes adding, 'All's devilish well'.

When their work was done they liberated my husband, and we remained with our poor friends most of the night, although I often looked towards the Retreat, and thought of my poor helpless mother and our tender little children. When we went thither we found the house in confusion; the robbers had not long left it. They took several articles of value of my mother's, my sister's, and our's; and made my mother's man-servant accompany them to the apartment where our children lay in their beds. They asked our little Elizabeth where her father kept his money. She cried, and said she did not know.

'I know', called out little Jane, 'where my father keeps his money'.
'Where, honey?'
'In his breeches pocket'.

They broke open my husband's desk, and scattered his papers about the room; we missed none of them, save three letters to me from Edmund Burke. The beauty of the pocket-book in which they were – a gift to me from his wife – no doubt caused it and them to be taken. I regretted my loss so much that I made a fruitless enquiry for them of the robbers on their next visit. It is probable these precious relics shared the fate of the guinea notes at Vinegar Hill, being used to light the pipes of the robbers.

They took a great deal of clothes, and broke the furniture, apparently to get at the contents, for they took a looking-glass off a chest of drawers, and

42 The Retreat was the former home of Richard Shackleton and the childhood home of Mrs Leadbeater. Betsy Shackleton gave a lengthy description of its contents: 'The idea of neatness and exactness is connected with the Retreat and with my grandmother. We entered a neat little paved yard, and then a very small hall or passage. At the right hand was the kitchen, and on the left was the parlour, which was covered with oil-cloth. I remember the patting of my aunt's feet on the floor ... Then the fire-place, with a low straight brass fender. A green, wooden-bottomed chair stood at one side, a window at her right hand, and my grandmother sat in a common arm-chair on the other side, a window at her right hand, and a clock behind her ... In short, I thought everything at the Retreat nicer and better than what we had at my father's' (Betsy Shackleton, 62).

laid it carefully aside. Perhaps, also, they recollected the superstitious notion that breaking a mirror brings bad luck to the breaker. In bursting open a wardrobe with the handle of a pistol, the charge exploded, and the ball passed through the bedstead in which lay little Jane. The room filled with smoke; the children screamed; the frightened servants ran in; and the robbers, also alarmed, hastened to see if the child was killed. She smiled in their faces, and told them not to be so frightened, for she was not hurt.

My dear mother appeared to be but little disturbed by this or the other scenes she had passed through; yet it is probable they accelerated her mental decay. We took the precaution of removing the whole family to sleep the following night at my brother's; but, though most welcome to continue there, we preferred returning to our own home as soon as we had it arranged after the attack, not believing a message from the audacious visitors that they would be with us again before next morning.

We richly enjoyed the satisfaction that morning brought us of a passing look at our dear Tom Eyre,[43] of whom we had lost sight of some years. he was travelling post, disguised in a round hat and great-coat over his regimentals. Afraid of endangering our safety by openly calling upon us, he had looked anxiously around as the carriage passed along the high road. At length he saw my husband and my brother in a field conversing together. He sent his servant for them, and my husband sent directly for me. I found him leaning on each of them, and was struck with the great alteration in his dear countenance. He looked extremely ill, and was then labouring under an attack of gout.

He said he had been twice in the West Indies since he had seen us. His health had suffered from fatigue, and the hardships he had undergone when encountering the French in Connaught had given it the finishing blow. He said that in this last expedition it was evident that they passed through an enemy's country, though their brave commander, Cornwallis, would not seem to observe it, and, where paper money was refused, paid down gold. Tom, now Lieutenant-Colonel Eyre, had the command of the French prisoners to Dublin. His wife was in England, for he said Ireland was no place for a woman now. He looked with longing eyes, filled with tears, upon the valley where he had sported in his childhood – lamenting that he could not see my mother, who had been one of his faithful guardians. He remounted his chaise; was soon out of sight, and we never saw him more.

As I sat at my work about eight o'clock that evening, my mind reverting mournfully yet sweetly to the past, the robbers knocked at the door. To the enquiry, 'Who is there?' the answer was returned, 'A friend;' and two

43 Thomas Eyre was enrolled in the Shackletons' school in 1764. Samuel, Robert, and Edward Eyre were also students (see *Leadbeater Papers*, vol 1, App. x–xi).

enemies entered, who demanded our watches and asked for money. One of them sat down, the muzzle of his blunderbuss turned towards me. I desired him to turn it away, and he did so. Doyle was one of them; his countenance was changing, becoming darkened by guilt. They asked me to go with them to our desk for money. I requested they would not awake the children, and they immediately spoke low. Finding I had very little money, one pretended to struggle with the other for the blunderbuss to shoot me; I was not afraid, except that by their awkward handling the piece might accidently go off. I had on these occasions very little fear, but I had also very little presence of mind. I was willing to give the robbers anything they demanded to get them away, and had no dexterity in preserving property. After ineffectual threats to procure more money, they wished me good night, and went again to Mary and Anne Doyle's; breaking their windows, robbing them, and striking dear Mary.

An impulse of general alarm caused many of the inhabitants to leave the village; some went to Dublin, and some to Athy. My husband took my mother, myself, and our two children to Carlow. Our poor neighbours looked sad and wept at seeing 'the old mistress' leave Ballitore under such circumstances. My husband returned next day, and very reluctantly I consented we should stay at Carlow for awhile, for fear is strengthened by flight from danger, and I was much less at ease at Carlow than at home, which I felt to be my right place. My thoughts dwelt also with poor Mary and Anne, but to them my husband was a protector. I became dreadfully terrified with the idea that Carlow would be attacked, especially one night when I was awakened by the sound of a horn, not recollecting that it only announced a mail-coach. Oh! the terror that blast on the horn gave me!

We now heard of the murder of William Hume[44] of Humewood. Mary Lecky[45] of Kilnock and her family were at Carlow, being expelled from her home by robbery and rough treatment. Elizabeth Lecky[46] of Ballykealy was also here, although a message had been sent to her that she should not be molested. Still the treatment inflicted on the equally beloved inhabitants of Kilnock made her tremble for her own large family.

---

44 William Hume of Humewood, Kiltegan, Co. Wicklow, commanded the Lower Talbotstown or Humewood Yeoman Cavalry. His unit enjoyed early success against the rebels on 25 May at the battle of Hacketstown, but he was killed in a skirmish near his home on 8 October (see Ruan O'Donnell, 'The Rebellion of 1798 in Co. Wicklow', in Ken Hannigan and William Nolan (eds), *Wicklow History and Society* [Templeogue, Ireland: Geography Publications, 1994], 350, 371). As a Whig, he had not been a hate-figure to the rebels, and his death was considered an accident of war (see L. M. Cullen, 'Politics and Rebellion: Wicklow in the 1790s', in ibid., 412, 421, 468).   45 Mary Lecky was probably the widow of Robert Lecky of Kilnock, Co. Carlow, who died in 1780. She was the mother of John Lecky of Ballykealy, Co. Carlow, and was thus a relative of the historian W. E. H. Lecky ('Lecky of Ballykealey', *Burke's Landed Gentry of Ireland* [1912], 390).   46 Elizabeth Goff, daughter of Jacob Goff of Horetown and sister of Dinah Goff (*qv.*), married John Lecky of Ballykealey in 1780. She died in January 1842 (Ibid.).

On our return to Ballitore, where 'the old mistress' was received with heartfelt gladness, we bade adieu to the sweet Retreat and settled in our own habitation, which though a smaller and much less commodious house, had the advantage of the close vicinity of our dear Mary and Anne Doyle, from whom we wished no more to separate, and to whom every fresh trouble more strongly united us. We felt ourselves like weak trees supporting one another against the storm. My mother lived with us. It was now in the fall of the year, but we could no longer look forward with comfort to the warm firesides and social evenings which we had often thought, whilst enjoying, made winter the pleasantest season of the year. We anticipated with too much certainty the dread and dangers of that which now approached, and scarcely dared to look beyond it. In fact, all about us was gloom.

I went one afternoon to the Retreat; the house was locked, and the family who took care of it had gone out. I entered at a window; the withered leaves entered with me, and the winds whistled through the empty rooms, once the warm nests of domestic delights. I went into the garden; the autumnal blasts had strewn it with leaves, which mournfully rustled under my feet, for no hand, as formerly, had swept them away. In the gardener's house lay poor John Fleming in malignant fever; as I approached it I heard his father addressing him in an anguished tone of voice. When I reached the door and enquired for him, the poor man answered, 'He died two hours before day! I had no one with me to send for the priest, so I prayed that God would do His will with him'.

I thought that this might have been an acceptable prayer, poured forth in the bitterness of an afflicted heart which had no human aid to look to. For him, poor youth, there was much to hope; he was a young man of uncommon mind, and of a very serious turn. He was much attached to the cause of the insurgents; but said during his illness that he hoped he had not much to answer for, as he had never wronged anyone of a shilling, and had never been present at the killing of a human being.

Shortly after our return from Carlow an attack on Boakefield terrified us more than one on ourselves could have done. We heard for nearly two hours repeated discharges of shot – then saw flames ascending. A dreary silence followed, broken at length by the noise of the robbers, and by a shot which they fired as they entered the village. We sat in fearful expectation of an attack upon ourselves, and could scarcely believe it when they passed us by; yet our anxiety for our neighbours' fate prevented our enjoying our own escape, and we longed for morning. When it came our worst fears were put to flight. No one at Boakefield had been injured, though on each refusal to admit them the banditti fired a volley with the regularity of disciplined men. Those within endeavoured to keep in positions where they could not be reached by the bullets, twelve of which penetrated the hall-door; the windows were shattered, and several pieces of furniture damaged. A servant escaped out of the back of the house and ran off to Timolin, where a party of army was stationed, to request their aid; they had been advised 'to leave the devoted hole to itself', and they took the advice. Soon afterwards this servant's life was attempted. The robbers at length got in at the back window; one of them, who appeared to be the commander, cried out, 'I know my doom, but we are starving. I am Captain Smith, and I scarce care what I do. Why would you not let us in? Are any of you hurt?'

He was answered that they had taken his band for the gang of robbers which were infesting the neighbourhood. 'We are no robbers', said he, 'and yet what else can you call us?' They did not take much out of the house, or offer any violence to the family, but made strict search for men who had been there, one of whom was actually hidden in the garret at the time. They desired the men to go out and save the stable, which they had set on fire; and then retired. Captain Smith and his band were soon after taken up and lodged in Baltinglass gaol.

A cheering circumstance diversified these gloomy scenes. Robert Baxter, our early and beloved friend who we believed had been for some years numbered with the dead, again appeared in Ballitore. He was now an officer in the Cavan militia, and called to see us on his route. His countenance was glowing with rapturous joy at the sight of his old friends and the well-remembered vale, and then shaded with regret at the havoc which time and war had made amongst the friends and the shades which he loved. His stay was very short; he introduced me to his wife as 'Molly Shackleton', and made us kiss in the street; then he rushed off without his hat to see our children, and was particularly struck with the beauty of our little Jane. That dear child had a great dread of military men ever since the fearful day which the children called 'Bloody First-day;' and she used to say to me, 'I love every body in the world, but I don't love the soldiers, because they killed the doctor, and he was a pleasant man!' I was therefore astonished to see her clasp Robert Baxter fondly round his neck and cling to him, though he was dressed in full regimentals, as if by sympathy she acknowledged and loved her mother's friend.

A general rebuilding of the ruined houses now took place, but even this work was in a great measure carried on by plunder. The stately trees of Ballitore were often missed in the morning, and we could hear at night the sound of their being felled and the creaking of the cars which took them away. Desolation threatened in various shapes – the darkness of the winter nights was illuminated by the fires of the houses burnt by the insurgents, and fatal was their vengeance. One man whom they thought they had killed and had thrown into a ditch, pulling down part of the bank upon him, was not fatally injured, struggled out of his grave, ran naked to

Baltinglass, and convicted his intended murderers. A large burial moved through Ballitore with a kind of indignant solemnity. It was that of a young man who had been hanged, and whose father, on his son's being apprehended, put an end to his own life. Such were the tragedies with which we were surrounded, and with which we had grown shockingly familiar.

Thus were we circumstanced when a sore domestic calamity seemed to fill up the measure of our sufferings. We thought we had a little respite from our foes, and we were once more assembled in peace around Mary and Anne's fireside, when our dear little Jane was trusted by me with a wax taper to go up stairs alone. The staircase was short, and her grandmother was in her own room with her attendant. I was not used to be so incautious, and the thought crossed my mind, 'Is it safe?' A distant voice seemed to reply, 'The child is so steady;' and all recollection of her left me till I heard her shrieks. Then the truth flashed upon me, and I accused myself of having murdered my child! She had gone into another room than her grandmother's, and had laid down the taper; it caught her clothes, and the flames were not easily extinguished. A kind of convulsion stiffened her for a moment; the burns though extensive were but skin deep, and those around us assured us she was in no danger. Alas, we were not aware that the fright she got had stopped the circulation of the blood. O! why were we not aware of it? Let this be remembered by others, and may no one else experience the distress caused by our error.

The dear child soon ceased to complain of pain, kissed all those about her, and was cheerful, yet all night was thirsty, wakeful, and cold, with but little pulse. In the morning her whole form and sweet countenance underwent a momentary revolution which I cannot describe. We had sent to Athy for a doctor, but he said nothing could be done. Meantime, unconscious that she was leaving us, the dear innocent got her book and her work into her bed, and repeated her little verses, spoke with her usual courtesy to all around her, and, happy in her short life, closed her eyes never more to open them just twenty-four hours after the accident happened. We who had lost our darling child of four years old felt deeply the deprivation, and struggled hard to submit to the will of Him who gives and takes away.

My grief was aggravated by self-accusation. I beheld my little cherub lie as in a placid sleep, her bloom not quite gone. I listened to those who desired me to reflect on the many fathers of families who lay buried in ditches, slaughtered in the prime of manhood and of usefulness; and to the widow who with tears reminded me that I still had my husband! I recollected how, a brief time ago, his precious life had seemed near departing, and I strove to extract consolation from the genuine sympathy bestowed by our friends; yet I thought no sympathy reached my heart so fully as once when I raised my eyes from contemplating the lovely remains of my child, and met those of a poor neighbour woman fastened upon me in silence, large tears streaming down her cheeks, her countenance filled with the deepest concern. She was a coarse-featured, strong, rough woman, and had forborne any expression by words of what she felt.

Our Jane was borne from our sight; the grave closed upon her for ever; her little playfellows bedecked it with flowers, and wept for their lost companion, while their schoolmistress and her husband mourned as for a favourite grandchild. Even in this season of universal dismay the loss of this dear child was very generally deplored; she was so beautiful, so engaging, so beloved – not like a thing of earth. So ended the year 1798. Oh! year of woe!

That year, that eventful year, which to me began with the fullness of joy, I saw depart laden with deep and piercing sorrow. Thus trouble takes its rounds; but 'shall we receive good at the hand of the Lord, and shall we not also receive evil?'

We were almost prepared to congratulate our precious child on her escape, and to think that her timid nature might have been terrified into imbecility, when, shortly after her death, the robbers paid us another visit, breaking in the windows in the solemn midnight, and scaring us out of our quiet slumbers to behold armed men in our very chambers. They discovered what we strove to conceal, for their search was very strict, and they took whatever suited their purposes; but withal treated us with civility and respect. They had been at other houses, and had just robbed a pedlar of goods to a large amount. Mary Doyle, whose face, even in that hour of terror, reminded me of the fine white marble figures I had seen in Westminster Abbey, pale, serious, smooth, and handsome, ventured to expostulate; but a false alarm that the soldiers were coming had more effect. We heard our little Elizabeth praying, as Ajax had once prayed, that the Lord would please to send us daylight.

Hearing that some of our plundered property had been found, and was in the custody of Squire Ryves[47] of Rathsallagh till it should be claimed, Mary Doyle and I went thither. The way appeared long, lonely, and drear. The large old mansion of Rathsallagh exhibited a melancholy picture. Its neglected appearance, barricaded windows, the absence of the female part of the family, and the presence of a military guard made us think our own

47 The identity of Ryves of Rathsallagh is uncertain. William Ryves of Whitestown, parish of Donaghmore, near Rathsallagh, Co. Wicklow, left a prerogative will dated 1797 (Vicars, *Index to the Prerogative Wills of Ireland*, 412). His son, Armstrong Ryves, married Mary Hobson, daughter of John Hobson of Tallagh, in June 1789 at Tubber (*Index to the Irish Marriages in Walker's Hibernian Magazine, 1771–1812*, 2:388). Cullen mentions a Captain Ryves, a moderate, who was disliked by the rebels for relying too much on legal procedures in examining men for information (Cullen, 'Politics and Rebellion: Wicklow in the 1790s', 468).

situation preferable, as we were permitted to enjoy domestic comfort. Some of our things were here, and while the squire restored them to us, he smiled, and warned us of our danger of being robbed again. He foretold but too truly, though for a while we heard only distant alarms, such as of the mail-coach and travellers having been robbed. Snowy weather, we thought, kept the plunderers from us, from apprehension lest the track of their feet should betray their haunts. The snow, however, melted, and a widow neighbour became the object of their pillage. She had charge of the post-office, so they got some money there.

A few nights after this they made a general inroad on the village, entering almost every house except my brother's. They had, in the course of their visits, got themselves intoxicated, and in that state beset our house. My husband told them he would open the door, and requested them not to break the windows; but they did break them, and entering, ordered him fiercely to prepare to go with them. He refused, saying, 'Do what you will to me here; I will not leave my family'.

'Ten of us were shot and hanged in Baltinglass'.

'I had no hand in hanging or shooting you'.

He had but a few shillings; they refused them, and enquired what o'clock it was. He told them he had been robbed of his watch. At this they took offense: 'Do you call us robbers? We are no robbers; we only want a little money; we want no watch. Did you ask him for a watch?'

They grew more and more furious, and struck at him with a hanger, which cut into the wainscot partition. They raised a gun at him, which he pushed aside. They presented a pistol; it burned priming.

My firm belief that they did not really intend murder preserved me in more composure than I could have thought; for there were six armed men threatening one armed and defenseless. But now the clatter of arms, the cries of three women who stood on the staircase, and the threats of those wicked men would have overcome me, had I not just then seen my husband escape from their hands.

The next moment was again terrible. Anne Doyle came in, holding her head with both hands, and saying in a tremulous voice that she believed she was killed. A ruffian had struck her with the butt-end of his pistol, and had wounded her head in two places. I saw a stroke aimed at the back of Mary Doyle's head, and averted it with my outstretched arm. She lamented aloud, and accused the robbers of having murdered her sister, not silenced by their offered blows, and their threats that they would kill her if she would not be quiet. At last one cried out, 'Hush, for God's sake!'

'Don't mention that name', returned Mary, 'He has nothing to do with such wickedness'.

They appeared to be struck with solemnity and distress with which she spoke, their countenances fell, and their accents became those of compassion. One man, who had his face hidden by a handkerchief, took her hand tenderly, and exclaimed, 'Surely you do not think it was I [who] hurt her?'

The next day an old woman came to enquire for Anne Doyle, and hinted that when the robbers thought we were rested they intended to pay us another visit; but before night a party of the Clare militia came in to protect the inhabitants. We could now sleep in our beds without fear of disturbance, yet deeply regretted that we owed this security not to confidence, but to force repelling force. The excesses of the military were not forgotten, and they did not appear to be cordially received by the lower class of people. The country was far from being settled; it was like the working of the sea after a storm. On the window-stools of the upper storeys of many gentlemen's houses were collected large stones, placed there to assist in repelling the attacks of robbers. Travelling carriages were escorted by military guards, and the mail-coach was guarded by two or more powerfully armed men.

To our particular feelings the public commotion was some relief, as it partially drew our thoughts into another channel than the contemplation of our affliction, and strengthened our hope that it was in mercy our darling child was called away. The marks of the flames which had caused her destruction and of the blood which flowed from our dear Anne's wounds together stained the wainscoat; which also bore the mark of the hanger aimed at my husband. These were easily obliterated, but the remembrance must last with life. I now perceived that my memory, which had been uncommonly good, was much impaired, and I imputed it to the series of repeated shocks which my mind had sustained. Such shocks had deprived many of health and some of reason, and we who were spared both had additional cause for thankfulness.

One day we saw two prisoners brought in who had robbed a gentleman in open daylight of the high road; the soldiers got the alarm, and quickly apprehended them. In a few days their lives were ended by martial law in Carlow. The soldiers having been withdrawn from Timolin, Pat Lalor's house was robbed, his daughter beaten, and he himself barely escaped with his life. One evening the village was alarmed by a soldier having shot another man. Two of the 'Ancient Britons', who had been sent on an express, entered a carman's stage-house, where were also some Kilkenny carriers. One of the dragoons, forgetting he had changed horses with his comrade, and knowing that his own pistol was not charged, snapped the pistol he held in his hand in jest at one of the carriers; it was loaded with death, and the young man instantly lay on the floor a bloody corpse; the soldier, standing over him, wringing his hands, exclaimed, 'Oh, what have I done!' He was tried and acquitted, much to the dissatisfaction of the country-people.

Several robbers were at this time shot or imprisoned. Amongst the latter was Doyle; he was in great danger, but he escaped death. We believed, notwithstanding, that the inclinations for plunder still continued, for the day the Dumfries fencibles left Ballitore several men of suspicious aspect appeared in the village, and our lower class of neighbours seeemed to exult in the departure of the military, and to be crest-fallen when another regiment came. It was on a fine day, and while the market was being held, that we saw pass through the village, escorted by a strong guard, two men yet living; but on the same car were their coffins. One had been convicted for burning the courthouse at Narraghmore, the other for the murder of Hannah Manders, and they were to suffer death at the places where their crimes had been committed. One of the men hung his head weeping, the other looked about as if stupified by terror. The march of the soldiers was slow and solemn, and the people in the market seemed afraid to notice the prisoners.[48]

Hugh Cullen now returned to his family from a long imprisonment, and, attended by his glad father, called to see his neighbours, who welcomed him back to life and liberty.

One of the curiosities of our village, our old neighbour Finlay McClane, after a severe conflict with death, yielded at last, having just completed his 110th year, and possessing his mental faculties to the last.

The sad account reached us about this time of the death of our dear Tom Eyre. He was on his way to Clogheen, where his regiment was quartered, and my sister Grubb[49] and he anticipated much pleasure in each other's society. His journey was arrested at Kilkenny by an attack of gout in the stomach, which speedily put an end to his life. At these tidings I mourned for him with sisterly sorrow, and wept bitter, inavailing tears, while retracing the pleasantest scenes of childhood.

I did not say in the right place how spring, though remarkably late this year, at length clothed the face of nature in more than wonted beauty. But, alas, it could not bring to our minds the sensations of gladness which it had formerly enjoyed. Our hearts dwelt on the recollection that our slaughtered neighbours, our murdered friends and our departed child had been enjoying life and health with us when the last fields were green.

---

48 These were probably John Whelan, alias Black Top, convicted of the murder of Hannah Manders, and [ ] Fitzpatrick, convicted of the murder of Thomas Young at Narraghmore. Musgrave states that they were 'executed where they had committed these horrid crimes' (Musgrave, 281). Later in 1800, Thomas J. Rawson apprehended three others, Howard, Keane and Bryan, who were convicted on the testimony of Margaret McIvers, Mrs Manders's niece. They were 'hanged and beheaded at Glassealy' (Ibid.; see also Thomas Bartlet, 'Bearing Witness: Female Evidences in Courts Martial Convened to Suppress the 1798 Rebellion', in Keogh and Furlong (eds), *The Women of 1798*, 71).   49 Margaret Shackleton married Samuel Grubb of Clonmel on 17 Apr. 1776. They had eleven children ('Grubb of Ardmayle', *Burke's Landed Gentry of Ireland* [1912], 282).

10

ANNE, COUNTESS DOWAGER OF RODEN

Anne Hamilton was born in May, 1730, at Dundalk, Ireland, the daughter of James Hamilton, 1st Earl of Limerick and 1st Earl of Clanbrassil (2nd creation), and his wife Lady Harriot, daughter of William Bentnick, 1st Earl of Portland. On 11 Dec. 1752, she married Robert Jocelyn of High Roding, Co. Tipperary, who was created 1st Earl of Roden in 1771.[1] Their son, Robert, Viscount Jocelyn and later 2nd Earl of Roden, commanded the First Fencible Light Dragoons, which defeated an army of Irish rebels at Rathfarnham on 25 May 1798, and later fought French troops under the command of General Humbert at the so-called 'Race of Castlebar'.

A pious woman, Lady Roden had returned to her home, Tollymore Park, in May of 1798, still in mourning over the death of her husband the previous summer. News of rebel activity at Larne prompted her daughter Harriot Skeffington to urge her to flee the estate for the safety of Belfast, and then to leave Ireland altogether for Scotland. She complied, and though she witnessed little of the actual rebellion, her obvious strong loyalist sympathies were reflected in her diary. She died at Belfast in 1802 and was buried at Dundalk.[2] Her diary, from which the following account is taken, was published posthumously in 1870.

THE ACCOUNT

Wednesday, May 23rd, [1798]. Louisa,[3] the Hutchinsons,[4] and I came to Tollymore Park. This day begun those dreadful scenes in and about Dublin, which, as we came farther north, we were ignorant of for two

---

1 'Roden of High Roding', in G.E. Cokayne, *Complete Peerage* (London: St Catherine Press, 1949), 11:62–3. See also *Burke's Peerage* [1975], 2280. An account of Lady Roden's experiences during the Rebellion may be found in Stewart, *Summer Soldiers*, 193–6.   2 The date given for Countess Roden's death varies. According to the *Complete Peerage*, she died on 16 April 1802 (Ibid.). However, the appendix of her memoir, *The Diary of Anne, Countess Dowager of Roden, 1797–1802* (Dublin: T. H. White, 1870) gives this date as 21 May 1802 (p. 180).   3 Lady Louisa Jocelyn, fifth daughter of the countess, married Col. Leonard Shafto Orde of Weetwood, Northumberland, 11 May 1801 (see *Diary*, App. G, 166–7). She died on 1 Sept. 1807 ('Orde of Weetwood Hall', *Burke's Landed Gentry* [1886], 1392).   4 They are defined as 'the Honourable Margaret and Prudence, sisters of Lord Donoughmore, and of John Low Hutchinson', *Diary*, App. G, 167).

days: dreadful indeed they are, but mercy has attended us, and Oh, surely it has attended me and supported me under the dreadful apprehension from reports yesterday that this shocking rebellion had broke out at Belfast and Drogheda, so that all I loved on all sides was in danger, except the single one who was with me; and even we appeared from that report to be between two fires, which would soon destroy us. God Almighty supported me for some hours that I endured this misery, and at last He granted me the mercy to know this report was false. His protection of my beloved son[5] in his brave undertaking against these unfortunate rebels, is a mercy for which my heart is too narrow to conceive or return praise. May it work in me more ardent love and implicit resignation to His most blessed will, who intends good to us in all His visitations. These threatenings continued; but the Province of Ulster was supposed to be quiet, nor was there any danger apprehended.

In this persuasion we remained for some days, and we were enjoying ourselves as comfortably as I could.

On *Thursday, June 7th*, Mr Moore and Mr William Moore came to see me, and gave me some instances that seemed to be convincing that the Province of Ulster was likely to continue quiet. In the evening, Gray asked me if I should not like to have some of the troops, that were at Bryansford, guard this house. I was rather startled at this question, as I apprehended he might have heard some alarming account; and he slightly said, No, and I refused the guard. In less than an hour after, I received an express from Harriot,[6] to inform me that there was a rising in Larne, which they hoped would be soon got under; but urging me most eagerly to set out immediately for Belfast, for which purpose she had sent her horses to meet me at Saintfield, and also an order from General Nugent[7] that the six dragoons that were stationed at Bryansford should escort me.

This account was most alarming. We waited for break of day, and set out in our chaise and Miss Hutchinson's chaise. Louisa recollected that Captain Wolseley was in the neighbourhood, and wrote to ask him to accompany us, which he most kindly complied with; and we found him upon our road at Clough. We got with perfect safety to Belfast, and saw nothing alarming. The two Miss Hutchinsons, Louisa, my three little children and our two maids, Davis and Miss H'.s footman, were all that went with us. Hammy Gray also accompanied us as far as Belfast. When

---

5 Robert, Viscount Joscelyn and 2nd earl of Roden, was born at Dundalk on 26 Oct. 1756. He succeeeded his father as Earl in 1797 and the following year commanded the First Fencible Light Dragoons. He died on 29 June 1820 at Hyde Hall, Herts (*Complete Peerage*, 11:63). **6** Lady Harriot Jocelyn, the eldest daughter of the countess, married, in 1780, the Hon. Chichester Skeffington, who was afterwards 4th earl of Massereene (see *Diary*, App. G, 168; *Burke's Peerage* [1975], 1772). She died on 7 July 1831 and was survived by an only child, Harriot, who married Thomas Henry Foster, 2nd Viscount Ferrard, 20 Nov. 1810.

we arrived within two miles of it, during all which time we had met nothing alarming, Captain Wolseley took his leave of me, as there were troops from thence to the town. In his return he narrowly escaped being taken upon that road which so few hours before we had travelled in safety. The next day Saintfield, where we had changed horses, was in the hands of the rebels.

June 8. We got to Belfast about ten o'clock, and found Harriot in a worse situation even than I expected. She had not seen Chitty[8] for two days and nights, during which time he had been in the battle of Antrim. It was a desperate one, where, by the brave but rash intrepidity of Colonel Lumley,[9] part of the 22nd were cut off, and the yeoman cavalry were probably saved by the means of Chitty's coolness and recollection. Poor Lord O'Neill[10] was murdered this day as he was going to a meeting of magistrates; not at all in the act of fighting. We were told Chitty was safe, but I could hardly believe it, not seeing them return; but after some hours the troop returned, and he safe with them. Lord O'Neill lingered some days at Lord Massereene's,[11] where he died.

Before we got to Belfast the only friends in whom Harriot could have any comfort were fled to Scotland, so that when I got to Belfast she was well nigh overcome; the only gleam of earthly comfort she had was seeing us. The troop had been delayed in their returning by conveying prisoners. They entered the town with the greatest acclamations through the streets. The emotion was strong upon this sight; but the doubt of the sincerity of

---

7 General Sir George Nugent (1757–1849) served in America, 1777–82, was present at the siege of Valenciennes in 1793, and the following year was stationed in Ireland. He was appointed major-general in 1796 and commanded troops in the north of Ireland in 1798. At Ballynahinch, he routed an army of rebels near the estate of Lord Moira, killing several hundred while losing only three of his own troops (see Thomas Bartlett, 'Defence, Counter-insurgency, and Rebellion: Ireland, 1793–1803', in Thomas Bartlett and Keith Jeffrey (eds), *A Military History of Ireland* [Cambridge: Cambridge Univ. Press, 1996], 282). Later, he served as Adjutant-General from 1799 to 1801 (*Dictionary of National Biography*, 14:705; Stewart, *summer Soldiers*, 80–1).   8 Chichester Skeffington, son-in-law of the countess and later 4th earl of Massareene, died on 25 Feb. 1816.   9 Lt. Col. William Lumley was the seventh son of the earl of Scarborough. Commanding a company of Light Dragoons, he played a prominent role in the battle of Antrim, leading a charge into the town of Antrim. His men were overrun, and he was shot through the ankle by a rebel bullet. After loosing many of his troops, he ordered a retreat (see Stewart, *Summer Soldiers*, 84, 108–10). He later served in Egypt, South Africa, and South America, and had a distinguished career with Wellington. He died in 1850.   10 John O'Neill of Shane's Castle, formerly Edenduffcarrig, Co. Antrim, was born in 1740. He matriculated at Trinity College and at Oxford, and served as M.P. for Randalstown and for Co. Antrim between 1761 and 1793. In 1793, he was created Baron O'Neill of Shane's Castle, and two years later was made Viscount O'Neill. He died 17 June 1798 at Lord Massareene's Castle, Co. Antrim, of wounds received from a pike in a skirmish with the rebels on 7 June (see *Complete Peerage*, 10:61–2; Musgrave, 547–54). 11 Clotworthy Skeffington, 3rd earl of Massareene (1742–1805), was the brother of Chichester Skeffington, who married Harriot Jocelyn, daughter of the countess.

these testimonies of joy dampened the luxuriant feel one might have had. When Chitty came to us he bore every mark of the most terrible feelings, joined to the most manly firmness and tenderness to us. The question was this day what we were to do. Chitty did not seem at this moment to advise us to leave Ireland, but we heard that General Nugent had thought it necessary to send Mrs Nugent away. Every hour brought accounts of increased disturbances. This day was passed, indeed, in a most agitated state, and on the next

Saturday, the 9th, Chitty seemed strongly of the opinion we ought to sail. He told me if an exceeding large force came upon the town, they might seize the boats, and leave us no means of escaping, and that there was now a very good little coal ship in which we might go. This day was also past in suffering, seeing him only for short minutes, when he rather wished to avoid than to see us. His eagerness to put us on board was very great, and at nightfall we (those I have named above) went down to the quay and embarked on board this little vessel (the Liberty, Captain Cargo). Poor Chitty put us on board, and was then obliged to leave us. Soon after, Harriot had the misery of hearing the trumpet sound to arms.

The river of Belfast is such a difficult passage, except with every favourable circumstance, that, as we had not these, we were soon a-ground, by the fault, as the Captain said, of the Pilot. All confidence being entirely lost in our countrymen, there was no security in our minds that this was not intended. As we lost a tide by it, and remained little more than a stone's throw from the land, if God had permitted them to see it, they might have made us a prey; but it was not permitted. There was an engagement near Saintfield, in which our troops were driven back, and this day, Sunday,

10th of June, the ladies upon the deck had the misery of seeing the York Fencibles flying over the bridge of Belfast, to which, as we lay a-ground, we were very near, indeed. We made very little way any part of this day, and got a-ground again. People were constantly coming to us from the town, by which we had the comfort of hearing that the Yeomanry Troop had not been out the night before, when that dreadful trumpet sounded. They had been so harrassed at Antrim, it was almost necessary to spare them this night if it was possible. This evening we had some prospect of sailing, but the Pilot (without whom the Captain dare not sail) did not come on board till barely time for the tide, and then half the crew had left us. All this appeared to me extremely suspicious, but as there was no mending our situation, it was needless to express my fears; there was terror enough spread amongst our fugitives by cruel and false reports which were continually brought from the town. While we were in this situation, Mr Salmon (Mr Skeffington's clerk) brought down the King's boat, out of which he replaced our crew, and worked jointly with them and a servant of

Mr Skeffington's (Denis), till twelve o'clock, to get us off, which they effected, and on this day,

Monday, June 11, we began to sail, and landed at Portpatrick, I think, between three and four in the evening. We brought with us a maid-servant and her child, who had lived many years in the family.

The ship was wonderfully crowded – we lay in the hold fifty-three, women and children – and tedious and woeful as the time we were confined there was, I never heard a complaint from any person, except the cries of the poor little innocent children. Harriot had brought some mattresses which were very useful; one of them, spread over some dressing boxes belonging to the passengers, was my bed for the most part of forty-five hours, and, I fear, I fared a great deal better than most of my companions. In one thing I fared well indeed, by the strength and spirit it pleased God to give me, never to sink at this strange and unexpected situation. I ought to mention every comfort it pleased God to give us, though I cannot probably tell half: our poor Captain, who I believe to be one of the best hearted creatures in the world, showed us such kindness and feeling as one could only have expected from a much higher style of education. When we landed, the town of Portpatrick was so completely full of military, going to Ireland, and fugitives from thence, that we had no hopes of a bed of any kind; we could only get a dirty bed-chamber in the inn to eat our dinner; but the regulating officer, Captain Carmichael, from whom we received every civility and assistance, found us out some rooms at the Minister's house, Mr McKenzie, who, with his wife, joined in affording us every comfort in their power. Mrs Nugent, who had got a lodging at an ale-house, gave Harriot and her child a bed in it. We remained this day.

Tuesday, June 12th, at Portpatrick, and had the satisfaction of seeing the troops embark for Ireland; one (Lancashire Greys) in the highest spirits. The weather was most favourable, and had been so from the time I left home.

As we could not hire any lodgings (for Mrs McKenzie would take nothing for her's), it was impossible to trespass upon the people who had so humanely received us, and besides I found our vicinity to Ireland occasioned us continually to hear reports of the most dreadful kind, which, though often false, distracted us all, but particularly Harriot. This made me wish to advance and on

Wednesday, June 13th, we went forward to Stranraer. Here the same difficulty occurred from the same causes as to lodgings. Two ladies, friends of Mr Arbuckle's[12] – the Miss Campbells – lent us some rooms; but even

12 James Arbuckle was Collector of the Customs at Donaghadee, Scotland. He married Lady Sophia Jocelyn, fourth daughter of the countess. She died in 1824 (see *Diary*, App. L, 169).

here our party was so large, Harriot and her child slept upon a couch and chairs, but that was, indeed, no inconvenience. Those ladies were remarkably kind to us. We then thought of going forward to Dumfries, where we were told we should get lodgings, and for which place we had letters from Captain Carmichael. We stayed this day and the next here, where we met Mr Bristow and his family, and on

Friday, June 15th, went on to Newtown Douglas, where we lay; and on

Saturday, the 16th of June, went on to Dumfries, where we met with great kindness from a gentleman – Mr Welwood Maxwell – to whom Captain Carmichael had recommended us. We stayed here on

Sunday, June 17th. Mr Maxwell went to Church with us, and showed us some lodgings; they were gloomy and disagreeable, and we disliked a close town for our children; besides, as I had come so far, I wished to get to my friends at Longtown.

Monday, June 18th. We set out for Longtown, and got there about three o'clock. I sent from the inn to let Mr and Mrs Graham know we were come. They came to us immediately. I was not disappointed in the hopes of their kindness, for nothing could exceed it – my own children could not have shown me more. They insisted upon our going to their house, which we all did this day,

June 19th. They wished us to continue with them, but this, while there was a house to be hired, we could not think of. They then found us out a most comfortable little dwelling at the end of the town, with a pretty garden. As the house was quite unfurnished, they lent us what furniture they could possibly spare, and interested Sir J. and Lady C. Graham so much for us, that they also supplied us with everything we could not hire. Mr Graham took Harriot to Carlisle to hire all the other things they wanted, and we were ready by

Saturday, June 23rd, to go to our new habitation, and thus day left Artharet, and were settled with as much comfort as in our anxious situation we could enjoy in that little place. I may say, from the moment we landed till this day, *July 23rd*, we met with nothing but the greatest kindness and benevolence, without one disappointment. Sir James and Lady Graham, I must believe (as I have good reason to trust their sincerity), grew equally attached to us with Mr and Mrs Graham. No words can express, nor no gratitude repay it. This was our situation while all we held dear that were not with us were suffering the horrors of this most accursed rebellion, the terrors of which left us no peace of mind; but, God be praised, nothing most dear to us has suffered. I persuaded Harriot to go to Harrogate, as I knew both she and her dear child wanted those waters; and I feared lest if Chitty was able to join her soon, seeing him tired of staying there before they had received the full benefit of them; and they left us this day. We remained at Longtown till the

12th September, in which time Mr Straton and Emily[13] came to us, but were obliged to return, as the severe fevers my little twins had, had detained us for six weeks, and prevented my setting out with them. Mr Arbuckle and Sophia also came and stayed with us till we came away. In this time the French had landed at Killala, and many other circumstances had occurred. We were obliged to travel so slow upon account of the children, that we did not reach Portpatrick till the 18th. Mr J. Arbuckle had the goodness to come to meet me, and we had a very pleasant passage on the 19th. We stayed that day at Donaghadee, the next day at Belfast, and got to Tollymore Park on Friday, September 21st.

In closing this little insignificant narrative of our situation for three months, let me deeply impress upon my mind the wonderful mercies that attended us from the beginning of our flight. Wherever we set our foot it pleased God to dispose the hearts of all we met to kindness and humanity towards us; and when we rested at Longtown, the tender friendship of the Graham family could only be equalled by the kindness of my dear children to me. We never suffered half of what our dearest concerns in Ireland did. Our spirits were not broken by the continual view of horrors which has nearly overcome some of those dear objects, and none of us have lost anything essential to our happiness or comfort. My dear little children were recovered, by the mercy of Providence, from desperate fevers, and I had the blessing of bringing them home in health, and seeing their strength returning every day. These are a small part of the mercies that were heaped upon me.

Whoever writes the history of this eventful unhappy summer, will particularly describe the astonishing mercies that have been granted to the defenders of religion and the laws in this distracted country – distracted by wickedness arisen to a pitch almost incredible, not yet subsided by the scattered remains of those unfortunate wretches who have either formed or were seduced into plans the most diabolical. The mercies to the country have been unspeakable; and to an individual, none that I know has received such as I have done – all my family safe and in credit, not the least of our property injured or diminished, and my dear, dear son appearing with such credit and honor as one in the first line of the protectors of his country.[14]

---

13 John Straton, Esquire, of Lisnawilly, Co. Louth, married Emily Jocelyn, the sixth and youngest daughteer of the countess (see the *Diary*. App. M, 169–170).   14 The second earl of Roden had commanded the First Fencible Light Dragoons, nicknamed 'The Roden Foxhunters', because recruiters had promised those who enlisted that they would have a day of fox hunting once a week (*Diary*, App. N, 170). Lord Roden was involved with two significant engagements against the rebels. At the end of May, 1798, Major-General Sir James Duff and an army of 600 men marched to Gibbetrath on the Curragh in order to receive the surrender of a gathering of rebels, who were then massacred. Musgrave's fabricated and inaccurate account states that the rebels 'wantonly and without provocation

These things ought to sink most deeply into my heart. How have I deserved such mercy? My own heart too truly tells me I am unworthy; by the mercy of God may I be directed to humble my heart in unfeigned penitence and perfect resignation. The grief that fills it is still often very great, though the cause of it ought to be matter of thanksgiving, and such I often make it to the best of my power, that the beloved scenes of this last dreadful year. I hope what I feel is pardonable, for sure the gift was worthy.

I have been very blameable in faults of temper, sadly so; surely such sorrow ought to soften, or it is not like humble resigned grief.

fired on the King's troops, of whom they killed one and injured three ... Ample vengeance was soon obtained; for above three hundred and fifty of the rebels were killed and several wounded, by Lord Jocelyn's Fencible Cavalry who fell in with them pell mell ...' (Musgrave, 242–3). A second incident occurred near Ballynamuck on September 8, when Lord Roden's Fencibles received the surrender of General Humbert and the French army.

11

MARIA EDGEWORTH

Maria Edgeworth of Edgeworthstown, Co. Longford was the predominant female literary figure in Ireland during the first half of the nineteenth century. She was born on 1 January 1767 at her mother's house at Black Bourton, Oxfordshire, the daughter of Richard Lovell Edgeworth and his first wife, Anna Maria, daughter of Paul Elers of Black Bourton. Her father, who lived from 1744 to 1817, was an author, militia leader, inventor, and M.P. in the Irish Parliament from 1798 to 1800. He married four times and was the father of a large brood of children.[1]

After being educated by several private tutors in England, Maria returned to the family estate, where she assisted in the education of her siblings and developed a close, confidential friendship with her father. She showed an early fondness for writing, publishing a defence of female education in 1795 under the title, *Letters to Literary Ladies*. Three years later in the autumn of 1798, she began a collaboration with her father under the title, *Practical Education*, in which they offered a series of discursive essays on educational theory.

The year 1800 marked the beginning of a prolific period of creativity and writing in Maria's life. It began with the publication of *Castle Rackrent*, her most famous novel, in which she offered a vivid portrait of the Irish gentry at the turn of the nineteenth century. Spurred by its success, Maria produced fifteen more books by 1818, including *Early Lessons, Moral Tales*, and *Belinda* in 1801; *Irish Bulls* in 1802; *Popular Tales* and *Modern Griselda* in 1804; *Leonora and Letters* in 1806; two series of short stories under the title, *Tales from Fashionable Life*, in 1809 and 1812; *Patronage* in 1814; *Harrington* and *Ormond*, published together in 1817; *Comic Dramas*, also published in 1817. Beginning in 1818, as she set to work finishing her father's memoirs and beginning a memoir of her own, she was afflicted by a weakness of the eyes that forced her to give up

1 The best account of the Edgeworth family history is Harriet Jessie Butler and Harold Edgeworth Butler, *The Black Book of Edgeworthstown and Other Edgeworth Memories, 1585–1817* (London: Faber and Gwyer, 1927). For a more succinct genealogy, see 'Edgeworth of Edgeworthstown', in *Burke's Landed Gentry of Ireland* (1912), 204–5. An excellent, concise biography of Richard Lovell Edgeworth appears in the *Dictionary of National Biography*, 6:383–5.

reading, writing, and needlework for several years. She eventually finished her memoirs, publishing them with her father's in 1820. Then Maria began a long period of domestic life at Edgeworthstown during which time she gave up writing. Her last two novels, *Helen* and *Orlandino*, were published in 1834, but they did not achieve the success of her earlier work. She corresponded with all of the major literary figures of her day and took a strong interest in the relief of the poor on her estate. She died at Edgeworthstown on 22 May 1849.[2]

The following account is taken from the second volume of Richard Lovell Edgeworth's Memoirs, which were completed by Maria.[3] It describes conditions in Co. Longford during the autumn of 1798, when neighbouring Co. Mayo was invaded by French troops under the command of General Humbert. The political views of the liberal Edgeworths did not typify those of other loyalist gentry in Longford at the time. Edgeworth's corps of yeomanry included both Catholics and Protestants, and in his role as a magistrate he attempted to display a scrupulous even-handedness toward Catholics. This liberality, coupled with the fact that Edgeworthstown remained undisturbed during the violence, led to suspicion that Edgeworth was rebel sympathizer, and the family became unpopular among many more conservative Protestants in the county. Maria's account of the rebellion provides an important glimpse of the divisions within the Protestant community at that time.

THE ACCOUNT

The summer of 1798 passed without any interruption of our domestic tranquillity. Though disturbances in different parts of Ireland had broken out, yet now, as in former trials, the Co. of Longford remained quiet; free at least from open insurrection, and, as far as appeared, the people well disposed. They complained, however, very frequently to my father of the harassing of certain new-made justices of the peace, and yeomen military, or, as the people called them, *scourers of the country*, who, galloping about

---

2 The principal biography of Maria Edgeworth remains Marilyn Butler's *Maria Edgeworth: A Literary Biography* (Oxford: Clarendon Press, 1972). Butler's account of the Edgeworths' experiences in 1798 follows closely Maria's own account and adds little new information. For two more recent studies of Maria's representation of 1798 in her literature, see Mitzi Myers, '"Completing the Union": Critical Ennui, the Politics of Narrative, and the Reformation of Irish Cultural Identity', in *Prose Studies: History, Theory, Criticism*, vol. 18 (Dec. 1995): 41–77. See also Mitzi Myers, '"Like Pictures in a Magic Lantern": Gender, History, and Edgeworth's Rebellion Narratives', in *Nineteenth Century Contexts* 19 (1996):373–412.
3 Richard Lovell Edgeworth and Maria Edgeworth, *Memoirs of Richard Lovell Edgeworth: Begun by Himself and concluded by His Daughter Maria Edgeworth*. 2 vols (London: 1820; Shannon, Ireland: Irish University Press, 1969).

night and day, would let no poor man sleep in peace. Our magistracy had at that time fallen below its proper level; many of the great proprietors of this county were absentees; and for want of resident gentlemen, magistrates were made of men without education, experience, or hereditary respectibility. During the war, and in consequence of what were called the war-prizes, graziers, land-jobbers, and middle-men had risen into comparative wealth; and instead of turning in due season, according to the natural order of things, into Buckeens and Squireens, they had been metamorphosed into justices of the peace and committee men, or into yeomen lieutenants and captains. In these their new characters, they bustled and bravadoed; and sometimes from mere ignorance, and sometimes in the certainty of party support or public indemnity, they overleaped the bounds of law. Upon slight suspicion, or vague information, they took up and imprisoned many who were innocent; the relations of the injured appealed to him, who was known to be a friend of public justice. I will not say *the friend of the poor*, though this was the name by which I have often heard him called. But this has become a hackneyed expression, degraded from its real meaning, since it has been used for party purposes, or by those who aim only at vulgar popularity.

In consequence to appeals made to him, my father made inquiry at public sessions or assizes into various cases of persons, who had been imprisoned. Sometimes such examinations, warrants, and commitals, were produced, or such explanatory letters were written to him by justices of the quorum, worded in such a blundering manner, so spelled, so scrawled, as to be almost illegible and quite incomprehensible. All this would have been ludicrous, had not the matter been too serious for ridicule, where the liberties and lives of human creatures were at stake. My father exerted himself upon all occasions to keep the law in its due course, representing, that, whether the accused were innocent or guilty, they were entitled to fair trial; that, till it was proved that they had forfeited the protection of our constitution, no persons should be treated as enemies or outlaws; that it was bad policy to make people detest the authority, which they were bound to obey, and on their obedience to which the safety of all ranks depends.

Those who were conscious of making themselves objects of dislike to the lower class of people were naturally afraid, that, if any disturbance arose, they should be the first victims; and cowardice combined with party prejudice, to increase their violence. They disregarded my father's representations; as far as they dared, resented his interference; and were in unfeigned astonishment at his opposite course of conduct. They found, that, when he was to judge of any action, he never inquired whether it had been committed by a catholic, or a protestant; nor would he use, or permit to be used before him, either as a magistrate or landlord, any of those party names, which designate and perpetuate party hatred. He would not even understand, that the term *an honest man*, pronounced with peculiar emphasis, meant, with one party, exclusively a *protestant*. The principle of 'shew me the man, and I will shew you the law', he considered as the opprobrium of magistracy. No fears of the timid, or cries of the violent; no personal views, no danger for himself of misrepresentation or odium, could in any one instance prevail upon him, even for the plea of public safety, or the necessity of the times, to strain a single point of law or justice. He believed that justice, like honesty, of which in fact it is only a more enlarged description, is always the best policy. He adhered therefore to the straight rule of right, without entering into any of the obliquies of expediency. The maxim, that extraordinary times call for extraordinary measures, he considered to be a principle, dangerous as it is vague; because those, who fancy they obey a mysterious legislative *call*, are often hurried on merely by the suggestions of their own fears, or their own passions; no judgment remaining to decide upon what is ordinary, or extraordinary. He thought, that no partial commotion, nothing less than a general earthquake of the state, should be suffered to disturb the balance of even-handed justice: when this is overturned, nothing remains but the sword.

Towards the autumn of 1798, this country became in such a state, that the necessity for resorting to the sword seemed imminent. Even in the county of Longford, which had so long remained quiet, alarming symptoms appeared, not immediately in our neighbourhood, but within six or seven miles of us, near Granard. The people were leagued in secret rebellion, and waited only for the expected arrival of the French army, to break out. In the adjacent countries military law had been proclaimed, and our village was within the bounds of the disturbed county of Westmeath. Though his own tenantry, and all in whom he put trust, were as quiet, and, as far as he could judge, as well disposed as ever, yet my father was aware, from information of too good authority to be doubted, that there were disaffected persons in the vicinity.

Numbers held themselves in abeyance, not so much from disloyalty, as from fear, that they should be ultimately the conquered party. Those who were really and actually engaged, and in communication with the rebels, and with the foreign enemy, were so secret and cunning, that no proofs could be obtained against them; while the eagerness to gain information laid proprietors in the middle and higher classes open to treachery, and to double danger from informers, who often gave them false clews, to involve them still farther in darkness and error. The object of such persons being in general to gratify provate malice, or to favor the escape of the guilty by turning suspicion upon the innocent.

Previous to this time, the principal gentry in the county had raised corps of yeomanry; but my father had delayed doing so, because, as long as the civil authority had been sufficient, he was unwilling to resort to military interference, or to the ultimate law of force, of the abuse of which he had seen too many recent examples. However, it now became necessary, even for the sake of justice to his own tenantry, that they should be put upon an equal footing with others, have equal security of protection, and an opportunity of evincing their loyal dispositions. He raised a corps of infantry, into which he admitted Catholics as well as Protestants. This was so unusual, and thought to be so hazardous a degree of liberality, that by some of an opposite party it was attributed to the worst motives. Many who wished him well came privately to let him know of the odium, to which he exposed himself – the timid hinted fears and suspicions, that he was going to put arms into the hands of men, who would desert or betray him in the hour of trial; who might find themselves easily absolved from holding any faith with a Protestant, and with one of a family, of whom the head, in former times. had been distinguished by the appellation of *Protestant Frank*. He thanked his secret advisers, but openly and steadily abided by his purpose. Suspicion he knew often produces the very evils it fears. Confidence he felt to be due to those, who had hitherto conducted themselves irreproachably, and who manifested at this moment, by every means in their power, strong attachment to him and to the government. These men had been exposed to some trial, and might be called upon to resist great temptations of passion and interest. On his own part, my father knew the risk he ran, but he braved it. Resident as he had long been in Ireland, his established character, his property, and his large family, afforded altogether so strong a pledge of his good intentions, that he considered himself as in a situation to set an example of that conduct, which he thought most advantageous for the country. The corps of Edgeworth-Town Infantry was raised, but the arms were, by some mistake of the ordnance-office, delayed. The anxiety for their arrival was extreme, for every day and every hour the French were expected to land.

The alarm was now so general, that many sent their families out of the country. My father was still in hopes, that we might safely remain. At the first appearance of disturbance in Ireland he had offered to carry his sisters-in-law, the Mrs Sneyds,[4] to their friends in England, but this offer they refused. Of the domestics, three men were English and Protestant, two Irish and Catholic; the women were all Irish and Catholic, excepting the housekeeper, an Englishwoman, who had lived with us many years. There were no dissensions or suspicions between the Catholics and Protestants in the family, and the English servants did not desire to quit us at this crisis.

4 These were Mary Sneyd (1751–1841) and Charlotte Sneyd (d. 1841), sisters of Honora Sneyd (d. 1779) the third wife of Richard Lovell Edgeworth. All three were daughters of Edward Sneyd of Bishton, Staffordshire. In spite of their relationship, they were on intimate terms with both Maria Edgeworth and Frances Anne (Beaufort) Edgeworth (1767–1865), the fourth wife of Richard Lovell Edgeworth.

At last came the dreaded news. The French, who had landed at Killala, were, as we learned, on their march towards Longford.⁵ The touch of Ithuriel's spear could not have been more sudden or effectual, than the arrival of this intelligence, in shewing people in their real forms. In some faces joy struggled for a moment with feigned sorrow, and then, encouraged by sympathy, yielded to the *natural* expression. Still my father had no reason to distrust those, in whom he had placed confidence; his tenants were steady; he saw no change in any of the men in his corps, though they were in the most perilous situation, having rendered themselves obnoxious to the rebels and invaders, by becoming yeomen, and yet standing without means of defence, their arms not having arrived.⁶

The evening of the day, when the news of the approach of the French came to Edgeworth-Town, all seemed quiet; but early the next morning, September 4, a report reached us that the rebels were *up* in arms within a mile of the village, pouring in from the county of Westmeath, hundreds strong. We could not at first believe their report. An hour afterwards it was contradicted.⁷ An English servant, who was sent out to ascertain the truth, brought back word, that he had ridden three miles from the village on the road described, and that he had seen only twenty or thirty men with green boughs in their hats, and pikes in their hands, who said '*that they were standing there to protect themselves against the Orangemen, of whom they were in dread, and who, as they heard, were coming down to cut them to pieces*'. This was all nonsense; but no better sense could be obtained. Report after report, equally foolish, was heard, or at least uttered. But this much being certain, that men armed with pikes were assembled, my father sent off an express to the next garrison town (Longford), requesting the commanding officer to send him assistance in the defence of this place. He desired us to be

---

5 Maria wrote to her aunt, Sophie Ruxton, on 29 August 1798: 'We who are so near the scene of action cannot by any means discover what *number* of the French actually landed; some say 88, some 1800, some 18,000, some 4,000. The troops march and countermarch, as they say themselves, without knowing where they are going, or for what' (Maria Edgeworth, *Life and Letters of Maria Edgeworth*, [Boston: Houghton, Mifflin, 1895], 1:57).   6 Maria wrote on 29 August: 'My father's corps of yeomanry are extremely attached to him, and seem fully in earnest; but, alas! by some strange negligence their arms have not yet arrived from Dublin. My father this morning sent a letter by an officer going to Athlone, to Lord Cornwallis, offering his services to convey intelligence or reconnoitre, as he feels himself in a most terrible situation, without arms for his men, and no power of being serviceable to his country' (Ibid.).   7 Maria wrote to Sophie Ruxton on 5 September: 'Yesterday we heard, about ten o'clock in the morning, that a large body of rebels, armed with pikes, were within a few miles of Edgeworthstown. My father's yeomanry were at this moment gone to Longford for their arms, which Government had delayed sending. We were ordered to decamp, each with a small bundle; the two chaises full, and my mother and Aunt Charlotte on horseback. We were all ready to move, when the report was contradicted: only twenty or thirty men were now, it was said, in arms, and my father hoped we might still hold fast to our dear home' (Ibid., 1:58).

prepared to set out at a moment's warning. We were under this uncertainty, when an escort with an ammunition cart passed through the village, on its way to Longford. It contained several barrels of powder, intended to blow up the bridges, and to stop the progress of the enemy. One of the officers of the party rode up to our house, and offered to let us have the advantage of his escort. But, after a few minutes deliberation, this friendly proposal was declined. My father determined, that he would not stir till he knew whether he could have assistance; and as it did not appear as yet absolutely necessary that we should go, we stayed – fortunately for us!

About a quarter of an hour after the officer and the escort had departed, we, who were all assembled in the portico of the house, heard a report like a loud clap of thunder. The doors and windows shook with some violent concussion; a few minutes afterwards the officer[8] galloped into the yard, and threw himself off his horse into my father's arms almost senseless. The ammunition cart had blown up, one of the officers had been severely wounded, and the horses and the man leading them killed; the wounded officer was at a farm-house on the Longford Road at about two miles distance.[9] The fear of the rebels was now suspended, in concern for this accident. Mrs Edgeworth[10] went immediately to give her assistance; she left her carriage for the use of the wounded gentleman, and rode back. At the entrance of the village she was stopped by a gentleman in great terror, who, taking hold of the bridle of her horse, begged her not to attempt to go further, assuring her that the rebels were coming into the town. But she answered, that she must and would return to her family. She rode on and found us waiting anxiously for her. No assistance could be afforded from Longford; the rebels were reassembling, and advancing towards the village; and there was no alternative, but to leave our home as fast as possible. No mode of conveyance could be hand for some of the female servants; our faithful English housekeeper offered to stay till the return of the carriage, which had been left with the officer; and as we hoped, immediately. As we passed through the village, we heard nothing but the entreaties, lamentations and objurgations of those, who could not procure the means of carrying off their goods or their families: most painful when we could give no assistance.

8 Maria identifies him as a Mr Murray, who was accompanied by Mr Rochfort and Mr Nugent. Rochfort was 'thrown from his horse, one side of his face terribly burnt, and stuck over with gunpowder. He was carried into a cabin; they thought he would die, but they now say he will live' (Ibid., 59). 9 Maria specified to her aunt that 'the ammunition cart, containing nearly three hundred barrels of gunpowder, packed in tin cases, took fire and burst, halfway on the road to Longford. The man who drove the cart was blown to atoms – nothing of him could be found; two of the horses were killed, others were blown to pieces and their limbs scattered to a distance; the head and body of a man were found a hundred and twenty yards from the spot' (Ibid.). 10 Frances Anne (Beaufort) Edgeworth, the fourth wife of Richard Lovell Edgeworth, was born in 1767 at Collon, Co. Louth. She was the daughter of the Revd Daniel Augustus Beaufort, the noted geographer, and his wife Mary,

Next to the safety of his own family, my father's greatest anxiety was for his defenceless corps. No men could behave better than they did at this first moment of trial. Not one absented himself, though many, living at a distance, might, if they had been so inclined, have found plausible excuses for non-appearance. The bugle was not sounded to call them together, but they were at their ranks in the street the moment they had their captain's orders, declaring, that whatever he commanded they would do. He ordered them to march to Longford. The idea of going to Longford could not be agreeable to many of them, who were Catholics; because that town was full of those who call themselves – I would avoid using party names if I could, but I can no otherwise make the facts intelligible – who called themselves Orangemen, and who were not supposed to have favourable opinions of any other religious persuasion. There was no reluctance shewn, however, by the Catholics of this corps to go among them. The moment the word *march* was uttered by their captain, they marched with alacrity. One of my brothers, a youth of fifteen, was in their ranks; another, twelve years old, marched with them.[11]

We expected every instant to hear the shout of the rebels entering Edgeworth-Town. When we had got about half a mile out of the village, my father suddenly recollected, that he had left on his table a paper, containing a list of his corps, and that, if this should come into the hands of the rebels, it might be of dangerous consequence to his men; it would serve to point out their houses for pillage, and their families for destruction. He turned his horse instantly, and galloped back for it. The time of his absence appeared immeasurably long, but he returned safely, after having destroyed the dangerous paper.

About two miles from the village was the spot, where the ammunition car had been blown up; the dead horses, swollen to an unnatural bulk, were lying across the road. As we approached, we saw two men in an adjoining field looking at the remains of one of the soldiers, who had been literally blown to pieces. They ran towards us, and we feared, that they were rebels going to stop us. They jumped over the ditch, and seized our bridles; but with friendly intent. With no small difficulty they dragged us past the dead horses, saying, 'God speed you! and make haste any way!' We were very ready to take their advice. After this, on the six long miles of the road from

daughter of William Waller of Allenstown, Co. Meath. At the time of her marriage on 31 May 1798, she was thirty-one years old (twenty-three years her new husband's junior). This disparity in age was a cause of initial concern for Maria, who was the same age as her new step-mother, but the marriage proved happy, and the two women established an intimate bond which lasted until Maria's death. Frances died on 10 February 1865, aged ninety-eight. See 'Edgeworth of Edgeworthstown', in *Burke's Landed Gentry of Ireland* (1912), 204–5.
11 Henry Edgeworth (aged fifteen) and Charles Sneyd Edgeworth (aged twelve).

Edgeworth-Town to Longford, we did not meet a human being. It was all silent and desert, as if every creature had fled from the cabins by the road side.

Longford was crowded with yeomanry of various corps, and with the inhabitants of the neighbourhood, who had flocked thither for protection. With great difficulty the poor Edgeworth-Town infantry found lodgings. We were cordially received by the landlady of a good inn.[12] Though her house was, as she said, fuller than it could hold, as she was an old friend of my father's, she did contrive to give us two rooms, in which we eleven were thankful to find ourselves. All our concern now was for those we had left behind. We heard nothing of our housekeeper[13] all night, and were exceedingly alarmed: but early the next morning, to our great joy, she arrived. She told us, that after we had left her, she waited hour after hour for the carriage: she could hear nothing of it, as it had gone to Longford with the wounded officer. Towards evening, a large body of rebels entered the village. She heard them at the gate, and expected that they would have broken in the next instant. But one, who seemed to be a leader, with a pike in his hand, set his back against the gate, and swore, that 'if he was to die for it the next minute, he would have the life of the first man, who should open that gate, or set enemy's foot within side of that place'. He said the housekeeper, who was left in it, was a good gentlewoman, and had done him a service, though *she did not know him, nor he her*. He had never seen her face, but she had, the year before, lent his wife, when in distress, sixteen shillings, the rent of flax-ground, and he would stand her friend now.[14]

He kept back the mob; they agreed to send him to the house with a deputation of six, *to know the truth*, and to ask for arms. The six men went to the back-door, and summoned the housekeeper; one of them pointed his blunderbuss at her, and told her, that she must fetch all the arms in the house; she said she had none. Her champion asked her to say if she remembered him – 'No; to her knowledge she had never seen his face'. He asked if she remembered having lent a woman money to pay her rent of flax-ground the year before? 'Yes', she remembered that, and named the woman, the time, and the sum. His companions were thus satisfied of the truth of what he had asserted. He bid her not to be *frighted*, 'for that no

---

12 Maria identifies it as 'Mrs Fallon's Inn' (Ibid.). 13 Mrs Billamore (see the Account of Frances Edgeworth in ibid., 1:60). 14 Frances Edgeworth attributed the hostility to the fact that the rebels had not plundered the house at Edgeworthstown. 'They had halted at the gate, but were prevented from entering by a man whom she [Mrs Billamore] did not remember to have ever seen; but he was grateful to her for having lent money to his wife when she was in great distress, and we now, at our utmost need, owed our safety and that of the house to his gratitude. We were surprised to find that this was thought by some to be a suspicious circumstance, and that it showed Mr Edgeworth to be a favorer of the rebels!' (Ibid.).

harm should happen to her, nor any belonging to her; not a soul should get leave to go into her master's house; not a twig should be touched, nor a leaf harmed'. His companions huzzaed and went off. Afterwards, as she was told, he mounted guard at the gate during the whole time the rebel were in the town.

When the carriage at last returned, it was stopped by the rebels, who filled the street; they held their pikes to the horses and to the coachman's breast, accusing him of being an Orange-man, because, as they said, he wore the orange colours (our livery being yellow and brown). A painter, a friend of ours, who had been that day at our house, copying some old family portraits, happened to be in the street at that instant, and called out to the mob, '*Gentlemen, it is yellow! – gentlemen, it is not orange*'. In consequence of this happy distinction they let go the coachman; and the same man, who had mounted guard at the gate, came up with his friends, rescued the carriage, and surrounding the coachman with their pikes brought him safely into the yard. The pole of the carriage having been broken in the first onset, the housekeeper could not leave Edgeworth-Town till morning. She passed the night walking up and down, listening and watching, but the rebels returned no more, and thus our house was saved by the gratitude of a single individual.

We had scarcely time to rejoice in the escape of our housekeeper, and safety of our house, when we found, that new dangers arose even from this escape. The house being saved created jealousy and suspicion in the minds of many, who at this time saw every thing through the mist of party prejudice. The dislike of my father's corps appeared every hour more strong. He saw the consequences, that might arise from the slightest breaking out of quarrel. It was not possible for him to send his men, unarmed as they still were, to their homes, lest they should be destroyed by the rebels; yet the officers of the other corps wished to have them sent out of the town and to this effect joined in a memorial to government. Some of these officers disliked my father, from differences of electioneering interests; others, from his not having kept up an acquaintance with them; and others, not knowing him in the least, were misled by party reports and misrepresentations.

These petty dissensions were, however, at one moment suspended and forgotten in a general sense of danger. An express arrived late one night, with the news that the French, who were rapidly advancing, were within a few miles of the town of Longford. A panic seized the people. There were in town eighty carabineers and two corps of yeomanry, but it was proposed to evacuate the garrison. My father strongly opposed this measure, and undertook, with fifty men, if arms and ammunition were supplied, to defend the gaol of Longford, where there was a strong pass, at which the enemy might be stopped. The offer was gladly accepted – men, arms, ammunition were placed at his disposal. He slept that night in the gaol with everything prepared for its defence; but the next morning news came that the French had turned off from the Longford road and were going towards Granard; of this, however, there was no certainty. My father, by the desire of the commanding officer, rode out to reconnoitre, and my brother[15] went to the top of the court-house with a telescope for the same purpose. We (Mrs Edgeworth, my aunts, my sisters, and myself) were waiting to hear the results in one of the upper sitting-rooms of the inn which fronted the street. We heard a loud shout, and going to the window, we saw people throwing up their hats, and heard huzzas. An express had arrived with news, that the French and the rebels had been beaten; that General Lake had come up with them at a place called Ballynamuck, near Granard; that 1,500 rebels and French were killed, and that the French generals and officers were prisoners.

We were impatient for my father, when we heard this joyful news; he had not yet returned and we looked out of the windows in hopes of seeing him, but we could see only a great number of people of the town, shaking hands with each other. This lasted a few minutes, and then the crowd gathered in silence round one man, who spoke with angry vehemence and gesticulation, stamping and frequently wiping his forehead. We thought he was a mountebank haranguing the populace, till we saw, that he wore a uniform. Listening with curiosity to hear what he was saying, we observed, that he looked up towards us, and we thought that we heard him pronounce the names of my father and brother in tones of insult. We could scarcely believe what we heard him say. Pointing up to the top of the court-house, he exclaimed, '*That* young Edgeworth ought to be dragged down from the top of that house'.

Our housekeeper burst into the room, so much terrified that she could scarcely speak.

'My master, ma'am – it is all against my master; the mob say they will tear him to pieces if they catch hold of him. They say he's a traitor, that he illuminated the gaol to deliver it up to the French'.

No words can give an idea of our astonishment. Illuminated! what could be meant by the gaol being illuminated? My father had literally but two farthing candles, by the light of which he had been reading the newspaper late the preceding night. These however were said to be signals for the enemy! The absurdity of the whole was so glaring, that we could scarcely conceive the danger to be real; but our pale landlady's fears were urgent, she dreaded that her house should be pulled down. We found, that the danger was not the less because the accusation was false; on the

15 Frances Edgeworth states that it was Henry who went to the top of the Court House (Ibid.).

contrary, it was great in proportion to its absurdity, for the people who could at once be under such a perversion of intellects, and such an illusion of their senses, must indeed be in a state of frenzy.

The crowd had by this time removed from before the windows; but we heard that they were going to that end of the town, through which they expected Mr Edgeworth to return. We wrote immediately to the commanding officer, informing him of what we had heard, and requesting his advice and assistance. He came to see us and recommended, that we should send a messenger to warn him of his danger and to request, that he would not return to Longford this day.[16] The officer added that, in consequence of the rejoicings for the victory, his men would probably be all drunk in a few hours, and that he could not answer for them. This officer, a captain of yeomanry, was a good-natured, but inefficient man, who spoke under considerable nervous agitation, and seemed desirous to do all he could, but not be able to do any thing. We wrote instantly, and with difficulty found a man, who undertook to convey the note. It was to be carried to meet him on one road, and Mrs Edgeworth and I determined to drive out to meet him on the other. We made our way down a back staircase into the inn yard, where the carriage was ready. Several gentlemen spoke to us as we got into the carriage, begging us not to be alarmed: Mrs Edgeworth answered, that she was more surprised than alarmed. The commanding officer and the sovereign of Longford walked by the side of the carriage through the town; and as the mob believed, that we were going away not to return, we got through without molestation. We went a few miles on the road towards Edgeworth town, till at a tenant's house we heard, that my father had passed by half an hour ago; that he was riding in company with an officer, supposed to be of Lord Cornwallis's or General Lake's army; that they had taken a *short cut*, which led into Longford by another entrance. Most fortunately not that at which an *armed* mob had assembled, expecting the object of their fury. Seeing him return to the inn with an officer of the king's army, they imagined, and we were afterwards told, that he was brought back a prisoner, and they were satisfied.[17]

The moment we saw him safe, we laughed at our own fears, and again doubted the reality of the danger, more especially as he treated the idea with the utmost incredulity and scorn.

Major (now General) Eustace[18] was the officer, who returned with him. He dined with us; every thing appeared quiet. The persons who had taken

16 Frances Edgeworth states that 'we sent a messenger in one direction to warn him, while Maria and I drove to meet him on the other road' (Ibid., 61). 17 Frances Edgeworth writes: 'We heard that he had passed some time before with Major Eustace; the mob seeing an officer in uniform with him went back to town, and on our return we found them safe at the inn' (Ibid.). 18 Probably Charles Eustace of Robertstown, Co. Kildare and of Corbally, Queen's Co. He became a Lieutenant-General in the Army and was later an M.P. in the Irish

refuge at the inn were now gone to their homes, and it appeared it was supposed that, whatever dispositions to riot had existed, the news of the approach of some of Lord Cornwallis's suite, or of troops who were to bring in the French prisoners, would prevent all probability of disturbance. In the evening the prisoners arrived at the inn; a crowd followed them, but quietly. A sun-burnt, coarse looking man, in a huge cocked hat, with a quantity of gold lace on his clothes, seemed to fix all attention; he was pointed out as the French General Homberg, or Sarrazin.[19] As he dismounted from his horse, he threw the bridle over its neck, and looked at the animal as being his only friend.

We had heard my father in the evening ask Major Eustace, to walk with him through the town to the barrack-yard to evening parade; and we saw them go out together without our feeling the slightest apprehension. We remained at the inn. By this time Col. Handfield, Major Cannon, and some of the other offciers, had arrived, and they were at the inn at dinner in a parlour on the ground-floor, under our room. It being hot weather, the windows were open. Nothing now seemed to be thought of but rejoicings for the victory. Candles were preparing for the illuminations; waiters, chambermaids, landlady, all hands were busy scooping turnips and potatoes for candlesticks, to stand in every pane of every loyal window.

In the midst of this preparation about half an hour after my father had left us, we heard a great uproar in the street. At first we thought the shouts were only rejoicings for victory, but as they came nearer, we heard screechings and yellings, indescribably horrible. A mob had gathered at the gates of the barrack yard, and joined by many soldiers of the yeomanry on leaving parade, had followed Major Eustace and my father from the barracks. The major being this evening in coloured clothes, the people no longer knew him to be an officer; nor conceived, as they had done before, that Mr Edgeworth was his prisoner. The mob had not contented themselves with the horrid yells that we had heard, but had been pelting them with hard turf, stones, and brickbats. From one of these my father received a blow on the side of his head, which came with such force as almost to stun him; but he kept himself from falling, knowing that if once he fell he should be trampled under foot. He walked on steadily till he came within a few yards of the inn, when one of the mob seized hold of Major Eustace by the collar. My father seeing the windows open, called with a loud voice, 'Major Eustace is in danger!'

Parliament (see 'Robertson-Eustace of Robertstown', *Burke's Landed Gentry of Ireland* [1912], 207).   **19** Col. Sarrazin was second in command to Gen. Jean Joseph Humbert. He conducted a reconnaissance mission, leading a body of 250 French and Irish troops at Ballina in Co. Mayo. Later, he fought at Castlebar, defeating the army of Gen. Lake. On 8 Sept. 1798, he was among those officers surrendering with Humbert and was brought to Dublin, where he and the other officers received the hospitality of the British (see Pakenham, 308, 310, 327).

The officers, who were at dinner, and who till that moment had supposed the noise in the street to be only drunken rejoicings, immediately ran out, and rescued Major Eustace and my father. At the sight of British officers and drawn swords, the populace gave way and dispersed in different directions.[20]

The preparations for the illuminations then went on, as if nothing had intervened. All the panes of our windows in the front room were in a blaze of light by the time the mob returned to the street. The night passed without further disturbance.

As early as we could the next morning we left Longford, and returned homewards. When we came near Edgeworth-Town, we saw many well-known faces at the cabin doors looking out to welcome us.[21] One man, who was digging in his field by the road side, when he looked up and saw my father, let fall his spade and clasped his hands; his face, as the morning sun shone upon it, was the strongest picture of joy I ever saw. The village was a melancholy spectacle, windows shattered and doors broken. But though the mischief done was great, there had been little pillage. Within our gates we found all property safe; literally 'not a twig touched nor a leaf harmed'. Within the house every thing was as we had left it – a map that we had been consulting was still open on the library table, with pencils, and slips of paper containing the first lessons in arithmatic, in which some of the young people had been engaged the morning we had been driven from home; a pansy, in a glass of water, which one of the children had been copying, was still on the chimneypiece. These trivial circumstances, marking repose and tranquillity, struck us at this moment with an unreasonable sort of surprise, and all that had passed seemed like an incoherent dream. The joy of having my father in safety remained, and gratitude to Heaven for his preservation. These feelings spread inexpressible pleasure over what seemed to be a new sense of existence. Even the most common things appeared delightful; the green lawn, the still groves, the birds singing, the fresh air, all external nature, and all seemed to have wonderfully increased in value, from the fear into which we had been put of losing them irrecoverably.

The first thing my father did, the day we came home, was to draw up a memorial to the Lord Lieutenant, desiring to have a court martial held on the sergeant, who, by haranguing the populace, had raised the mob at

20 According to Frances Edgeworth, 'the military patrolled the streets, and the sergeant who had made all the disturbance was put under arrest. He was a poor, half-crazed fanatic' (Ibid.). 21 Maria wrote on 9 September 1798: 'When we got into town this morning we saw the picture of a deserted, or rather a shattered village – many joyful faces greeted us at doors of the houses – none of the windows in the new houses in Charlotte Row were broken: the mob declared they would not meddle with them because they were built by the two good ladies, meaning my aunts' (Ibid. 1:62).

Longford;[22] his next care was to walk through the village, to examine what damage had been done by the rebels, and to order that repairs of all his tenants' houses be made at his expense. A few days later, Government ordered, that the arms of the Edgeworth-Town infantry should be forwarded by the commanding officer at Longford. Through the whole of their hard week's trial, the corps had, without exception, behaved perfectly well. It was perhaps more difficult to honest and brave men passively to bear such a trial, than any to which they could have been exposed in action.

When the arms for the corps arrived, my father, in delivering them to the men, thanked them publicly for their conduct, assuring them, that he would remember it, whenever he should have opportunities for them, collectively or individually. In long after years, as occasions arose, each, who continued to deserve it, found in him a friend, and felt, that he more than fulfilled his promise. Now that he could look back upon suspicions and accusations, now that events had decided upon guilt and innocence, and had shown who were, and who were not, implicated in this rebellion, he had the satisfaction of feeling, that, though he had trusted much, he had not in *many* instances trusted rashly. In some few cases he was deceived. – Who in Ireland at that time can boast, that he was not? Some few, very few indeed, of his tenantry, on a remote estate- alas too near Ballynamuck, did join the rebels! These persons were never readmitted on my father's estate.

In some cases it was difficult to know what ought to be done: for instance, with regard to the man who had saved his house from pillage, but who had joined the rebels. It was the wise policy of Government, to pardon those, who had not been ringleaders in this rebellion; and who, repenting of their folly, were desirous to return to their allegiance, and to their peaceable duties. My father sent for this man, and said he would apply to Government for a pardon for him. The man smiled, and, clapping his pocket, said, 'I have my *Corny* here safe already, I thank your Honour; else sure I would not have been such a fool as to be showing myself without I had a *purtection*'. – A pardon signed by the Lord Lieutenant, Lord Cornwallis, they called a *Corny*.

---

22 Maria wrote to her aunt Sophie Ruxton on 19 September 1798 that 'when Colonel Handfield told the whole story of the Longford mob to Lord Cornwallis, he said he never knew a man so much astonished. Lord Longford, Mr Pakenham, and Major Edward Pakenham have shown much warmth of friendship upon this occasion' (Ibid., 1:63). Later on 3 October, she wrote: 'My father went to Dublin the day before yesterday, to see Lord Cornwallis about the Court of Inquiry on the sergeant who harrangued the mob' (Ibid., 1:64). Frances Edgeworth noted later that 'the sergeant was to have been tried at the next session, but he was by this time ashamed and penitent, and Mr Edgeworth did not press the trial, but knowing the man was, among other weaknesses, very much afraid of ghosts, he said to him as he came out of the Court House, 'I believe, after all, you had rather see me alive than have my ghost haunting you!' (Ibid., 1:65).

We observed, and thought it an instance of Irish acuteness and knowledge of character, that this man was sure my father never would *forget him*, though he gave him nothing at this time. When my father said, that, though we were obliged to him for saving the house, he could not *reward* him for being a rebel; he answered, 'Oh, I know that I could not expect it, nor look for any thing at all, but what I got – *thanks*'. With these words he went away satisfied.

A considerable time afterward my father, finding that the man conducted himself well, took an opportunity of serving him. Rewards my father thought fully as necessary and as efficacious as punishments, for the good government of human creatures: therefore he took especial care, not only to punish those who had done ill, but to reward, as far as he could, all who had done well.

Before we quit this subject, it may be useful to record, that the French generals, who headed the invasion, declared they had been completely deceived as to the state of Ireland. They had expected to find the people in open rebellion, or, at least, in their own phrase, *organized* for insurrection; but to their dismay, they found only ragamuffins, as they called them, who, in joining their standard, did them infinitely more harm than good. It is a pity, that the lower Irish could not hear the contemptuous manner, in which the French, both officers and soldiers, spoke of them and of their country. The generals described the strategems, which had been practised upon them by their good allies. The same rebels frequently returning with different tones and new stories, to obtain double and treble provisions of arms, ammunition, and uniforms – selling the ammunition for whiskey, and running away at the first fire in the day of battle. The French, detesting and despising those by whom they had been thus cheated, pillaged, and deserted, called them beggars, rascals, and savages. They cursed also without scruple their own Directory, for sending them, after they had, as they boasted, conquered the world, to be at last beaten in an Irish bog. Officers and soldiers joined in swearing, that they would never return to a country, where they could find neither bread, wine, nor discipline; and where the people lived on roots, whiskey, and lying.

These, my father observed, were comfortable words for Ireland. National antipathy, thus felt and expressed between the invaders and the Irish malcontents, would be better security for the future quiet and safety of the country even than the victory. Full of these thoughts, unconcerned about himself, and in excellent spirits, he succeeded in turning our attention to new objects. The Longford mob completely vanished from our imagination. Reflecting upon what had passed, my father drew from it one useful conclusion for his own future conduct – that he ought to mix more with society, and make himself more generally known in Ireland.

At all times it is disadvantageous to those, who have the reputation of being men of superior abilities, to seclude themselves from the world. It raises a belief, that they despise those with whom they do not associate; and this supposed contempt creates real aversion. The being accused of pride or singularity may not, perhaps, in the estimation of some lofty spirits and independent characters, appear too great a price to pay for liberty and leisure; they will care little, if they be misunderstood or misrepresented by the vulgar; they will trust to truth and time, to do them justice. This may be all well in ordinary life, and in peaceable days: but in civil commotions, the best and the wisest, if he have not made himself publicly known, so as to connect himself with the interests and feelings of his neighbours, will find none to answer for his character, if it be attacked, or to warn him of the secret machinations of his enemies; none who on any sudden emergency will risk their own safety in his defence: he may fall and be trampled upon by numbers, simply because it is nobody's business or pleasure, to rally to his aid. Time and reason may right his character, and may bring all who have injured, or all who have mistaken him, to repentence and shame, but in the interval he *must* suffer – he *may* perish. There is no absurdity of ignorance, or grossness of calumny, from which he may hope to be secure. He may be conceived to be a traitor, because he would not be a tyrant; he may be called a rebel, for offering to defend a loyal garrison; and may well nigh be torn to pieces by a mob, for having read the newspapers by two farthing candles.

BIBLIOGRAPHY

MANUSCRIPT SOURCES

Adams, Jane, Manuscript narrative. Ms. No. 21,142. British Library, London.

Barber, Jane, 'Recollections of the Summer of 1798'. (typescript) Wexford County Library, Wexford; copy in National Library of Ireland (ir. 920041).

Caulfield-Troy Correspondence, Troy Papers, Dublin Diocesan Archives.

Ferns Diocese Marriage Licenses Index. National Archives of Ireland.

Goff, Dinah, Ms. No. 5116. Trinity College Dublin.

Goff Papers. Ms. No. T1621/1-2. Public Record Office of Northern Ireland.

Leslie, James, 'Biographical Succession List of the Clergy of Dublin Diocese'. Unpublished typescript. Representative Church Body Library, Dublin.

Lett, Barbara, Manuscript narrative. Ms. No. 4472-3, National Library of Ireland; also Ms. No. 2066 (s. 3. 18) Trinity College Dublin.

Pounden, Alicia, Manuscript narrative. Ms. T.720, Public Record Office of Northern Ireland.

Richards, Elizabeth, Diary. Original reputedly in The Hague, Netherlands; a copy of the original is kept at Rathaspick Manor, County Wexford. A transcribed copy by the Revd Thomas H. Orpen is in the National Library of Ireland, Microfilm 36486.

PUBLISHED SOURCES

Ainsworth, J.F. 'Report on the Lett Diary of the 1798 Rising in Co. Wexford', *National Library Report on Private Collections*, no. 221.

Atkinson, Thomas. *The Irish Tourist* (Dublin, 1814).

Bartlett, Thomas, 'Bearing Witness: Female Evidences in Courts Martial Convened to Suppress the 1798 Rebellion', in Keogh and Furlong (eds), *The Women of 1798*, pp. 64–86.

——, 'Defence, Counter-insurgency, and Rebellion: Ireland, 1793–1803', in Bartlett and Jeffrey (eds), *A Military History of Ireland*, pp. 247–93.

——, and Keith Jeffrey (eds), *A Military History of Ireland* (Cambridge, 1996).

Beatty, John D., 'Protestant Women of County Wexford and their Narratives of the Rebellion of 1798', in Keogh and Furlong (eds), *The Women of 1798*, pp. 113–36.

Brady, W. Maziere, *Clerical and Parochial Records of Cork, Cloyne, and Ross* (London, 1863).

Brownrigg, Mrs, 'Wexford in 1798: An Account of Events by an Eye-witness', ed. by Francis Joseph Bigger. *South East of Ireland Archaeological Society Journal*, 1–2 (1895–96), pp. 268–78, 16–22.

Burke, J.B., *Genealogical and Heraldic Dictionary of the Landed Gentry of Great Britain and Ireland for 1850* (London, 1850).

——, *Burke's Landed Gentry* (London, 1850).

——, *Burke's Landed Gentry of Ireland* (London, 1904).

——, *Burke's Landed Gentry of Ireland* (London, 1912).

——, *Burke's Peerage and Baronetage* (105th ed., London, 1975).

Butler, Harriet Jessie, and Harold Edgeworth Butler, *The Black Book of Edgeworthstown and Other Edgeworth Memories, 1585–1817* (London, 1927).

Butler, Marilyn, *Maria Edgeworth: A Literary Biography* (Oxford, 1972).

Byrne, Miles, *Memoirs of Miles Byrne* (2 vols., Paris, 1863).

Cantwell, Brian, *Memorials of the Dead: Wexford* (6 vols., Wicklow, n.d).

Caulfield, James, *Reply of Right Revd Dr Caulfield, Roman Catholic Bishop and of the Roman Catholic Clergy of Wexford to the Misrepresentations of Sir Richard Musgrave, bart.* (Dublin, 1801).

Cleary, Brian, 'The battle of Oulart Hill: Context and Strategy', in Keogh and Furlong (eds), *The Mighty Wave: The 1798 Rebellion in Wexford*, pp. 79–96.

——, 'Sowing the Whirlwind', *Journal of the Wexford Historical Society* 14 (1992–3), pp. 8–79.

Clifford, Andrew J. 'Swanzy Will Abstracts', *Irish Genealogist* 9 (1997), pp. 441–93.

Cloney, Sean, 'The Hessians', *Journal of the Wexford Historical Society* 14 (1992–3), pp. 113–28.

——, 'South-west Wexford in 1798', *Journal of the Wexford Historical Society* 15 (1994–5), pp. 74–97.

Cloney, Thomas. *Personal Narrative of 1798* (Dublin, 1832).

Cokayne, G.E. *The Complete Peerage* (13 vols., London, 1929).

Comerford, Patrick, 'Euseby Cleaver, Bishop of Ferns, and the Clergy of the Church of Ireland in the 1798 Rising in Co. Wexford', *Journal of the Wexford Historical Society* 16 (1996–7), pp. 66–94.

Croker, T. Crofton, *Researches in the South of Ireland* (1823. 2nd ed. Shannon, 1969).

Cullen, L.M. 'Politics and Rebellion: Wicklow in the 1790s', in Hannigan and Nolan (eds), *Wicklow History and Society*, pp. 411–501.

——, 'The 1798 Rebellion in Wexford: United Irishman Organisation, Membership, Leadership', in Whelan and Nolan (eds), *Wexford History and Society*, pp. 248–95.

De Montfort, Simon L.M. (ed), 'Mrs Pounden's Experiences During the 1798 Rising in Co. Wexford', *Irish Ancestor* 8 (1976), pp. 4–8.

Dickinson, James, *A Journal of the Life, Travels, and Labour of Love in the Work of the Ministry, of that Worthy Elder, and Faithful Servant of Jesus Christ, James Dickinson* (London, 1745).

Dickson, Charles, *The Wexford Rising in 1798: Its Causes and Its Course* (Tralee, n.d).

Dictionary of National Biography, ed. by Sir Leslie Stephen and Sir Sidney Lee (21 vols., Oxford, 1982).

O'Donnell, Ruan and Bob Reese. 'A Clean Beast: Crofton Croker's Fairy Tale of General Holt', *Eighteenth-Century Ireland* 7 (1992), pp. 7–42.

Edgeworth, Maria, *Life and Letters of Maria Edgeworth* (2 vols. Boston, 1895).

Edgeworth, Richard Lovell, and Maria Edgeworth, *Memoirs of Richard Lovell Edgeworth: Begun by Himself and Concluded by His Daughter Maria Edgeworth* (2 vols. 1820. 2nd ed. Shannon, 1969).

Elliott, Marianne, *Partners in Revolution: The United Irishmen and France* New Haven, 1982).

Emmet, Thomas Addis, *Memoir of Thomas Addis and Robert Emmet* (2 vols. New York, 1915).

Farrar, Henry, *Irish Marriages: Being an Index to the Marriages in Walker's Hibernian Magazine, 1771 to 1812* (2 vols. London, 1897).

Farrell, William. *Carlow in '98: The Autobiography of William Farrell of Carlow* ed. by Roger McHugh (Dublin, 1949).

Flood, W.H. Grattan, *History of the Diocese of Ferns* (Waterford, 1916).

Furlong, Nicholas, *Fr John Murphy of Boolavogue, 1753–1798* (Dublin, 1991).

Gahan, Daniel, 'The Black Mob and the Babes in the Wood: Wexford in the Wake of Rebellion'. *Journal of the Wexford Historical Society*, no. 13 (1990–91), pp. 92–110.

——, *The People's Rising: Wexford, 1798* (Dublin, 1995).

Goff, Dinah W., Divine *Protection through Extraordinary Dangers during the Irish Rebellion of 1798* (Philadelphia, 1856).

Goodall, David, 'Dixon of Castlebridge', *Irish Genealogist* 6 (Nov. 1984), pp. 629–641.

——, 'A Divided Family in 1798: The Grays of Whitefort and Jamestown', *Journal of the Wexford Historical Society* 15 (1994–5), pp. 52–66.

——, 'Frayne of Co. Wexford', *Irish Genealogist* 4 (Nov. 1970), pp. 213–220.

——, 'Freemen of Wexford', *Irish Genealogist* 5 (1974–77), pp. 103–21, 314–34, 448–63.

——, 'Hatchell of County Wexford', *Irish Genealogist* 4 (Nov. 1972), pp. 461–76.

Goodbody, Olive C., *Quaker Records Dublin, Abstract of Wills* (Dublin, 1957).

Gordon, James, *History of the Rebellion in Ireland in the Year 1798* (London, 1803).

Gough, Hugh and David Dickson (eds), *Ireland and the French Revolution* (Dublin, 1990).

Gurley, Leonard Beatty, *Memoir of Revd William Gurley* (Cincinnati, 1850).

Hancock, Thomas, *The Principles of Peace, Exemplified by the Conduct of the Society of Friends in Ireland During the Rebellion in the Year 1798* 3rd ed. (New York, 1974).

Handcock, Thomas, 'Reminiscences of a Fugitive Loyalist in 1798', *English Historical Review*, 1 (1886), pp. 536–544.

Hannigan, Ken and William Nolan (eds.), *Wicklow History and Society* (Templehogue, 1994).

Harrison, Richard S. *Biographical Dictionary of Irish Quakers* (Dublin, 1997).

Hay, Edward, *History of the Irish Insurrection of 1798* (Boston, n.d.).

Holt, Joseph. *Memors of Joseph Holt: General of the Irish Rebels*, ed. by T. Crofton Croker. (London, 1838).

Hore, P. H. *History of the Town and County of Wexford* (6 vols. London, 1911).

Jackson, Charles. *A Narrative of the Sufferings and Escapes of Charles Jackson, Late Resident of Wexford* (4th ed. Dublin, 1802).

Jones, Henry Z. *Palatine Families of Ireland* (2nd ed. Camden, ME, 1990).

Kavanagh, Art, and Rory Murphy. *The Wexford Gentry* (2 vols. Bunclody, 1994–96).

Kavanagh, Patrick F. *A Popular History of the Insurrection of '98* (Dublin, 1920).

Keogh, Daire. *'The French Disease': The Catholic Church and Radicalism in Ireland, 1790–1800* (Dublin, 1993).

——, and Nicholas Furlong (eds), *The Mighty Wave: The 1798 Rebellion in Wexford* (Dublin, 1996).

——, and Nicholas Furlong (eds), *The Women of 1798* (Dublin, 1998).

——, 'Sectarianism in the Rebellion of 1798: The Eighteenth Century Context' in Keogh and Furlong (eds), *The Mighty Wave: The 1798 Rebellion in Wexford*, pp. 37–47.

Kneschke, Ernst Heinrich. *Neues Allgemeines Deutsches Adels–Lexikon* (Leipzig, 1863).

Landreth, Helen. *The Pursuit of Robert Emmet* (New York, 1948).

Leadbeater, Mary. 'Annals of Ballitore'. *Leadbeater Papers* (2 vols. London, 1862), pp. 13–416.

Leslie, James B. *Ferns Clergy and Parishes* (Dublin, 1936).

'List of Claimants for the Relief of Suffering Loyalists', *Journal of the Irish House of Commons* (Dublin, 1800).

A List of the Subscribers to the Fund for the Relief of Widows and Orphans of Yeomen, Soldiers, &c. Who Fell in Suppressing the Late Rebellion (Dublin, 1800).

Lucas, Richard. *General Directory of the Kingdom of Ireland, 1788* (Dublin, 1789).

Madden, Richard R. *The United Irishmen: Their Lives and Times* (3 vols., London, 1860).

Maxwell, William H. *History of the Irish Rebellion in 1798* (London, 1845).

McDowell, R. B. 'Personnel of the Dublin Society of United Irishmen', *Irish Historical Studies* 2 (1940), pp. 12–53.

Musgrave, Sir Richard. *Memoirs of the Different Rebellions in Ireland* (1801; 4th ed. Fort Wayne, 1995).

Myers, Mitzi. '"Completing the Union": Critical *Ennui*, the Politics of Narrative, and the Reformation of the Irish Cultural Identity', in *Prose Studies: History, Theory, Criticism* 18 (Dec. 1995):, pp. 42–77.

——, '"Like the Pictures in a Magic Lantern": Gender, History, and Edgeworth's Rebellion Narratives', in *Nineteenth Century Contexts* 19 (1996), pp. 373–412.

O'Donnell, Ruan, 'The Rebellion of 1798 in County Wicklow', in Hannigan and Nolan (eds), *Wicklow History and Society*, pp. 341–378.

O'Flannigan, Patrick, Paul Ferguson, and Kevin Whelan (eds), *Rural Ireland 1600–1900: Modernisation and Change* (Cork, 1987).

Ogle, T. Acres. *The Irish Militia Officer* (Dublin, 1873).

O'Kelly, Patrick. *History of the Rebellion of 1798* (Dublin: 1842).

O'Neill, Kevin. 'Mary Shackleton Leadbeater: Peaceful Rebel', in Keogh and Furlong (eds), *The Women of 1798*, pp. 137–162.

O'Reilly, Andrew. *Reminiscences of an Emigrant Milesian* (3 vols. London, 1853).

O Snodaigh, Padraig, 'Notes on the Volunteers, Militia, Yeomanry, and Orangemen of County Wexford', *The Past* 14 (1983), pp. 5–48.

Pakenham, Thomas. *The Year of Liberty* (Englewood Cliffs, 1969).

Power, T.P. and Kevin Whelan (eds), *Endurance and Emergence: Catholics in Ireland in the Eighteenth Century* (Dublin, 1990).

Ranson, Joseph (ed). 'A 1798 Diary by Mrs Barbara Newton Lett, Killaligan, Enniscorthy', *The Past* 5 (1949), pp. 117–149.

Richardson, John Grubb. *Six Generations of Friends in Ireland, 1655 to 1890* (London, 1895).

Roden, Anne, Countess Dowager of. *The Diary of Anne, Countess Dowager of Roden, 1797–1802* (Dublin, 1870).

Sands, David. *Journal of the Life and Gospel Labours of David Sands* (London, 1848).

Shackleton, Betsy. *Ballitore and Its Inhabitants Seventy Years Ago* (Dublin, 1862).

Skrine, Helen, 'A Glimpse of Bagenal Harvey', *Journal of the Wexford Historical Society* 14 (1992–93), pp. 92–100.

Snoddy, Oliver. 'The Volunteers, Militia, Yeomanry and Orangemen of Co. Kildare in the 18th Century', *Journal of the Co. Kildare Archaeological Society* 15 (1971), pp. 38–49.

Snowe, William. *Statement of Transactions at Enniscorthy* (Bray, 1801).

Spedding, John Carlisle. *The Spedding Family* (Dublin, 1909).

Stewart, A. T. Q. *The Summer Soldiers: The 1798 Rebellion in Antrim and Down* (Belfast, 1995).

Taafe, Frank. 'Some Ballitore Shackletons'. *Carloviana* 36 (1988/89), pp. 22–23.

Taylor, George. *A History of the Rise, Progress, Cruelties, and Supression of the Rebellion in the County of Wexford in the Year 1798* (Belleville, 1864).

Tenison, C. M. 'The Private Bankers of Cork and the South of Ireland', *Cork Historical and Archaeological Society Journal* 2 (1893), 184–186, 205–206.

Vicars, Arthur. *Index to the Prerogative Wills of Ireland, 1536–1810* (Dublin, 1897).

Walsh, Dan. *100 Wexford County Houses: An Illustrated History* (Enniscorthy, 1996).

Watson, Edward, 'Memories of Col. Jonas Watson', ed. by Hilary Murphy, *Journal of the Wexford Historical Society* 15 (1994–95), pp. 115–118.

Wheeler, H. F. B. and A. M. Broadley. *War in Wexford* (London, 1920).

Whelan, Kevin. 'The Catholic Community in Eighteenth-Century County Wexford', in Power and Whelan (eds), *Endurance and Emergence: Catholics in Ireland in the Eighteenth Century*, pp. 129–170.

——, 'The Catholic Priest in the 1798 Rebellion', in Whelan and Nolan (eds), *Wexford History and Society*, pp. 296–315.

——, 'Politicisation in County Wexford and the Origins of the 1798 Rebellion', in Gough and Dickson (eds), *Ireland and the French Revolution*, pp. 156–178.

——, 'Reinterpreting the 1798 Rebellion in County Wexford', in Keogh and Furlong (eds), *The Mighty Wave: The 1798 Rebellion in Wexford*, pp. 9–36.

——, 'The Religious Factor in the 1798 Rebellion', in O'Flanaghan, Ferguson, and Whelan (eds), *Rural Ireland 1600–1900: Modernisation and Change*, pp. 62–85.

——, and William Nolan (eds.), *Wexford History and Society* (Dublin, 1987).

Wigham, Maurice J. *The Irish Quakers: A Short History of the Religious Society of Friends in Ireland* (Dublin, 1992).

Young, Joseph J. *Parish of Narraghmore* (Naas, 1957).

Zimmermann, Georges-Denis. *Songs of Irish Rebellion: Political Street Ballads and Rebel Songs, 1780–1900* (Dublin, 1967).

INDEX